P9-CCF-498

PRESIDENTIAL ELECTIONS

PRESIDENTIAL ELECTIONS

Strategies of American Electoral Politics

Sixth Edition

UNIVERSITY LIBRARY
UW-STEVENS POINT

Nelson W. Polsby
Aaron Wildavsky

Charles Scribner's Sons
New York

Copyright © 1964, 1968, 1971, 1976, 1980 Aaron Wildavsky and
The Polsby Daughters' Trust
Copyright © 1984 Emily Polsby and the Wildavsky Children's Trusts

Library of Congress Cataloging in Publication Data

Polsby, Nelson W.
    Presidential elections.

    Includes bibliographical references and index.
    1. Presidents—United States—Election.   I. Wildavsky,
Aaron B.   II. Title.
JK528.P63 1984   324.973   83–16410
ISBN 0–684–17991–1
ISBN 0–684–18052–9 (pbk.)

This book published simultaneously in the
United States of America   and in Canada—
Copyright under the Berne Convention.

All rights reserved. No part of this book
may be reproduced in any form without the
permission of Charles Scribner's Sons.

1 3 5 7 9 11 13 15 17 19   F/C   20 18 16 14 12 10 8 6 4 2
1 3 5 7 9 11 13 15 17 19   F/P   20 18 16 14 12 10 8 6 4 2

PRINTED IN THE UNITED STATES OF AMERICA.

JK
528
.P63
1984

For our children, in more ways than one:
LISA, EMILY AND DANIEL POLSBY
ADAM, SARA, BEN AND DAN WILDAVSKY

Preface

The central purpose of this book is to provide what for want of a better name might be called civic education. We think people are entitled to information about the choices they make—not merely about the alternatives presented, but also about the processes that produce alternatives. Presidential elections in the United States involve significant choices for millions of Americans and in one way or another affect nearly everyone else on earth. Thus, it has seemed to us worthwhile to offer a discussion of the entire presidential election process, a discussion that is unsentimental, nonpartisan, and explicit about how and why things happen as they do. Ideally, this should help people follow events and participate in them. It should also help to minimize the production of false expectations, and supply an antidote to the unrealistic and cynical views of politics that tend to develop when people do not understand why things turn out less well than they had hoped.

We suggest that civic education plays an important part in the risky business of self-government. Among other things, it alerts people to changes that are likely to affect their lives. Over the past fifteen years, changes in presidential elections have had such effects. For example, between 1972 and 1976 the Democratic party forbade unit voting and made it easier for more than one candidate to come into the national convention with a chance to

win. This attempt to increase political competition was largely nullified by
the national television networks. The networks, following their own need to
generate excitement over their early nomination coverage, exerted pressure
on delegates and party leaders to decide on their preferences early in the
election season and consequently to start a bandwagon. Thus, a rule change
that made it more difficult for a single candidate to sew up the nomination
before the nominating convention was overwhelmed by the gradual growth
of television's focus on just one leader. Between 1980 and 1984, the Democrats made some more changes. This time they required the states to choose
their delegates during a more restricted period of three months. Here again,
the attempt was to keep the networks from focusing on just one state by
making sure that more than one state's selection process would take place on
each day set aside for delegate selection. The effect will probably be to help
the front runner, who will have the resources to run everywhere at once, and
to hurt all other prospective candidates.

It is now clear that the changes in the nominating process of the past few
elections add up to a fundamentally different role for political parties. This
should be understood and debated before these changes accumulate into an
inexorable and inevitable pattern. The question is whether our parties will
seek office by maintaining and nurturing consensus or will become organizations purely of factional advocacy. Every party must do—and does—some
of each: reconciling conflicting views and advancing the interests of factions.
But how much of each? The balance has been altered in favor of factionalism
to the detriment of consensus building. There would be no great difficulty in
this if it were not that sometimes the policy positions advocated by party
activists tend to be unpopular with most other people. Thus, it is possible for
the nominating process to produce candidates who appeal to the people who
become delegates but not to voters. This happened to the Democrats in 1972
and to the Republicans in 1964. In 1976 a Democratic president was elected
who could boast that he owed nothing to anybody—certainly not to the
leaders of his own party. In 1980, he failed to be reelected, the first such
failure of an incumbent since Herbert Hoover lost in 1932, in the middle of
the Great Depression. If our national parties no longer aspire to perform the
integrative function of keeping the country together, what agencies will do
so? This is one question that we must keep in mind while pondering the real
functions of such mechanisms as the formulas for financing elections and the
methods for allocating delegates on the basis of votes in primaries.

Another way of approaching the role of political parties in presidential
elections is to ask whether their purpose is to express the shades of opinion

among their own activists or to govern the nation. If their purpose is expression, then rules maximizing the most minute differences are in order. If their purpose is to govern, then rules for maximizing cohesion are appropriate. Evidently, both the capacity to express differences and the ability to govern effectively are necessary. The issue is one of proportion. As our system is presently structured, the danger is that expressiveness will overwhelm effectiveness. Yet the need for effectiveness does not seem to have abated, judging from widespread complaints about the activities of the so-called single-issue special-interest groups. Crises over such issues as Social Security and the production of huge budget deficits suggest that there is still a need for institutions whose functions are to moderate opinions and structure difficult issues so that they can be resolved. Political parties have traditionally been those institutions. As the California Committee for Party Renewal says:

> Only political parties can compromise and incorporate the wishes of a wide range of citizens in programs that encompass a multitude of issues and stretch across a greater span of time than a brief term of office that may or may not be renewed. Only political parties can marshall the resources and develop the strategy to recruit, train, support and guide a succession of highly qualified individuals to advance those programs during their terms in office. Only political parties can provide an effective means of holding elected representatives accountable to the people who elect them on the basis of such programs, by being ready to deny their resources to unworthy incumbents seeking reelection. Only political parties can put forward a broad panel of spokespersons in defense of such programs informing and educating the citizenry in a debate which extends beyond the short-range electoral prospects of particular candidates. In short, only political parties can provide us with the cohesion, continuity and accountability necessary to make democracy work.[1]

We agree.

We have tried in this book not merely to keep up with changes in the rules governing candidate selection, political campaign contributions, party delegate participation, voting eligibility, and the like, but in addition to organize and synthesize these into the general view of political resources and political strategies that has informed our approach to presidential elections from the beginning. As always, we are confident that our understanding of these matters is imperfect, as the unfolding of events will make only too clear. We have, however, attempted to stay abreast of political life in America and to shift our gaze toward those elements of the system that seem most important in shaping the strategies and outcomes of politics in the 1980s, just as earlier editions attempted the same tasks for the 1960s and 1970s. We only hope that what we say in this edition is sufficiently interesting so that four years hence it will still seem worthwhile for us to try again, in another edition, to come nearer to the mark.

Twenty years is a long useful life for a book—especially a book about something as volatile as American politics. When we wrote the first edition of *Presidential Elections,* in the early 1960s, the rules and practices of the presidential nomination and election process had not changed for decades. Since then, they have done nothing but change. Anyone who claims that there is no such thing as real or fundamental change in American politics need only glance at the necessary amendments to our account of what has happened over the years. Procedures for making nominating decisions, the kinds of people who are influential in making them, the characteristics of the delegates, and their basic dispositions toward politics have all undergone drastic alterations. Our one confident expectation is that the growth industry of chronicling changes from one edition to the next will not suffer decline.

For over a decade, from the Second Edition in 1968 to the Fifth Edition in 1980, we have argued, with as much cogency as we could muster and as much passion as propriety would permit, that the party system was in trouble. The worst wounds, we felt, were self-inflicted: changes in rules that drove out deliberation by party leaders in favor of choice through a plethora of primaries that involved more people but in a less consequential way. The results of primaries were added together by passive arithmetic, and early primaries, magnified by the coverage of the news media, had an enormous impact on later decisions. It thus became evident that national nominating conventions had lost their decision making ability, ratifying rather than choosing presidential candidates. By the 1980 conventions, which were even drearier than usual, foregone choices were presented in a dream-like encounter with a predetermined destiny. The preferences of political scientists, reporters, and other professional observers began to change. They, too, had become worried about the decline of deliberative party decision making. The result has been a number of serious proposals to bring party professionals and public officials back into the nominating conventions in significant numbers. The body of this book contains the story. Here, in our preface, we wish to observe that if the Sixth Edition contains less advocacy, that is because the main lines of our thinking have become much more commonly accepted.

This is not to say that Rip Van Delegate, who has been sleeping for the past thirty years, would find presidential elections totally unrecognizable. For as so often happens in the history of reform, the new does not necessarily entirely displace the old but, rather, coexists with it. The professional party stalwarts of the First Edition, who wanted party unity in order to win the presidential election, are still here and active, although increasingly they are outnumbered by the amateur purists of the Second and Third Editions, who would rather be right and remain a minority than wrong and maintain a majority. State primaries and state conventions are still around, but the proportions have changed to give delegates selected in primaries—especially the early primaries—a greatly dominant voice. Money is still, as Jess Unruh once said, the mother's milk of politics, but it is now raised differently than it was, and it must be spent earlier and in different and more dispersed feedings. State caucuses and candidate organizations still matter a great deal at the conventions, but increasingly they must ally themselves with organized caucuses of young people, women, black people, Mexican-Americans, and other demographic groups. All this explains why so much of what we write has to be qualified by saying that this is how things once were, or that our remarks apply to some actors some of the time but not to all actors most of the time or to any of them all of the time.

It would be fair to say, since we last wrote, that concern over the effectiveness and the cohesion of American government has increased. Perhaps the rise of unease has something to do with the decline of political parties. And perhaps the decline of parties has something to do with the way in which nomination and election to the presidency, once celebrated as the central source of party unity, has changed and contributed to the problem instead of the solution. In this edition, therefore, we pay even more attention than in the past to the prospects of the American party system, not to what it has been but to what it is becoming and what it ought to be.

We are pleased to acknowledge that in this edition, as in all the others, our work relies heavily upon the contributions of our colleagues in the profession of political science, who have done so much to increase knowledge about parties, voters and elections. Some of these colleagues have given us aid and comfort more directly, and we thank, in particular: Byron Shafer, who through his Russell Sage Foundation Project sponsored visits by one of us to both national party conventions in 1980, Herbert Alexander, Louise Lindblom, Richard Brody, Steve Wayne, and Joseph Gorman, all of whom helped us gather material for this edition. Readers of the last edition whose thoughts helped us shape this one include Henry Brady and Donald Pfarrer, and we continue to be grateful for the work that has stood the test of time that Bill Cavala and Byron Shafer put into earlier editions. The sizable effort that we have made to update this book was greatly facilitated by the help of Joseph White in Berkeley, and especially by the prodigious exertions of Michael Goldstein in Washington. We also appreciate the hospitality of our good friends Douglas Bennet and Norman Sherman of the Roosevelt Center for American Policy Studies, and of Rena Lacey, who put the entire manuscript into the Center's word processor. The Center has, in its short existence, already carved out a special place for itself in the world of Washington think tanks, and not only because of its graciousness toward visitors.

Finally, we acknowledge that our families have been uppermost in our minds as we wrote this revision. Now that so many of our children have reached college age, it gives us special pleasure to dedicate the contents, as well as the proceeds, of this book to them.

Washington, D.C.   N.W.P.
Berkeley, California   A.W.
April 20, 1983

Contents

Preface   vii

☆ **Introduction**
POLITICAL STRATEGIES AND
PRESIDENTIAL ELECTIONS   I

☆ **Chapter 1**
THE STRATEGIC ENVIRONMENT:
PARTICIPANTS   5

Voters
Interest Groups and Voting Blocs
Parties
The Electoral College
Conclusion

☆ **Chapter 2**

THE STRATEGIC ENVIRONMENT: RESOURCES   **53**

The Distribution of Resources
Money
Control over Information
The Role of Television
Incumbency as a Resource: The Presidency
Incumbency as a Liability: The Vice-presidency
Convertibility of Resources

☆ **Chapter 3**

THE NOMINATION PROCESS   **93**

Before the Primaries
Primaries
State and District Conventions
Prenomination Strategies
At the Convention: Housekeeping
Candidates and Their Organizations
Delegates and Caucuses
Delegate Behavior in Multiballot Conventions
The Balloting
The Vice-presidential Nominee
The Future of National Conventions

☆ **Chapter 4**

THE CAMPAIGN   **147**

Three Underdog Strategies
The Strategies in Application: 1964 to 1980
Party Realignment and the 1980 Election
Theory and Action
"Ins" and "Outs"
Organizations and Accidents
Where to Campaign
Domestic Issues

Foreign Affairs
Social Issues
Presentation of Self
Television Debates
Getting a Good Press
Mud-Slinging and Heckling
Feedback

☆ Appendix
FORECASTING THE OUTCOME   199

☆ Chapter 5
REFORM   208

The Political Theory of Policy Government
The Evolution of a Second Branch of Party Reform
Reform by Means of Participatory Democracy: An Appraisal
Three Specific Reforms
An Appraisal of the Nomination Process
An Appraisal of Permanent Voting Enrollment
An Appraisal of the Electoral College
Party Differences and Political Stability
Is Party Reform Relevant?

☆ Chapter 6
AMERICAN PARTIES AND DEMOCRACY   267

Elections and Public Policy
Parties of Advocacy versus Parties of Intermediation

Notes   283

Index   345

PRESIDENTIAL ELECTIONS

Political Strategies and Presidential Elections

This book is about the winning of the presidential office. Although many writers have alleged that the president occupies a great and lonely eminence, the presidential office exists within a cultural and political tradition that shapes the ways in which it is won and, later, the ways in which presidential power is exercised. We will, however, not speak further here about the exercise of executive power. Rather, the task before us is to make plain the context within which the battle for presidential office is waged, to discuss the strategies of contending parties, and, if possible, to explain why some strategies are used by some contestants and other strategies by others. In this way we hope to elucidate a significant area of our common political life.

Our thesis is a simple one: that strategies of participants in a presidential election make sense once we understand the web of circumstances in which they operate. This principle applies to candidates and their managers, to delegates at nominating conventions, to party workers, and to voters. Strategies are courses of action consciously pursued toward well-understood goals. Watching strategies helps us to learn how political leaders use the constraints and opportunities of their environment to achieve their goals.

Both the political strategies of participants in presidential elections and

1

the circumstances that give rise to them are relatively stable, persistent features of our political system. We have had a two-party political system with the same two major parties for well over a hundred years. Presidential nominees have been picked (or at least ratified) by national party conventions for an even longer period.[1] Presidential candidates have always been faced with such problems as deciding whether more or less emphasis on their party affiliation will help them gain votes. Contemporary evidence that party preferences are not distributed evenly among the electorate helps explain, for example, why the strategy of recent Democratic candidates has been to emphasize their party label, while Republicans have been more inclined to minimize their connection with their party.

Political strategies that persist over a period of time are reasonably easy to identify, even when they are colored by the distinctive styles and personalities of particular candidates. We hope, therefore, to achieve a level of discussion that goes beyond the special circumstances of 1984 or any other year, and say something about American presidential elections in general. This task is not made easier by the undeniable fact that the rules of the game themselves have undergone changes over time; but it has not been made impossible. Our intention is to show how changes in the rules affect how politicians behave in presidential election politics. In fact, the very rapidity with which the rules have recently changed makes clearer than ever the importance politicians ascribe to them. Their disagreements over the rules reveal that real differences in outcomes are at stake when the game is played by one set of rules or another.

In large measure, a description and analysis such as ours is possible because of the efforts of dozens of scholars who have reported upon and investigated, with ever-increasing detail and accuracy, the component parts of the American political system. The purpose of this book is to synthesize these reports for the enlightenment and use of interested citizens. But we cannot forecast the outcome of any particular election, and we have no desire (at least, not here) to advise people how to vote.

In the first two chapters we identify the characteristics of the American political system that make up the strategic environment within which the pursuit of the presidency takes place. The would-be president must come to terms with voters, who enter each election period as complex bundles of already formed habits, attitudes, and loyalties. Candidates must deal with interest groups and parties which activate these habits. And they must pay attention to the rules by which votes are counted. In the second chapter, we discuss the comparative availability to candidates of certain key resources, such as money and control over information.

These two chapters lay out a framework for much that follows in the third and fourth chapters. These deal, successively, with the various steps of the nomination and election processes. At this point in the book, we discuss a variety of classic strategic "moves," such as entering or not entering primaries, the manipulation of interpretations of primary results, the starting and stopping of bandwagons at national party conventions, the selection of areas of the country in which to campaign, and the choice of issues to emphasize. In Chapters 3 and 4, we relate those moves to their necessary preconditions in terms of resources and also relate them to their probable consequences.

In the fifth chapter, we discuss significant reforms that have altered the strategic framework of presidential elections, as well as reform proposals that would in some respects reconstitute the party system and redistribute resources among presidential candidates. Reforms and reform proposals are often debated rather abstractly on their presumed merits, without being related to any concrete consequences. We hope to provoke fresh insight into the subject by looking at reforms in the light of the new distribution of benefits and handicaps which we believe they allocate to various participants in presidential elections.

Finally, in Chapter 6, we state in general terms the properties of political parties as they are emerging in the framework provided by contemporary presidential elections. In particular we juxtapose the emerging parties of advocacy with the persisting fact that in our system public officials receive few specific and meaningful policy directives from the electorate. We show that while our political system discourages both strict application of majority rule and mandates on specific policies, it is still meaningful to speak of our form of government as democratic, open, and responsive—as well as flexible, tough, stable, and resourceful. Whether these qualities will persist, however, depends on the maintenance of major political parties that will continue to reconcile divergent interests. The capacity of parties to mediate between citizen and government and among sectors of society is now under severe strain. Insofar as there is a tendency for activists to grow further away, not only from each other, but from the bulk of citizens who identify with party labels, it is worthwhile considering whether parties ameliorate, reflect, or in fact exacerbate differences. Activists who care mostly about programmatic and ideological correctness are becoming more significant than those who care mostly about political cohesion and winning elections in the presidential nominating process. The final chapter calls attention to this trend and asks what are the gains and costs of moving in this direction.

While some scholars doubt that political parties have in fact declined as much as we say, there can be little doubt that the functions parties once performed now have to be shared with other forces.[2] Once upon a time, political parties virtually monopolized election campaigns. Now they share with or relinquish to candidates and their professional specialists the jobs of recruiting people to run the campaign, ascertaining popular preferences, and communicating with voters. The financing of elections, the making of issues, the recruitment and advertising of candidates now belong to a variety of interest groups, media people, and self-starting candidates, all of whom compete as well as cooperate with political parties. True enough, the financial base and training capacity of national parties has improved, but so has the ability of rival institutions. Thus the traditional division of labor—public officials and interest groups making policies and political parties nominating and electing candidates—has become blurred. Interest groups have become much more important at the electoral level, in which they once participated only sporadically, while intensifying their activities at the policy level. Parties, by contrast, have diminished in electoral importance *and* in the coordination of public policy (keeping certain issues out of politics and mobilizing support or opposition on others). When is the last time we heard of national parties influencing the president or Congress? The crucial connections between electoral and policy politics have become attenuated.

Presidential elections are important to us as citizens. They constitute a major (though, of course, not the only) means of guiding our future. They also remind us of our heritage of political responsibility and freedom, a heritage that is increasingly precious.

Chapter 1

The Strategic Environment: Participants

Political strategies are worked out within a framework of circumstances that are in part subject to manipulation but in greater part are "given." This fact of life also applies to the strategies of aspirants to the presidency, who must construct extremely complex plans of action within a context of hundreds of relevant circumstances, most of which lie beyond their control. Some of these circumstances are contingent upon and relate to the strategies and resources of other participants in the election process. Other circumstances are more stable and have to do with features of the American political system that are in place before the contest starts. These features provide advantages and handicaps differently to Democrats and Republicans, to incumbent presidents and challengers, to household names and newcomers. In this chapter and the next, we shall deal with these "givens" of the political system to show how they shape the decisions of presidential election strategists.

☆ Voters

Voters vary in their party loyalties, the strength of their commitment to their views, and their interest in politics. Most of them are not interested in most

5

public issues most of the time.[1] In a society like ours, it apparently is quite possible to live comfortably without being politically concerned. Political activity is costly and eats up time and energy at an astounding rate. To be informed and politically active on strategic problems in nuclear politics or on the operations of a municipal electric plant is not a matter of a few moments of reflection. One must attend meetings, listen to or participate in discussion, write letters, attempt to persuade or be persuaded by others, and engage in other time-consuming labor. This means foregoing other activities, like devoting extra time to the job, playing with the children, and watching TV. So far as we can tell it is these other activities rather than public affairs that are the primary concerns of most people, and the costs of participation in public affairs appear, for most people, to be greater than the returns. Only a few people receive financial rewards or hold jobs or are acclaimed in the public arena, considerations that might lead them to devote the time and effort required to participate. It is only in regard to a few issues, such as prolonged unemployment or rapid inflation or sudden and sharp tax increases, that most citizens find it worthwhile to attend to politics rather than do other things.

Even so, there are a few people who are continuously interested in a wide variety of issues. These are usually public officials, interest-group leaders, newspaper editors, and academics—all people whose occupations require political interest. There is a larger number who have specialized interests in specific policy areas. These may include public officials, officers and members of civic organizations and interest groups, citizens who are directly affected, and a sprinkling of others who make a hobby of being interested, including seekers after causes and people who like to get their names on letterheads. These political activists, who may or may not themselves be leaders, are different from ordinary voters, as we shall see.

The fact that individuals vary enormously in their degree of interest has profound implications for political life. For ordinary citizens, interest is a necessary condition of influence. The interested tend to go to meetings where public affairs are discussed and decided. They tend to belong to political parties and to work in various ways to help the party of their choice. They cultivate their access to public officials. They tend to care more about the outcomes of public policies and to communicate their concerns to decision makers. And so they become more influential.

Differences in interest also influence voting behavior: people who are interested in politics tend to vote, and those who are uninterested tend not to vote.[2] Who is included in these two groups? In general, the better-educated people are more active and interested in public affairs. They also tend to be better off financially and more settled in their communities.[3] This is also the population from which the Republican party draws disproportionate support, which consequently gives it a substantial advantage among voters who tend to turn out most reliably for presidential elections. On the other hand, the low-turnout groups, normally Democratic, tend to be numerically greater than the high-turnout groups. Furthermore, traditionally Democratic groups may be clustered in a way that maximizes their strength in presidential elections by being located in areas that are favored by the Electoral College system of vote counting. We shall return to this topic later.

How do voters make up their minds whom to support? Most people vote according to their habitual party affiliation.[4] In other words, because they always support a particular party, many people will have made up their minds how to vote in 1984 before the candidates are even chosen. These party regulars are likely to be more interested and active in politics and have more political knowledge than people who call themselves political "independents."[5] But they rarely change their minds. They tend to listen to their own side of political arguments and to agree with the policies espoused by their party. They even go so far as to ignore information which they perceive to be unfavorable to the party of their choice.[6]

If party is so important in giving a structure to voters' pictures of reality and in helping them choose their preferred presidential candidate before the candidate is even nominated, we had best inquire where people get their party affiliations. There seems to be no simple answer to this. The party affiliations of most voters seem to be governed by a number of forces. An individual lives in a social context and inherits a social identity that contains a political component. People are Democrats or Republicans, in part, because their families and the other people with whom they interact are Democrats or Republicans.[7] Most individuals come into close contact with affiliates of only one party.[8] And just as people tend to share characteristics with their friends and families, such as income and educational level, religious affiliation, area of residence, and so on, so they also tend to share party loyalties with them.[9]

Of course, we all know of instances where people do not share various status-giving characteristics with their parents and at least some of their friends, so it should come as no surprise that sometimes children do not share the politics of their parents. No doubt political differences tend to run together with the other kinds of differences. But by and large, voters retain the party loyalties of the primary groups of which they are a part.

The overall result is to give each of the major political parties reservoirs

of voting strength they can count on from year to year. Republicans traditionally do well in the small towns and rural areas of New England, the
Middle Atlantic states, and the Midwest. They draw their support from
people who are richer and better educated than Democratic supporters,
occupy managerial or professional positions or run small businesses, live in
or move into the well-to-do suburban areas, and are predominantly Protestant. Democrats draw great support from the large cities. Wage earners,
union members, Catholics, black voters, and many of the descendants of the
great waves of immigrants who entered this country in the latter half of the
nineteenth century—Jews, Irish, Poles—all contribute disproportionately to
the Democratic vote.[10]

One may ask how these particular groups came to have these particular
loyalties. We must turn to history to find answers to this question. Enough
is known about a few groups to make it possible to speculate about what kinds
of historical events tend to align groups with a political party.

Let us take a few examples. We all know about the "Solid South," which
from the Civil War until the era of George Wallace and Barry Goldwater was
predominantly Democratic in its presidential voting. For all those years,
resentment against the harsh Reconstruction period under the leadership of
the Republican party was reflected in the election returns. Less well known
is the fact that the South was not unanimous in its enthusiasm for the Civil
War or in its resentment of Reconstruction. In many states of the Old South,
there were two kinds of farms: plantations on the flat land, which grew cash
crops, used slaves, and, in general, prospered before the Civil War; and
subsistence farms in the uplands, which had a few or no slaves and, in general,
were run by poorer white people. This latter group formed the historical core
of mountain areas that year after year, well into the latter half of the twentieth
century, voted Republican in presidential elections in western Virginia and
North Carolina, eastern Tennessee and Kentucky, and southeastern West
Virginia.[11]

The voting habits of black citizens, where they have voted, have been
shaped by several traumas. The Civil War freed them and made them Republicans. The Counter-Reconstruction disenfranchised them, and the growth of
American industry brought them north, where a crushing burden of economic destitution was added to racial discrimination. The differing effects of
the Great Depression of 1929 on black voters in the North brought them into
the New Deal coalition, and the Northern black voter has remained Democratic ever since.[12] As black voters have observed Democratic politicians

espousing causes in which they believe, they have increased their already high levels of support.

If, for some people, the historical events of the Civil War and the depression shaped their political heritage, for others the critical forces seem less dramatic and more diffuse. It is possible to see why the poor become Democrats, since the Democratic party in recent years has been so welfare-minded; but why do the rich lean toward the Republicans? Perhaps, in part, this is a reaction to the redistributive aspirations of some New Deal programs and the inclination of Democratic presidents to expand the role of government in the economy. But in all probability it is also a response to the record of the congressional wing of the Republican party, which so thoroughly dominated the post-Civil War era of industrial expansion. In this era, Republican policies vigorously encouraged—and to a degree underwrote—risk taking by private businessmen, granted them federal aid in a variety of forms, and withheld federal regulation from private enterprise.

Sometimes party affiliation coincides with ethnic identification because of the political and social circumstances surrounding the entry of ethnic groups into the country. In southern New England, politics was dominated by the Republican party and by "Yankees" of substance and high status during the decades following the Civil War. During these decades, thousands of Irish people streamed into this area. The Democratic party welcomed them; the Republicans did not. Soon the Democratic percentage of the two-party vote began to increase, and Irish politicians took over the Democratic party.[13]

In the Midwest, events such as American involvement in two wars against Germany under Democratic auspices seem to have shaped the political preferences of Americans of German descent toward the Republicans.[14]

Specific candidates of special attractiveness or unattractiveness may under certain circumstances sway voters to leave the party of their choice. The extraordinary elections of President Eisenhower are one example of this. His appeal to Democrats was quite amazing. But this was possible partially because these Democrats did not perceive Eisenhower as a partisan figure, but rather as a nonpartisan war hero. It is not surprising, then, that his personal popularity did not greatly aid other Republicans who ran with him, or the Republican party, once he no longer headed the ticket. As the figures in Table 1.1 indicate, the candidacy of George McGovern had the opposite effect; it propelled Democrats out of their party.[15]

Most of the time issues have much the same sporadic and peripheral effect as candidates. Let us see why. We can say to begin with that at least three

Table 1.1

Vote by Groups in Presidential Elections since 1952

	1952		1956		1960	
	Stev.	Ike	Stev.	Ike	JFK	Nixon
	(percent)		(percent)		(percent)	
NATIONAL	44.6	55.4	42.2	57.8	50.1	49.9
SEX						
Men	47	53	45	55	52	48
Women	42	58	39	61	49	51
RACE						
White	43	57	41	59	49	51
Nonwhite	79	21	61	39	68	32
EDUCATION						
College	34	66	31	69	39	61
High School	45	55	42	58	52	48
Grade School	52	48	50	50	55	45
OCCUPATION						
Professional						
and Business	36	64	32	68	42	58
White Collar	40	60	37	63	48	52
Manual	55	45	50	50	60	40
Members of						
Labor Union						
Families	61	39	57	43	65	35
AGE						
Under 30 years	51	49	43	57	54	46
30–49 years	47	53	45	55	54	46
50 years and older	39	61	39	61	46	54
RELIGION						
Protestants	37	63	37	63	38	62
Catholics	56	44	51	49	78	22
POLITICS						
Republicans	8	92	4	96	5	95
Democrats	77	23	85	15	84	16
Independents	35	65	30	70	43	57
REGION						
East	45	55	40	60	53	47
Midwest	42	58	41	59	48	52
South	51	49	49	51	51	49
West	42	58	43	57	49	51

	1964		1968			1972	
	LBJ	Gold.	HHH	Nixon	Wallc	McG.	Nixon
	(percent)		(percent)			(percent)	
NATIONAL	61.3	38.7	43.0	43.4	13.6	38	62
SEX							
Men	60	40	41	43	16	37	63
Women	62	38	45	43	12	38	62
RACE							
White	59	41	38	47	15	32	68
Nonwhite	94	6	85	12	3	87	13
EDUCATION							
College	52	48	37	54	9	37	63
High School	62	38	42	43	15	34	66
Grade School	66	34	52	33	15	49	51
OCCUPATION							
Professional							
and Business	54	46	34	56	10	31	69
White Collar	57	43	41	47	12	36	64
Manual	71	29	50	35	15	43	57
Members of							
Labor Union							
Families	73	27	56	29	15	46	54
AGE							
Under 30 years	64	36	47	38	15	48	52
30–49 years	63	37	44	41	15	33	67
50 years and older	59	41	41	47	12	36	64
RELIGION							
Protestants	55	45	35	49	16	30	70
Catholics	76	24	59	33	8	48	52
POLITICS							
Republicans	20	80	9	86	5	5	95
Democrats	87	13	74	12	14	67	33
Independents	56	44	31	44	25	31	69
REGION							
East	68	32	50	43	7	42	58
Midwest	61	39	44	47	9	40	60
South	52	48	31	36	33	29	71
West	60	40	44	49	7	41	59

Table 1.1 (continued)

	1976			1980		
	Carter	Ford (percent)	McC.	Carter	Reagan (percent)	Andrsn
NATIONAL	50	48	1	41	51	7
SEX						
Men	53	45	1	38	53	7
Women	48	51	*	44	49	6
RACE						
White	46	52	1	36	56	7
Nonwhite	85	15	1	86	10	2
EDUCATION						
College	42	55	2	35	53	10
High School	54	46	*	43	51	5
Grade School	58	41	1	54	42	3
OCCUPATION						
Professional and Business	42	56	1	33	55	10
White Collar	50	48	2	40	51	9
Manual	58	41	1	48	46	5
Members of Labor Union Families	63	36	1	50	43	5
AGE						
Under 30 years	53	45	1	47	41	11
30–49 years	48	49	2	38	52	8
50 years and older	52	48	*	41	54	4
RELIGION						
Protestants	46	53	*	39	54	6
Catholics	57	42	1	46	47	6
POLITICS						
Republicans	9	91	*	8	86	5
Democrats	82	18	*	69	26	4
Independents	38	57	4	29	55	14
REGION						
East	51	47	1	43	47	9
Midwest	48	50	1	41	51	7
South	54	45	*	44	52	3
West	46	51	1	35	54	9

*Less than one percent

SOURCE: *Gallup Monthly Opinion Index,* December 1976, December 1980.

preconditions must be satisfied for a voter's opinion about an issue to change his vote.[16] First, a voter must know about the issue; second, he must care about it at least a little; and third, he must be able to distinguish the positions of the parties and their candidates on the issue. Data from public opinion polls tell us that most people are not well informed about the content of issues most of the time.[17] All but major public issues are thus eliminated for most people. And even these major issues may enter the consciousness of most people in only the most rudimentary way.

Once a voter has some grasp of the content of a public policy and learns to prefer one outcome over another, he must also find public leaders to espouse his point of view. Finding differences on policy issues between parties is not always easy. Party statements on policy may be vague because leaders have not decided what to do. They may deliberately obfuscate an issue for fear of alienating interested publics. They may try to hold divergent factions in their parties together by glossing over disagreements on many specific issues. Even when real party differences on policy exist, many voters may not be aware of them. The subject may be rather esoteric to the common under- standing, or the time required to master the subject may be more than most people are willing to spend. By the time we get down to those who know and care about and can discriminate between party positions on issues, we usually have a small proportion of the electorate. This proportion is evidently grow- ing, as befits an increasingly educated electorate that responded to the rela- tively high-temperature presidential elections of the 1960s. Even so, the number of ideologically sophisticated voters appears to be no larger than 30 percent.[18] What can we say about these people?

Their most obvious characteristic is interest in and concern about issues and party positions. But these are precisely the people who are most likely to be strong party identifiers, who are characterized by a deep devotion to party, which makes it most unlikely that they will shift allegiance just because of a disagreement on one or two issues.[19] The number of issue-oriented "independents" who are left must be very small, especially if we consider that most of them lean toward one of the two major parties.[20] It is not unlikely that these people are distributed about equally on both sides of major policy questions, so that the total number of votes changed by the impact of any specific issue is bound to be minute.

We still have some preconditions to satisfy, however, before even these changes can be accepted as certain. One is that there must not be other issues that are also highly salient to voters and that work the other way. For if voters were willing to change their votes on one particular issue, why should

they not switch their support back because of another? There usually are
many issues in a campaign; only if all or most of the issues pointed voters
in the same direction would they be likely to switch their votes. But what is
the likelihood that parties will arrange their policies along a broad front,
forcing large numbers of "independent" voters from or into the fold? It is
low, but not impossible. In 1964 the Republicans may have done so. And in
1972 the Democratic candidate, George McGovern, "was perceived as so far
left on the issues that Nixon was generally closer to the electorate's average
issue position . . . on 11 out of 14 separate issues."[21]

Although it is true that the less knowledge a person has about public
affairs, the more likely he is to vote for a candidate of the opposite party, it
is important to distinguish between those who only have a little knowledge
and those who have none at all. For the voter who is utterly without any
contact with the political world, except at the polls, has no reason whatsoever to change his customary party vote. Thus changes in vote from one
party to another are likely to be concentrated among those who receive a
little but not a great deal of information about parties, issues, and candidates.[22]

Recent studies have more thoroughly penetrated the problem of issue
voting. One seeks to demonstrate that there is considerable issue content in
the citizen's behavior at the polls by showing that those who change party
from one election to the next generally are sympathetic to some key policies
of their new party. The "standpatters," on the other hand, generally are in
sympathy with major policies of their party.[23] Whether the citizen is taught
what to believe by his party or finds a party in accordance with his beliefs
cannot be determined from evidence presently available.

We can now see that a strong issue orientation is likely to guide voting
decisions under some circumstances. One set of circumstances occurs when
an issue becomes so intensely important that the voter is willing to lay aside
his party preferences and his preferences on other issues. An unpopular war,
severe economic deprivation (whether or not it is related to governmental
policies), a fixation on such issues as keeping water free of fluoride, have at
times led to the required intense feeling. The pocketbook nerve seems especially sensitive.[24] The inflation of 1977 to 1980 hurt President Carter, and the
high unemployment of 1981 and 1982 hurt Republican congressional candidates; it remains to be seen whether the Republican nominee for president
in 1984 will escape from its lingering effects even should the economic
situation improve.

Another case where issues might matter occurs when a party is seen to change across the spectrum of policies, as the Democrats appeared to do in 1972, or, more rarely, when the voter himself undergoes such a broad-scale change of heart. Finally, in a historical sense we can say that issues may have a lasting impact on voting behavior through the ways in which they shape the party affiliations of whole generations of voters. But if parties and their leaders make the issues and give them meaning for most people, then most people are not likely to change their party allegiance based upon their own reasoned look at issues. A depression, a civil war—events felt immediately and personally by millions—have activated new voters and thereby precipitated the great changes in party allegiances, not debates on the merits of this or that comparatively minor matter. The sheer brute impact of great events does more to change electoral outcomes over the long run than any single policy problem.

Issues can be forced on presidents and presidential candidates by events, interest groups, the news media, or some combination of these. Had President Carter wished to downplay Iran's taking of American hostages, the daily coverage on television would have made it difficult. Inability to resolve what had become defined as a major crisis eventually hurt Carter at the polls. President Reagan's attempt to keep negotiations on nuclear disarmament on the back burner until his defense build-up had gone further was at least partially thwarted by the widespread and intense nuclear freeze campaign. The dramatization of the plight of the unemployed on television, and the continuous charges in news media that Reagan's tax and expenditure cuts were "unfair," presented him with an issue he undoubtedly would rather have avoided.

Candidates and party leaders, rather than events alone, define the party's stand on issues. Cataclysms change past allegiance only if party responses win approval or disapproval from voters. The "Responsible Electorate," as V. O. Key called it,[25] may change its views of the parties, but the best guess is that the changes reflect appraisals of past party performance, rather than changes in issue preferences. As far as we are able to tell, voters adopt most of their issue orientations at the instigation of the parties: strong party identifiers are more likely to learn more and care more about issues, in part, precisely because this process reinforces their party identification.[26] Issue preferences may be adjusted to fit party views, rather than the other way around.[27] The Reagan administration's concerted effort to reduce the size of government by cutting domestic spending, for instance, is in part a response to the demands of party activists who supported the president. Citizens respond to this issue by intensifying their identification with the Republican party if they agree, and with the Democratic party if they disagree. People do not readily change their party identifications, so instead they may interpret party positions to fit their positions. This means that there are few issues that are not made by parties and political leaders, and hence few party identifiers are lost as a result of the policies adopted by the party of their choice.

The complex relationship between issues and electoral outcomes was illustrated by two issues in the especially heated 1968 election: the war in Vietnam and what was delicately called the "social issue"—racial conflict, crime, and law and order. Both issues had enormous public exposure and excited the passions of the politically aware. Yet the most sensitive and sophisticated analysis we have of how these issues related to public opinion shows that party identification had "fifty times the net impact of the Vietnam issue"[28] in determining whether voters favored Nixon or Humphrey for president. Party was so powerful that it cannot be considered on the same scale with other forces. Figure 1.1, which summarizes the impact of various

Figure 1.1

Domestic Policy More Important Than Vietnam and Urban Issues Combined: Issue Forces and the Presidential Vote, 1968

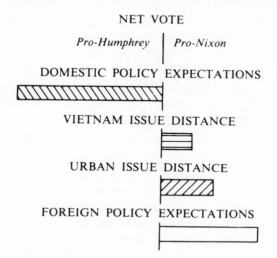

SOURCE: Richard A. Brody et al., "Vietnam, the Urban Crisis and the 1968 Presidential Election: A Preliminary Analysis," prepared for delivery at the 1969 meeting of the American Sociological Association, September 1969.

issues on the 1968 presidential vote, shows that domestic policy issues (the bread-and-butter matters of social welfare, employment, and prosperity) were considerably more important than Vietnam and social issues combined. Like other Democrats before him, Humphrey gained on domestic policy because voters saw themselves as closer to him than to his Republican opponent. Richard Nixon gained on the foreign policy side because of the Democratic image as the party of war.

Why was the Vietnam issue so unimportant? Most voters found Senators Robert Kennedy and Eugene McCarthy too "dovish" for their taste and Governor George Wallace much too "hawkish." The candidates of the major parties were rather close to the voters' preferences, with Nixon coming in a little ahead. Vietnam, Page and Brody argue, was an extremely "hot" issue. But the candidates managed to convince much of the electorate that their positions differed little, while those respondents who saw a difference tended to make that perception fit their preexisting bias—Democrats feeling closer to Humphrey and Republicans to Nixon, regardless of their own personal opinions.[29] It is difficult for an issue to have a major impact on an election outcome when the voters do not differentiate greatly among the candidates with respect to that issue. So, once again, we come back to party as the more important organizer of voters' ideas and sentiments.

When voters perceive a vast chasm separating them from one of the candidates, as they did with George McGovern in 1972, the importance of issues relative to party is bound to grow. The research group at the Michigan Center for Political Studies estimates that in 1972, party identification and issue differences each accounted for approximately one-third of the total vote. In this election Nixon received almost all Republican votes (94 percent), two-thirds of independents' votes (66 percent), and nearly half the votes of people calling themselves Democrats (42 percent). This was a better showing among Democrats than Dwight D. Eisenhower managed in his landslide year of 1956, when he got 28 percent of the Democratic vote. Why did this happen? Because "McGovern was seen as quite distant from the population's policy preferences. . . ." The Michigan group concludes that "a candidate such as McGovern who may represent only one segment of the national policy preference spectrum may capture control of a political party that shares his policy preferences but cannot go on to win an electoral victory under contemporary conditions of polarization."[30] This suggests that if most voters disagree with a candidate, and know they disagree with him, they are likely to vote against him.

Merely to list the functions that party identification performs for voters

—reducing their costs of acquiring political information, telling them what side they are on, organizing their information by ordering their preferences, letting them know what is of prime importance—is to suggest the profound significance of parties for voting behavior. Politics is complex; there are many possible issues, relevant political personalities, and choices to be made on election day. Voters who follow their party identification, however, can simplify their choices and reduce to manageable proportions the time and effort they spend on public affairs simply by voting for their party's candidate. Voters with strong party identifications need not puzzle over each and every issue. They can, instead, listen to the pronouncements of their party leaders, who inform them what issues are important, what information is most relevant to those issues, and what position they ought to take. Of course, citizens with greater interest in public affairs will want to investigate matters for themselves. Even so, their party identification provides them with important guides for the many matters on which they cannot possibly be well informed. All of us, including full-time participants like the president, have to find ways to cut information costs on some issues.[31] For most people who vote, identification with one of the two major political parties performs that indispensable function most of the time.

Has there been a decline in party identification? From 1952 to 1964, the overall amount of party identification among voters remained stable. From 1964 onward, many more Americans identified themselves as independents. Indeed, by 1974, self-styled independents outnumbered Republicans five to three and came near to the number of Democrats. It is important to distinguish, however, between pure independents, who exhibit no party feeling, and partisan independents, who lean toward the Democratic or Republican party. Partisan independents are far more knowledgeable and participate much more actively in politics; they also evidence a far greater tendency to vote, and they give large proportions of their vote to the party toward which they lean.[32]

Partisan independents continue to vote their party preferences (less frequently than strong party identifiers but more frequently than weak ones), and pure independents do not vote much at all. Party identification was considered strong in 1952; at that time 23 percent of the voting public declared themselves to be independents: 10 percent leaning to the Democrats, 7 percent leaning to the Republicans, and 6 percent pure independents. By 1980 the proportion of self-styled independents had risen to 37 percent—13 percent pure, 11 percent Democratic and 13 percent Republican. Thus while the number of pure independents has doubled, they are not a large fraction of the voting population. It is easy to overstate the political impact of the decline in party identifiers, in view of the fact that the increase among independents is divided between hidden party supporters and general nonvoters.[33]

Continuity in the identification of individuals with their parties remains high, especially when compared with their tendencies to continue with the same views of public policy (.85 compared to .35).[34] However, there have been massive defections of identifiers from the major parties in presidential voting in recent elections. From 1952 to 1968, Democrats defected about twice as often as Republicans (19 percent to 10 percent). Since 1972, Republican defection rates have stayed about the same, but Democratic defections have increased (to a mean of 27 percent).[35]

Do defections mean a long-term drop in party identification, or are they a short-term response to particular events and specific candidates? No one can say for sure. One interpretation of the difference between the classic characterization of the 1960 study, *The American Voter,* of party identification as a durable standing decision and Morris Fiorina's more recent view of it as a "running balance sheet on the two parties"[36] has been contributed by Donald Kinder, who finds that citizen assessment of party performance on major dimensions of public policy—war and peace, employment, inflation, race—do matter.[37] However, most changes of party identifications involved switching in and out of the independent category rather than between the parties.[38] As Kinder sums up:

[P]arty identification is *not* immovable: it both influences and is influenced by the performance of government, by policy disagreements, and by the emergence of new candidates. . . . The loyalty citizens invest in party is at least partly a function of what governments and parties do, and what they fail to do. . . .

We should not press this too far, however. Although party identification does respond to political events, it does so sluggishly. It is one thing for Republicans to feel less enthusiastic toward their party after a period of sustained national difficulty presided over by a Republican administration; it is quite another to embrace the opposition. The latter seldom happens. In this respect, the running balance sheet metaphor is quite misleading. The strongest message of the evidence reviewed here may be the durability of party identification, how difficult it is to budge people from their commitment to party.[39]

What might challenge or supplant parties as organizers of issues, present-
ers of alternatives, and publicizers of public affairs? The personal efforts of
candidates may substitute for party leadership, and so may the mass media.
We have called attention to their increasing role. Presumably an indicator of
the corresponding weakness of parties is the decline in partisan identification
among voters.[40]

While fewer party identifiers may mean that parties are weaker, this does
not mean that people are less likely to give themselves a party label because
they are dissatisfied with parties. Some people undoubtedly like to call themselves independents because being independent is valued in our political
culture. As we have seen, about two-thirds of the people who claim that
status actually vote rather steadily for one party.[41] There has also been a
long-term increase, from about 2.1 percent in 1964 to 9.7 percent in 1980,
in survey respondents who do not call themselves independents but also have
no party preference. These people seem rather indifferent to the parties. What
evidence we have suggests that they are not "turned off" by the parties, but
have "tuned out."[42]

Amid these subtleties in the analysis of party identification, what may we
safely conclude? We can begin by saying that party as a value and an orientation point is less important than it once was, but it is still very important.
Most people—especially most voters, since those without any preference are
not likely to vote—identify with or lean towards one party or the other. There
are always defections, however, and the parties cannot automatically count
on all their identifiers to give unqualified support in every election. Party
identification does not translate automatically into party-line voting. Voters
may tend to be loyal, but they can also be driven away.

This, more or less, explains the direction of voting. But why do people
turn out to vote at all? Clearly, some people vote and some people do not.
In the last few presidential elections only about 55 percent of those eligible
by virtue of age actually voted.[43] And of course the numbers are even lower
for midterm national elections for Congress, where there is no presidential
contest.

In order to vote, people must register as voters according to regulations
and procedures that vary somewhat from state to state. Voting itself takes
place not on a holiday, as in some countries, or over a weekend, but on a
regular workday, customarily the first Tuesday after the first Monday in
November. The number of people voting is usually so large that, as one
observer calculated, it is less likely that an individual vote will decisively

Table 1.2
Turnout in Presidential Elections, 1968–1980
(percentage of age-eligible voters)

1968	1972	1976	1980
60.9%	55.5%	54.3%	53.2%

SOURCE: U.S. Bureau of the Census, *Statistical Abstract of the United States 1981* (Washington, D.C., 1981), p. 496.

affect an electoral outcome than that the voter will be struck by lightning on his way to the polling place.[44]

Since there are barriers to voting, since the link between one's vote and a policy result is tenuous, and since the variety of choices on an American ballot can be overwhelming, we should not be surprised that some people do not vote. There is, however, something to be explained in the decline since 1960 in voting rates. One possible explanation, building upon observations in the early voting literature,[45] is that decline in party identification contributes to a decline in voting.[46] Another relates decline in voting to a sense that the system will not respond anyway, a phenomenon that we would argue may also be related to party weakness.[47] Party strength can also be important in a way not related to attitude: strong party organizations knock on doors and get out the vote.

Party feeling is not, however, the sole source of the impulse to vote. The socioeconomic status and general educational level of voters also matter, both of which correlate with a voter's general level of social connectedness. The sense of membership in society gives people a stake in events and increases the likelihood that they will be part of a group that is particularly interested in current politics. As people get older, for example, their ties to their social environment become stronger and more numerous, and they tend to vote in greater numbers. When people move about, their ties loosen and they vote less conscientiously; but as they settle down, they vote more frequently. The more educated people are, the more different connections they maintain with the outside world in the form of membership in voluntary organizations, and the more likely they are to vote.[48]

Group membership, then, is a factor in voting rates and other forms of participation. Naturally one's group affiliations also influence one's voting choice. Therefore it is useful to consider more thoroughly the strategic role of interest groups in presidential elections.

☆ Interest Groups and Voting Blocs

Interest groups are collections of people who are similarly situated with respect to one or more policies of government and who organize to do something about it. The interest groups most significant for elections in our society are those having one or more of the following characteristics:

1. They have a mass base, that is, are composed of many members.

2. They are concentrated geographically, rather than dispersed over the entire map, or they are connected by modern technology, such as computerized mailing lists or low-cost WATS phone lines.

3. They represent major resource investments of members—such as in the case of the *producers* of bicycles, whose entire livelihoods are tied up in the group involved, as against the *consumers* of bicycles, for whom investment in a bicycle is not anywhere near as important.

4. They involve those characteristics that give people status in society—such as race or ethnicity.

5. They involve feelings about a single issue that are so intense as to overpower concerns about other issues.

6. They are composed of people who are able to participate actively in politics; that is, people who have time and money to spare.

Interest groups may be more or less organized and more or less vigilant and alert on policy matters that concern, or ought to concern, them. They are not necessarily organized in ways that make them politically effective; very often the paid lobbyists of interest groups spend more time trying to alert their own members to the implications of government policies than they spend lobbying with politicians.[49]

In American politics, interest group activity is lively and ubiquitous, even when it is not particularly effective or meaningful in terms of policy outcomes. We shall be concerned with three characteristics of interest groups. First, membership in these groups may be quite important in giving voters a sense of affiliation and political location. In this respect, interest groups act much the way parties do, helping to fill in the voter's map of the world with preferences, priorities, and facts. Second, interest groups are important because of their partisan political activities; they may actively recruit supporters for candidates and aid materially in campaigns. Third, interest groups may influence party policy by making demands with respect to issues in return for their own mobilized support. The extent to which interest groups can "deliver" members' votes, however, is always problematic; to a great extent interest group leaders are the prisoners of past alliances their group has made. Even so, the black vote, the farm vote, the labor vote, the youth vote, the consumer vote, and many other "votes" are bandied about as though they were political commodities that can be manipulated easily in behalf of one or another candidate. Indeed in the case of some of the most vocal groups, they have no membership at all and only exist as lobbying organizations.[50]

When the use of election statistics and opinion polls was in its infancy, claims to guarantee support or threats to withdraw it could be analyzed only intuitively, and no one could tell with any certainty whether these claims had substance. The appearance of voting studies and the development of public opinion analysis have created new opportunities for the purveyors of bloc votes and new difficulties for the interested but necessarily amateur citizen and public official. How are they to evaluate these important political claims backed up by impressive and complicated arrays of data?

The usual argument is that if one or another candidate captures the allegiance of a particular bloc, that bloc's pivotal position or large population in a state will enable the fortunate aspirant to capture all of the electoral votes and thus win the election. But of course no one combination of states totaling more than a majority of electoral votes is more critical, valuable, or pivotal than any other such combination. In a fairly close election the defection of any number of combinations of states to the other side would spell the difference between victory and defeat.

Appeals to various groups are conditioned by time, place, and circumstance. There is little doubt that under *some* conditions during *some* elections *some* social characteristics of voters and candidates may have *some* relevance to the election results. Finding the conditions under which specified social characteristics become relevant to voter choice is difficult. We know that in a competitive political system various participants (parties, interest groups, leaders) put forward candidates and issues designed to capture the allegiance of various groups. Rarely is it possible to appeal to one group alone, not only because there are so many different groups, with all sorts of conceptions of policy, but also because each individual may have many social characteristics that are potentially relevant to his voting decision. While some people may be so single-minded that they have only one interest that is important in determining their vote—color, religion, ethnic background, income, feelings about abortion or the Equal Rights Amendment or the environment—most of us have multiple interests that sometimes conflict. Ecological interest groups, for example, may have less success in areas where environmental concerns conflict with employment opportunities than in areas where the two do not conflict. The worse the economic conditions, the stronger the difficulty. Concern about increasing unemployment may influence how some voters feel about governmental support of people who are not working. Much depends on the tides of events, which may bring one or another issue to the forefront of the voter's consciousness and incline him toward the candidate he believes best represents his preferences on that matter.[51] Today, the enormous size of governmental transfer payments in money, such as Social Security, and in goods, such as food stamps, may lead recipients and providers alike to see a close cash connection between public policy and their individual welfare. Long-term social trends, as well as candidates' strategies, have much to do with the impact of appeals to bloc votes.

In each election members of the various groups that make up the American voting population turn out to vote, dividing their loyalties in varying ways between the major parties. To determine the contribution that a particular group makes to a party, it is necessary to know three things: how big the group is, how many of its members actually vote, and how devoted its members are to one party or another.

For example, let us look at the contribution of votes of poor people— defined as those whose incomes are below a specified amount that fluctuates according to the price changes in a constant market basket of goods—to the Democratic party. Basing his analysis on Michigan Center for Political Study polls, Robert Axelrod has shown that the contribution of the poor to the total Democratic vote has fallen from 28 percent in 1952 to only 5 percent in 1980.[52] This trend can be accounted for in any—or all—of three ways: (1) more of the nonpoor voted Democratic in 1980, diluting the contribution of the poor; (2) fewer poor people voted Democratic in recent elections; (3) there are simply fewer poor people, by the standard definition, and this dilutes their vote. This last is certainly true: in 1952, poor people made up 36 percent of the U.S. adult population; the proportion defined by the standard measure as poor had sunk to 16 percent in 1969 and 9 percent in 1980, partly (but not entirely) because of inflation.

While the poor have not been an important part of the Democratic coalition in recent years, black people have established themselves as a substantial component: from 5 percent to 7 percent in 1952–1960 to 12 percent in 1964, and 19 percent in 1968. In 1972 the percentage rose again, to 22 percent. In 1976, their contribution fell for the first time, reaching 16 percent, largely as a result of the return of many Democratic voters who defected in 1972; in 1980 the percentage was again at 22 percent. Since the black population has remained a relatively constant 11 percent of the total population, their vastly increased contribution through 1980 was the result of a near doubling of their turnout throughout the nation and of their high loyalty to the Democratic party.

While union members and their families made up a third of all Democratic votes in the 1950s, their contribution fell slightly to 28 percent in 1968 and rose again to 32 percent in 1972, where it stayed in 1976 and 1980. They are important to the party because a quarter of all adults are in union families, their turnout is reasonably good, and they vote more Democratic than other people. Although only half of union members voted Democratic in 1980, the overall defection among other Democrats was so great that union members still voted 9 percent more Democratic than others. Whereas union families contributed four times as many votes as black people to the Democratic party in 1960, unionists contributed fewer than twice as many Democratic votes as blacks in 1980.

Catholics comprise roughly a third of the population and they provide a third of all Democratic votes. In 1952 and 1956, Southerners still voted about 10 percent more Democratic than the rest of the country. In more recent elections they have been slightly more Republican than other people, though they moved back to the Democrats in 1976 and 1980, when a Southerner headed the Democratic ticket. They gave a quarter of their votes to the third-party movement of George Wallace in 1968. Black Southerners stayed with the Democrats in that year, but white Southerners split their presidential vote among all three parties.

A major change has been the increase in the votes of young people, that is, those under thirty years of age. Until 1972, they were not part of any party coalition and their low turnout reduced any impact that their 18 percent of the population might have given them. Now things may be different. Because the voting age has been lowered to eighteen, and because of the baby boom after the Second World War, their proportion of the population has increased to 28 percent, more than half again what it was a few years ago. Their turnout in 1972 was only 9 percent less than the overall average compared to 15 percent less in 1968. Their loyalty to the Democratic party, moreover, never exceeding 3 percent since 1952, had increased fourfold to 12 percent in 1972.[53] Whether youth was so important to the Democrats in 1972 mainly

Table 1.3

Participation in National Elections, by Population
Characteristics: 1968, 1972, 1976, and 1980

Persons in thousands, as of November. Covers civilian noninstitutional population. For 1968, persons 18 years old and over in Georgia and Kentucky, 19 and over in Alaska, 20 and over in Hawaii, and 21 and over elsewhere;

		1968		
	Persons of voting	Persons reporting they voted		Percent reporting they did
Characteristic	age	Total	Percent	not vote
TOTAL	116,535	78,964	67.8	30.0
Male	54,464	38,014	69.8	27.6
Female	62,071	40,951	66.0	32.1
White	104,521	72,213	69.1	28.9
Negro	10,935	6,300	57.6	38.5
18–20 years old	432	144	33.3	64.1
21–24 years old	11,170	5,707	51.1	45.6
25–34 years old	23,198	14,501	62.5	35.8
35–44 years old	22,905	16,223	70.8	27.1
45–64 years old	40,362	30,238	74.9	22.8
65 years old and over	18,468	12,150	65.8	31.9
Median age (years)	45.2	46.7	(x)	(x)
Metropolitan residence	75,756	51,503	68.0	32.0
Nonmetropolitan residence	40,778	27,461	67.3	32.7
North and West residence	81,594	57,970	71.0	29.0
South residence	34,941	20,994	60.1	39.9
Years of school completed:				
8 years or less	30,430	16,592	54.4	45.5
9–11 years	20,429	12,519	61.3	38.7
12 years	39,704	28,768	72.5	27.5
More than 12 years	25,971	21,086	81.2	18.8
Employed	70,002	49,772	71.1	28.9
Unemployed	1,875	977	52.1	47.9
Not in labor force	44,657	28,215	63.2	36.8

for 1972, 1976, and 1980, persons 18 years old and over in all states. Includes aliens. Figures are based on a population sample. Differences in percentages may also be due to overreporting of voting by persons in the sample. Excludes persons who did not report whether or not they had voted.

| Characteristic | Persons of voting age | 1972 Persons reporting they voted | | Percent reporting they did not vote |
		Total	Percent	
TOTAL	136,203	85,766	63.0	37.0
Male	63,833	40,908	64.1	35.9
Female	72,370	44,858	62.0	38.0
White	121,243	78,166	64.5	35.5
Negro	13,493	7,032	52.1	47.9
18–20 years old	11,022	5,318	48.3	51.7
21–24 years old	13,590	6,896	50.7	49.3
25–34 years old	26,933	16,072	59.7	40.3
35–44 years old	22,240	14,747	66.3	33.7
45–64 years old	42,344	29,991	70.8	29.2
65 years old and over	20,074	12,741	63.5	36.5
Median age (years)	42.4	44.9	(x)	(x)
Metropolitan residence	99,248	63,799	64.3	35.7
Nonmetropolitan residence	36,855	21,967	59.4	40.6
North and West residence	93,653	62,193	66.4	33.6
South residence	42,550	23,573	55.4	44.6
Years of school completed:				
8 years or less	28,065	13,311	47.4	52.6
9–11 years	22,277	11,587	52.0	48.0
12 years	50,749	33,193	65.4	34.6
More than 12 years	35,113	27,675	78.8	21.2
Employed	80,164	52,899	66.0	34.0
Unemployed	3,735	1,863	49.9	50.1
Not in labor force	52,305	31,004	59.3	40.7

27

Table 1.3 (continued)

Characteristic	1976			
	Persons of voting age	Persons reporting they voted		Percent reporting they did not vote
		Total	Percent	
TOTAL	146,500	86,700	59.2	40.8
Male	69,000	41,100	59.6	40.4
Female	77,600	45,600	58.8	41.2
White	129,300	78,800	60.9	39.1
Negro	14,900	7,300	48.7	51.3
18–20 years old	12,100	4,600	38.0	62.0
21–24 years old	14,800	6,800	45.6	54.4
25–34 years old	31,500	17,500	55.4	44.6
35–44 years old	22,800	14,400	63.3	36.7
45–64 years old	43,300	29,800	68.7	31.3
65 years old and over	22,000	13,700	62.2	37.8
Median age (years)	41.5	45.1	(x)	(x)
Metropolitan residence	99,600	58,900	59.2	40.8
Nonmetropolitan residence	47,000	27,800	59.1	40.9
North and West residence	99,400	60,800	61.2	38.8
South residence	47,100	25,900	54.9	45.1
Years of school completed:				
8 years or less	24,900	11,000	44.1	55.9
9–11 years	22,200	10,500	47.2	52.8
12 years	55,700	33,100	59.4	40.6
More than 12 years	43,700	32,200	73.5	26.5
Employed	86,000	53,300	62.0	38.0
Unemployed	6,400	2,800	43.7	56.3
Not in labor force	54,100	30,600	56.5	43.5

Characteristic	1980			
	Persons of voting age	Persons reporting they voted		Percent reporting they did not vote
		Total	Percent	
TOTAL	157,100	93,100	59.2	40.8
Male	74,100	43,800	59.1	40.9
Female	83,000	49,300	59.4	40.6
White	137,700	83,900	60.9	39.1
Negro	16,400	8,300	50.5	49.5
18–20 years old	12,300	4,400	35.7	64.3
21–24 years old	15,900	6,800	43.1	56.9
25–34 years old	35,700	19,500	54.6	45.4
35–44 years old	25,600	16,500	64.4	35.6
45–64 years old	43,600	30,200	69.3	30.7
65 years old and over	24,100	15,700	65.1	34.9
Median age (years)	40.7	44.6	(x)	(x)
Metropolitan residence	106,700	62,700	58.8	41.2
Nonmetropolitan residence	50,500	30,400	60.2	39.8
North and West residence	106,500	65,000	61.0	39.0
South residence	50,600	28,100	55.6	44.4
Years of school completed:				
8 years or less	22,700	9,600	42.6	57.4
9–11 years	22,500	10,200	45.6	54.4
12 years	61,200	36,000	58.9	41.1
More than 12 years	50,800	37,200	73.2	26.8
Employed	95,000	58,800	61.8	38.2
Unemployed	6,900	2,800	41.2	58.8
Not in labor force	55,200	31,400	57.0	43.0

x—Not applicable

SOURCE: U.S. Bureau of the Census, *Current Population Reports,* series p-20, Nos. 192, 253 and 359. From *Statistical Abstract,* 1974, p. 437; 1977, p. 491; 1981, p. 499.

because older citizens deserted George McGovern's candidacy in droves or whether age will emerge as a permanent divider of the parties remains to be seen. In recent years, first-time voters by reason of age have on the whole voted Democratic for president.

The Republican coalition appears to be constituted as follows: white people, who comprise approximately 90 percent of the U.S. population, vote anywhere from 3 to 5 percent more Republican than Democratic. The comparatively small size of the black population means that even in 1960, when Richard Nixon got about a quarter of the black vote, 97 percent of his total came from whites; 99 percent of his vote came from whites in 1968, 98 percent in 1972. Ninety-nine percent of Ronald Reagan's votes in 1980 came from whites. If one can conceive of nonunion families and Protestants as "groups" in the usual sense, they make up about 75 percent of the population and vote 5 percent more Republican than the nation as a whole. The Republican party gets its vote, then, from white people, nonunion members, Northerners, and Protestants outside the central cities. Although Republicans received 60 percent majorities or better from all of these groups in 1972, they were able to attract at most 53 percent from any of them in 1976, and no more than 56 percent in 1980.[54]

One of the largest groups of all, women, provides an example of a group membership whose meaning may be changing. At one time gender could not be shown to have a strong partisan effect; what weak tendency existed at the time of The American Voter (1960) showed women as slightly more Republican.[55] In 1980, however, women were substantially less pro-Reagan than were men,[56] and thus made up a much larger part of the Democratic than of the Republican coalition. We do not know, however, whether this division is permanent. Throughout 1981, differences between men and women appeared

Table 1.4
First-time Voters (by age) in a Presidential Race

	1980	1976	1972	1964
Republican	38.2%	41.7%	49.3%	22.4%
Democratic	41.8	50.0	50.2	77.6
Anderson	18.2			

QUESTION: Who did you vote for in the election for President?

SOURCE: 1980 American National Election Study, Center for Political Studies, University of Michigan.

in public opinion polls that asked about party identification, and it became commonplace to refer to President Reagan's "gender gap."[57] Yet *The New York Times'* 1982 election-day surveys showed only small differences between men and women voters.[58]

The case of the "women's vote" should alert us to some of the complexities of group interest. Not all women are the same—richer women are more Republican and poorer more Democratic, just like men. Thus group memberships are crosscutting. Within a group, its "interests" may be of greatest interest to only a subset of members. Thus the Equal Rights Amendment, a "women's issue," is of greatest importance to *highly educated* women. A difference between men and women may also reflect not failure in appealing to one, but success at appealing to the other. Thus there can be "women's" issues like abortion and "men's" issues like gun control for hunters, and what can be read as a defection of women from the Republicans may equally mean a defection of men from the Democrats.[59] Moreover, a difference in one election may or may not prefigure a permanent difference in basic coalitions; as Celinda Lake argues, the particular candidate choices in 1980 may have maximized the possibility of a gender gap.[60]

As Table 1.3 indicates, *turnout* varies enormously among different groups in the population, rising with income, occupational status, education, and age. Since Republicans are disproportionately located in the high-turnout groups and Democrats in the low, this tends to give Republicans electoral advantages that in some measure, varying from election to election, make up for the preponderance of Democrats in the potential electorate. It is possible, then, to analyze party coalitions in terms of the group memberships of the people who vote regularly for one party or another. Likewise, it is possible to consider the differential impact of different candidates on these various groups.

The picture of voters and interest groups we have drawn thus far can be generalized. Presidential campaigns and elections are events that activate the personal loyalties of voters. The amount of new information about candidates or issues that citizens ordinarily need in order to vote or hold casual conversations about the election is slight, because the political component of their personal identities is reasonably stable and familiar to them. So long as their main reference groups do not change, party loyalty and membership in interest groups provides a shortcut to voter preferences and minimizes the costs of getting information about the specifics of the issues and candidates in any particular election year.

Interest groups act as intermediary agencies that help voters to identify their political preferences quickly by actively soliciting their members' interest in behalf of specific candidates and parties and, more importantly, by providing still another anchor to the voter's identity. This helps the voter fix his own position quickly and economically in what otherwise would be a confusing and contradictory political environment.

Although interest groups in the past have differed over policy, they have not (at least since the acceptance of industrial unions in the 1930s) denied the rights of opponents to advocate their policy preferences. But, in one significant respect, that is no longer true. "Public interest" lobbies have attacked the legitimacy of "private interest" groups. Intermediary organizations are groups such as political parties, labor unions, trade associations, religious groups, that link citizens and their government. Many are "special interest" groups—groups, that is, with special interests in public policy. Part of the program of public interest groups is to reduce the power of private, special interests and substitute their own services as intermediary organizations. Typically, public interest groups have fewer—sometimes vastly fewer —members than private interest groups.[61] They rely on the mass media to carry their messages to the population at large, and their success is an indication of the extent to which American voters now rely on mass media rather than group membership to get their political orientations and opinions.

Laws have been passed and constitutional amendments proposed that restrict the amounts of money unions and corporations can contribute to political campaigns and use in lobbying. On the whole, however, these laws have been unsuccessful in curbing interest group activity. What has happened is that interest groups have found new ways within the law to advance their interests. One such device is the political action committee. From 1974 to 1977 the number of political action committees (PACs) organized by business and unions more than doubled, increasing from 608 to 1,222. By 1980, there were 2,075. The bulk of this increase was accounted for by the rise in corporate PACs from only 89 in 1974 to 550 in 1977, and 1204 in 1980.[62] PACs are created to collect and disburse political contributions. They must contribute to more than one candidate, and the amount they may give to any one candidate is limited. In 1976, amendments to the Federal Election Campaign Act enabled individual companies or labor unions to establish multiple PACs, thus multiplying the amount of money that can be funneled to any single candidate. Surprisingly, corporate PACs have not favored Republican campaigns as much as might be expected. Instead, the predominant trend in congressional elections has been to support incumbents over challengers, and

since nationwide there are far more Democratic than Republican office holders, Democrats have gained accordingly.[63]

While an individual citizen is still prohibited from contributing more than
$25,000 to federal candidates during any given year, the decision in *Buckley*
v. *Valeo* (1976) removed any such restrictions from PACs. Thus, "a corporate or union political action committee can collect donations and contribute
an unlimited sum of money to unspecified numbers of candidates or committees so long as no single contribution exceeds $5,000."[64] In addition, once a
PAC "contributes to five or more federal candidates, [it] can make unlimited
independent expenditures . . . on behalf of candidates or parties. . . ." (e.g.,
advertising on behalf of a candidate in print or electronic media).[65] Not
surprisingly, prospective presidential candidates themselves are organizing
PACs as a way of developing political alliances.

The rise of PACs to prominence is ironic. In the 1950s, reformers thought
that it would be a good idea to convert local parties, which were based on
jobs and conviviality, to more idealistic concerns. It was thought that the
replacement of a politics of patronage with a politics of issues would lead to
party government in which informed activists could hold public officials
responsible for their policy positions. As government grew and parties weakened, however, two things happened: business corporations, concerned about
what government was doing to them, founded and reinvigorated their own
interest groups, and other citizens formed and joined new groups to press
their particular concerns. Instead of integrative party government, therefore,
the weakening of parties facilitated further fragmentation into what are called
"single-issue special interest groups," such as those concerned with busing,
gun control, abortion, and other matters. The emphasis on issues has led to
further fragmentation, one of whose manifestations was the explosive growth
of political action committees.

A second irony is that the PACs have been created in response to congressional efforts to restrict the role of money in elections. In 1943, Congress,
following up its earlier act against corporate spending, forbade direct spending by labor unions. Soon thereafter, the more militant of the union federations, the Congress of Industrial Organizations (CIO), formed a political
action committee financed by a separate fund collected from its membership,
as well as a National Citizen's Action Committee to solicit contributions
from the community at large. When the labor federations merged in 1955,
the new AFL-CIO created its own Committee on Political Education
(COPE) to collect and inject money into campaigns. COPE is commonly
regarded as the model of the modern PAC.

But that was only the beginning. Government intervened again in 1971, 1974, and 1976 with the passage of the Federal Election Campaign Act (FECA) and subsequent amendments. By limiting the amount any individual or company could contribute, FECA reduced the role of large contributors while at the same time giving incentives for the formation of groups of small contributors. Once the courts decided that money raised and spent in politics was protected under the First Amendment as a necessary adjunct to political speech and expression, the way was open for committees to proliferate, each concentrated on the issues and candidates of their choice.[66] With no obligation to govern, no limit on new committees, and no necessary connection to any other issue, PACs became an electoral rival to political parties. Now governmental intervention is being proposed as a further remedy for the presumed ills caused by the last round of intervention. The question to be considered is whether to try once more to limit PACs or to reduce their influence.

Public interest lobbies have sought to weaken the power of party leaders and strong party identifiers as compared with citizens who are weakly identified with parties and who emerge during a particular election campaign or in response to a current issue. The stress on ease of entry into internal party affairs—more primaries, more conferences, more frequent and more open elections to party bodies—leads, given the fact that party membership occurs in the first place by self-activation, to the domination of parties by activists who have time and education and are able to take the trouble to go to meetings. What kinds of people have these characteristics? Among others, they are the middle- and upper-middle-class professionals who predominate in supporting Common Cause, Nader's Raiders, and other public interest lobbies. Thus, among interest groups, if money matters less as a resource, business matters less; if time and talk matter more, ordinary workers matter less. As leaders of labor, business, and the parties lose power, organizers of public interest lobbies gain.

Two advantages have helped public interest groups flourish. One is a product of modern technology and the other has been generated by government. The use of computerized mailing lists has permitted these groups to tap contributions from large numbers of people who do not otherwise participate directly in group activities, but rather become a privileged audience of spectators to group leaders' battles over public policy. This opportunity for vicarious participation not only produces ready cash, but also simplifies somewhat the tasks of leadership. Instead of having to satisfy an active membership that might make contradictory demands, only the top leadership need be considered. Leaders of public interest groups are frequently poorly paid, accepting low income as a sacrifice for their cause. Moving from one group to another, they reduce organization overhead by providing experienced lobbying at small cost.

The second advantage is that public interest groups are regulated by the Internal Revenue Service; people who contribute to them are entitled to count these monies as tax deductible. Where deductibility is inconvenient for the entire group, it often establishes a separate educational or litigious "arm." Without tax deductibility, the survival of some of these groups would be in doubt. The tradeoff is that they engage in educational activities rather than overt lobbying, which may be a distinction without a difference. In addition, some of these groups achieve a status as legally authorized interveners before regulatory commissions, a role that entitles them to payment for their activity. In this sense, such public interest groups are partially subsidized by government.

Around two-thirds of public interest activists identify with the Democratic party, compared to about 40 percent of the general public. When asked to place themselves on the usual political scale, about three-fourths of activists in public interest organizations saw themselves, in American terms, as liberal or radical.[67]

What does the ordinary mail-order member get from these public interest groups that keep asking for contributions? After all, the benefits these groups seek are available to all; no one can be excluded from clean air or honest government. Why, then, do not more people become free riders, gaining the benefits but not paying the costs? Robert C. Mitchell suggests one possible answer:

> these [member] contributions are compatible with behavior of the egoistic, rational, utility-maximizing kind because the cost is low, the potential cost of not contributing is high and the individual has imperfect information about the effectiveness of his or her contribution in obtaining the good or preventing the bad.[68]

The main distinction Mitchell makes is between public goods and public "bads," i.e., bad things imposed on everyone unless steps are taken. Thus, vicarious participation in countering threats to civil liberties or the environment can be had relatively cheaply. For a few dollars a year contributors can plausibly argue to themselves that they are participating in an effective effort at preventive social action.

☆ Parties

A third aspect of the social framework—along with voters and interest groups—that will help us to account for the strategies of participants in presidential elections is the nature of political parties in this country. Here we discuss parties as organizations, rather than as symbols for voters. As organizations parties are devoted to maintaining or increasing their own opportunities to exercise political power primarily through sponsoring candidates for public office.

By "political power" we mean the ability to make decisions or to influence decision making by governments. Instrumental to this goal is access to those offices and officials legally entitled to make such decisions.[69] Access, in turn, depends in part upon participation in staffing the government, either by selecting officials to fill appointive offices (patronage) or by significantly influencing the nomination and election of elected officials. Since elected officials are usually empowered to select appointed officials, access to them is often instrumental to the dispensation of patronage. There are, of course, numerous ways of gaining access to public officials, but their original selection is the primary avenue of access used by political parties.[70]

An additional goal that political parties may from time to time seek is the expression of the political views of their most active and influential members. People vary in their ability to make their views known to and accepted by a party organization. When party activists seek power primarily over the party, and only secondarily over the government, we refer to them as "purists." Purists wish their views to be put forth by the parties without much equivocation or compromise, and although they otherwise seek to win elections, they do not care to do this at the expense of self-expression.[71] Whereas a party politician might promote his own views to the point that it costs his party's candidate the election, the purist never pursues electoral victory to the point that it impedes the expression of his views. In the purist conception of things, instead of a party convention being a place where a party meets to choose candidates who can win elections by pleasing voters, it becomes a site for passing resolutions and for finding a candidate who will embody the message delegates seek to express.

At each level of government, the elected chief executive (mayor, governor, president) generally has the most political power. As a result the party organizations depend more upon controlling these offices than on any other source for their political power. In addition, parties are accountable for the activities of chief executives elected with their endorsement. Accountability means that when the party endorses a candidate, it designates him as its agent before the electorate. The fortunes of the party depend on the success of party candidates. Candidates come and go, but parties and electorates remain. The party organizations, therefore, are quite concerned about selecting suitable officeholders, since it is assumed that the actions and identities of these men and women will in the long run determine the extent and location of the party's appeal within the electorate and its record of success at the polls.

Just as the party is greatly dependent upon its officeholders for its political power, these officeholders in turn often have great discretion in the distribution of rewards to the party. Party members expect that officeholders will seek to strengthen themselves within the organization by the judicious dispensation of favors and patronage. As people who have won office at the head of party tickets, elected chief executives will probably come closer than other individuals to possessing the control over the party organization that will enable them to impose their own preferences on party organizations. Indeed, where parties are weak, they may become mere appendages of the major officeholders who use the label and manipulate the machinery until the next ad hoc collection of activists mobilizes around a new leader.

State party organizations are not simple in their internal workings. Sometimes elected chief executives run them; sometimes they are run by coalitions of party chieftains representing the local organizations of several large cities or counties. Sometimes party officials and elected officials work cooperatively; sometimes they work at cross-purposes. A strong national committeeman in a state party organization whose party occupies the presidency may find he is the main avenue of access in the distribution of federal largess if there are few elected officeholders in the state with whom he might have to share power. On the other hand, there are instances of governors who have felt that their chances of continuing personal victory would improve if they thoroughly disassociated themselves from the party whose label they nominally bore, causing the party organization in the state to shrivel on the vine. A strong party organization, well led, can force on an executive choices suitable for the party's purposes even if they conflict with alternative choices more likely to enhance the executive's position. A weak party organization may have the actual conduct of election campaigns torn entirely from its grasp, as happens with increasing frequency at the national level, where presidential candidates, once nominated, have all the authority and most of the money. Leaders of party organizations frequently are at odds with the party's elected officeholders for a variety of reasons. Many elected officials see their party leaders as potential threats to their positions; many party leaders see the officeholders as ungrateful louts with whom the organization is unfortunately saddled.

Even so, what party leaders ordinarily care about most is getting their candidates into office and keeping them there. Other considerations are usually secondary. Party leaders are neither for nor against policies in the abstract; they are concerned with policies as means to the end of officeholding. If new policies help win elections, they are for them; if they help lose elections, they are against them. If officeholders are popular, party leaders have to accept them; if they are unpopular, threatening to bring the party into disrepute, party leaders will turn against them. Where parties are purist, however, activists control candidates. Their purpose is to espouse policies of which they approve. If they can do that and win, so much the better for them; if the price of purism is defeat, so much the worse for the candidate. If a choice has to be made by purist activists, purism outside office is better than power in government.

It is not the case that party officials lack all interest in issues. As Herbert McClosky found as far back as the mid-1950s, party officials exaggerate much more than they minimize policy differences among their citizen supporters.[72] Table 1.5, which is based on a recent CBS survey, reveals considerable issue distance between members of the Republican and Democratic national committees and party supporters. Democratic committeemen are more liberal and Republican committeemen more conservative than their party's rank and file.

Though political party leaders try to pursue policies which they believe will enhance their political power and to avoid unpopular points of view, it is clear that they are far from indifferent to the substance of policy. Because they are more interested and active than most citizens, party leaders also tend to care more about the policies with which they have to deal. In fact, some politicians who hold public office make a specialty of being policy oriented. At times they may deliberately incur some unpopularity in order to serve their policy preferences, although they are unlikely to go so far as to lose an election on purpose. The heavy losses of the Republicans in the 1964 election and the presidential landslide against the Democrats in 1972 are extreme cases, and they are instructive. For in general, political party leaders regard policy as a result of an interaction among legitimate political demands—as a bargainable product—and not, as purists regard it, as an inflexible set of logical or ideological imperatives.[73] President Reagan favors tax cuts but in 1982, when other aspects of his program were at stake, supported a tax increase. Similarly, Walter Mondale, the early front runner for the 1984

Table 1.5

Views of Members of the Democratic and Republican National Committees and Party Supporters, 1981

	DEMOCRATIC		REPUBLICAN	
	Committee	Rank & File	Committee	Rank & File
Political Philosophy				
Liberal	36%	24%	1%	11%
Moderate	51	42	31	33
Conservative	4	29	63	51
Military/Defense Spending				
Increase	22	48	89	60
Decrease	18	13	1	5
Keep Same Level	51	36	7	31
Equal Rights Amendment				
Favor	92	62	29	46
Oppose	4	29	58	44
Too Much Government Regulation of Business				
Agree	35	59	98	72
Disagree	49	30	1	22

SOURCE: Adapted from Martin Plissner and Warren Mitofsky, "Political Elites," *Public Opinion* (October/November 1981), pp. 47–49.

Democratic nomination, has been for free trade but, in the course of seeking labor support, came out for protection in the automobile and steel industries.

How strong are the major political parties? The answer depends in part on which parties we have in mind at what time. Congressional parties are generally believed to have experienced a decline in partisanship since the turn of the century. But the Republican party in the House of Representatives showed a high level of cohesion in the 1970s and gave President Reagan remarkably unified support in his first year of office. House Democrats did not vote together nearly so often but if one eliminated certain Southern Democrats, the "Dixiecrats" of the 1940s and 50s and the "boll weevils" of the late 1970s and early 1980s, the remaining mainstream and liberal Democrats would have looked a lot more cohesive. The national committees of the two parties waxed and waned in strength—in the 1940s and 1950s a politically informed person might even have known the names of the national chairmen. The Republican National Committee, under Chairman William Brock, began in the late 1970s to raise large sums of money from a broad network of individual donors to provide aid to state parties, and to help candidates and state parties professionalize their operations.[74] The Democratic National Committee, more haltingly and less successfully, began to follow suit.

In spite of considerable efforts by the national Democratic party to tighten up qualifications for voting in presidential primaries, political parties in America as yet do not have elaborate procedures of membership, dues, and formal organizational structure. They are constituted differently in different localities and exist primarily to make nominations for and elect candidates to a variety of state and local offices. They are regulated by state law and are often quite cohesive up to the state level. Given the vast diversity among state and local parties and the periodic changes they undergo, it is not easy to characterize their effectiveness. At the turn of the century and through the 1940s, state party politics in most states was dominated by incumbent governors or national committeemen. There were virtually no permanent state party organizations. Central committees were, so far as is known, largely dormant. By the early 1960s, a few state chairmen were paid full time, and most but not all states had a permanent party headquarters, as well as at least one paid professional.[75] As a sign of the times, by 1980 the long-standing practice of moving the state party headquarters to the home of the chairman had in most states been abandoned.[76]

Owing to the lamentable lack of research on state parties, we cannot say how many states now have permanent headquarters with professional staff who recruit candidates, raise money, and help campaigns. But the best evidence suggests their number is growing.[77] State chairmen now have seats on the national committee. They mediate between national rules and state practices. They are conduits for the growing services—recruitment, polling, fund raising, issue development, vote mobilization—provided by the national parties.[78]

At the national level, what used to be a loose federation of state parties is slowly being converted—by changes in party rules and by judicial decisions —into a more centralized structure. The most obvious indicator of continuing decentralization is that national parties are organized on a geographical basis with the state units as the constituent elements. The party organizations from different states meet formally by sending delegates to national committee meetings, and most importantly, by coming together at national conventions to nominate a president. The strongest indicator of nationalization is the guidelines that are set out at the national level which, especially for Democrats, are becoming increasingly important in determining who these delegates will be.[79] Still, it is the states who choose their representatives to national party bodies; the national committees and conventions do not choose officers of state parties. On the Democratic side, the permanent national party organization is not in a position to help the state parties, having neither the funds, nor the personnel, nor the contacts to contribute substantially to the nomination or election of candidates for Congress or local offices, who must run within state boundaries.[80] For the Republicans, however, things are changing, owing to the large amounts of money now available to the national party for use in recruiting, training, and helping elect Republicans in local constituencies.[81]

The operation of the so-called presidential coattail, whereby a popular president brings out supporters who also vote for other candidates of his party, is uncertain. It does not help state parties and candidates who must try to win every year in numerous elections at the state and local level. At best, coattails operate every four years and then only if there happens to be a strong presidential candidate on the ballot.[82] And there is also the possibility (nowadays perhaps probability) that reverse coattail effects will operate as unpopular presidents do damage to other members of their party running for office.

The state parties have substantial powers enabling them to share in making national policy when they are strong enough to be influential in the nomination and election of senators and congressmen. Increasingly, members of Congress are self-starters who do not depend on state parties. But where the older relationship still holds, the states have a share in federal patronage through their congressmen and senators as well as their own sources of patronage. The very circumstance that the states are separate constitutional entities engenders a drive for autonomy as those who hold places of prestige and profit in the state governments and parties seek to protect their jurisdictions, much as the framers of the Constitution hoped they would. Federalism, however, is much more than a legal fact. The states have great vitality because there are distinct, numerous, and vigorous ethnic, religious, racial, and economic groups that are disproportionately located in specific geographic areas and that demand separate recognition. State organizations, therefore, become infused with the purposes of groups who use their state parties for the recognition and enhancement of their separate identities and needs. Italians in Rhode Island, Jews and black people in New York, dairy farmers in Wisconsin, wheat growers in Kansas, "gay rights" advocates in California, and many others make the idea of a noncentralized party system a reality.[83]

Each of the state parties is composed of different people with somewhat different interests to protect and demands to make. Control over state parties must be exercised from within each state, since the various states do not control one another and the national party exercises only partial control. This is the essence of what is meant by a decentralized party system in which power is dispersed among many independent state bodies. Efforts, which in recent years have been quite successful, to centralize control of the criteria for delegate selection to national conventions may lead state parties to adopt two sets of rules—one for state and local nominations and another for federal —leading to even greater fragmentation of the party system.

Thus, despite rule changes which have tended to nationalize the parties, they remain in many respects coalitions of state parties which meet every four years for the purpose of finding a candidate and forging a coalition of interests sufficiently broad to win a majority of electoral votes. Increasingly, though, the national conventions exist mainly to ratify the results of the numerous primary elections that precede them. State parties are not always as effective as candidates themselves in mobilizing support among primary electorates, and so it is less and less true that presidential nomination processes entail making a coalition of state parties and party factions—Southern and Northern Democrats, coastal and Midwestern Republicans—who disagree on some major policy issues. Instead of compromise and coalition building, prospective candidates must build personal organizations state by state, mobilize their followers, and energize their individual factions in state primary elections. The cumulative effect of coming out ahead of other contenders—not necessarily winning a majority—is what makes for a successful presidential candidacy. By downgrading the necessity for compromise within the party and emphasizing the benefits of factional mobilization, the new rules of the presidential nomination process, which we discuss in the next chapter, expose the parties to certain risks. The most significant of these are the risks of spectacular failure in the general election, or, worse, an inability to govern in the event of a victory because of a failure to see the need for coalition building.[84]

The two major parties, as we have seen, cull their electoral support from somewhat different groups in the population, *but* no party has a monopoly of support from any of these groups; each party draws significant, and often indispensable, support from almost all categories.[85] In a close election the ability of a party to increase its support within one group from, say, 20 to 30 percent may be crucial, even though that group still votes overwhelmingly for the opposition. The strategic implications of these remarks color all of national campaign politics: when they are trying to win, the parties try to do things that will please the groups consistently allied to them without unduly alienating other groups.

The temptation for political parties to avoid specific policy commitments in many areas, therefore, is very great. The American population is so extraordinarily varied—crisscrossed by numerous economic, religious, ethnic, racial, sectional, and occupational ties—that it is exceedingly difficult to guess at the total distribution of policy preferences in the population at any one time, except for questions that have already been settled between the parties, such as national defense, Social Security, and unemployment compensation.[86] It is even more difficult to predict how these aggregations of actual and potential interest groups might react to shifts in party policy positions, and still more hazardous to prophesy what different policy commitments might do to the margin of votes required for victory. This pervasive problem of uncertainty makes the calculation of gain from changes in policy positions both difficult and risky, and suggests that the interests of parties and candidates frequently are best served by vague, ambiguous, or contradictory policy statements that will be unlikely to offend anyone. The advantages of vagueness about policy are strengthened by the facts that most citizens are not interested in policy or are narrowly focused on a few issues, and that only a few groups demand many specific policy commitments from their parties and candidates.

Yet, despite all this, political leaders and parties do make policy commitments that are often surprisingly precise, specific, and logically consistent. Thus, we must consider not only why the parties sometimes blur and avoid commitments on issues, but also why they often commit themselves to policies more readily than their interest in acquiring or retaining office would appear to require.

Part of the answer may arise from the fact that the parties serve slightly different functions for their own activists than for people who vote but are otherwise largely disengaged from politics. Party activists are people who are much more interested in politics and attentive to political issues than the general population. The interest and attentiveness of political activists leads them to formulate and elaborate political opinions and preferences. Their desires to make these preferences internally consistent and consistent with the preferences of their party certainly lead to demands upon the party leadership for policy positions that are reasonably clear and forthright.[87] Activists also mutually reinforce their opinions when they interact with one another, which further leads them to press their opinions upon their party. When candidates compete for support of voters with the same general political outlook, as a large flock of Republican hopefuls did in 1980, the positions they take in the primary season may even exaggerate their policy differences.

There are some differences between the parties in the social identities of party activists. Activists in both parties have disproportionately high social and economic status, but activist Democrats are more likely to come from working-class backgrounds; activist Republicans, on the other hand, are more middle class. These differences may be reflected in the noticeable tendency of the two parties to support policies intended to benefit the members of the social strata from which their active members are drawn.[88]

The interest groups most closely allied with each party also make policy demands that parties must meet to some extent. While it is true that voters are generally uninterested in specific policies, interest group leaders and their full-time bureaucracies are manifestly concerned. If they feel that the interests they represent are being harmed, they may so inform their members or even attempt to withdraw support from the party at a particular election. Should voters find that groups with which they identify are opposed to the party with which they identify, they may temporarily support the opposition party, or they may withdraw from participation and not vote at all. Consequently, the party finds that it risks losing elections by ignoring the demands of interest groups. The demands of many of these groups conflict, however. If unions object to antipollution devices because they increase costs and decrease car sales, for example, labor and ecology groups cannot both be equally satisfied. If the costs of increasing worker safety compete with the costs of welfare payments, both cannot be obtained at the same level. Therefore, the parties may attempt to mediate among interest groups, hoping to strike compromises which, though they give no one group everything, give something to as many groups as they can. The increasing number of single-issue groups, of course, makes mediation difficult, as Jimmy Carter discovered when Catholic bishops, who wanted a strong anti-abortion stand, rejected his effort to remind them of a common interest in social welfare policies.

The contradictory pulls of vagueness and specificity are further exemplified in Jimmy Carter's 1976 campaign. He slid by such potentially divisive issues as amnesty for draft evaders or resisters—"a classic example of how to say something and not piss off people," as his press advisor Jody Powell put it—by saying he preferred pardons, which implied wrong had been done but had been forgiven. On the proposed B-1 Bomber, Carter said the decision should be made by the next president, leaving listeners to guess what he might do. On abortion, he was personally opposed but fudged on the role of government. This led a speechwriter to quit with a public blast, declaring, "I am not sure what you believe in other than yourself." Yet, time after time, as in his proposal for a more progressive income tax or for a ten-cent-a-gallon duty on import of oil, candidate Carter was attacked when he became specific. His poll-taker, Pat Caddell, attempted to resolve the dilemma during the campaign:

> We have passed the point when we can simply avoid at least the semblance of substance. This does not mean the need to outline minute, exact details. We all agree that such a course could be disastrous. However, the appearance of substance does not require this. It requires a few broad, specific examples that support a point.[89]

Not being magicians, candidates have a hard time coming up with many "broad, specific" policies. Throughout the years the opposing political parties have become identified with somewhat different policies. When new candidates arise they may bring with them somewhat new policy preferences. But there are bound to be many areas of policy on which they are not informed or do not have strong preferences. In such cases the existing set of policies traditionally associated with the parties provides the candidates with a useful economizing device. They can accept the going positions and concentrate on the policies that they may wish to revise, supplant, or present anew. The "neoliberals" in the Democratic party, for example, can accept its traditional welfare goals while advocating more efficient methods of achieving them, including an industrial policy to increase the wealth from which these traditional policies can be better supported. This tack is bound to be popular with the party faithful, who have been brought up on the rallying cries of the past, who have learned to prefer what their party prefers, and who respond with vigor and enthusiasm to the cues provided by mention of their party's chief stocks-in-trade. Just as voters commonly use parties as a means of cutting their information costs on issues and candidates, and activists use them as reference groups, so may candidates use the parties' traditional policy positions to ease their burden of innovation.[90]

Political parties today, however, are not as reliable as guideposts for the faithful as they once were. For forty years the New Deal structured the nature of political conflict in the United States. Those who were for or against a greater role for the federal government, for or against public or private electric power, for or against medical care for the aged and a host of other issues, knew immediately where they stood. When the Republicans lost the 1964 election with Barry Goldwater, huge Democratic majorities were elected to both houses of Congress, and the Eighty-ninth Congress effectively enacted the agenda of the New Deal. This sharply altered the content of partisan conflict at the national level. Since then new issues have arisen in bewildering profusion and new groups have come to public attention, clamoring to determine the shape of public policy. Such issues as environmental pollution, law and order, prayer in schools, gun control, and abortion have not yet taken on firm identification with either major political party. Hence there is more fluidity in political life, more leeway for the presidential nominees to set their party's course, and less opportunity for them to rely on the past policy positions associated with their respective parties.[91]

President Reagan has contributed to the reinvigoration of party differences with his efforts at across-the-board reduction of nondefense federal expenditures accompanied by significant tax cuts. It is important to note that during the 1980 campaign he argued for this in only the most general way, with many assurances that nobody would suffer untoward consequences, because of his belief—embodied in what is sometimes called "supply-side economics"—that the return of large sums of money to the private sector would spark a resurgence of the economy leading to increased government tax revenues. This has not happened. But the President's program has impelled congressional Democrats to strengthen their commitment to Social Security and a variety of other social programs.

In the past, a relatively few party leaders controlled the decisions of a large proportion of the delegates to conventions. Delegates to national conventions were chosen as representatives of the several state party organizations, apportioned according to a formula laid down by action of previous national conventions. While it is true that official decisions are made by a majority vote of delegates, American party organizations were often centralized at state and local levels. This meant that such hierarchical controls as actually existed on the state and local levels asserted themselves in the national convention. Until recently the probabilities were fairly good that both major parties at any given time would have succeeded in electing a substantial number of governors and mayors of important cities; the chances were also fairly good, therefore, that a substantial number of delegates would be controlled hierarchically. Some states, of course, were badly split, with no one holding the lever to much more than his own vote.[92]

Normally, state party organizations are unified by incumbent governors. Without the centralizing forces of state patronage and coherent party leadership embodied by a leader in the governor's chair, state parties tend to fragment into territorial jurisdictions that can be played off one against another by astute aspirants for the presidential nomination. The lack of strong leadership at the state level also means that within the delegation a set of presidential preferences and strategies for pursuing them is less likely to be worked out in advance and agreed upon by all elements. Decentralized state parties thus become happy hunting grounds for early starters in the presidential sweepstakes. They can move into a vacuum, make alliances and receive commitments, and build delegate strength from the ground up.

The importance of governors at national conventions (and along with them hierarchical control of state delegations) has diminished over the past quarter-century. There has been a little noticed but important long-term decline in the number of governorships that are up for election in years during which presidents are also running for office, as Table 1.6 indicates. From the thirty-three governorships that were open to election in 1944, the number declined to twenty-one in 1972 and ten in 1980. Many states are changing the two-year gubernatorial term to a four-year term and are providing for the gubernatorial election in the middle of the president's term of office. This is intended to isolate gubernatorial elections from national electoral currents, but it may also mean that the number of state delegations to national party conventions controlled by governors will decrease as the motivation of governors to protect their own fortunes by finding popular presidential candidates also decreases. This trend thus far has had its most pronounced effect upon the Republican party, where the number of Republican governors up for election in presidential years has declined from twenty in 1944 to three in 1980.

This fact helps account for the willingness of Republican delegates to nominate Barry Goldwater even though he could reasonably have been expected to hurt the party's chances in many states. There were Republican state leaders in 1964 who winced at the thought of a disastrous defeat in November, but there were fewer such leaders than there might have been because there were fewer (that year, sixteen) Republican governors at the Republican convention. The advantages accruing to Goldwater by declaring an early candidacy under these circumstances are obvious. Governors might have had

Table 1.6
Number of Gubernatorial Elections
in Presidential Election Years
(Excluding Hawaii and Alaska)

Year	Number of Elections
1944	33
1948	31
1952	31
1956	31
1960	27
1964	26
1968	25
1972	21
1976	24
1980	10

SOURCE: *World Almanac,* 1944, 1948, 1952, 1956, 1960, 1964, 1968, 1972, 1976, 1980.

Number of Republican Governors
up for Election in Presidential Election Years
(Excluding Alaska and Hawaii)

Year	Number of Republican Governors up for Election
1944	20
1948	19
1952	15
1956	16
1960	11
1964	7
1968	8
1972	11
1976	6
1980	3

SOURCE: *World Almanac,* 1944, 1948, 1952, 1956, 1960, 1964, 1968, 1972, 1976, 1980.

sufficient hierarchical control over their delegations to keep them from precipitously joining the Goldwater bandwagon. The absence of central leadership on a state-by-state basis meant that delegates were freer to follow their personal preferences and also free to weigh ideological considerations more heavily than they could have if they had been responsible to a leader who would suffer badly if Republicans were defeated for state offices. Similar considerations have affected Democrats in recent years, as a look at the decline in the attendance of senators and congressmen at national conventions reveals. From 1952 to 1968, senators and congressmen frequently played a role in the nomination process. But not since the reforms of 1968 and beyond have gone into effect, as Table 1.7 reveals, have they even put in an appearance in significant numbers as national convention delegates. This separation of the nomination process from subsequent processes of governing is as good an index as any of the precipitous decline of party power. Increasingly, those who do the selecting have not been the same as those who live most intimately with the results. Recognition of this defect has led the Democratic party to adopt the recommendations of its Hunt Commission to reserve delegate seats for a large number of the party's officeholders. It remains to be seen whether they will actually participate actively in the selection process, and thus feel greater responsibility to a candidate they have helped select.

Table 1.7
Convention Attendance of Democratic Elected Officials

	Percentage of Democratic U.S. Senators who were voting delegates or alternates	Percentage of Democratic U.S. Representatives who were voting delegates or alternates
1956	90%	33%
1960	68	45
1964	72	46
1968	68	39
1972	36	15
1976	18	15
1980	14	15

Data were drawn from official Convention Calls for each year.

SOURCES: Commission on Presidential Nomination and Party Structure (Morley A. Winograd, chairman), *Openness, Participation and Party Building: Reforms for a Stronger Democratic Party* (Washington, D.C., January 1978), p. 18; and Nelson W. Polsby, "The Democratic Nomination," in Austin Ranney, ed., *The American Elections of 1980* (Washington, D.C., 1981), p. 57.

We have been saying that the distinctive functions of political parties—selecting candidates and campaigning for office—have atrophied in favor of entrepreneurship by candidates working through the mass media. Since candidates select and campaign for themselves through the media, it would not be surprising if the electorate, observing what has happened, pays more attention to the prime movers, the candidates, and less to their party labels. There is good evidence that this is exactly what has happened. As Martin Wattenberg reads the data provided by the Inter-University Consortium for Political and Social Research,

> One possible explanation for why parties have declined in importance is that for various reasons candidates no longer need the parties in order to win elections. . . .
>
> In other words, the stands which candidates take on the issues may no longer be linked to voters' perceptions of the parties. The parties may still stand for certain broad principles and groups, but when it comes to specific policies, candidates now stand above parties rather than with them. . . .
>
> In summary, at least a partial answer to the question, "Why the growing neutrality towards the parties?" seems to be that fewer people are translating their likes and dislikes about the candidates and the candidates' stands on specific issues into likes and dislikes about the parties. . . .
>
> The reason for party decline has not been that people no longer see any important differences between the parties. . . . Rather, the problem which the parties must face is that they are considered less relevant in solving the most important domestic and foreign policy issues of the day. In the voters' minds, the parties are losing their association with the candidates and the issues which the candidates claim to stand for.[93]

For the parties to regain their association with the candidates, the balance of initiatives, now running from candidate to party, has to be reversed.

☆ The Electoral College

Another element of the strategic environment within which the drama of a presidential election is played is that peculiarly American institution, the

Electoral College. American presidential elections are not decided by popular vote. Instead, popular votes are collected within each state, and each state casts all of its electoral votes for the candidate receiving the most popular votes within the state. This "winner take all, loser take nothing" approach is called a "unit rule."[94] We will explain some consequences of this rule presently.

Each state is allowed as many electoral votes as it has senators and representatives in Congress. Thus, all states, no matter how small, have a least three electoral votes. This means that sparsely populated states are overrepresented by the Electoral College. In 1980, 156,762 Alaskans influenced the disposition of three electoral votes, which gives a ratio of one electoral vote for every 52,254 voters. In New York, on the other hand, 6,201,959 voters went to the polls and voted for thirty-six electors, a ratio of one electoral vote for every 172,277 voters. In California, 8,587,063 voters for forty-seven electors produced a ratio of one electoral vote for every 182,703 voters.[95] One might conclude, therefore, that each Alaskan had about four times as much influence on the final outcome as each Californian. But this is not entirely valid.

Why not? Because the unit rule of the Electoral College provides that the candidate having the most votes in a state receives the entire electoral vote of the state. This means that each Alaskan was influencing the disposition of all three of Alaska's electoral votes, and each Californian was helping to decide the fate of all forty-seven of California's votes. Ask any politician whether he would rather have three votes or forty-seven—the answer is immediately apparent. Thus the Californian gets more attention, which means the candidates may promise more to California voters even though each one of them does not matter so much. In fact, the present method of electing the president tends to give greater power to the large, populous states, not the small, empty states, because the large states can deliver to the winner large blocs of the votes he needs to win. Consequently, presidential nominees tend to come from big states and tend to run on platforms likely to appeal to interest groups that cluster there. They concentrate their campaigns in the big population centers, and, as politicians know, they stand or fall on the big state votes.[96] In 1976, for example, Jimmy Carter and Gerald Ford used strategies that emphasized the same seven states—New York, New Jersey, Pennsylvania, Ohio, Illinois, Michigan, and California—with Carter adding Indiana and Ford including Texas.[97]

☆ Conclusion

As politicians develop their strategies for winning nomination and election to the presidency, they will have to keep in mind numerous facts about participation that exist in their political environment and probably are not subject to change by anything they may do. Among these are the following facts:

1. Most voters are not sufficiently concerned with specific policies to change their votes in response to policy appeals.

2. Voters vote the way they do out of party habit.

3. Voters may not *turn out* in great numbers, and therefore it is necessary to use intermediary organizations and party activists to help turn out one's own voters.

4. Parties usually seek to win elections but may occasionally prefer to express the views of their activists as their major goal.

5. Either party has a reasonably good chance to win the election; the Democrats because they are in the majority, the Republicans because they are much more likely to turn out.

6. Intermediary organizations such as interest groups and party organizations can be activated by policy commitments and reaffirmations and promises of access to governmental decision making.

7. Each party consists of a loose coalition of interest groups and state and local parties.

8. Increasingly, primary electorates determine presidential nominations.

9. The Electoral College puts a premium on votes from large two-party states.

Most or all of these basic facts about participants are well understood by presidential candidates and their managers. In addition, they must consider certain basic facts about the other resources available to them, to which we now turn.

Chapter 2

The Strategic Environment: Resources

★ The Distribution of Resources

Certain resources that, at any given time, are disproportionately available to Democrats and Republicans play a significant part in the strategic environment of presidential elections. Possession of the presidential office, skill in organization, knowledge of substantive policies, a reputation for integrity, facility in speechmaking, ability to devise appealing campaign issues, wealth, stamina—all can be drawn upon to good advantage in a presidential campaign. There are more resources available to parties and candidates than any one book could deal with exhaustively. But some resources obviously are going to be more important than others, and the importance of different resources varies from occasion to occasion. It would be sensible to regard as especially important those resources that one side monopolizes—such as the presidential office—and those resources that can be easily converted into other resources, or directly into public office—such as money, which can be used to buy competent staff, newspaper space, television time, and so on.

Although political resources are distributed unequally between the parties, in a competitive two-party system such as ours the inequalities do not all run in the same direction. Sometimes Republican candidates reap the benefits; sometimes Democrats do. One result of these inequalities of access to different resources, however, is that different strategies are more advantageous to each of the two parties. Let us examine the effects on election strategies of three resources commonly held to be extremely important—money, control over information, and the presidential office.

☆ Money[1]

Presidential campaigns are terribly expensive. Radio and television appearances, newspaper advertising, travel for the candidate and his entourage, mailings of campaign material, buttons and placards, maintaining a network of campaign offices, taking polls, and raising money itself—all cost a great deal of money. It is estimated that the various committees (the Republican and Democratic national committees, the House and Senate campaign committees of both parties, and various ad hoc volunteer committees that spring up in each campaign) at the national level spent approximately $20 million in 1960, $25 million in 1964, over $44 million in 1968, roughly $100 million in 1972, nearly $90 million in 1976 and $143 million in 1980.[2] Substantial sums were also spent by state and local organizations on behalf of the presidential candidates. Total political costs for all candidates at all levels of government amounted to something like $200 million in 1964, $300 million in 1968, $425 million in 1972, $540 million in 1976, and $1.2 billion in 1980.[3] The huge costs involved inevitably raise serious questions about the relationship between wealth and decisions in a democracy. Are presidential nominating and electoral contests determined by those who have the most money? Do those who make large contributions exercise substantial or undue influence as a result? Is the victorious candidate under obligation to "pay off" his major financial contributors? Do those who pay the piper call the tune?

This was certainly the reasoning that inspired the post-Watergate political reforms of the mid-1970s, which attempted to take money as an influence out of presidential elections.[4] A federal election fund has been established, and the two major parties are entitled to draw upon it in equal amounts to finance the conduct of their general election presidential campaigns. The fund is available to the candidates of the two parties provided they do not collect or disburse money from any other source or coordinate their campaigns with citizens who are spending their own money in the candidates' behalf. Under this system, each major party spent $34 million in 1980, not an overwhelming sum, given the size of the electorate. This proved to be adequate, however, at least to move the presidential candidates around the country and to get them on television. Missing were billboards, buttons and bumper stickers, and evidence of strong coordination between local and national presidential campaigns. The omission of these sorts of efforts may well have contributed to President Carter's impression, once he was elected in 1976, that he owed his election to nobody.[5]

Federal contributions also are available to contestants in primary elections, on a matching basis, insofar as they are able to raise money in small denominations from a variety of states. The best methods for qualifying for a federal subsidy of a primary campaign are (1) to make appeals through the mails and via personal appearances at fund-raising events to known party contributors and (2) to hold benefit performances, since the donated services of celebrities have been held to be exempt from contribution limitations. Thus, being able to raise money through mass means is a newly significant skill, conferring special power on professional practitioners of the arts of mail solicitation and celebrity hunting. These are the new fat cats of campaign finance, along with the professional managers of PACs, the all-purpose campaign contribution clubs set up to comply with strict federal rules limiting campaign contributions by individuals and various sorts of corporate entities.[6]

Before these elaborate limitations were established, however, the evidence was slight that presidential elections were unduly influenced, never mind "bought," by monied interests. In the general election—that is, after the primaries—Republicans did spend more than Democrats in most places, but the difference was not as overwhelming as some would suppose. The Democratic percentage of major party postnomination expenditures from 1932 to 1972 varied from a low of 33 percent in 1972 (when McGovern lost) to a high of 51 percent in 1960 (when Kennedy won).[7] Although the Johnson forces spent more money in 1964 than Kennedy's had in 1960 (the Democrats in 1964 managed to spend $12 million), Goldwater's forces spent $17.2 million, significantly more than Johnson's.[8] Total expenditures of both parties were high in absolute terms, but outlays per voter per party were quite modest, running in the 1972 election to about $1.31 for each of the 76.02 million voters.[9] "Contrary to frequent assertion," says Alexander Heard, who in 1960 published a comprehensive study of party finance, "American campaign monies are *not* supplied solely by a small handful of fat cats. Many millions of people now give to politics. Even those who give several hundred dollars each number in the tens of thousands."[10]

From 1956 through the 1960s, roughly 10 percent of the population contributed in presidential election years. Data from the Michigan Survey show that 10 percent of a national population sample said they had contributed in 1956, 12 percent in 1960, and 11 percent in 1964. Translating these numbers into individuals, 8 million people in 1956, 10 million in 1960, and 12 million in 1964 contributed to political campaigns.[11] The bulk of the money to run campaigns, however, came from people who contributed over $100. For the years before 1956, two-thirds of the campaign war chests at the national level were made up of contributions of over $500, and an additional one-fifth came from contributions of over $100. At the local level, where approximately six-sevenths of election expenses were met, the proportion of gifts over $500 declined to one-half or one-third. The figures on contributors for 1952 will perhaps give some idea of the numbers. Around 3 million people made some contribution. At least one gift of $100 was made by 150,000 contributors, $500 by 20,000 of these people, and $10,000 or more was given by 200 of these individuals.[12]

The most obvious and most important conclusion in our view is that even in the era when the parties were free to spend whatever they could raise and were not subjected to the limitations of the public finance law, money did not buy election victories. The candidates and party with the most money did not always win. Otherwise, Republicans would have won every election in the past forty years, and we know, in fact, that Democrats won eight of the twelve presidential contests from 1932 to 1976. Nor does there seem to be a correlation between the amount of money spent and the extent of electoral victory in national elections.[13] In 1968, for example, the Republican party outspent the Democrats by more than two to one, yet they won the election by a mere half-million out of the 72 million votes cast. One would expect that money would flow into the coffers of the party that is believed to have the best chance of victory. Yet with the possible exception of 1968, there does not seem to have been a single presidential election in this century that any competent observer believes would have turned out differently if the losing candidate had spent more money than the winner. We can at once eliminate all the Democratic victories because the Democrats spent less than the Republican losers. Dwight Eisenhower was so popular that his two elections now seem to have been certain, whether or not he had a substantial campaign surplus. No doubt part of the reason he had so much money to run with was his personal appeal to the people who contribute to campaigns, and they might well have given to him even if he had run as a Democrat. Nixon in 1968 had a great deal of money—indeed, probably a surplus—and Humphrey had less than he needed to make an effective race. Because the final outcome of the election was so close and the financial situations of the two major parties so disparate, 1968, it may be argued, is the single exception to the rule. Even so, it seems more plausible to argue that it was not lack of money but rather the deep divisions within the Democratic party (only trivially reflected in a diminution of contributions) that hurt even more. Had Vice-president Humphrey, the most creative liberal legislator of the quarter century after the Second World War, with impeccable credentials on civil rights and social welfare, received a rousing send-off instead of emerging bloody and half-beaten from the Democratic Convention, the election results might well have been different. But the party could not contain its differences on the Vietnam war.

In 1972, the Committee to Reelect the President raised a colossal amount of money—and, judging from the revelations of Watergate, spent much of it foolishly. Had they not possessed money to burn, it is doubtful whether a break-in at the Democratic party headquarters would have ranked high enough to consider funding. The Democrats, meanwhile, had to make do with much less (though more than in 1968), but nobody believes that more money would have helped Senator McGovern's hapless candidacy. The Republicans who won in the period from 1900 to 1928 did so with large majorities, as befits the party that then enjoyed the allegiance of most of the voters. The problem, then, is not to explain why money is crucial, but, on the contrary, to explain why it is not.

No one doubts that money is important; parties and candidates, not to speak of ordinary mortals, can hardly function without it. If a candidate could not raise any money, or only a pitifully small amount, he would be dreadfully handicapped and might not be able to run at all. But this situation has never arisen—although Humphrey in 1968 came close—after the national convention has made its choice. The crucial question is not the total spent by the candidates but the difference in the amounts they spend. The first part of our explanation, therefore, is that the differences in spending ordinarily have not been so great as to give any candidate an overwhelming advantage. So long as the poorer candidate could raise the minimum amount necessary to mount a campaign—that is, to hire employees, distribute literature, go on radio and television a few times, get around the country, and so on—he could do most of what he has to do. In other words, spending more than the minimum amount necessary to run a campaign did not confer significant advantages. Like other goods, money is subject to diminishing returns. People may get tired of being bombarded with literature and harangued by speakers. The candidates sometimes worry about overexposure lest they go the way of certain television celebrities who were seen once too often. Accusations of "trying to buy the election" may arise if too much time is taken on television. Indeed, there may be resentment if favorite programs are taken off the air to accommodate a candidate who seems to have had more than his say. We know that many voters are relatively impervious to bombardment by the opposition, and all the handouts in the world will not make them change. The actual result of an extensive assault by the richer party may be to give those who oppose that party additional reasons to intensify their opposition.

Given the necessary minimum amount of money, the less-affluent candidate can count on a good deal of free publicity. Presidential campaigns are deemed newsworthy by the news media and are extensively reported. While Democrats may get somewhat less space than Republicans in the shrinking number of newspapers that openly display their partisanship in their news columns, they still get some, and they do better in the magazines and on the air. To some extent the candidates can make news. John Kennedy's grappling with the religious issue, Harry Truman's assaults on the opposition, Dwight Eisenhower's dramatic promise to go to Korea, Jimmy Carter's efforts to rescue the hostages in Iran or to negotiate them out, all made headlines at little or no financial cost. The television debates in 1960, 1976, and 1980 attracted millions of viewers, numbers far in excess of the usual political broadcasts for which fees had to be paid.

The factor of skill must also be considered. Money can be spent for unrewarding purposes which actually rebound against the candidate. Democratic strategists during the 1930s were delighted at the expenditures made by the Liberty League on behalf of the Republican candidate. The strategists considered the expenditures to be an ideal target for their charges that the Republicans were the party of privilege. Much of the negative advertising during the elections of 1980 and 1982 was regarded as more of a burden than a benefit to the candidates it was supposed to help. Money spent may unwittingly get the opposition to the polls. As Edward Kennedy showed in 1980, a poor performance on television may harm a candidate no matter how much is spent. The man who says the wrong thing may deeply regret the wealth that made it possible for him to disseminate his statement widely. The methods by which money is raised, as Nixon learned to his sorrow, may do more to hurt a president when he is in office than they ever did (or could have done) to help when he was campaigning.

Other things being equal, of course, it would be nice to have more money to spend than the other fellow. But conditions are rarely, if ever, equal. The fundamental party allegiances of the population, the state of the economy, religious and ethnic affiliations, the personalities of the candidates—all appear to be more significant in determining the outcomes of elections than the differences in total party spending. Despite the cries of harried party money raisers, the Democrats always seemed to come up with enough to get by. There is always the hope of victory. The winner can expect to have his deficits covered at the next round of party "victory" fund-raising drives. It remains true that the most expensive election is the one you lose.

Money probably makes a greater difference at the prenomination stage than later on. Eisenhower and Taft each spent about $2.5 million on their nominating campaigns in 1952.[14] McGovern spent $12 million in 1972 on the way to his nomination.[15] Jimmy Carter spent $12.4 million in 1976 and—as an incumbent president—$19.6 million in 1980.[16] Of course, inflation explains much of this growth in spending. The candidate who wishes to enter primaries and conduct a national drive to obtain delegates may be dissuaded through lack of the minimum amount necessary to get started. The low visibility of primaries and the lack of attention paid to them by citizens may give an advantage to those with more to spend. Money, however, is only one factor. Estes Kefauver in 1952 put on a vigorous campaign despite his relative lack of wealth. Had he not been bitterly opposed by party leaders, or had he won all the primaries he entered, as Kennedy did in 1960, he might have won the nomination. As it was, Kefauver lost to Stevenson, whose command of wealth was the least of his political assets. In 1968, Nelson Rockefeller spent over $7 million in his effort to impress Republican delegates with his strength in the public opinion polls, but the effort was fruitless.[17] In 1976, Jimmy Carter won the nomination of his party through the primaries without a great campaign war chest, and incumbency, not money, was his great resource in 1980. It was not Ronald Reagan but John Connally who had the most Republican money in 1980, but Reagan won anyway.[18]

One can always argue that a small sum at the critical moment, if only one knew when beforehand, might have been crucial. "If I'd only known then what I know today," Morris Udall lamented to an interviewer, referring to his decision (because of a money shortage) to stop advertising during the last week of the 1976 campaign in Wisconsin, where he lost by 5,000 out of 670,000 votes.[19] Since Udall came in second six times, losing three times to Carter by a tiny margin, any number of "it might have beens" (including an entry by Senator Henry Jackson into New Hampshire, which might have prevented Carter from getting started) might well have made the difference.

Thus, it cannot successfully be argued that a candidate who ran so long and so often in so many primaries lost because he lacked money for a week.

Skill and strategy in using resources matters as much as having them. Witness a memorandum written to Morris Udall by his campaign manager: "We've got a reputation, frankly, as the sloppiest campaign in memory. No one knows who is in charge. . . ."[20] In 1976, Birch Bayh's indecision about entering primaries, Henry Jackson's taking Pennsylvania for granted, Hubert Humphrey's waiting until the California primary, when it was too late, Jimmy Carter's failing to see Maryland was not for him and getting involved in a pointless scrap with Governor Jerry Brown of California, all this and more mattered. It also mattered that Carter's strategy of running early and everywhere was a good strategy that paid off. Carter not only was able to run because he could raise money, he was able to raise money on the strength of his early victories.

Other candidates, however, may have been adversely affected by lack of funds. Nelson Rockefeller in 1960 is a curious example. Apparently he decided not to contest the Republican nomination that year, in part because he could not raise the cash, or, one assumes, the enthusiasm that cash contributions symbolize among like-minded party financiers. During the 1960 Kennedy-Humphrey primary campaigns in West Virginia, charges of vast Kennedy spending were made. Certainly, Kennedy's ready cash did him no harm. In retrospect, however, it does appear that he was decidedly more popular with the voters than his rival, Hubert Humphrey.[21] Would more money have enabled Humphrey to turn the tide? Humphrey's campaign was badly managed and severely underfinanced, and in part this led the press to accord him less serious treatment than he might otherwise have merited. Had Humphrey had as much money to spend on campaigning as Kennedy, for as long a period of time, the tide might conceivably have turned in the other direction.[22] There were, nonetheless, other candidates—Johnson and Symington, for example—who had plenty of money but who chose not to contest the primaries.

It is exceedingly difficult to get reliable information on an event that involves a decision *not* to act, such as a political candidate's decision not to run because he could not raise the money. There is, of course, no literature on this subject. But undoubtedly there have been some prospective candidates whose inability to raise the cash has proved fatal to their chances of being considered for the nomination. Whether this failure represents inability to satisfy the monied classes or to convince enough people that the candidate is serious and worthy is difficult to say in the abstract. A more important question concerns whether there has been systematic bias in favor of or against certain kinds of candidates that consistently alter the outcomes of presidential nominations. We can immediately dismiss the notion that the richest person automatically comes out on top. If that were the case, Rockefeller would have triumphed over Goldwater in 1964 and Nixon in 1968, and Taft over Eisenhower in 1952. In 1976, Ronald Reagan's personal wealth eclipsed Gerald Ford's, as, in 1980 Edward Kennedy's did Jimmy Carter's. Nevertheless, in both instances, the incumbent president beat the challenger.

The ability to raise money is not only a matter of personal wealth but also of being able to attract funds from others. Does this mean that only candidates attractive to the wealthy can run? The question is not so much whether it helps to be rich but whether candidates who favor the causes of the rich have the advantage over those who favor the poor. There is little evidence to support such a view. Given the nature of the American electorate, no candidate would openly admit to being the candidate only of the rich. Candidates holding a variety of views on economic issues—most of which are highly technical—manage to run for the nominations of both parties. If candidates are generally chosen from among people who differ but little on most substantive issues, the reason is not because the rich are withholding their money from the more radical candidates. Rather it is because the distribution of opinions in the electorate renders the radicals' cause hopeless. Our conclusion is that it is nice to be rich; some candidates who lack funds may be disadvantaged. From the standpoint of the total political system, however, the nomination process does not appear to bar candidates who are otherwise acceptable to the electorate.

The Federal Election Campaign Act Amendments of 1974 were explicitly designed to reduce the influence of money in the electoral process. Whether they will actually accomplish this goal is difficult to calculate. The reform bill does establish a $1,000-per-person limit on contributions to any one candidate's primary, runoff, and general election campaigns, together with an overall limit of $25,000 on contributions by a single individual to all federal candidates in any one year. Organizations of all kinds are limited to $5,000 per candidate per contest. Since there is no limit on how large or small a donating group may be, or on how many donor organizations there are, it is possible that state and regional affiliates of businesses, unions, consumer groups, or what have you could each contribute the maximum amount up to a total of $250,000. This is the loophole through which PACs are being formed, and, in recent years the number of such organizations is growing.

Political action committees (PACs) raise money from individuals to employ in campaigns, either as direct contributions to a candidate or to fund separate but complementary campaigns. The latter was the technique of the National Independent Conservative Political Action Committee (NICPAC), which in both 1980 and 1982 ran negative ad campaigns against liberal incumbents. Most PACs are products of established organizations—unions, corporations, trade associations, "public-interest" lobbying groups—and thus are vehicles for those organizations' leaders to collect funds from members. The degree to which donors to PACs are in one way or another coerced into giving is yet to be researched. A few PACs, like NICPAC, were created by direct mail entrepreneurs.

PACs are controversial; in spite of the large membership of some, they symbolize "special interest" use of money in politics. Already, looking to the 1984 campaign, a number of Democratic hopefuls have appealed to this sentiment by foreswearing use of PAC funds in seeking the nomination. Since presidential nomination campaigns operate with federal matching grants and with spending limits, such "sacrifice" is easier in presidential campaigns than in congressional races. Indeed, much of the fear of PACs focuses on their use to influence Congress, with congressmen on committees with jurisdiction over a given matter receiving funding from the interested PACs.

The president of Common Cause, Fred Wertheimer, says "PAC money has a major and negative impact on the legislative process. Not only do PAC contributions provide access and influence for the donors, but special interest PACs have played a key role in the growing fragmentation of our political process."[23]

A PAC practitioner, Bernadette A. Budde, Political Education Director, Business-Industry Political Action Committee, argues the contrary viewpoint:

PACs are a positive force in American politics for a number of reasons. First, and most important, participation in a PAC provides an opportunity for personal involvement in politics. What once might have seemed an obscure, remote activity engaged in by candidates and a few activists is now within the reach of all citizens. Second, PAC dollars offer opportunities for candidates without personal wealth to run for office. Third, PACs help to elect candidates who, while perhaps not supported by a major party, do represent the view of a large segment of the electorate. Fourth, PACs assist candidates in effectively managing their campaigns and budgets. Finally, PACs reinforce the basic concept of American politics—that all viewpoints can be heard and that public policy is best formed when created in a context of open competition between interests.[24]

One can argue both that PACs reduce citizen activity and that they increase it. The relation of PACs to parties is still developing. Their rise may be a symptom of party decline, for if parties controlled the resources for election, candidates would not need PACs. To the extent that PACs orient themselves to candidates rather than parties, they contribute to party decline by increasing the ability of candidates to build their own organizations. Yet PACs may in the long run be useful to parties. As PACs proliferate (there are now over 4,000), they need to cooperate, and for PAC leaders as for voters parties can become organizing symbols. The ideological PACs—which probably should include not just NICPAC and Jesse Helms' National Congressional Club, but the labor unions as well—line up virtually on party lines.

Richard Richards, former chairman of the Republican National Committee, expressed the tensions in the emerging relationship of PACs and parties. Ideological PACs that openly affiliate with a party, he believes, are useful in accumulating small contributions whose donors may "even sit on the Committee and watch how it is spent and allocate the money to people who have [their] interests at heart. . . ." The Independent Expenditure Committees, like NICPAC, which can spend as they please so long as they do not formally coordinate their activities with a party or candidate, make Richards unhappy. He feels that they can confuse the campaign and compete with the party for the loyalty of candidates. "The candidates say," he continues, "The party didn't do anything for me. I don't owe the party anything."[25]

Michael Malbin describes the developing interaction between the rise of PACs and the professionalization of campaigns:

Paid professionals are less likely than individual corporate executives to give candidates early "seed money" for sentimental reasons. On the other hand, the professionals are more likely to share political information about competitive races, and move together to influence those races during a campaign's closing weeks. Professionals working for business groups also tend to be more "practical" and less ideological than individual corporate contributors. They are less likely to be satisfied with such honorific rewards as ambassadorships, and more interested in electing people who will at least listen to their technical legislative concerns.[26]

More important than PACs for presidential elections are the 1974 act's provisions for public financing of presidential primaries, conventions, and campaigns. To be eligible for matching public funds, candidates in a presidential primary have to raise, on their own, at least $100,000, including $5,000 from each of twenty states or more. Only the first $250 of each individual contribution can be matched by the federal government, up to a total of $5 million for each candidate, providing that no one primary candidate receives more than 25 percent and no party more than 45 percent of the monies available. It is clear that early money, widely dispersed in modest amounts, will be thrice blessed: once for helping a candidate get an early start, once for generating federal matching, and once for multiplying the disparity in private contributions by government aid. If three candidates raised $100,000, $200,000, and $300,000, the difference among them would be half as much ($100,000 and $200,000) before matching as afterward ($200,000 and $400,000).

The two major parties get $3 million apiece for their national conventions from the Presidential Election Campaign Fund. This fund comes from the money automatically assigned to it from the U.S. Treasury when citizens check the proper box on their tax forms. Minor parties may receive lesser amounts based on the percentage of the total vote their candidates have received in a past or current election. Thus new parties have to compete at a disadvantage. To the extent that past presidential elections are used as a basis for calculating support, there is also a danger that a lapse of four years will distort a party's popularity, and the outpouring of third-party sentiment in one year will subsidize the perpetuation of the party four years later, when popular sentiments have shifted. This feature of the election law may keep John Anderson in the limelight in 1984, owing to the magnitude of the protest vote in his favor in 1980.

During the presidential election campaign the major parties can get more than $20 million each from the public fund.[27] They may forego this sum if they choose to do so and opt for private financing instead. It is likely, however, that they will settle for the public bird in the hand. If they go public, they cannot also raise money privately, and this release from private fund raising is a blessing few presidential nominees are likely to reject. They may also suspect that choosing private financing would alienate some voters. Again, minor parties are eligible on a proportionate basis, depending on the votes they received at the last general election, so long as they obtained a minimum of 5 percent of the vote.

Each candidate, finally, is required to establish a single central campaign committee through which all campaign contributions are funnelled and re-ported. Specific banks must be designated as depositories of campaign funds. Many committees may be called to contribute funds, but only one can be chosen to spend them. These stipulations add to the already strong disclosure provisions of the 1971 Federal Election Campaign Act, the attempted cir-cumvention of which was exposed during the Watergate revelations and subsequent trials and convictions.

There were difficulties with the 1971 act and the 1974 amendments. The act was cumbersome, requiring reporting of small sums, and discouraged local campaign activity. It was also parsimonious, providing too little money to conduct adequate national campaigns. And it caused political candidates and parties to become dependent on the timing of regulatory decisions. As these and other problems became apparent, the act was altered again in 1979 so as to allow state and local parties to do more and to lessen the reporting requirements for all concerned. Herbert Alexander and Brian Haggerty have written an admirable summary of this detailed piece of legislation, which imposed new changes upon old ones.

Among its major provisions, the new amendments:
—Exempted candidates who receive or spend $5,000 or less on a campaign from filing disclosure reports; the same applied to party committees under certain circumstances.
—Raised the level for itemized reporting of contributions and expen-ditures from over $100 to in excess of $200, and raised from $100 to $250 the threshold for reporting independent expenditures.
—Reduced the maximum number of reports a candidate is required to file during a two-year cycle.
—Permitted an individual to exclude from reportable contributions an amount up to $1,000 in behalf of a candidate or $2,000 in behalf of a political party, in volunteer expense connected with providing his home (as for a fund-raising event), food, or personal travel.
—Allowed state and local party groups to buy, without limits, but-tons, bumper stickers, handbills, brochures, posters, and yard signs for voluntary activities, and to conduct voter registration and get-out-the-vote drives on behalf of presidential tickets without financial limit.
—Increased from $2 million to $3 million the allotment of federal funds for the Democrats and Republicans to finance their nominating conventions.[28]

If readers think it takes accountants and lawyers to keep up with all this, they are on their way to uncovering another reason for the increasing costs of campaigns.

Watergate was in part a scandal about campaign finance. It was revealed, for example, that the Justice Department negotiated a settlement of an anti-trust suit with the ITT Corporation soon after an ITT subsidiary, the Sheraton Corporation, agreed to supply $400,000 worth of services to the Republican party if the party would locate its 1972 national convention in San Diego. Sheraton's offer was only part of a package put together by San Diego civic leaders, in competition with other cities around the country whose visitors' bureaus also wanted to attract one or both national party conventions.[29]

Now that the law provides a publicly financed $3 million to each national party for its national convention, it forbids parties to spend more than that on the conventions. It is unclear, however, whether this ban includes the various "in kind" services that traditionally have been provided: automobiles from the major manufacturers, free hotel rooms for the national committee roughly on a ratio of one free room for every ten paid for, special police protection and trash collection service, and so on. This is one of the most difficult of the questions faced by the bipartisan Federal Elections Commission established for the purposes of monitoring compliance with campaign expenditures laws and distributing public money under provisions for public financing of elections.

There are four broad issues raised by the new regulations on money. The least troublesome is the issue of public disclosure of campaign financing. In federal campaigns, all contributions in excess of $200 and expenditures by candidates and committees in excess of $1,000 must be publicly reported under the Federal Election Campaign Act of 1971. The availability of this information led Common Cause in 1972, and others since, to compile and publish lists of contributors to congressional campaigns. These compilations document the unsurprising news that some senators and congressmen attracted donations from contributors having business before the committees on which they sat, and that some Senate and House races attracted money from sources far away from the state or district concerned. As well they might; a few hundred thousand dollars invested in Delaware or South Dakota could help to elect a sympathetic congressman or senator as readily as several million dollars invested in New York or California.[30]

When these contributions are matters of public record, voters can decide for themselves whether or not their representatives are still able to represent them adequately. Against this clear public gain must be weighed the possible chilling effects of publicity on the financial angels of small, unpopular parties. Safeguards against this problem are not at present in the law, and so far First Amendment protections of free speech have not been successfully invoked against disclosure on these grounds.[31]

A second feature of the new law is a provision for the public financing of presidential election campaigns, which, as we have said, currently offers nearly $30 million of public funds to each of the major parties, lesser amounts to minor parties, and matching sums to presidential candidates in primary elections. Among the policy issues raised by public financing are: How much should minor parties get? Shouldn't some method be found so that people rather than legislatures allocate public funds to the parties of their choice? In light of the nearly $100 million spent by the major party candidates in 1972, the last presidential year before public finance went into effect, isn't $60 million too low to provide adequate political communication in a nation as large and diverse as ours?

United to this last question is, of course, the question of whether private expenditures should be prohibited where public expenditures are used. Any limitation on campaign expenditure limits political communication, a class of speech that one would think would be especially protected by the First Amendment. In practical terms, limits on campaign spending—now in force in all federal elections—constitute an incumbent's protective device, since challengers almost always have the greater burden of making their names known. When expenditures are limited, political competition is inhibited. At present, however, the courts have held that Congress can set expenditure limits as a condition of accepting public subsidy except when politicians are spending their own money, which it is their unlimited right under the law to do.

The final issue raised by recent legislation is the issue of limitations on contributions. Here, once again, a First Amendment problem is encountered, since voluntary political contributions by citizens of their own money as a means of political advocacy can readily be construed as exercise of free speech. Against this must be weighed a general public interest in seeing to it that politicians are not unduly influenced by people who have large financial interests. May not those who contribute or raise money in large amounts thereby gain influence not available to others? Aware that the answer to this question is not a simple one and certainly does not dispose of the First Amendment problem, we would say, "Yes, but not overly much." As one fund raiser said of Washington: "This town works on personal relationships.

Any time there's an opportunity to develop those relationships, it's a plus. The most anybody figures they can get in this business is access. You can't buy a vote. What you can do is say, 'Listen, I've helped you.' "[32]

What contributors or fund raisers (the financial middlemen) get to begin with is access to centers of decision making. Control over money certainly makes it easier to get in "the door" and present one's case. Persons of wealth, however, are likely to have substantial interests that would provide them with good access whether or not they made contributions. If no significant interest feels disadvantaged by what these contributors want, they may well be given the benefit of the doubt. But in matters of great moment, where the varied interests in our society are in contention, it is doubtful whether control over money goes very far with a president. There are many reasons for this.

In the first place, there are many issues on which a candidate is likely already to be publicly committed. Suggestions that he change his position during the campaign are likely to be met with little favor. If the matter is important enough to be mentioned, it has to be considered in relation to its vote-getting potential. Forced to make a choice, nominees are far more likely to prefer votes to dollars. And even if a miscalculation is made in public, candidates generally prefer not to reverse their field and appear vacillating and inconsistent. Money may be given in the expectation of future favors. To spell this out in detail would appear unseemly, however, and is likely to be rejected outright.[33] The moral sense of the candidates would most likely forbid such a thing. If not, the good political sense of their advisers (certainly after, if not before, Watergate) would suggest that the consequences of discovery are much worse than any possible benefits. Thus, any strings attached to a gift are likely to be vague and cloudy, subject to all sorts of interpretations. When they are not, the risks of exposure are so great that the costs of corruption are as likely to be as high for the contributors as for the public.

Once a president assumes office, he is in a much stronger bargaining position. Contributors are likely to need him much more than he will need them: he can do more to affect their fortunes than they can to affect his. A president may at that point refuse to acknowledge any alleged agreement of policy concessions in return for contributions. Wealthy contributors frequently give to both parties and, in any case, are often found on opposite sides of public issues. For candidates to give in to one of them may simply incur the wrath of others.

A decline in contributions from one source may be made up by funds from another. The president's need to gain or maintain support from voters, the limits placed on his powers of decision by what congressmen, bureaucrats, and interest groups will accept, and his own preferences all place drastic constraints on benefits contributors get from campaign contributions. In brief, money becomes much less important to the things a president needs to do while he is in office. Contributors may be heard to complain in the hurt tones of Henry C. Frick, who, after visiting Theodore Roosevelt at the White House, said, "We bought the son of a bitch and then he did not stay bought."[34] The foregoing analysis should help to explain why presidential politicians do not "stay bought," whatever their debt to their financial supporters.

It would be amazing if the exponential growth in the regulation of private industry did not lead businessmen to seek advantages and governmental officials to confer them. The fact is that what government does—an airline route or a television license here, a tax ruling or an import quota there—can have an enormous impact on the fortunes of private people. Businessmen, we have learned from investigations of the fund-raising practices of the Nixon Committee to Reelect the President, feel they must act defensively. They may give to a campaign fund not so much to steal a march on their competitors as to make sure they are not left behind. Thus, for example, airlines may give to protect their routes.[35] Because government power is so pervasive, businessmen, not knowing when or where they might need a friend, frequently give to the campaigns of both parties. Deregulation makes this less necessary. So does public finance of elections.

Though the parties usually seem to raise enough money to get by, the activities that go into finding money are likely to give the candidates a few traumatic experiences. Each successive presidential campaign tends to be run by different people, who have to start from the beginning. When Adlai Stevenson was nominated in 1952, he downgraded large contributions and appointed Beardsley Ruml his chief fund raiser. Ruml tried to get most of what he needed from small contributions, and he got more than usual from small givers, but not nearly enough.[36] His predecessor was Edwin Pauley, who raised funds for Truman. Pauley was an oilman who had a wide acquaintanceship among the wealthy. He was adroit in having his claims recognized by such groups as road builders and construction firms, who could expect to benefit from Democratic policies. Until the Kennedy campaign, the Democrats continued to live, at best, from hand to mouth, day to day, crisis to crisis. In 1948 President Truman found himself stranded without funds on his campaign train in the middle of Oklahoma. Few people wished to contribute to what was thought to be a sure defeat. The governor and a few others on the train decided that this could not be allowed to continue and found the money. Humphrey was nearly out of money in the midst of his seemingly hopeless 1968 campaign when a plea for funds was inserted as an after-thought at the end of a nationwide television speech from Salt Lake City, in which he pledged a bombing halt in Vietnam. Enough money came in to pay for the program twice over. Again, the essential wherewithal was forthcoming, but the attendant tension is hardly the best atmosphere in which to conduct a political campaign.[37] In 1964, "when Republican chances of victory over Johnson were never rated much brighter than those of a snowflake in Austin," the Republicans raised more money than they had in any previous campaign. And, in contrast with previous campaigns, the money came not from big business but primarily from "small donations sent in by hundreds of thousands of contributors, many of whom had never before contributed to a national campaign." The GOP collected 651,000 small, individual contributions in 1964. Candidates who generate intensely enthusiastic personal followings seem to be more capable of raising money from small contributors than less charismatic representatives of the parties. For example, George Wallace always raised a great deal of money this way, and in 1976 he was the first Democrat to qualify for federal primary matching funds, some eighteen months before the election.[38]

One of the more promising fund-raising gimmicks, the selling of advertisements in the program book of the Democratic National Convention at $15,000 a page, had to be abandoned in 1965 because of adverse publicity. Lacking this source, Humphrey turned in 1968 to the device of securing loans to cover campaign expenses as they arose. Prominent contributors would sign notes with banks and would then be paid back as funds from more traditional sources (such as dinners) arrived. Most of the Democratic debt left over after the 1968 campaign involved these outstanding loans.[39]

After the election of 1960, President Kennedy shifted the emphasis in fund raising back from numerous small contributors to a few large ones. A Presidents' Club ($1,000 a year) was formed, whose members were rewarded with invitations to White House social functions and other notable occasions. Under Johnson this club became the primary source of Democratic fund raising to the detriment of formerly broad-based efforts (such as Dollars for Democrats). The plan worked well in 1964 (when 4,000 members joined), but as Johnson's popularity declined, so did the membership (to 200 in 1966). From 1966 to 1968, Johnson was involved too deeply in other problems to concern himself with party affairs and the decline in broad-based efforts continued.[40]

In order to pay off the sizable debt left over from the 1968 presidential campaign, the Democrats took to the airwaves and put on a number of fund-raising telethons. These raised more than $2 million each, after costs. In recent years the Democrats have also practiced other methods of debt reduction, including the painful business of negotiating with creditors to see if they would settle for less than 100 cents on the dollar. Political parties and candidates, in consequence of these sorts of maneuvers, have gotten a name for themselves as bad credit risks. As a result, television stations and newspapers usually require payment in advance. Airlines and the telephone company—both regulated industries, after all, and hence vulnerable to the wrath of newly elected officials—have been edging gingerly toward similar requirements.

Campaign reform laws have encouraged candidates to switch to the attraction of small donations by mass appeals through the mails. Mail solicitation has become a large and sophisticated business, and a whole new class of professional political managers who know about such things—which mailing lists yield the best results, how to write a mail solicitation, how to organize and account for returns—has grown up.[41]

Today the financing of presidential elections is broken into two phases: before the nomination, where federal subsidies supplement the fund-raising activities of candidates, and after the nomination, where federal subsidies provide all the money to the major parties to run their presidential campaigns. Expenditures independent of candidates by political action committees—buying ads on television or in the newspapers, or campaigning via direct mail, for example—are permitted by law, and play an increasing part in presidential elections. However, this sort of independent access to the voting public is by no means as pervasive as the ordinary access to voters provided to those nonpoliticians who own and operate the news media.

☆ Control over Information

Control over information is thus a major political resource. Information does many things other than help voters to change their minds—that rare phenomenon. It helps people keep in touch with the progress of the campaign, gives the party faithful indications of the effectiveness of their side, and acquaints voters with the candidates' major arguments. Information helps to guide and channel both the enthusiasm and content of participation, and therefore control over information and its dissemination is a significant political resource.

As we scan the major information media it appears that, generally speaking, newspapers are somewhat more partisan in their straight news coverage than are radio and television stations. A political party that feels discriminated against over the air can complain to the Federal Communications Commission, which may take such complaints into account when the offending station's broadcast license is up for renewal. This makes station management jumpy and is a strong incentive for balanced coverage.[42] There is no such legal limitation on the "freedom" of newspapers and magazines to be one-sided in the presentation of the news, and, indeed, it has again and again been discovered that the printed media avail themselves rather extensively of this freedom. Many newspapers enjoy monopoly positions in their communities, and much of the detailed political information available comes from the press. For these reasons the character of press coverage of presidential elections is a matter of strategic importance.

Historically, partisanship in news coverage has generally tended to favor the side that is most often endorsed editorially by the press, namely, the Republicans. Repeated studies have shown that the Republicans usually are the favorite party of the newspaper executives who determine editorial policy in most newspapers. They have also shown that whatever biases exist in news reporting, in placing stories in papers, in location and size of headlines, and so on, systematically have favored the Republicans.[43] The election of 1964, when newspapers gave a slight edge to President Johnson, provided the only exception; in 1968 newspapers returned to form.

Yet, paradoxically, Democratic candidates for president do not seem to be harmed excessively by pro-Republican sentiments in the press, even among voters who rely heavily upon newspapers as sources of civic information. In recent decades Democrats like Franklin Roosevelt, Harry Truman, John F. Kennedy, and Jimmy Carter have gained office despite the fact that a vast majority of the press was editorially against them. If electoral votes had been apportioned within each state by the number of newspaper endorsements for each candidate, the 1976 count would have been Ford 538, Carter 0. If they had been apportioned on the basis of the circulation of these papers, the count would have been Ford 489, Carter 49. The actual result, of course, was Ford 240, Carter 297. In 1980, a Republican year, the numbers were Reagan 444, Carter 46 (with 48 electoral votes in states where newspaper endorsements were evenly balanced) on the basis of the number of endorsements. On the basis of newspaper circulation, Reagan 385, Carter 139 (and 14 for ties). The actual result was Reagan 489, Carter 49.[44]

Despite the seeming Republican edge, the days of the crusading editor

THE STRATEGIC ENVIRONMENT: RESOURCES

who owned his own paper and used it as a vehicle to propagate his own political doctrines are largely gone. In our time, newspapers with substantial circulations are much more likely to be part of a corporate chain devoted primarily to making money for their stockholders.[45] The costs of publication are high. In order to show a profit, papers must have a high circulation and a good deal of advertising. This is difficult to achieve in the midst of competition among several papers and with television and accounts for the trend toward consolidation. Reader attention is gained by emphasizing human-interest stories—sports, crime, local personalities, and the high jinks of movie stars. Especially outside the major metropolitan areas, political news, though it does have a place, is downplayed because most readers are not terribly interested in politics. An excessive emphasis upon public affairs, therefore, is unlikely so long as appeal to readers is a prime consideration. This certainly has drawbacks for civic education. But for present purposes, it means that the possibilities for political propaganda are much less than they otherwise might be, because public affairs do not get much space.[46] Advertising is gained by convincing businessmen that it will pay them in terms of increased sales. The periodic appeals of conservatives requesting businessmen to place or withhold advertising as a form of political coercion usually fall on deaf ears, because the motives of those who pay are commercial rather than political. Both the paper and its advertisers are likely to shy away from political controversy: it tends to make enemies rather than friends and is commonly believed to be "bad for business." The result is that much of the time newspapers are rather bland. Such political opinions as they do express are watered down so they will not give offense. Their political opinions, far from being their central concerns, tend to be sporadic and aimless, rather than representative of a coherent political ideology.[47]

These tendencies are strengthened by a prevailing belief that papers ought to be nonpartisan in their news stories and present both sides of the issues of the day. However much the norm of impartiality may be honored in the breach, it provides a standard that to some extent holds down partisanship. More than that, the belief that newspapers should report what happens rather than editorialize in their news columns has many other attractions for editors. It enables them to avoid the hostilities engendered by political controversy; it lessens problems of editorial judgment, thus decreasing their work load; it enables them to select items that they think will enhance their readership; it provides editors with a defense against the charge of giving too much prominence to causes and candidates that may be unpopular with advertisers or influential readers. The norm of impartiality leaves the papers open to manipulation by political strategists who can create sensational news stories. During the heyday of Senator Joseph McCarthy, for example, newspapermen slowly became aware of the extent to which they had aided him by publicizing his charges because they were "news," rather than ignoring or carefully evaluating them.[48] During presidential campaigns, application of the same standard gives the candidate who is opposed by newspapers the opportunity to enter at least some of its news stories because whatever he says is "news." If he should be an incumbent, his exposure will be greater because the president of the United States gets attention for the smallest things that he and his family do.

The desire to cut costs has at least one favorable consequence for increased impartiality in news stories. There is today a growing reliance on material put out by the giant news services, the Associated Press, United Press International, and to some extent the *New York Times, Los Angeles Times,* and *Washington Post* services. These news-gathering agencies serve a wide clientele having a broad spectrum of opinions. They therefore endeavor to prepare stories that will prove acceptable to various shades of opinion.[49] Presenting what happened with a minimum of slanted commentary is a good way to do this, though the wire services are by no means perfect in this respect. The final product, however, is closer to the canons of impartiality than would be the case if each paper prepared stories in accordance with its editorial position.

While it remains true that candidates favored by newspapers receive better treatment and somewhat greater coverage than others, there is one compensating factor in presidential campaigns that has not received the attention it deserves. Although the papers are generally conservative and Republican, political correspondents are comparatively more liberal and Democratic.[50] The stories they send, though subject to the mercies of the editor in the home office, to a certain extent redress the balance on the paper. This is particularly the case in the rather subtle question of how candidates are portrayed. The feeling that some candidates are more responsive, more open, more friendly, more intelligent than others may get communicated through little human-interest stories and result in an impression contrary to that preferred by the owners of the paper. This is about the extent to which journalists' biases get into the news columns, however. Most of the same standards of professional practice that constrain right-wing partisanship by publishers also damp down left-wing partisanship by journalists. As Michael Robinson has shown, while reporters may lean to the left, it's hard to find this bias in their copy.[51]

In 1960 John F. Kennedy, who was popular with reporters, got some favorable extra attention. Richard Nixon, who was not so popular with them, quite understandably complained.[52] By 1968, Nixon was a battle-scarred veteran who could watch with grim satisfaction as the press pursued the early Republican frontrunner, the relatively inexperienced George Romney. Jules Witcover comments:

Romney, Nixon reasoned correctly, had not yet learned the lessons about the press that Nixon's experience had taught him, and even if he had, he could not go into hiding. A moratorium on politics by a former Vice-President, Presidential candidate and conspicuous globe-trotter would make little difference, since his face and his views already were widely known in the country; Romney, however, needed exposure in large doses on the national scene if he hoped to graduate to the status of a national candidate. That exposure, Nixon was confident, would be Romney's downfall. . . . Meanwhile, Nixon himself could sit back, let Romney's destruction happen, and emerge all the stronger by virtue of the contrast between the way he and Romney conducted themselves in the pre-election year shakedown.[53]

In 1972, Nixon carried his strategy of avoidance even further, programming himself into local television spots in key places around the country and totally bypassing exposure to possible hostile questions from news correspondents.[54] He used the norm that the president's statements are news to get the coverage he wanted. Ronald Reagan, with his affable personality and long experience in show business, did exceedingly well with the men and women of the media in 1980. Jimmy Carter's efforts to portray him as an ogre, insensitive to poor people, or a war-monger were contradicted by Reagan's media coverage. By comparison, President Carter had far less favorable press notices.

Are ordinary citizens actually influenced in their opinions and voting choices by the newspapers they take? We use the word "take" advisedly, because the fact that a newspaper enters a home is no guarantee that its political news and editorials will be read. Most people pay little enough attention to politics; they often read nothing or just scan the headlines without taking away much of an impression. Analyses of tons of newspaper clippings showing political propaganda by newspapers mean nothing insofar as the effect is concerned if these stories are never read.

When stories and editorials are perused with some care, the reader's perception of what has been written may differ markedly from the writer's intentions. An editorial may not be clear in intent, particularly if it is hedged by qualifications or watered down to minimize offense, as is often the case. Frequently, the reader pays attention only to those parts of the piece that substantiate his own opinions. Opinion studies have demonstrated the remarkable capacity of people to filter out what they do not wish to hear and come away with quite a different impression than an objective analysis of an editorial or article would warrant. Indeed, the reader may interpret the story to mean precisely the opposite of what it intends. A criticism of Harry Truman for being vituperative, for example, could be taken as a commendation of his fighting spirit, just as a condemnation of Jimmy Carter for being obstinate could emerge as praise for his high principles.[55]

Stories and editorials may also be interpreted as they were meant to be and still be rejected as invalid. There is a great deal of suspicion of the press in the United States.[56] Party identification is so powerful that it is likely to overwhelm almost anything a paper says. Obviously, millions of citizens have no difficulty remaining and voting Democratic while reading Republican newspapers. Group loyalties are another force that may lead to rejection of opinions in newspapers. Face-to-face groups in unions, on the job, in fraternal, religious, and ethnic organizations, may generate opinions of their own. If these differ from those in the newspaper, the group is provided with defense against the persuasion of the press. Group pressures of this kind are likely to be far more influential than what is written in a paper. The group may also reinforce what the paper says, but this represents an intensification rather than a change of opinion.[57]

Consider a puzzle concerning the political impact of the *New York Daily News,* a tabloid with a circulation in the millions. It is apparent that if those who read the *News* all through the 1930s and 1940s had voted against Franklin D. Roosevelt, as the paper repeatedly recommended in vitriolic terms, Roosevelt certainly would never have carried New York City by the huge margins he did. At the same time it seems strange that so many people who not only voted for but revered FDR in New York continued to read a newspaper whose editorials bitterly attacked their hero. The Democratic readers of the *News* apparently managed to get the best of both worlds. They read the paper they liked and voted for the man they favored without noticing the apparent contradiction. For them, clearly, there was no contradiction. They either did not pay attention to the editorials, or they blocked out the unfavorable ones completely, or they interpreted them to mean something favorable to FDR. Voting studies document instances where people who wanted to vote for Harry Truman in 1948 convinced themselves that the incumbent president was against price controls; some people who preferred Dwight Eisenhower in 1956 apparently had no difficulty in believing that he surely favored medical care for the aged.[58]

Or, let us consider the case of the opposite of the *New York Daily News,* the gray, sober, responsible *New York Times.* After the *Times* came out for John F. Kennedy in the closing weeks of the 1960 presidential campaign, various political pundits speculated on the probable impact of this endorsement by so august and respectable a source. Our theory about voting behavior would lead us to be wary of claiming much influence for the *Times,* not because its readership is too indifferent to heed a call to reason, but because of the kind of people who read this paper. One has to be terribly interested in politics to read through the *Times* as far as the editorial page. Precisely because of this interest, *Times* readers are likely to identify with a major party and to resist changing their allegiance. A call from the *Times,* therefore, however respectable, could hardly shake these devoted party people in their fundamental loyalty. The vacillating, the doubtful, and the uninformed who cannot make up their minds are far more likely to read comic books or *Modern Romance* than the *New York Times,* with its surfeit of "dull" news about political events.

No doubt the monopoly position of most newspapers in local communities makes the dissemination of opposing views more difficult than it might be in the presence of competition from a newspaper of a different outlook. But there are ways of getting around this. Other publications may enter the home—magazines and pamphlets that are religious, ethnic, union, fraternal, and even political in their focus—and these may contain contrary notions of public policy and candidate preference. True, only a relatively few persons read the political magazines, but these people are likely to be opinion leaders, people who take an active interest in public affairs and from whom others seek advice. The availability, therefore, of little magazines of many shades of opinion permits the opinion leaders to receive and then disseminate on a personal basis information that may counteract whatever is in a newspaper. And there is the pervasive influence of television, which has put so many afternoon newspapers out of business, and is now the favorite means by which citizens inform themselves of the rudiments of the daily news.[59]

What, then, is the significance of newspapers in presidential campaigns? We have suggested that the press is by no means immensely influential. Its major importance probably lies in two directions: presenting some kind of information about the candidates and the campaign to its readers and intensifying the predispositions held by people who tend to agree with the paper's preferences. Under some circumstances, also, a united press can force politicians to pay attention to a particular range of issues, not by telling people what to think so much as, in Bernard C. Cohen's lapidary phrase, telling them what to think *about*. Candidates would undoubtedly rather have the press on their side than against them. But they can and do win in the face of opposition from the press.

It may be that the newspapers people read subtly condition their attitudes in ways now unsuspected and that this has some effect on their opinions and voting choices.[60] One study, by Robert S. Ericson, suggests that when a newspaper in a monopoly position endorses a presidential candidate, that endorsement slightly influences the prevailing trend. Ericson found no influence for the press in 1968, a close election, but some in the polarized contest of 1964, when the usual Republican predominance lessened, and in 1972, when it intensified. The press matters more, it appears, as a conveyer of information during landslides, when its effect on the outcome matters less.[61]

Whatever impact the press has varies enormously with circumstances. Against a well-known and immensely popular president (such as Franklin Roosevelt in 1936 or Lyndon Johnson in 1964) with publicity resources of his own, the impact of the press may be negligible. Against a little-known candidate, such as Adlai Stevenson in 1952, the attitudes communicated by the press—say, aloofness, overintellectuality, indecisiveness—may be more significant. Yet we know from voting studies that in 1952 Stevenson was favorably regarded by Democrats who identified him with his party.[62] The sheer number of different issues that may become relevant during a presidential campaign may either neutralize or intensify the influence of the press, depending on whether they are "pocketbook" issues that are grasped with relative ease by voters or "style" issues that owe their existence as issues to the attention paid them by the mass media.

It might appear that radio and especially television have significant impact on electoral outcomes because more people get their news from these sources today than from any other. This may well be true for local, state, and congressional elections, where voter interest and information is low. It is even probably more true for primary elections at these levels, where sheer name recognition may count a great deal. But, whatever may be true under other conditions, it evidently does not hold for presidential elections. Studying several gubernatorial, congressional, and presidential elections, Gary C. Jacobson found "only a small, statistically insignificant relationship between the candidate's relative proportion of broadcast media exposure and the proportion of the votes he receives" at the presidential (but not at the other) levels. In presidential contests, he explains, voters reach their saturation level of exposure long before any disparity in attention to or communications from the candidates makes the difference.[63]

☆ The Role of Television

The role of television in presidential elections is so complicated that it deserves special mention. As a news medium, television reaches more voters than the newspapers. As an advertising medium, it soaks up enormous amounts of the money allocated to candidates under the law.

Television news coverage, while for the most part strictly impartial after the parties make their nominations, plays a significant role in determining who wins the nomination in the first place. Early in the nomination process, when there are many prospective candidates, those candidates who are "taken seriously" by the news media, and especially by television, have a much better chance to survive the primaries and caucuses. Because the delegates to national party conventions are picked mostly by primary electorates, favorable exposure to mass electorates through the mass media—expensively by buying advertisements, or inexpensively by receiving news coverage —is absolutely necessary for hopeful candidates.

There is a tendency, brought on by the brisk competition among the three major television networks, for television news to deal rather ruthlessly with candidates, declaring them "winners" and "losers" with great rapidity on primary election nights, based on projections from early returns and exit polls. The competitive pressure to see a pattern even when the outcome is not terribly clear is overwhelming. Thus, on the night of the early-bird Iowa caucus in 1976 Jimmy Carter was proclaimed a big winner for bagging 29 percent of the vote. This was more than any of his rivals—the next in line was Birch Bayh with 11 percent—but far less than the 39 percent that went to uncommitted delegates.

Television journalists, in common with their brethren in print, make every effort to nail down "expectations" against which the performance in early primaries of candidates can be measured: Lyndon Johnson beat Eugene McCarthy as a write-in candidate in New Hampshire in 1968, but McCarthy did so much better than "expected" that the fact of his strong showing dominated the news and shortly drove Johnson out of the race altogether.

So television interacts powerfully with the delegate-selection process—

especially early on, before popular images of the various candidates are fully established—and makes a difference to political outcomes. This is not to say that television as a medium is politically biased; on the whole the producers of the main news programs try very hard to guard against that.[64] However they do, inevitably, make decisions in order to get or keep viewers. This affects their reporting.

The media want excitement. That is what sells newspapers and captures viewers for the television news. From this need to compete follows a proclivity to adopt a horse-race metaphor and before election evening to overemphasize the closeness of races. Even when the results of surveys appear conclusive, the media suggest the race is still open. A close race keeps the adrenaline flowing. So, according to the study by C. Anthony Broh, reporters

> 1) avoid predictions if they are definitive; 2) avoid reporting percentages if they are not close; 3) report the attitudes and preferences of subgroups that cast doubt on the outcome; 4) compare polls to a time period that can demonstrate a narrowing or constantly close gap between the candidates; 5) report voter reaction to spectacles of the campaign; 6) distort results that do not generate excitement; and 7) question the validity of polls that show a wide gap. Furthermore, they interpret methodological ambiguities involving undecided voters and sampling error in ways that maximize shifts in campaign support.[65]

Decisions favoring horse-race excitement and sensationalism eventually produce premature closure on apparent winners, not only on election night, but also in the course of interpreting to viewers what has happened. Consequently, the news media tend to start bandwagons early in the election season and hasten the outcome of nomination processes.

Similarly, after the nominations are made, if equal-time provisions of the Federal Communications Act are waived by a special act of Congress, as they sometimes are, the networks are able to give or withhold legitimacy to third-party candidates more or less at will. This greatly affects the capacity of such candidates to mount a credible challenge to the candidates of the two major parties. For example, in 1980 John Anderson lost ground steadily after he was excluded from the televised debate between major candidates, more or less at Jimmy Carter's insistence.

Because they lend themselves easily to television coverage primary elections and other "open" delegate selection mechanisms that lead to pledged delegates receive a lot of attention from television journalists.[66] This has made it hard for state party leaders to maintain control over party nominations. In effect the news media have been a major influence in transferring power over the nomination process from state party leaders to candidates and primary electorates.[67]

As an advertising medium television has gained greatly from the laws requiring a strict accounting of candidate expenditures. As compared with the numerous decentralized commitments of money that might occur in a grass-roots campaign, it is relatively easy to keep close watch over expenditures by buying television time for the presidential candidate's campaign. This has tended to centralize campaigns, and to make candidates increasingly dependent on television to carry their message. No wonder, then, that public relations specialists and experts at the use of television have increasingly turned up on presidential staffs since the days when actor-director Robert Montgomery coached candidate Eisenhower.[68]

We conclude that newspapers, magazines, and television stations do not conspire together (or within their own industries) to control the outcomes of nominations and elections. Nor, despite inevitable biases, do single papers or networks, so far as we know, overtly attempt this task. Similarly, although they try, as we have seen, candidates do not succeed in molding or manipulating the media to their liking. What we see most often is behavior that is not essentially manipulative or conspiratorial but mutual and interactive. The media and the candidates depend on each other for news to report and for favorable reporting to such a degree that each anticipates the actions and reactions of the other. Observers are correct in noting the extent to which the media are not merely part of the campaign, but centrally important to the campaign. No candidate has enough time or money or energy to reach all or most of the people necessary to get nominated and elected. There was a time, as far back as 1968 or 1972, when it was still possible for a candidate to go from small early primaries to larger later ones, gaining strength along the way. Nowadays there are too many primaries and too many groups and too many voters to manage without the media. In addition, most people get their news from the media, and early reports of progress are essential to later success. Therefore, candidates must estimate how their actions are likely to appear in the news. Such questions as which primaries to enter or how much emphasis to put on them or how much attention to pay to which issues must be considered from the standpoint of the impression they will create on television. Gerald Ford's advisors came to the conclusion that he was not a terribly effective campaigner (news of his appearances seemed to be associated with declines in his popularity at the polls), so they decided to keep him in the White House as much as possible, campaigning for president by being president.

Candidate choices continuously interact with media interpretations. R. W. Apple's *New York Times* story on the 1976 Iowa primary was widely credited with making Carter a front runner. Had Morris Udall not spent too much time in Iowa and not enough in New Hampshire, as hindsight suggests, he might have come out ahead in the New Hampshire primary, appeared on the covers of *Time* and *Newsweek*, and been lionized by the press and shown on prime time. And, for all we know, had there not been numerous network and newspaper polls before the 1976 Republican convention showing Ford ahead, Reagan might have been able to maneuver better against a background of uncertainty. Knowing that dramaturgical stereotypes (who the good guys are, who the leaders are, who's out in left field, and so on) tend to persist, and that the front runner of today may be carried along only by early exposure, journalists may seek to resist perpetuating them.[69] This, however, is hard to do, because it must be done within certain rules of the news-gathering business. Newspapers and television news programs require leads. Since ignoring an act can be as dangerous as attending to it, since under- and overexposure may be evident only in retrospect, and since they need news, the media are swept along by the tide of events to which they contribute and in which they swim, very much like the rest of us.

☆ Incumbency as a Resource: The Presidency

The presidency is one resource which, in any given election year, must of necessity be monopolized by one party or the other. When an incumbent president seeks reelection, he enjoys many special advantages by virtue of his position. He is, to begin with, much better known than any challenger can hope to be. Everything the president does is news and is widely reported in all the media. The issues to which the president devotes his attention are likely to become the national issues because of his unique visibility and capacity to center public attention on matters he deems important. To this extent, he is in a position to focus public debate on issues he thinks are most advantageous. The president can act and thereby gain credit. If he cannot act, he can accuse Congress of inaction, as Truman did in 1948, and Ford did in 1976. Should he face a crisis in foreign affairs, and there are many, he can gain by doing well or by calling on the patriotism of the citizenry to support its chief executive when the nation is in danger.

A significant example of this took place during the 1980 campaign, when Iranian students seized the American embassy in Teheran on November 4, 1979, just as Edward Kennedy announced that he would run for the Democratic nomination against the incumbent president, Jimmy Carter. Before the hostage crisis began, Kennedy was outdistancing Carter in the polls by 54 percent to 31 percent (with 15 percent undecided). Soon, however, Democrats rallied around the flag, and Carter's ratings shot up to 48 percent, with 40 percent for Kennedy and 12 percent undecided. Carter announced that he would suspend active campaigning, and he used his crisis responsibilities as a reason to refuse to meet his rivals in debate. He continued to campaign from the White House rose garden, however, and with great success.[70]

Unfortunately, the crisis dragged on too long, and President Carter's popularity ultimately suffered a serious decline, reverting to its precrisis level. Thus this episode also shows that the president cannot count on continued popularity if his policies do not appear successful to the electorate. President Nixon, to make a similar point in a different context, made repeated use of national television to mobilize support for his Vietnam policy. So long as his administration's actions were in accord with general public desires for withdrawal, even if gradual, the president did well in the polls. When he sent troops into Cambodia instead of withdrawing them from Vietnam, however, it was less clear that his fellow citizens approved of that course of action.[71]

As the symbol of the nation, the president can travel and make "nonpolitical" speeches to advance his candidacy subtly, while his opponent is open to charges of "blind partisanship" in what are becoming unceasingly troubled times. Should his opponent claim that he can do a better job, the president need hardly make the obvious response that he is the only candidate who has had experience in a job for which there exists no completely appropriate prior training. Presidents, moreover, as Nixon did in 1972, can campaign by doing their jobs, while challengers, as McGovern discovered, have to manufacture positions that may dissolve upon close scrutiny or criticism.

The life of the incumbent, however, is not necessarily one of undiluted joy. If the economic situation takes a turn for the worse, if lines lengthen at gas stations, if a race riot erupts, if another nation comes under Communist influence, he is likely to be blamed. Whether he is really to blame or not, as president he is held responsible and has to take the consequences. Herbert Hoover felt deeply the sting of this phenomenon when the people punished the political "in-group" for a depression that Hoover would have given much to avoid. So, too, President Carter found himself fighting inflation with higher interest rates and spending less on social welfare than Democrats normally like to deliver.[72]

The incumbent has a record; he has or has not done things, and he may be held accountable for his sins of omission or commission. Not so the man out of office, who can criticize freely without always presenting realistic alternatives or necessarily taking his own advice once he is elected. Gerald Ford was hurt by his pardon of Richard Nixon. The "missile gap" of 1960 turned out to be something of a chimera after Kennedy got into the White House, and he never found it possible to act much differently toward the Matsu-Quemoy situation near mainland China than did Dwight Eisenhower, despite their overpublicized "differences" about this question during the campaign. Richard Nixon could complain about the problem of "law and order" in 1968 without promising anything more concrete than a new attorney general, which he would have appointed anyway. In 1980 candidate Reagan said "ask yourself if you are as well off today as you were four years ago" and voters—for the most part erroneously—responded as Reagan had, in the negative.[73] Candidate Reagan was able to blame "stagflation," the unwelcome combination of high inflation and unemployment, on President Carter. Had the recession widely predicted for the last year of the Carter administration occurred at that time, or even in the first few months of Reagan's tenure in office, the incoming president would have been in a wonderful position to argue that his program was the cure for whatever ailed the nation. And so he did for his first year in office. Even as inflation declined, however, unemployment rose as the recession arrived during Reagan's second year. Whether or not Carter was responsible for inflation or Reagan for unemployment, each chief executive was accountable for what happened during his term of office. Thus the considerable Republican losses in the 1982 congressional elections, combined with the ability of Democrats to blame the Republican president for unemployment, placed Reagan in the same difficult defensive position his predecessor had been in. The incumbent is naturally cast as the defender of his administration and the challenger as the attacker who promises better things to come. We cannot expect to hear the man in office say that the other fellow could probably do as well or to hear the challenger declare that he really could not do any better than the incumbent, although both statements may be close to the truth.

While his opponent can to some extent permit himself to be irresponsible or carried away by exuberance, the president cannot detach himself from office while campaigning, and he must recognize that other nations are listening when he makes statements. The president's very superiority of information may turn out to be a handicap, as he cannot make certain statements or reveal his sources for other statements without committing a breach of security. His opponent can attack his record, but the incumbent may have difficulty finding a comparable record to assail on the other side —unless, of course, a McGovern or Goldwater comes along who succeeds at making his proposals the issue. The memory of McGovern undoubtedly influenced those who have come after him, especially Jimmy Carter and Ronald Reagan, to be less specific during their campaigns than they might otherwise have been.

Barring catastrophic events—depression, war, scandal—the president's power is most certainly strong enough to assure him of renomination within the limits imposed by the anti-third-term (the Twenty-second) amendment to the Constitution. This is not merely because his is the greatest, most visible office in the land, with all sorts of patronage and other controls over the potential delegates. There is, in addition, the fact that his party can hardly hope to win by repudiating him. To refuse him the nomination would, most politicians feel, be tantamount to confessing political bankruptcy or ineptitude.

This rule was bent but not broken in 1980 by Kennedy's opposition to Carter and in 1976 by the Reagan challenge to Ford. Nor was it broken in 1968. President Johnson had scheduled the Democratic convention to coincide with his birthday in anticipation of his renomination. The fact that his birthday fell in late August left his successor as nominee, Hubert Humphrey, with little time to heal the wounds and raise the money needed for victory in November. The challenges of McCarthy and Kennedy in that year demonstrated, however, that the costs of party insurgency are high: not only do insurgents rarely win their party's nomination; their party also usually loses the election in such years. It was not only the fact that Senator Edward Kennedy sought to take the nomination away from incumbent Jimmy Carter in 1980, but also that he persisted right up through the convention, refusing to give Carter his wholehearted endorsement, that hurt the President. Consequently candidate Carter was unable to focus on his Republican opponent as early as he would have liked.

The presidential power over national conventions has historically extended to (1) the right to renomination, or to designate the party nominee, effectively exercised in almost all of the conventions since the Civil War in which the president interested himself in the outcome; (2) the power to dictate the party platform; (3) the power to designate the officers of the convention; (4) the power to select many delegates. This privilege was especially potent historically in the case of Republican delegations during the days of the one-party Democratic South, when Republican presidents, until the passage of the Hatch Act, drew upon a corporal's guard of federal patronage appointees to man this sizable convention bloc.

The constitutional amendment limiting presidents to two terms may eventually change the power of a two-term incumbent radically, but we doubt it. The party still must run on the presidential record, and the outgoing president still seems likely to control the management of the convention. Before President Roosevelt broke the two-term tradition, outgoing presidents controlled conventions even when no one expected them to run again. Presidents Truman and Johnson were also very influential in 1952 and 1968, when they were not candidates for reelection.[74]

There are those who believe that, like other democratic countries, the United States is going through a crisis of ungovernability.[75] In this view, any incumbent is vulnerable because he cannot satisfy the expectations of increasingly well-educated and articulate critics and their audiences in the electorate, who want results but are not willing to pay the costs. The presidency, therefore, becomes an albatross, and successive presidents are doomed to defeat. We do not fully accept this thesis, but note that it becomes far more plausible with the decline of parties that are capable of transmitting demands to leaders as well as moderating and channeling public opinion. It is one thing to demand that government take on new responsibilities; it is another to couple that demand with a refusal to give government the necessary resources, especially acceptance of its authority to carry out these tasks. Without parties to mediate between leaders and followers, government is indeed in a double bind: damned if it doesn't act and damned if it does.

☆ Incumbency as a Liability: The Vice-presidency

Yet the incumbent president does have some advantages; it is the candidate who seeks to succeed an incumbent of his own party who suffers the most. His is the unhappy lot, as Stevenson discovered in 1952, Nixon in 1960, and Humphrey in 1968, of getting the worst of all possible worlds. He suffers from the disadvantages both of having to defend an existing record and of being a new face. He cannot attack the administration in office without alienating the president and selling his own party short, and he cannot claim he has experience in office. It may be difficult for him (think of Hubert Humphrey on Vietnam) to defend a record he did not make and may not wholly care for. His is the most difficult strategic problem of all the candidates.[76]

Thomas Riley Marshall, the genial Hoosier who was Woodrow Wilson's vice-president, once observed that the office he had in the Capitol was so little protected from tourists that they used to come by and stare at him like a monkey in the zoo. "Only," he complained, "they never offer me any peanuts." This is the way vice-presidents have viewed their constitutional office, not just its physical setting, for a long time. "Not worth a pitcher of warm spit" was the bowdlerized version of John Nance Garner's rueful conclusion in the mid-1930s. "A mere mechanical tool to wind up the clock" was the way the first vice-president, John Adams, described himself. "My country has in its wisdom contrived for me the most insignificant office that was the invention of man."

The main constitutional function of the vice-president is to wait. Clearly this is not much of a job for a major political leader who is used to active leadership. Yet suppose a sudden tragedy should befall the president. Can we afford in the inevitable days of uncertainty that follow such an event to replace him with anything less than a major political leader who can step into the breach immediately, do the president's job, and do it well? This is the first and fundamental dilemma of the vice-presidency and as the quotation from John Adams amply testifies, it has been with us since the founding of the Republic. From this dilemma flow the problems characteristic of the modern vice-presidency.

We can date the modern vice-presidency from April 12, 1945, the day Franklin Roosevelt died. The next day his successor, Harry S Truman, remarked to some newspapermen: "Boys, if you ever pray, pray for me now. I don't know whether you fellows ever had a load of hay fall on you, but when they told me yesterday what had happened, I felt like the moon, the stars and all the planets had fallen on me." Truman had been a respected but not a leading senator before he assumed the vice-presidency. In his three months in that office Vice-president Truman saw President Roosevelt only a few short times. As vice-president he had not been told of the Manhattan Project to build the atomic bomb. Sticking closely to the duties prescribed under the Constitution, Mr. Truman spent the vast bulk of his time on Capitol Hill, presiding over the Senate. His knowledge of the affairs of the executive branch and of foreign and military operations was the knowledge of an experienced legislator and not the inside information routinely available to top policymakers in the Roosevelt administration. Mr. Truman wrote later,

"It is a mighty leap from the vice presidency to the presidency when one is forced to make it without warning."

Since Harry Truman made the leap in the waning days of World War II the world has grown more complicated, and so has the presidency. Efforts have accordingly been made to update the vice-presidency to meet modern conditions. The vice-president now sits with the National Security Council as a matter of right; under President Eisenhower, the vice-president attended all meetings of the cabinet at the president's invitation and presided in the president's absence. In addition to his Capitol Hill quarters, Vice-president Johnson had a suite of offices in the Executive Office Building adjacent to the White House. For a while President Nixon moved Spiro Agnew to an office down the hall from his own. Nelson Rockefeller was not only made head of the Domestic Council by President Ford, but also was allowed to bring in his own men as top staff assistants in this presidential agency. Vice-president Mondale, with an office in the White House only a few doors away from the Oval Office, was given an unprecedentedly full, though junior, partnership by President Carter. Vice-president Bush's relations with President Reagan were complicated by worries among the Reagan staff about Mr. Bush's future ambitions, a common enough difficulty between presidents and vice-presidents, somewhat exacerbated in this case by their differences in age and in political outlook. But Bush kept a White House office. And he has played a part in smoothing over difficulties faced by allied nations in interpreting presidential rhetoric on arms control.

Since 1945, presidents have made greater efforts to involve vice-presidents in various administrative activities: goodwill tours abroad, occasional attempts to promote legislation on Capitol Hill, honorific jobs "coordinating" programs to which the president wants to give a little extra publicity, and, especially, political missionary work around the country—speeches and appearances on behalf of presidential programs. These are the tasks of the modern vice-president. In return for continuous briefing on the entire range of problems confronting the government, vastly improved access to the president, and a closer view of the burdens of the presidency, the modern vice-president must carry some of these burdens himself. Which burdens he carries, how many, and how far are up to the president. Naturally a vice-president may withhold his cooperation; but if he does, he impairs his relationship with the president. This is bound to affect his capacity to fulfill the constitutional obligation of the vice-presidency, which is to be genuinely prepared in case of dire need.

No vice-president is in any sense the second in command in a president's administration. In truth, he is entirely removed from any chain of command in the government. This guaranteed the independence of the vice-president in the days of Aaron Burr, John C. Calhoun, Charles Dawes, and other free spirits who have occupied the office. Today, the situation is quite different: it is much easier for high members of a president's administration to maintain independence from the presidency. Top administrative officials can constitute a loyal opposition on government policy within the executive branch because their obligations run in at least three directions: upward to the president, downward to the agencies whose programs they supervise within the administration, and outward to the clientele their agencies serve. Political executives serve the president best who serve their clients with devotion and promote the interests of their agencies with vigor. Executives know, moreover, that if in the process they conflict too much with presidential plans or priorities the president can always fire them. If the president fails them in some serious way, they can resign, as Attorney General Richardson did when President Nixon ordered him to remove Special Prosecutor Archibald Cox during the memorable "Saturday Night Massacre" of October 1973, or as Secretary of State Cyrus Vance did from the Carter administration in 1979 over the aborted rescue mission to Iran.

The vice-president can hardly fulfill his constitutional responsibilities by resigning, nor, in midterm, can he be dismissed. He has no anchor in the bureaucracy, no interest group constituency. Thus, uniquely in the executive branch, the modern vice-president must discipline himself to loyalty to the president.

This sometimes has painful consequences for vice-presidents, especially when they attempt to emerge from the shadow of the president and run for the presidency on their own. It is scarcely necessary to note Vice-president Humphrey's difficulty in persuading opponents of the Vietnam war that he and President Johnson were not Siamese twins. Voters with longer memories may recall Vice-president Richard Nixon's similar problem in 1960, when Senator Kennedy wanted to get the country "moving again." Mr. Nixon somehow had to offer a new program of his own while defending the eight Eisenhower years, wrapping himself in the mantle of his popular predecessor but taking no notice of the occasional potshots the general peevishly took at him. Neither Nixon nor Humphrey was fully able to run independently on his own record.

There seems, in short, to be no way for a vice-president to avoid the dilemmas built into the office. Unless he is scrupulously loyal to the president, he cannot get the access to the president that he needs to discharge his constitutional function; when he is loyal to the president, he is saddled, at least in the short run, with whatever characteristics of the president or his program the president's enemies or his own care to fasten on him. He sits there in the limelight, visible, vulnerable, and for the most part, powerless.

Nevertheless, as long as vice-presidents have some chance eventually to run for the presidency, as they presently do, and are not arbitrarily excluded from further consideration as independent political leaders in their own right, there will be plenty of takers for the vice-presidential nominations. This contributes to the strength of political parties. Vice-presidential nominees can balance tickets, help to unite a warring party, and campaign effectively with party workers and before the public—as, for example, Senator Lyndon Johnson did with conspicuous success in the election of 1960, and both George Bush and Walter Mondale did in 1980. Thus, vice-presidential nominees can help elect a president. It is after the campaign is over that the vice-president's problems begin.

☆ Convertibility of Resources

Clearly, the social framework within which presidential election strategies must be pursued distributes advantages and disadvantages rather importantly between the parties. We have attempted to explain why the unequal distribution of key resources such as money and control over information do not necessarily lead to election victories for the parties and candidates who possess and use most of these resources. Might there not, however, be a cumulative effect that would greatly assist those who possessed both more money and more control over information? This effect may exist, but it could not be of overwhelming importance, since the Democrats, who are usually disadvantaged in both respects, have won most elections since the 1930s. We can suggest a few reasons for Democratic strength despite these disadvantages. First, the Democrats are able to convert other resources into money and control over information, thereby narrowing the gap during campaigns. Second, the Democrats have superior access to other important resources which may overwhelm the Republican superiority in money and control over the media of information.

Once the Democratic party assumed the presidency in 1933 and held it for twenty years, it was able to use the resource of official position to collect campaign funds because contributors wanted access to the winner. The Democratic candidate could also get greater news coverage because the president's activities are newsworthy no matter what his party. The alliance of the Democrats with the large industrial unions has, at times, meant that the party has received contributions in the form of personal electioneering, for which the Republicans had to lay out cash or do without. The superiority (perhaps the mere existence) of Democratic organizations in cities of large population with strategic impact on the Electoral College has sometimes led to the availability of election workers who did not have to be paid in cash—at least not in cash the presidential candidate had to raise during the campaign. The appeals of the Democrats to ethnic, racial, and religious groups has meant that publications of these specialized groups might serve to offset the preponderant Republican ownership of the daily press.

The fact that the Democrats have approximately a one-and-a-half-to-one lead over Republicans in party identification is perhaps the most effective resource in the Democratic arsenal. Apparently it is more than enough to compensate for whatever advantages the Republicans gain through wealth and the mass media. For unless the Democrats oblige, as they have done more often than not since 1968, to contrive to lose presidential elections— by fighting bitterly among themselves and by writing self-defeating rules that lead to unpopular nominees—the voters will elect a Democrat by following their usual partisan dispositions. To be sure, other factors—turnout, for example—are not always equal; otherwise the Republicans would never win. But in the sheer numbers of nominal supporters the Democrats are ahead at the start. Republicans need a break to win; Democrats just have to mobilize their natural majority.

Implicit in these remarks is the proposition that the Democrats in our era ought to be better able than the Republicans to convert their resources into success at the polls. That is, the party identification of a significant majority of the electorate can more easily be turned into victory than money or control over information can be turned to winning the allegiance of citizens to a different party. Party identifications change but slowly and change significantly only under the impact of events that profoundly affect the mass of citizens and that cannot be manipulated easily, if at all, by political leaders. No one really knows short of that how to go about changing the party identifications of masses of people in the same partisan direction.

The Republicans can use their advantage in turnout to overcome the Democratic advantage in party identification. They can try to make party identification seem less relevant at election time by putting up an attractive candidate who is "above" partisanship. They can capitalize on errors by Democrats or on dissatisfaction with a Democratic administration. No one can claim to predict the outcomes of elections yet to come; certainly we cannot. Nothing that has been said here means that a Republican might not win handily, as Nixon did in 1968 and 1972, and Reagan did in 1980, after the Vietnam issue decimated the Democratic party leadership, and the party undertook to reform itself in a way that gave advantages to factional rather than coalition-building candidates.[77] Speaking in terms of probabilities over several elections, however, it seems to us that the Democrats are likely to win more often than they lose. When Republicans win, the cause will normally be found in something the Democrats did to make it possible.

Chapter 3

The Nomination Process

Obtaining the presidential nomination of a major political party in this country has never been easy. Today, however, this process has grown even more time-consuming, expensive, and complicated. This is because of rules governing the conduct of candidates, activists, and party regulars in the preprimary period, during the actual delegate selection phase, and at the national party conventions themselves.[1]

☆ Before the Primaries

Once upon a time, not so long ago, there was a gap between one presidential election campaign and the next one four years later. This gave a little breathing space during which, we assume, politically active citizens occupied themselves with such unexciting business as, for example, making a living (for those out of office) or governing (for those in office). What has caused this gap to shrink so drastically, in spite of the entreaties of reformers and the bleats of journalists?

As we see it, the spreading out of preconvention party skirmishing, extending first to the primary phase and now to an ever-lengthening preprimary period, is, in part, a result of rules changes over the last decade. These changes govern delegate selection to the national convention, and especially the national convention of a party that has no incumbent president eligible for reelection.

The rules changes have increased the number of people each candidate for the nomination must reach, and, if possible, convince of his worthiness. The more people you have to reach, the more time and money it takes to do the job. We reserve for later a consideration of whether this can be called a democratization of the candidate-selection process. There is something to be said on both sides of that proposition. For the moment, however, let us put ourselves in the shoes of the candidate for a presidential nomination who confronts the following rules of the game:

1. For Democrats, all convention delegates must be selected according to rules mandating that state parties "assure that such delegates have been selected through a process in which all Democratic voters have had full and timely opportunity to participate. . . ."[2] This must be done by all states within a three-month period (which three months to be determined by the Democratic National Committee), and each individual state must set candidate filing deadlines thirty to ninety days before the election. Delegates selected in crossover primaries (where those not registered in the party are allowed to vote) or in single-member delegate districts are not permitted under the rules, which also prohibit all other winner-take-all arrangements. This process must result in state delegations that are evenly divided between men and women.[3]

2. Candidates of either party may be eligible for the funding of their primary up to $4.5 million each if they can raise at least $5,000 cash in each of twenty or more states before the primary (only the first $250 of each contribution being eligible for matching).

3. In the Democratic party, any candidate in a statewide primary who receives more than a certain percentage of the vote obtains a proportionate share of the delegates per district, up to a maximum of 25 percent.

The first overall constraint on the system is that the more people you have to convince, the longer it takes. And so the nomination process is getting longer. The second overall constraint is that the more restrictions that are placed upon the expenditure of money, the harder it is for newcomers to public notice to get into the race. And this too dictates an earlier start to the campaign. Anybody whose name is known ahead of time—movie stars, sports figures, incumbents of high office—gets a boost. The upshot of these constraints is to make it more (rather than less) important for serious candidates to contest primary elections. Moreover, proportionate rules for counting votes encourage Democrats to contest more primaries for the simple reason that there are delegates to be had. And primaries generate attention, which means more people will be enticed out of the woodwork to make financial contributions that the government will then match.

In part, no doubt, candidates will be reading the lessons of the postreform era of 1972, 1976, and 1980 into future election years. For among the axioms of conventional wisdom to bite the dust in 1972 was the notion that an early announcement of candidacy was a sign of a weak candidate, and that it therefore behooved front runners to avoid an early disclosure of their plans, with all the inconvenience and running around that an active campaign entails. This coyness destroyed the chances of the early Democratic front runner, Senator Muskie. In 1976, this lesson was greatly reinforced as Jimmy Carter, an outsider, parlayed early, narrow wins in Iowa, New Hampshire, and Florida into the presidency itself. Thus the congressional elections of 1978 were barely over before a variety of Republicans announced their candidacies for the 1980 race and began to qualify for federal support. And two Democratic candidates qualified for the 1984 federal subsidy by the end of the first week of 1983.[4]

In some respects, the 1972 preconvention race in the Democratic party provided an interesting transition between old and new practices. Democratic party rules were written in such a way as to placate the element of the party that was most disaffected in the debacle of 1968, namely, the left wing. This may have been done in part because party leaders who both acquiesced to and enforced these changes were reasonably confident that placating the left in this fashion would merely legitimize throughout the party the eventual selection of a broadly based, centrist candidate.[5] Early in the 1972 election season, at least two such candidates were extremely visible to party leaders: Senator Edward Kennedy and, after the Chappaquiddick incident put Kennedy out of action, Senator Edmund Muskie of Maine. By early 1971, Muskie was leading President Nixon in Gallup trial heats. Consequently, giving in on party rules must have seemed to centrist party leaders a low-cost proposition. As the leading Democrat in all polls, Muskie concentrated his early efforts upon securing endorsements from party notables. However, by the time of the primary elections, when Muskie got around to announcing his candidacy formally, Senator George McGovern had already won the allegiance of and organized the most energetic segment of the party. McGovern's was the only organization that employed grass-roots activists in large numbers. Like Goldwater among Republicans in 1964, McGovern won not because he was the most popular candidate among his fellow partisans, but because he was best organized to move into state primaries and state party conventions and take them over from party regulars.

So the lessons of the preprimary period have become clear: before the primary season begins candidates must organize to achieve personal visibility. Visibility is important because in order to win it is necessary to appeal to voters in primary elections. Organization is important because that is what it takes to turn out voters. Because many candidates begin the election season with presidential hopes, the course of selection is a winnowing process in which the successive hurdles of the primary weeks knock off more and more hopefuls until only one survivor is left. Before the primaries the candidate's tasks are to raise money and to give his personal attention to states that will select candidates early in the process. Increasingly it is thought that this sort of work cannot be done by a public official who at the same time holds a responsible job. Politicians remember that Jimmy Carter did nothing but campaign for the presidential nomination for a full year before the first primary of 1976, and that Edmund Muskie chose to attend to his Senate responsibilities in 1971, when he should have been out campaigning. In the run-up to the 1984 election, Walter Mondale was far better off as an ex-senator and ex-vice-president than he would have been as an incumbent office holder. With this much in his mind, the Majority Leader of the Senate, Tennessee Republican Howard Baker, announced at the height of his influence that he would not be a candidate for reelection to the Senate.

Of course to be "taken seriously" by the news media a candidate should have won a statewide election for public office. In addition, the news media pay attention to signs that candidates are hiring competent campaign staff—fund raisers, lawyers, accountants, poll takers, media buyers, advance men, speech writers, issue analysts, spotters of political talent in the early states —and establishing a beachhead in these first battlegrounds. All this activity is highly visible to the increasingly watchful news media, who in turn pronounce candidates to be "serious" or "not serious," with attendant consequences for public visibility and credibility with donors of campaign funds.

Preprimary activities thus take up more and more time and absorb more and more resources in preparation for the primary elections themselves, which by 1984 will select delegates in thirty-four Republican and thirty-two Democratic state elections.

☆ Primaries

From 1968 to 1972 the Democratic Commission on Party Structure and Delegate Selection developed a set of rules and guidelines subsequently adopted by the national party concerning the selection of delegates to national party conventions. They wanted to make delegate selection more open and representative. So they issued eighteen new regulations that opened up meetings to all comers, gave those who came the right to vote, scheduled their choices closer to the election, and included various demographic groups in proportion to their size in the population. This had the immediate effect of greatly increasing the number of primaries. Seeing that their delegates could be challenged in eighteen new ways, state party leaders in numerous states decided to let all the candidates contend in what they assumed would be regarded as fair and open primaries. Thus, from 1968 to 1975 fourteen new states adopted primaries as their method for choosing delegates to the Democratic National Convention. More important, as a study by James Lengle and Byron Shafer explains:

> The increase in the number of "effective" primaries was even greater . . . because (required) reforms upgraded previously less significant arenas into serious campaign sites. In fact, the biggest rise in the number of delegates along the primary route came not from new entries but from changes in old ones. In 1968, nearly half of all primaries had been "advisory," i.e., either voters would express a Presidential preference but delegates would be chosen *independently* in party conventions, or, more commonly, a Presidential preference could not be logically connected with the separate vote for delegates. By 1972, the linkage between candidate preference and delegate selection had been tightened so much that the free agents of past primaries —"favorite sons," "bosses," and "uncommitted" delegates—had almost disappeared.[6]

Primaries are important largely because most delegates are selected in them and because the results represent an ostensibly objective indication of whether a candidate can win the election. The contestants stand to gain or lose far more than the growing number of delegate votes that may be involved. Success in early primaries—even those, like New Hampshire, where there are only a handful of delegates at stake—takes on enormous importance because the mass media focus on front runners, giving them a great advantage in publicity. This makes front runners' appeals for money both directly to groups of fat cats and through the mails more successful, bringing advantages in the later primaries, where name recognition is a significant determinant of the vote. It also greatly reduces the capabilities of lagging candidates to catch up.

This means that early and vigorous participation in primaries is now the only strategy available to serious presidential aspirants. As his political advisor, Hamilton Jordan, told President Carter, "It is absolutely essential that we win the early contests and establish momentum. If we win the early contests, it is difficult to see how anyone could defeat us for the nomination. Conversely, if we lose the early contest(s), it is difficult to see how we could recoup and win the nomination." In order to improve the President's chances, his preconvention organization managed to advance the dates of several Southern primaries, where he expected to do better, and to delay Connecticut's for a month. All this was done in 1979 before the rival organization of Senator Edward Kennedy had gotten started.[7]

It was not always thus. It made no sense for a man situated as Richard Nixon was in 1960—the heir-apparent—to enter a primary unless he believed that he was quite certain to win. This stricture applied with special force to any candidate who was well ahead in delegate support. All he could gain was a few additional votes, while he could lose his existing support by a bad showing in the primary, since this might be interpreted as meaning that he could not win the election. The candidate who was far behind or who had to overcome severe handicaps, however, had little or nothing to lose by entering a risky primary. If he won, he demonstrated his popularity; if he lost, he was hardly worse off than if he had not entered the primary at all. Such was the case when John F. Kennedy quieted the apprehensions of Democratic politicians about the religious issue by winning in Protestant West Virginia.[8] In 1964 Goldwater needed a primary victory in California to show uncommitted delegates that he had voter appeal, even though at the start of the primary campaigns he had been a prominent candidate. He accepted the risk of losing the nomination if he lost the primary because he needed proof of popularity to get the votes necessary for nomination.[9] Nixon, who had lost the presidency in 1960 and the governorship of California in 1962, had a similar problem in 1968. He had to enter the primaries in order to dispel his "loser" image.[10]

Those who live by the primary may be done in by it as well. In 1980, after Governor Jerry Brown of California received only a tenth of the primary vote in New Hampshire, he staked his all in the Wisconsin primary, where, coming in a distant third, he terminated his candidacy. Similarly, when Senator Edward Kennedy lost the Illinois primary in 1980 to President Carter two to one in votes and 165 to 14 in delegates, it was widely believed that inability to win in an industrial, ethnic, populous state where he had the support of the famous Chicago machine, doomed his chances.[11] On the Republican side, John Anderson tried to distinguish himself as a Republican moderate by espousing conservative financial policies and liberal social policies. But he was unable to win a single primary: after a loss in Wisconsin, where he had placed his last hopes, he withdrew from the Republican nominating contest, emerging as an independent candidate for president. Anderson was too far out of line with the preferences of people who vote in Republican primaries.[12]

A significant part of the nomination process now includes trying to manipulate what the mass media say about primary elections both before and after they take place. In a primary with many contenders, a defeated candidate may attempt to gain advantage from what may be regarded as an ambiguous result by claiming that the man who actually won was allied to him ideologically. The results may then be viewed as a victory for the ideology rather than defeat for the candidate. After Robert La Follette had won an overwhelming victory in the 1912 Republican primary in North Dakota, Theodore Roosevelt issued a statement "claiming an immense progressive victory." He even went beyond this to count the La Follette delegation as part of the Roosevelt camp once it had cast "a complimentary vote for La Follette."[13] Rockefeller supporters in 1964 hailed the New Hampshire Republican primary, which Henry Cabot Lodge won, as a defeat for Goldwater and a victory for the moderate wing of the Republican party. Something similar went on in 1968; supporters of both Eugene McCarthy and Robert Kennedy claimed that all those who had voted for either man in the primaries had voted against Hubert Humphrey, who was nowhere on the ballot.[14]

One strategy for primaries, the write-in, offered the maximum possibility of gain with the minimum possibility of loss. If a candidate got virtually no votes, he could easily explain this by saying that he did not campaign and that it is difficult for people to write in names. If he received over 10 percent of the vote, he could hail this as a tremendous victory under the circumstances. In Nebraska in 1964, Nixon received 35 percent of the vote as a write-in in the primary and it was "claimed that 'Nebraskans have nominated the next Republican candidate for President . . .' a claim that was forgotten after the Nixon debacle in Oregon just three days later."[15]

If a write-in candidate won, or came close, he could build his victory up to the sky, stressing the extraordinary popularity required to get people to go to all the trouble of writing in a name.[16] But the man who was behind could not rest content with being able to explain away a poor showing; he had to win to establish himself as a contender. The strategy of the write-in, consequently, was most accessible to the candidate who was ahead and hoped to solidify his position while minimizing his risks.

Today, of course, the write-in strategy is moribund; it can be used only by an incumbent president who expects no serious opposition in primary elections. Everyone else must enter primary elections, and almost certainly all of them.

Because so many candidates enter primaries, the results may be ambiguous, with a scattering of votes spread among many candidates. Nevertheless, the news media require interpretations that sort out winners and losers more decisively and so, as we have seen, how results are interpreted is often even more important than the actual numbers. The contestant who loses but does better than expected may reap greater advantage from a primary than the one who wins but falls below expectations. It is, therefore, manifestly to the advantage of a candidate to hold his preelection claims down to minimum proportions. Kennedy tried in 1960 to follow this advice in Wisconsin—he claimed Humphrey had been Wisconsin's third senator—but the press, radio, and television took note of his extensive organization and of favorable polls and in advance pinned the winner-by-a-landslide label on the senator from Massachusetts.[17] Early predictions in the 1968 New Hampshire primary were that Eugene McCarthy would receive somewhere around 10 percent of the vote. When he eventually polled 42 percent—against Lyndon Johnson's 48 percent write-in vote—it was widely interpreted as a victory, in part because it was so unexpected.[18] George McGovern benefited from a similar process in 1972.

Consider the contest between George Bush and Ronald Reagan in 1979 and 1980. Basing his bid on Jimmy Carter's early-bird strategy in Iowa, Bush built a strong organization there, making twenty-one visits within a year. He did very well in the Iowa state convention. Overnight, Bush became a serious contender, so serious that he could not lower expectations for future engagements. His second-place showing in New Hampshire might have been acceptable, or at least less worthy of negative notice, had he not won in Iowa. His loss in New Hampshire also had the effect of giving credibility to John Anderson's bid to become the main alternative to Ronald Reagan. Barely beating Anderson in the Massachusetts primary a week later, Bush did not regain his role as the major opponent to the front runner until the spring of 1980, when it was too late. As his then-campaign manager, James Baker, said, "We had solved the George Who problem in Iowa. We did not answer the question of George Why."[19]

Ronald Reagan's 1980 strategy was interesting because he changed management in midstream. He began by emulating Gerald Ford in 1976, running as if he already had the nomination sewed up. He refused to debate other Republicans on the grounds this would be divisive. He made only a few campaign stops in Iowa, and bought a mere half-hour of television time. So he lost. He lost even worse because he was expected to win. Fearing that failure to establish himself early would lose him the nomination, Reagan changed campaign managers and began to run as hard as he could. He gave more speeches, put on more commercials, engaged in debates, established stronger organizations in primary states, and otherwise energized his efforts.[20]

Attempting to arrange expectations so that the media will give favorable interpretations of primary results has become an art form. In 1976 in New Hampshire "liberal" candidates Morris Udall and Birch Bayh developed "two-track" interpretations in which there would be a centrist victor (from among Carter, Jackson, and Wallace) and a liberal victor (from among Harris, Sanford, Shriver, Bayh, and Udall). They wanted the liberal or progressive who received a plurality to be considered by the press to be the victor even if he did not actually win. Alas for this interpretation, not every candidate ran; Senator Henry Jackson decided it was best to avoid starting with a defeat as he had in 1972, and so he stayed out of the New Hampshire race. Although Jimmy Carter did not call himself a conservative, he was the main beneficiary of Jackson's decision not to enter. Jackson expected to run well in certain districts in Florida, winning perhaps a plurality of delegates statewide, but not necessarily coming out in front when the entire vote was tabulated. To make the most out of his expected heavy vote in and around Miami and to minimize his expected weaknesses elsewhere, his staff spoke of the state as containing some fifteen primaries—one for each of its congressional districts. When the expected happened, some of the story stuck, but the sheer complexity of reporting so many separate contests frustrated the strategy, and Jackson appeared the loser.[21]

The significance of primaries has, not surprisingly, risen with the importance of public opinion polls. As knowledge of popular opinion has increased, the news media have disseminated the information. Why should politicians guess if they can get direct access to public opinion through polling? The result has been a sequence in which leaders in opinion polls go on to contest primaries, and the winners of the contested primaries do well in future polls and proceed to take the nomination—not always, to be sure, but very often. William H. Lucy, who has studied the matter, concluded in 1973:

> There have been several strong relationships between polls, primaries, and presidential nominations since 1936. At those 20 national conventions, the nominee has been the pre-convention poll leader 19 times. The preprimary poll leader became the nominee 85 percent of the time. The preprimary poll leader continued as the postprimary poll leader 90 percent of the time. Only once has the preprimary poll leader lost primaries and then permanently lost the poll lead. Ninety percent of the winners of the seriously contested primaries who also led the final preconvention polls won the nomination. And 75 percent of the cumulative winners of seriously contested primaries were nominated.[22]

The political consequences are as clear to Lucy as they are to us.

> If primary winners are nearly always nominated, then it behooves would-be leaders to bargain with candidates early in the primary process in order to be on board when their support is still valued. Or, if the preprimary poll leader is nearly always nominated, then this fact would be a cue for party leaders to start to choose sides even before the primaries began. In addition, if candidates leading the polls believed that success in the primaries depended but little on support by political leaders, then the assets with which they would be willing to negotiate with political leaders might be reduced in number and value. As compared with political leaders, those with plentiful campaign funds or media skills might increase their bargaining potential. If primaries were not important enough, however, the Democratic Party has made sure they will not be overlooked.[23]

Though the demand for more primaries came, as we have seen, from politicians challenging their party establishments, the cause was quickly picked up by the networks. The role of television journalists, Richard Rubin contends, lay "in legitimating the process as *the* genuinely democratic way to choose convention delegates." Television, unlike print journalism, finds it easier to cover exciting primary races rather than processes of deliberation and negotiation among a few party leaders in caucuses and conventions. The special needs of television, Rubin writes, are

> reflected by the medium's broad use of sports analogies (such as the "horse race") to describe primary campaigns. Television needs a shorthand method to compress and dramatize events, and has settled comfortably on sporting phrases to describe and simplify a complex process. Candidates are "leading the pack," "closing fast," "sagging in the stretch," and "gaining ground," as the medium strives to treat their competition in language suggestive of movement and vitality.
>
> The "game analogy" is prominent in the treatment of all media, but its prominence, as Thomas Patterson has demonstrated, is greater on television (and in weekly news magazines) than in newspapers. The looser story line in newspaper versus television reporting and a larger "news hole" enables it to move beyond these analogies to cover intricate, complex, and talky political activities in more detail than television easily accommodates.[24]

Aside from "the vastly disproportionate time given primaries compared to other selection methods," the primaries were often called open and democratic and the winner labeled the popular choice of the voters even if the results were ambiguous.[25]

By reporting as they do, the electronic media alter the character of presidential nominations. Since voters lack the guidance that the endorsement of political parties provides during elections, and since primary events are often full of uncertainty, media reporting of who is ahead or behind or how seriously candidates should be taken assumes considerable importance. Were political parties able to select their own candidates, the media would matter much less. But with primaries replacing caucuses and conventions, it is fair to say that candidates have to care much more about how they do on television than on whether they please leaders of their party.

The political parties have acted in a way that makes it difficult to avoid primaries. It is no one thing but the whole confluence of events that has conspired to reemphasize primaries. Now that the national party conventions ratify rather than choose candidates, the function of reducing uncertainty about which candidates are ahead and behind is transferred from successive ballots to the sequence of primaries.

National party conventions nowadays are convocations of the party faithful only when an incumbent president is due for renomination. Otherwise, the convention is the last stage in a process in which primaries are playing an increasing role. In 1968, only seventeen states selected delegates by primary; in 1972 twenty-three states did so, and in 1976 the number was thirty. In 1980 thirty-two states used primaries, while in 1984 the number will decrease to twenty-six states. Obviously, the number of delegates selected in this fashion is on the rise, from 36.7 percent in 1968 to roughly two-thirds in 1972, and about the same in 1976 and 1980.

So, now, who runs in primaries? In an increasing number of states, *all* recognized candidates are placed on the ballot by a state official whether they wish to enter the fray or not. A convergence of opinion, whether justified or not, that no candidate is legitimate without exposure in primaries makes it difficult to stay out. The more primaries there are, the harder they are to miss. And there is an added inducement for candidates to enter. Delegates on a statewide basis are allocated proportionally, which means that even losing candidates can frequently pick up a few delegates.

Since primaries have become so important—indeed, indispensable—for presidential nominations, it behooves us to learn more about how they operate. Which candidates, and which interests they represent, are advantaged or disadvantaged by primaries? Will radicals, conservatives, or moderates do better or worse with more extensive use of primaries? Are citizens' preferences more or less likely to be reflected in the results? If not citizens, then whose preferences will be met? How do the rules for counting votes affect the results? We begin with this last important question because it turns out that the way votes are counted in large measure determines whose preferences count the most. We draw our examples mostly from the Democratic primaries of 1972 and 1976.

No one pretends that primaries are perfect representations of the electorate that either identifies with a particular political party or is likely to vote for the party's leading vote getter. For one thing, voters are not allowed to rank their preferences, so a candidate's popularity with voters who give their first-choice votes to others is unknown. It is quite possible for a candidate to be the first choice of the largest clump of voters but to be only the fourth or fifth choice of all voters taken together. In 1972, for example, the candidates of the Democratic party right and left—Wallace and McGovern, respectively —won pluralities in more states than any other candidates, yet they also attracted widespread opposition. This opposition was ineffectively expressed in the primary process. Voter turnout in primaries is usually much lower than in the general election and is likely to contain a larger proportion of dyed-in-the-wool party supporters than would be true in a general election. Austin

Ranney has shown that average turnout in primaries is approximately 27 percent of all people of voting age, compared with roughly double that in the presidential election.[26] It is not so much low turnout, however, as the combination of low turnout with plurality elections that biases the results. In 1972 Senator McGovern had a plurality in six states. In those states his proportion of the vote compared with the total vote cast in the general election ranged from 4 to 22 percent. Clearly, his primary voters could not have been a representative sample of those who actually voted in November.[27]

Nevertheless, it may appear that McGovern was entitled to most of the primary delegates because he won more often than any other candidate. This would depend, however, on how the votes were counted. There are three basic ways of counting votes. One is winner take all: whichever candidate gets a plurality of votes in the entire state gets all the delegates. Another is proportional: all candidates who pass a certain threshold, say, 15 percent, divide the delegates among them in accordance with their percentage of the vote. A third is congressionally districted: after delegates are allotted (by population or past party vote or both) to districts, the candidate who wins a plurality gains all of the votes in that area. What would happen if all the votes in the 1972 Democratic primaries were recomputed by following any one of the three rules consistently, rather than according to the actual melange of rules that determined the 1972 delegate allocation? Which candidates and, more importantly, which interests would have prevailed?

Consider the situation in Pennsylvania. Had it been run under a winner-take-all rule, Humphrey would have gained all 182 votes. Under the actual districted rule, however, Humphrey received only ninety-three votes, substantially more than the sixty-six he would have gotten had proportional rules been in effect. Two close students of the situation point out: "In fact, the *difference* [in delegates] between winning Pennsylvania Winner-Take-All and . . . proportionately is greater than the total number of delegates available in twelve out of the first fifteen primaries."[28] The point is not that Humphrey "wuz robbed," since McGovern might well have been nominated anyway, but that the rules matter a great deal. And they contributed to the interpretation of the results: McGovern's thirty-nine votes were considered excellent in a state where he was not expected to run well, and Humphrey's total of ninety-three was downgraded for the opposite reason, whereas the entire 182 would have been considered a real victory.

Comparing 1972 delegate strength in fifteen primaries held before California's, one can see the enormous differences in results given by varying the rules. The reason the actual results differ from the three pure plans is that the candidates were helped and harmed in different ways. McGovern evidently gained in that he would have done worse if any of the three pure plans had been used. Had the district rule been uniformly employed, Wallace would have been the leading candidate before the California primary.

Rumination about the three rules reveals the kinds of constituencies (and hence interests) they are likely to favor. Winner-take-all gives more power to populous and competitive states, which have a large number of delegates. These are, by and large, the states of the Northeast and California, known for their large concentration of urban voters, ethnic minorities, and union laborers. The proportional rule favors noncompetitive areas because in these places a high degree of support for a single candidate pays off. Among Democrats, such areas are found in the South, West, and Midwest. The congressional district rule would fractionate the large states, where many candidates could get some support, but not the smaller, less competitive ones that have a few homogeneous districts. That is why Governor Wallace did so well wherever the proportionate rule was in force. It should be evident, as Lengle and Shafer conclude, that

> the widespread adoption of Districted primaries after 1968, or the prohibition of Winner-Take-All primaries after 1972, were not, then, just inconsequential decisions to hand out delegates via a certain mechanism. They were far-reaching, if almost accidental, choices about the type of candidates who would bear the party's standard, the type of voters who would have the power to choose those standard-bearers, and the type of issues with which both groups would try to

Table 3.1

How the Rules of the Game Affected Delegate Distributions, 1972 Democratic Primaries

	Winner take all	Proportional	Districted	Actual Results
Humphrey	446	314	324	284
Wallace	379	350	367	291
McGovern	249	319	343	401.5
Muskie	18	82	52	56.5
Others	0	27	6	59

SOURCE: James Lengle and Byron Shafer, "Primary Rules, Political Power, and Social Change," *American Political Science Review* 70 (March 1976), pp. 25–40.

shape history. They were, in short, a decision on how to (re)construct the Democratic party.[29]

The Carter primary results in 1976 are not easy to assess. For one thing, he won most primaries by such tiny margins that almost any setback, however slight, might have sunk him without a trace. For another, the crucial importance of looking good early in order to enhance future prospects means that determining whether certain rules help or hinder various candidates is in part a matter of timing. If one counts the late California primary of 1972, which George McGovern won under the winner-take-all system, for example, then winner-take-all was good for McGovern. In the early primaries, which kept McGovern going, had winner-take-all applied, he might not even have been in the race by the California primary. Two further things can be said: one is that most electoral devices overreward winners, and this is no exception; the other, which is more striking, is that Carter did much better in the states that had primaries for the first time in 1976. According to Gerald Pomper, "The Georgian won nearly two-thirds of the delegates from these thirteen new primary states. . . . Without the aid of these supporters, it is quite conceivable that Carter would have been denied the Democratic nomination."[30] Carter was far weaker in the states with longer histories of primary participation or which still chose delegates in caucuses. In these two areas, where state parties presumably had greater influence, he won only about a third of the delegates.

Most of the delegates picked in the new primaries were in the southern or border states, home territory for both Jimmy Carter and the resurgent Republican conservatism that favored Ronald Reagan.[31] Had winner-take-all rules prevailed early on in 1972 and 1976, the chances of moderate Republicans and Democrats, with their strength in the industrial Northeast would have been much better. Once a candidate is ahead, proportional voting rules help put him over the top whether he wins or not. That is how Jimmy Carter won the nomination in 1980, although he lost five of his last eight primaries.

The rules of the Democratic party require selection of delegates by either proportional or congressional district rules. Who will benefit? District rules provide more sites for electioneering than any other. Hence they will favor candidates with intense followings. Prior to 1976 this appeared to mean that ideological intensity was a prerequisite for success under district rules. However, Carter's performance as a moderate in 1976 muddies this contention. It now appears that any leader who can mobilize a faction effectively for whatever reasons can win. Will this prove more difficult over the long run for moderates? After all, moderates, who may appeal to rank-and-file voters in the general election, may be too bland to develop a devoted following within the party, and hence run the risk of losing out. In the absence of an unusually appealing moderate, therefore, the Democratic convention hazards being faced with a choice between candidates of relatively committed radical and conservative factions. This would test the capacity of the internal machinery of the party to reconcile differences from within.

It could be said that primaries are more important than general elections because primaries do more to limit the choices available to voters. Despite the great importance of primaries in presidential selection, little research has been devoted to them. And since the effects of primaries are cumulative, it is especially important to study how earlier events affect later ones. Larry Bartels argues that the nomination victories of Republican Gerald Ford and Democrat Jimmy Carter in 1976 were due to the accumulation of momentum, with over half of Carter's support in primaries coming from his early successes.[32] Perhaps the most interesting preliminary finding comes from a study by Richard Brody and Larry Rothenberg showing that voter turnout declines toward the end of the primary season.[33] This makes sense to us; if the early primaries dominate the process, then it would follow that people would see less purpose in turning out for later ones.

☆ State and District Conventions

In 1980 approximately 71 percent of the delegates at the Democratic convention were chosen in primaries. State and district conventions chose the other 29 percent. In the past this process has provided relatively few contests over the selection of delegates. But taking over the state and district conventions that chose the delegations to the party convention was the heart of Barry Goldwater's strategy in 1964 and an important aid for George McGovern in 1972. Jimmy Carter's 1976 showing in the early Iowa convention—where he beat all his competitors except "uncommitted"—was a central feature of his strategy.[34] The anti-Johnson forces' belated realization in 1968 that state conventions contained so much of the action prompted them to demand, and get, substantial changes in the rules governing the selection of delegates for the next convention. These included abolition of unit-rule voting in state and district conventions and a rule that delegates to the national convention had to be chosen in the year of the convention itself rather than at some earlier time, as had been the case in some states.[35]

In the past, attempts by candidates to influence delegates chosen outside of primaries were usually made after these delegates were selected by state parties. The first strategic requirement for the candidate seeking to influence these delegates was an intelligence service, a network of informants who would tell him which delegates were firmly committed, which were wavering, and which might be persuaded to provide second- or third-choice support. Advance reports on the opportunities offered by internal division in the state parties, the type of appeal likely to be effective in each state, and the kinds of bargains to which leaders were most susceptible were also helpful. The costs of this information were high in terms of time, money, and effort, but it was worthwhile to the serious candidate who needed to know where to move to increase his support and block his opponents.

These days no one wants to wait for delegates to be chosen before trying to influence them. The idea is for candidates to get their supporters selected as delegates. By the time they are selected, delegates are likely to be committed to a particular candidate or point of view. In any event, they cannot be selected before the year of the election. The same forces that persuade candidates to begin their drive for the nomination ever earlier—by February 1983 four men had announced their candidacies for the 1984 Democratic nomination, one solid year before the first primary election—impel them to begin the hunt for delegates ahead of time.[36] Since fund raising must go on in at least twenty states to attract federal matching money, it can be combined with delegate selection. Primaries are important, too, because the publicity candidates get and the signs that they are doing well encourage both contributions and volunteers, and persuade the news media to take them seriously.

The major change between past and present, however, stems from weaknesses in the party system. When and where there were strong state party organizations in the past, aspiring candidates had to deal with them. Decisions on whether to enter a primary or influence delegate selection were mediated through party leaders. If party leaders thought a contest in a state would be divisive, candidates would have to worry about incurring their enmity. The decline of state parties in the nomination process has lowered these obstacles. Relatively small numbers of activists without a continuing connection to the party may mobilize around a cause or a candidate and, by appealing to primary electorates, overwhelm the party regulars. If the test is numbers of followers who will come to a particular meeting, rather than present party position or past service, the activist surge is bound to carry the day, as McGovern and Goldwater demonstrated so well. Had there been no primary in Texas during 1976, for example, Jimmy Carter would not have been able to challenge Senator Lloyd Bentsen's "favorite son" candidacy without coming to terms with established elements of the Texas Democratic party.

Aspirants for nomination vary greatly in the degree to which they know other politicians throughout the country. Men like Richard Nixon, Hubert Humphrey, and Barry Goldwater, who traveled extensively and gave assistance to members of their party, simply needed to keep their files up to date in order to have a nationwide list of contacts. When the time came they knew from whom they could request assistance in gathering information, persuading delegates, and generally furthering their cause. Candidates who lacked this advantage, however, had to take special steps in order to build up their political apparatus. In paving the way for Franklin D. Roosevelt's nomination in 1932, James A. Farley began early by sending invitations to Roosevelt's inauguration as governor of New York to party leaders throughout the country. Most invitations were refused, but a valuable correspondence grew out of this approach. Farley next sent a small manual containing a few facts about the New York Democratic party organization to people throughout the country. The response encouraged a follow-up pamphlet which presented, without comment, the New York gubernatorial vote in every county since 1916. It was intended to be impressive testimony of FDR's vote-getting ability. When many people wrote back expressing an interest in FDR's candidacy, offering suggestions, or just saying "thanks," Farley replied with a personal message and endeavored to keep up the contact through further letters, phone calls, and even a phonograph record. Later, in 1931, Farley took a trip through the West, ostensibly to visit the Elks Convention in Seattle, but actually to contact over 1,000 party leaders in all but three states west of the Mississippi. Upon Farley's return, every one of his contacts received a personal letter.[37]

This is more or less the method candidates must use in building their personal organizations in state after state, and especially those states early in the process. In addition, candidates have to be well known to get a start. Instead of heading toward the Elks, a candidate's managers march toward the media. Senators Eugene McCarthy in 1968 and George McGovern in 1972 and former Governor Jimmy Carter in 1976 increased their visibility by doing better than expected in early primaries. They were thus able to build on past successes to create future ones until their luck ran out or they were nominated. Now everybody believes, and with good reason, that the early aspirant gets the nomination. Candidates will need more publicity than they used to have and they will need it earlier than they used to have it to compete in the future.

The delegates to national party conventions are selected state by state, in conventions or primaries or by a combination of the two methods.[38] They are the outcomes of processes that are slightly different in their legal requirements and political overtones in each of the states, the District of Columbia, and the territories—all of which send delegations to both party conventions. Increasingly, however, these requirements are subject to supervision at the national level.

National parties, in the wake of the *LaFollette* decision of the Supreme Court,[39] have taken a strong hand in determining such matters as who may participate in the selection of state delegations, the demographic composition of delegations, and the timing of selection processes. This has led to various sorts of maneuvering by state parties. The abolition of winner-take-all elections and the Democrats' establishment of a relatively narrow band of time during which delegates must be selected have inspired some states to move the date of delegate selection as far forward as possible, so as to increase their influence on the overall outcome. In 1980, the manager of President Carter's renomination was especially active in attempting to manipulate the sequence in which delegates were to be chosen, so as to maximize favorable news coverage for the President.[40] Thus, as convention time approaches, more and more states will have selected delegates who are already pledged to various candidates.

☆ Prenomination Strategies

The formal selection of a presidential nominee is the business that dominates the convention. From this it follows that decisions preceding the presidential nomination are important or unimportant largely depending upon their implications for the presidential nomination. Decisions not taken unanimously that precede the presidential nomination in the convention are almost always tests of strength between party factions divided over the presidential nomination. These decisions are usually more important for the information they communicate on the strength of the candidates than for their actual content. Here are two famous examples: the vote in the 1976 Republican convention on early disclosure of vice-presidential choices by candidates, and the seating of Virginia in the 1952 Democratic convention.[41]

In 1976, in a last-ditch effort to stave off a narrow defeat for the nomination, Ronald Reagan named a moderate Republican senator, Richard Schweiker of Pennsylvania, as the man he would pick as his running mate if he were to be nominated. Reagan forces attempted to change the rules so as to force President Ford to disclose who he would name. They failed to do so, signaling to everyone that Ford had enough votes to win.[42]

In the 1952 Democratic convention, the issue was the seating of the Virginia delegation. Adlai Stevenson's patron, Colonel Jack Arvey of Illinois, describes the strategic problem from his perspective:

> Cook County Chairman Joe Gill and I were having dinner . . . when one of our ward committeemen came running over to tell us an important roll call vote was under way on the seating of Virginia . . . Gill and I hurried back into the hall. Illinois had already been recorded 45–15 against seating Virginia. It suddenly dawned on us what was happening. The strategy of the Kefauver backers and the Northern liberal bloc was to try and make impossible demands on the Southern delegates so that they would walk out of the Convention. If the total Convention vote was thus cut down by the walkout of delegates who would never vote for Kefauver, then the Tennessee Senator would have a better chance of winning the nomination. Our Illinois delegation quickly huddled and then changed our vote to 52–8 in favor of seating Virginia.

> The eight opposed included Senator Douglas and other backers of Kefauver.[43]

Perhaps the first strategic decision facing an avowed candidate is whether to attempt to become a front runner by raising enough money in twenty states to qualify for the federal subsidy of his primary campaigns, entering primaries, barnstorming the country, and publicly seeking support at state conventions. The advantage of this strategy is that a candidate may build up such a commanding lead (or appear to) that no one will be able (or will try) to stop him at the national convention. The possibility that a candidate might become unstoppable early, reinforced by the larger number of primaries, the prospect of a federal subsidy for primary contestants, and the proportionate allocation of delegates obviously makes early entry more desirable for all candidates than it has been in the past. The disadvantage is that an open campaign may reveal the inability of some candidates to acquire support or may lead other candidates to band together to stop the front runner. Being a front runner depends for its success, then, upon the front runner's ability to predict accurately both how he will fare compared with others in open competition and what others will be able to do when they discover his lead. He may, for example, try to anticipate whether this activity will stimulate a coalition of opponents who are otherwise unlikely to get together. Exactly this happened to Jimmy Carter in 1976 when, after an initial period of disbelief, everyone else in the race, without formal coordination, directed their fire at him. If such a coalition seems likely, the candidate may issue communications playing down the extent of his support. But this tactic may discourage new supporters who would have been attracted by a display of strength. Since even losers stand to gain delegates if they get 15 percent of the vote in early primaries—although they must get higher percentages in later ones—and since funds depend on visibility, running openly is much more attractive than it used to be. Indeed, increasingly it is mandatory.

The dark horse is a possible candidate who picks and chooses among primaries and avoids much open campaigning. Like Stuart Symington in 1960, or Richard Nixon in 1964, the dark horse is content to be everyone's friend and no one's enemy.[44] As Abraham Lincoln wrote to a supporter in 1860 describing his dark-horse strategy: "My name is new in the field, and I suppose I am not the first choice of a very great many. Our policy, then, is to give no offense to others—leave them in a mood to come to us if they shall be compelled to give up their first love."[45] The strategy of the dark horse is to combine with others to oppose every front runner. His hope is that when no front runner is left he will appear as the man who can unify the party by being acceptable to all and obnoxious to none. The dangers the dark horse faces are that he will enter the convention with too little support to make a strong bid or that some other dark horse will prove preferable. How much support is enough to make a serious bid but not enough to be shot at as a front runner? How far behind the front runner can a candidate permit himself to get without becoming entirely lost from sight? Either an intuitive ability to guess or an exceedingly accurate apparatus for collecting information on the present strength of candidates, as well as on the likely effect of different levels of strength on other delegates, must be part of the serious dark horse's equipment.

The best chance for a dark horse in the future is likely to be a deadlocked convention. Well-known party leaders who have run before and have achieved great visibility, like Hubert Humphrey or Edmund Muskie in 1976, can afford the luxury of hoping lightning will strike without doing too much to stimulate it. But the fact that both these men lost out to a new and inexperienced face is a lesson that future dark horses are bound to heed. If the candidates who contested the primaries and arrived at the convention with pledged delegates are unacceptable to a majority, presumably the party will either have to go back to someone it passed over or break up. Increasingly, however, by convention time there is a clear front runner, and dark horses have too few delegates to affect the outcome. Where once it was useful to be the second choice of 90 percent of all delegates, today first choices—even of as few as 30 percent—are far preferable. This is a good measure of the changes that recent reforms have wrought in the nomination process. Whether the country will do better with presidents who are the strong preference of party minorities or the weak preference of party majorities remains to be seen. One key test for presidents selected by modern processes will come when they attempt to gather the support they need to govern—or, even more significantly, what happens to them and to their governments if they neglect to make the attempt. The warning words of a British observer, Anthony Teasdale, merit careful consideration:

> One irony of the primaries may thus be that in the name of greater democratic participation, nominations more often go to those less representative of party opinion. A second irony seems to be that in pursuit of more authoritative and legitimate government, primaries often favour candidates with less governmental experience, reduce the usefulness of party, increase popular expectations of politicians, and generally make America more difficult to govern. . . .
>
> Above all, by establishing direct personal contact between candidates and the mass electorate, primaries erode the importance of party as an intermediary between the elected and the elector in the United States. Candidates establish their own national organization, with their own mobile campaigners now imported into States as necessary. In government, this weakens the attachment of party loyalty which might give the President additional leverage to secure action on his proposals in Congress and the States.[46]

☆ At the Convention: Housekeeping

While the selection of a site for the convention has often been interpreted as one of the preballot indicators of various candidates' strength, in the past it usually was the rather routine outcome of the weighing of one major and several very minor factors. The major factor was the size of the convention city's proffered contribution to the national party committee. This contribution—in cash or in services—came partly from the city government but mostly from various business groups—hotels, restaurants—which stood to profit from a week-long visit of 6,500 delegates and alternates, their families and friends, and thousands of media representatives, dignitaries, and other convention personnel. The cloud over the offer of several hundred thousand dollars by the Sheraton hotel chain as part of San Diego's bid to host the 1972 Republican convention, as well as the reaction to Watergate, has changed all that. The federal government now makes available a sum of $3 million to each of the national parties to finance their nominating conventions, thereby lessening the pressure to acquire cash contributions or contributions in kind. A variety of other factors, however, may tip the balance between cities. Among these are the quality of facilities, the suitability of the convention hall to the television networks, hotel and entertainment accommodations, and the caliber of the local police force. For example, Philadelphia's James Tate headed as large and as loyal a Democratic organization in 1968 as Chicago's Richard Daley, and his city was closer geographically to Lyndon Johnson in Washington, but Philadelphia simply could not provide 20,000 first-class hotel rooms.[47] All things being equal, an incumbent president is likely to prefer a city near enough to Washington (or to his home if, like Ronald Reagan, he likes to vacation there) to allow him to keep close tabs on convention business and travel easily back and forth to the convention while at the same time playing his role away from it as "president of all the people." And, naturally, the president's wishes will not be furthest from the minds of the members of the site-selection committee of the national committee, which does the choosing. In addition, they will have in mind some other marginal factors. The Republicans in 1968, by selecting Miami Beach for the first Republican convention ever held south of the Mason-Dixon Line, may well have facilitated a "southern strategy" if they intended to pursue one. Both parties prefer to bring their publicity and their business to cities and states where the mayor and the governor are friendly members of the party, since this may give added access to (and control of) public facilities. The aloof attitude of California's Governor Jerry Brown toward the site-selection committee of his party evidently tipped the decision of the Democrats toward New York City in 1976 and away from Los Angeles.[48] In 1984, the fact that the party chairman, Charles Manatt, was a Californian, may have tipped the balance back to San Francisco for the Democrats. The desire to maintain the autonomy of the convention from demonstrators in 1972, which resulted from the Democratic debacle in Chicago in 1968, led to a choice of Miami Beach, where a causeway facilitated crowd control.

The time of a convention varies between mid-July and late August. There are two general statements to made about it. One is that the "out" party will normally hold its convention before the "in" party, on the theory that its candidate will need more of a publicity boost earlier. In 1960, 1972, 1976, and 1984 this put Democrats before Republicans, and in 1964, 1968, and 1980 it was the other way around. Also, if there is an incumbent president, he will schedule the convention to fit his timetable. At its most momentous, the convention may coincide with an international peace offensive; in 1968, the date of the Democratic convention seems to have been set with nothing more in mind than the president's birthday.

Once assembled, the national convention is a mass meeting in which the participants necessarily play widely varying and unequal roles. The candidates and their chief supporters are busily, perhaps frantically, perfecting their organizations and trying to maintain their communication with as many of their delegates as they can. In the old days, "bossed" or "pledged" delegations were either actively supporting their candidate or negotiating for the disposal of their votes. The leaders of these delegations were the people who conducted negotiations among the delegations when an impasse developed. There were also factional leaders and independent delegates within state delegations who played an important part in determining what their delegation or a part of their delegation would do. They bargained *within* their delegation rather than *among* the various state delegations. Now, the roles of both of these relatively autonomous types of politicians are bound to be sharply diminished, since more and more delegates will come to the convention pledged to one or another presidential candidate. This will mean that candidate organizations, not state party leaders, will have to do the bargaining. But it will be hard for them to bargain if they cannot transfer the votes of their supporters. In setting the stage for their balloting, therefore, we will deal first with candidates and their organizations and then with the delegates —leaders of large delegations, independent delegates, state factional leaders, and finally the rank-and-file delegates.

☆ Candidates and Their Organizations

At the national convention, before the balloting for the presidential nomination starts, one or more days are consumed in a variety of party rituals:

making speeches, seating delegates, presenting the platform, and so on. During that time delegates and their leaders mill about, exchanging greetings and gossip. It is this set of circumstances that challenges even the most efficient candidate organization.

There is a wide divergence among candidate organizations. They range from the comprehensive, integrated, and superbly effective to the fragmented, uncoordinated, and virtually nonexistent. We can only suggest the range of organizational alternatives through some general comments and a few examples.

The first modern candidate organization at a national convention, tied together with sophisticated communications equipment, was the expensively mounted organization of Senator John F. Kennedy in 1960. His communications network provided him with a continuing and accurate stream of vital information.[49] He wanted detailed personal information about as many delegates as possible in order to know how they were likely to vote and how they might best be persuaded to stay in line or to change their minds. More than a year before the convention the Kennedy-for-President organization started a card file containing information on people throughout the nation who might be delegates and who might influence delegates. Included on each card was the prospective delegate's name, occupation, religion, party position, relation (if any) to the Kennedy family or its leading supporters, ambitions, policy preferences if strongly held, and likely vote. This was brought up to date before convention time and entries were made in a central register as new information developed. Thus when it appeared that a delegate needed to be reinforced or might not vote for Kennedy, his card was pulled and the information was used in order to determine the best way to convince him.

In order to keep an up-to-date and, when necessary, an hour-by-hour watch on developments within the state delegations, the Kennedy organization assigned an individual coordinator to each state. This person might have been a delegate or an observer, such as a senator or a member of the candidate's staff. When it was deemed inadvisable to choose a delegate for fear that any choice would alienate one faction or another, a person outside the state was chosen. These liaison men kept tabs on individual delegates and maintained a running record of the likely distribution of votes. When necessary, the liaison men sent messages to the candidate's headquarters and reinforcements were sent to bolster the situation. At the Kennedy headquarters the seriousness of the report would be judged and a decision made on how to deal with it. Senator Kennedy himself might call the wavering delegate, one of his brothers might be dispatched, a state party leader might intervene, or some other such remedy might be applied.

In the hurly-burly, crush, and confusion of convention activity, it cannot be assumed that messages sent are received or that decisions are communicated to those who must carry them out. The Kennedy organization took great care to prepare a communications center that would receive messages and locate the recipients and that could send out instructions and receive feedback on the results. Each key staff person was required to phone his whereabouts periodically to a central switchboard. This made it possible for the Kennedy forces at the convention to deploy and reassign their people on a minute-by-minute basis as developments required.

A system set up only to deal with emergencies would have limited usefulness to a candidate who wanted regular reports so that he could appraise them in a consistent way. Every morning every liaison man assigned to the Kennedy headquarters attended a staff meeting at which he deposited with the secretary a report on his activities for the previous day. These reports were sent to what was called the "secret room" and the information was transferred to state briefing files. From these files, a daily secret report on delegate strength was written and given to the candidate and his top advisers.

At the morning staff meetings, Robert Kennedy, who acted as campaign manager for his brother, would ask each liaison man for his estimate of the number of Kennedy votes. Keenly aware of the dangers of seeming to want high estimates, Robert Kennedy challenged the liaison men if he felt that their estimates were too high, but not if they appeared too low. On occasion he would reprimand a liaison man for including a delegate as a certain Kennedy supporter when other information indicated that this was not true. The success of this procedure was indicated by the fact that when the alphabetical balloting had reached Wyoming on the first (and last) ballot, the Kennedy organization's estimate of their delegate strength was proved correct within a one-vote margin.[50]

The danger of confusion and mishap is multiplied during the balloting because the convention floor is filled and it is difficult to move about freely. To deal with this, the Kennedy organization arranged for telephones on the convention floor. Six were set up beneath the seats of chairmen of friendly delegations who were seated around the gigantic convention hall. These phones were connected to the Kennedy headquarters outside the hall. Inside the headquarters, staff members sat near the telephone and simultaneously scanned several television sets to look for possible defections. Had the pretested telephones failed to work, walkie-talkie radios were available to take their place.[51]

By comparison with the Kennedy efforts, most of the organizations that have successfully nominated presidential candidates in American history have been uncoordinated, diffuse affairs. For example, in 1952 none of the various factions in the Democratic party that favored the nomination of Adlai Stevenson had the wholehearted cooperation of their candidate; information gathering was casual and tactical maneuvers were in some cases hit upon accidentally or as afterthoughts. The factions working for the Stevenson nomination did not cooperate to a significant degree and squabbled on occasion. Yet Stevenson was nominated; his success came about because he was the second choice of an overwhelming number of delegates who could not agree on any of their first choices and the first choice of a significant number of leaders in spite of his disinclination to pursue the nomination in an organized fashion.[52]

We have devoted so much space to the Kennedy organization because, unlike the Stevenson example, it became a harbinger of the future. McGovern's in 1972 was like it only more so—more telephones, more communications apparatus, more file cards. These extremely organized efforts created some tension within the McGovern camp because delegates who prided themselves on independent thinking did not always appreciate a series of communications on each issue coming before the 1972 convention telling them how to vote or—equally insulting—allowing them a free choice if a given matter was not considered important.

The McGovern organization worked wonderfully on the platform. A free vote was permitted on giving Indians first choice in the distribution of federal land. Proposals for a guaranteed national income of $6,500 and for minority rights for homosexuals were opposed and defeated. Last-minute additions to reassure supporters of Israel and a commitment to keep troops in Western Europe were supported and passed. Commands went down the line, obedience came up the line, since it was all for the cause.

At the 1976 convention, Jimmy Carter was superbly organized but did not need to be because his nomination was already in the bag. An interesting contrast emerged at the more closely contested Republican convention. Following recent practice, the President Ford Committee installed an effective communications apparatus. Rather than rely entirely on the geographic leaders of their earlier delegate monitoring operation, the President Ford Committee divided the convention floor into zones, whose floor leaders wore red hats, tied by telephone to the Ford trailer and to subleaders responsible for each state. By contrast, Ronald Reagan relied on style and ideology rather than hierarchy and division of labor. As a convention leader said, "Our conservatives don't like to be told what to do, and they don't need to be. The Ford people need all that hardware because they can't count on their delegates to vote with them consistently." F. Christopher Arterton, who observed the convention, believes that at crucial moments, as when the Mississippi delegation caucused on the floor before a crucial vote, Reagan "was handicapped by key coordinators having to fight their way through jammed aisles."[53]

By the 1980s, all serious candidates bring to the convention as part of their normal equipment a full complement of electronic communications gear. All have trailers parked in the convention hall in which they monitor trends on the floor and entertain friends and allies. What was extraordinary about the Kennedy effort in 1960 has, with the passage of time and the progress of technology, become commonplace.

☆ Delegates and Caucuses

There are three identifiable categories of convention activists: (1) a small number of managers of candidate organizations; (2) a shrinking proportion of state leaders who control votes other than their own and who participate in high-level negotiations on the disposition of these votes; and (3) leaders of caucuses representing interest groups and demographic categories. The rise of these caucuses deserves special comment.

The demographic identities of the delegates to the Democratic National Convention since 1972 have been determined in part by the kinds of people who supported candidates who won delegates in primaries and state conventions. Since 1972 new rules have modified the demographic makeup of the delegations. The Democratic Commission on Party Structure and Delegate Selection, headed by George McGovern, required state parties to take "affirmative steps to encourage representation . . . of young people [and] . . . minority groups in reasonable relationship to their presence in the population of the States."[54] The best study we have of the immediate effects of this requirement is William Cavala's aptly titled article "Changing the Rules Changes the Game," which deals with California. After observing what happened there, we shall note the effects on the composition, policy preferences, and behavior of delegates as a whole.

California had a winner-take-all primary in 1972, the last in the country. According to past practice, the candidate who won this primary election would choose his delegates on the basis of recommendations made by his leading supporters around the state. The major criterion for delegate selection was the degree to which a possible delegate's past record or present resources suggested he could help the party in the coming campaign. Thus high party officials, officeholders, and financial contributors, most of whom are white, male, and over thirty, fit the bill.

This traditional system had its drawbacks. It gave candidates a splendid opportunity to unmake friends by failing to appoint people to the delegation. And space was always limited. This meant a certain amount of bargaining; people who wanted to be selected could refuse to help with the campaign or delay their contributions until they had first been rewarded with a delegate's position. Thus California political leaders did not oppose changes in the rules that imposed de facto quota requirements and removed the choice of delegates to the congressional district level. At the time, this seemed to be an opportunity to connect convention rewards with party performance.

In each congressional district, delegate selection meetings were held on behalf of each candidate well in advance of the primary. Some of these meetings were dominated by traditional interest group forces. But these were mostly the meetings of the traditional centrist candidates—Humphrey, Jackson, and the early front runner, Muskie. Not so the meetings of the eventual winner of the primary, George McGovern. At the McGovern district meetings there were large turnouts of white liberal activists who had not previously been involved in local and state politics. "In contrast to campaign professionals," Cavala writes, "who saw delegates as basically campaign personnel, the assembled activists viewed them as moral ambassadors. . . ."[55] Thus prior experience in campaigns was often viewed as a disqualification, presumably on the ground that the nominee had been tainted, and offenders were hooted down. Activists found the instructions on quotas congenial because they believed in both demographic (race, age, sex) and issue representation. They soon broke up into black, Spanish-American, and women's caucuses, whose members bargained with one another for representation. The concern of these caucuses was with group interests rather than party or candidate interests. Hence women who had been active for McGovern were slighted in these mini-caucuses in favor of those whose attention was focused on women's rights. Racial minorities received a double bonus. The McGovern campaign committee urged extra representation in districts where minorities predominated in order to enhance electoral prospects. This was done. But they did not anticipate that areas with few minority people would also feel it necessary to have minorities on their slate.

What about white males over thirty years of age? They, presumably, did not have a shared interest requiring separate representation. Only 8 percent of the McGovern delegates selected at district meetings met this description. Jewish males, who had in the past supplied a great deal of money for Democratic politics in the state of California, and many of whom backed McGovern, were evidently not considered a minority because they were nowhere to be found. To find Jews one had to look at the female side of the delegation. The final result was a delegation consisting of 41 percent minority-group members, whose presence in the general California population hovered around 18 percent.

As an aid in obtaining party unity during the campaign for the general election, the primary winner traditionally chooses a few delegates from the losing slates. A few members of the winning slate are asked to resign, and supporters of other presidential nominees are salted in. However, the new breed of delegates refused to give up a single place. Consequently, organized labor, which had supported Humphrey, had hardly any representation in the California delegation, and officeholders were noticeable by their absence. Hence the manpower and money these groups provided in the campaign came to McGovern late and in smaller amounts.[56]

At the convention, the McGovern organization and the state delegations increasingly came to be recognized by delegates as the places where instructions originated and were delivered.[57] In the future, however, if conventions are more closely contested and if demographic groups become more experienced, they may become an important part of the strategic environment. For if state delegations lack leaders (that is, people who can deliver at least one delegate's vote other than their own) candidates may seek to simplify their task by bargaining with larger numbers through group caucuses. In 1976 state delegations remained crucial; they were less so in 1980. And in 1980 group caucuses were better organized and able to monitor their membership on the Democratic side. They also appeared for the first time in 1976 among Republicans. There, as Jeffrey L. Pressman observed, the Republican norm against blatant interest-group politics—telling delegates to do this or that—worked against the influence of formal caucuses.[58]

Whether the prospect of power will increase or decrease the willingness of these groups to seek common goals no one can say. At this time party rules regarding primaries give delegates little freedom of choice at the convention so long as their candidate is still running. Thus at the Democratic convention there are many delegates of the requisite variety, but all are pledged to one candidate or another. Demographic caucuses have some impact on party platforms and convention resolutions, however, and so it is worth knowing how representative delegates were who were chosen under the new quotas as compared with delegates in previous years and what their preferences were compared with those of voters who identified with the Democratic party.

The new rules have succeeded in increasing the proportion of blacks, women, and youth at the past three Democratic conventions. In 1972 black people were overrepresented compared with their proportion in the total population (16 percent to 11 percent), but this accurately mirrored their proportion (17 percent) among Democratic party identifiers. Black delegates were at the Republican convention in rough proportion (5 percent) to their 4 percent of party identifiers.

Women in 1972 constituted 40 percent of Democratic delegates, a three-fold increase over the 1968 Democratic convention. Youth (i.e., those under age thirty) comprised 23 percent (as compared to 3 percent in 1968) of delegates for the Democrats, while they constituted 28 percent of the population over eighteen and 25 percent of Democratic party identifiers. Around 16 percent of youth identified with the Republican party, but this group made up just 8 percent of Republican delegates. Although people over sixty-five made up 15 percent of the general population, only 4 percent of that age group was at the Democratic convention and 9 percent at the Republican.

This breakdown covers only certain sorts of groups; what happens if we stratify delegates by income and education? At the end of 1971, 48 percent of Democratic identifiers had a family income of less than $9,000; another 30 percent had incomes of from $9,000 to $15,000. Thirty-six percent of Democratic delegates had incomes of over $10,000; and another 50 percent had family incomes of over $20,000. The gaps between rank-and-file and delegate income were even greater on the Republican side. Forty-three percent of Republican identifiers had incomes of under $10,000, as compared with 23 percent of delegates with incomes of under $20,000; 15 percent of Republican identifiers had incomes of over $15,000, and 23 percent of Republican delegates had incomes of over $50,000.[59]

Educational differences were even more striking. About three in five delegates from both parties had college degrees, compared to one in four among rank-and-file Democrats and one in three of rank-and-file Republican identifiers. Among the Democratic delegates, 65 percent of McGovern's people had college degrees, compared to 33 percent for Wallace, 40 percent for Humphrey, and 56 percent for Muskie. Professional people predominated among the delegates, with lawyers in the forefront, except among McGovern supporters, where teachers were predominant.

Who was absent? Mainly the representatives of capital and labor. Self-employed businessmen constituted only 8 percent of Democratic delegates (compared to 29 percent in 1968) and made up 18 percent of Republicans, not much for the alleged party of business. Workers were hardly to be seen. As Jeane Kirkpatrick concludes, "The delegates to both conventions were an overwhelmingly middle to upper class group. . . ."[60]

In 1976, the percentage of minority delegates to the Democratic Convention receded to 11 percent, women dropped to 33 percent, and youth fell to 15 percent. But income and education were equally skewed among 1976 Democratic Convention delegates. The "median income of the delegates to the convention exceeded $18,000, while the national median was under $6,000. . . . Six percent of the convention delegates had incomes of less than $10,000 per year while 44 percent of the Democratic rank-and-file had incomes of less than $10,000 per year." In 1976 over 50 percent of the Democratic delegates had at least a bachelor's degree, versus only 9 percent of the rank-and-file. Nineteen seventy-six also saw a high of 51 percent of delegates who were professionals versus only 5 percent of delegates who were either blue-collar or clerical workers.[61]

The 1980 conventions show the cumulative effects of quotas and of party rules, the one nearly nullifying the other. Ninety-seven percent of Democratic delegates, being pledged in advance, had no choice of whom to vote for; half of those were women and 15 percent were black. They did get pro-Equal Rights Amendment and jobs for minorities planks in the platform, but these were not binding on the candidate. Only 3 percent of Republican delegates were black but the women rose to 30 percent.[62]

There are other, long-standing differences between the delegates of the two parties. A tiny 2 percent of Republicans were liberal, and a mere 6 percent of Democrats were conservative. Overall (see Table 3.2) delegates were far more liberal or conservative than the general population. The data, which come from a CBS News survey, reveal that Republican delegates tended to be older, more Catholic or Jewish, and held many more union cards. Of the Democrats who were union members, almost all belonged to white-collar unions or held white-collar jobs as officials in blue-collar unions. Though their level of education was quite similar, the median income of Republican delegates was around $10,000 a year more than Democrats. An estimated one-third of the Democrats were governmental employees, partly due to the large number of teachers who made up the National Education Association contingent of

Table 3.2

	Democrats	Republicans	Overall U.S.
Liberals	46%	2%	19%
Moderates	42	36	43
Conservatives	6	58	30

SOURCE: CBS News Delegate Survey, 1980. Characteristics of the public are average values from seven CBS News/*New York Times* polls, 1980. Adapted from Warren J. Mitofsky and Martin Plissner, "The Making of the Delegates, 1968–1980," *Public Opinion* (October/November 1980), p. 41.

delegates, while the proportion of governmental employees among Republicans was 21 percent, about the same as in the population at large.[63]

What difference does this substantial disparity in policy preferences among activists, politicians and voters make? In some years, depending on the presidential candidate in question, it makes more of a difference than in others. Herbert McClosky's classic study comparing delegates to the 1956 conventions with ordinary voters uncovered an important source of difficulty for the Republican party that has persisted through the years; Republican voters and Democratic voters tend to think more or less alike on most policy issues and ordinary voters of both parties in turn have attitudes close to those of Democratic leaders but relatively removed from the attitudes of Republican leaders.[64] This suggests that Republican activists, by satisfying themselves with a candidate and platform, would court unpopularity and defeat. Indeed the 1964 experience is frequently cited as evidence of this.

In 1972, quite similar risks passed to the Democratic camp. On the broadest range of issues, Democratic delegates, especially McGovern delegates, were far from most citizens, including supporters of the Democratic party. In fact (see Table 3.3), they differed from the preferences of Democratic voters on most issues even more than did Republican delegates. On welfare policy, most voters gave priority to work, while most Democratic delegates were more interested in eradicating poverty. On busing, only 3 percent of the McGovern delegates were strongly opposed, in contrast to 71 percent of voting Democrats. On law and order, over three-fourths of the delegates cared more about the rights of the accused, compared to one-third of the voters. On Vietnam, 7 percent of the voters but 57 percent of the McGovern delegates were opposed to giving any aid whatsoever after American withdrawal. Only on inflation did Democratic voters and delegates agree on the importance of governmental action.

Table 3.3

Differences Between Democratic Rank-and-File Identifiers and Selected Groups of Convention Delegates, 1972
(The larger the number, the greater the difference)

Attitudes toward:	McGovern	Humphrey	Delegates for: Wallace	Muskie	Republican	Democratic
Welfare	110	35	46	60	19	76
Busing*	147	54	26	67	9	108
Crime	107	45	54	54	21	79
Civil rights leaders	94	59	74	69	4	67
Welfare recipients	76	69	32	50	1	64
Political demonstrators	123	61	5	68	5	90
Police	33	7	11	7	18	16
Military	97	5	30	30	29	52
Blacks	34	45	6	37	73	46
Conservatives	89	42	66	48	41	64
Liberals	78	24	99	37	73	46
Union leaders	10	43	52	21	52	15
Politicians	55	76	16	66	75	57
Inflation*	21	5	30	9	20	14
Abortion*	89	43	2	67	50	68
Laying off women first*	54	32	4	38	18	42
Women's liberation†	61	32	55	21	57	25
Business interests†	57	2	2	15	45	35
Black militants†	93	26	15	32	9	61
Vietnam	109	29	14	62	34	79
Ideological Self-Classification†	83	40	80	54	59	59
MEAN DIFFERENCES	77.0	36.9	34.2	43.5	31.6	54.9

*These data on rank-and-file identifiers—used to compute differences—were taken from the CPS Pre-Election (Post-Convention) Study.

†These data on rank-and-file identifiers—used to compute differences—were taken from the CPS 1972 Post-Election Study.

The remaining data on rank-and-file identifiers were taken from the Pre-Convention Study.

N.B.: The difference scores above were computed from preponderance scores carried to the first decimal place.

SOURCE: Jeane J. Kirkpatrick, "Representation in the American National Conventions: The Case of 1972," *British Journal of Political Science* 5 (July 1975), p. 304.

Politics involves feelings not only about issues but also about groups. Toward one group—politicians—delegates in both parties were more favorable than voters. On unions, business, and liberals, Democratic voters and delegates were together. But on political demonstrators, civil rights leaders, black militants, the military, and people on welfare, Republican delegates were closer to Democratic voters, who were very far indeed from Democratic delegates. On all issues and group attitudes, McGovern delegates differed more with Democratic voters than the supporters of any other candidate, including George Wallace.

Differences between Republican and Democratic voters persist. Democrats are more liberal on crime, welfare, and busing, and are more sympathetic to union leaders, the aspirations of black citizens, and demonstrators. But, as Kirkpatrick emphasizes, in 1972, ". . . the same issues and symbols which separated the Democratic from Republican voters still further separated Democratic voters from their own party elite."[65] Were these differences caused by the new quota rules of the Democratic party or by divergences between voters and activists on other grounds? All McGovern supporters shared the same political attitudes whether they were male or female, white or black, young or old. Thus the quotas clearly cannot be blamed for the disparity in views between 1972 Democratic delegates and voters. It is possible that the entire process that brought delegates to the Democratic convention, and not the quotas, made them less representative on issues than delegates used to be. Perhaps what happened is that activists in both parties, enjoying high social and economic status but without professional commitment to party unity or party organization, grew at once farther apart from one another and from the voters. The participant sectors of the parties were far more polarized in 1972 than they had been in the 1940s and 1950s in two directions—one party from the other at the elite level, and elites in both parties from their followers.[66]

There is certainly good reason to believe this *a priori,* since at the 1972 convention a majority of delegates voted for George McGovern, who lost 40 percent of the vote of Democratic identifiers in the general election. In addition, there are the striking differences in policy attitudes between McGovernites and the rest of the Democratic party, as displayed in Table 3.3. But the question remains: Were these the only Democratic activists? Or could we find a population of Democratic party leaders whose attitudes fall closer to the mainstream of the voting population?

Evidently we can. A 1972 survey comparing the policy preferences of Democratic and Republican county chairmen with rank-and-file party identifiers discloses findings "rather similar to McClosky's"—Republican chairmen were much more conservative than most voters, whereas Democratic chairmen and voters had more congruent preferences.[67]

There is something about having a winning presidential candidate, however, which helps to tone down ideological extremism after a while. A scholar who has made a study of political attitudes among Republican delegates suggests that while many of the former Goldwater activists remained active in Republican organizations, after 1964 they made individual ideological accommodations to the more moderate forces that captured the GOP. In the short run, the Nixon candidacies may have tempered the conservative zeal of many former Goldwater supporters and resulted in their "professionalization." The comments of a state committeewoman who was recruited as a Goldwater volunteer in 1964 characterizes this pragmatic evolution: "I was a Republican amateur in 1964 but I wouldn't support Goldwater today. Our leader must reflect majority opinion, namely the views in the middle because a man is elected to represent this country's beliefs, not to force his own on the country. Nixon is doing a great job at this even though conservatives have given him a hard time. . . . After the primary we worked for the ticket because party unity is the result of both free discussion and being a good loser if necessary."[68]

Why might Democratic delegates be different? According to Austin Ranney, a political scientist and a member of the McGovern commission that wrote the rules for 1972, "Most of the guidelines were consciously designed to maximize participation by persons who are enthusiasts for a particular presidential aspirant or policy *in the year of the convention.*"[69] Evidently enthusiasts for McGovern were indeed different. If a more centrist Democratic candidate had emerged from the 1972 convention, the discrepancies we are exploring might not have existed or been noticed. But centrist and moderate candidates are relatively poor at stimulating the enthusiasm among party activists that is increasingly needed to win under the current guidelines. They may, however, be aided by the public attention generated by the media after the earliest tests of candidates' strength, as with Carter in 1976.

☆ Delegate Behavior in Multiballot Conventions

By the time of the nominating convention, most delegates are pledged and a probable winner has emerged. The convention merely ratifies the result. Sometimes there is a little suspense if the numbers are close, as the Republicans demonstrated in 1976 with Ronald Reagan's down-to-the-wire battle with President Ford. And so it is still worthwhile to explore what happens in the increasingly rare instances of multiballot conventions, where decisions are actually made. Under these circumstances, there is uncertainty at the time of the convention about who will be the nominee. In an uncertain convention, delegates crave information on what is going to happen and when. For some of them, of course, the convention is a spectator sport, since they will be acting under instructions from the voters in their state primary or from their state party leaders. Even so, they will want to know who is ahead and who is behind and what the chances are of majority agreement on one of the leading candidates. Rumors are rife because no one has been able to establish an unshakable claim of victory, because it is to the advantage of more than one aspirant to be thought to be winning, and because people like to speculate. In the grip of uncertainty, the delegates grasp for any objective information that may be gleaned from the events of the convention itself.[70]

Before the balloting on the candidates begins at the convention, there often are votes on the seating of contested delegations, a plank in the platform, or some rule governing convention life (such as a loyalty pledge), or there is conflict over who is to be permanent chairman. If some of the candidates become identified with one or the other side on these preliminary votes, the results may be considered a test of who is likely to win the nomination. Thus, candidates who choose sides may prejudice their chances of nomination. They must calculate the effects of the loss of such a vote. In 1932, Franklin Roosevelt nearly lost his bid for the nomination by coming out against the two-thirds rule then required for nomination. Fortunately, FDR's supporters at the convention discovered that the opposition to the change in rules was greater than the opposition to FDR, and he beat a hasty retreat from his previous position.[71]

A challenge to the seating of delegates may also tell the story. Eisenhower's victory in 1952 was signaled by challenges to Taft delegates, and McGovern showed he would win in 1972 by beating Humphrey's forces on California. The decision of the credentials committee to allow contested delegates from California, who intended to support McGovern, to vote on the challenge was an early and significant sign. At the Democratic convention of 1980, the Carter forces beat back an attempt instigated chiefly by Kennedy supporters to change the rules so as not to require delegates to vote for the candidates to whom they had been pledged. Since a majority of the delegates were already pledged to Carter, Kennedy's only hope was to give them room to change their minds. As soon as this effort failed, Kennedy withdrew his candidacy altogether.

Many of the same strategic considerations hold in relation to conflicts that may develop over the permanent chairman. This struggle may be important because the chairman has significant procedural powers at the convention. He can speed up adjournment to give a particular candidate time to make bargains, or he can harm another's chances by refusing to recognize a state delegation about to go over to that candidate at a crucial moment. The importance of being chairman was demonstrated at the 1920 Republican convention, when Senator Henry Cabot Lodge wanted to permit party leaders to find a way out of an impasse that had developed. Shortly after the fourth ballot, Senator Reed Smoot of Utah moved to adjourn the proceedings. A resounding "no" echoed throughout the auditorium as Lodge put the motion to a vote and immediately declared the convention adjourned.[72] Twenty years later, at another Republican convention, Senator John Bricker of Ohio asked Chairman Joseph Martin for a recess before the sixth ballot; this would have given the Taft and Dewey forces time to make a deal. Partial to the Willkie cause, however, Martin refused the request and the balloting continued, ending with victory for Willkie.[73] A similar situation developed at the 1976 Republican convention when the Ford forces gaveled through a voice vote on the foreign policy plank instead of risking a roll call that might have shown less strength than was desirable for their candidate.

Unless victory appears assured, it may be unwise for a candidate to challenge a popular chairman. An alternate strategy is to accept an unfavorable chairman but to put forth a stream of publicity stressing the chairman's partiality, so that he feels under continuous scrutiny and may bend over backward to avoid charges of favoritism. Nowadays, however, the usual practice is for representatives of the leading candidates to agree upon major personnel of the convention—keynote speaker, permanent chairman, platform committee chairman, credentials committee chairman—well ahead of the convention itself. If they do not, the outcome of the ensuing struggle over the chairmanship becomes a signal of the strength of the contenders, depending on whether the person they favor gets the position.

Virtually any action can take on added significance if it reveals information hitherto unavailable to all. In the 1932 Democratic convention a vote on seating a contested delegation was taken under conditions that freed many delegates from the unit rule. This revealed which delegations were closely divided, information that imposition of the unit rule had helped to hide.[74]

Such apparently trivial matters as the date or the site of the convention may take on special meaning if those decisions are believed to affect the fortunes of candidates. The fact that the 1844 Democratic convention was delayed while Martin Van Buren's letter opposing the annexation of Texas was having its effect was known at that time to be prejudicial to his chances. Locating the 1928 Democratic convention in Houston, Texas, was widely interpreted as a move to mollify Southerners and led to the conclusion that this was necessary because party leaders intended to nominate Al Smith.

While candidates are being nominated, and during the balloting, demonstrations—which are largely prearranged—take place on the floor. These raucous displays are meant to let everyone know that a candidate has many loyal supporters. A demonstration at a crucial moment, it is hoped, might ignite the spark of enthusiasm among the multitude of uncertain delegates. But, as supporters of Adlai Stevenson learned in 1960, this can work only when delegates are really uncertain and uncommitted.

Despite the fact that everyone seems aware of what is going on, the same old tricks are played at every convention. Part of the reason is that once a practice has begun, unanimous consent is necessary to eliminate it; otherwise, the candidate who received no ovation would be deemed to have no support or not enough sense to stimulate applause artificially. Another part of the rationale behind demonstrations should be clear from our argument: reliable information may be so scarce that, despite all warnings, delegates may be swayed (as was the Republican convention of 1940 that nominated Wendell Willkie) by the most immediate, tangible evidence before them—the roar of the crowd. But this would become a factor today only if delegates were exhausted by balloting that did not lead to a decision. Uncertainty plays no part when delegates come to ratify a choice already made for them in the primaries.

☆ The Balloting

Politicians who wish power in government try to contribute to the majority essential for the nomination of the candidate they believe will be the winner. This explains the so-called bandwagon behavior which has been seen in operation at many conventions. When politicians believe that one presidential aspirant is certain of nomination, they will attempt to go on record as voting for that aspirant as quickly as possible. Delegates committed to a favorite son candidate will trade their votes for access (or what they hope will be access) to the candidate they think most likely to win nomination. Note the differences in these two statements. In the first, delegates *know* which candidate will win and hope to earn his gratitude by voting for him. In the corollary, delegates are less certain of the outcome, hence their commitment to an aspirant is more costly for him. The prospective candidate, in these circumstances, often makes promises of access to delegates in return for their support.

Purists among the delegates will try to keep pure. If they can't get all they want, they may search for a candidate who is ideologically and stylistically compatible. A compromise candidate, however, would be far less congenial to them. If they get on any bandwagon, it is more likely to be one taking them out of the convention. Splitting the party would be better, so far as purists are concerned, than injuring their integrity.

Aspirants who lead in votes for the nomination must actually win the nomination by a certain time or else their chances of eventually winning decline precipitously, even though they remain temporarily in the lead. This is true when delegate support is given to candidates in anticipation of victory. When this victory doesn't materialize quickly, delegates may question their initial judgment. Thus, the longer candidates remain in the lead without starting a bandwagon, the greater the possibility that their supporters will vote for someone else. In order to maximize access, delegates prefer to support the eventual winner before he achieves a majority. They are therefore guided by what they expect other delegates to do and are constantly on the alert to change their expectations to conform to the latest information. This information may be nothing more substantial than a rumor, which quickly takes on the status of self-fulfilling prophecy as delegates stampede in response to expectations, quickly realized, about how other delegates will respond. The strategies that a candidate adopts depend, therefore, not only on showing that he can win, but also on his position in the convention. So long as he keeps gaining support, no matter how slightly, he is still in contention, because it is assumed that he may have more strength in reserve. But the front runner who begins to manifest any decline, or even in some cases a leveling-off in votes, on successive ballots can expect uncommitted delegates to conclude that he has shot his bolt and begin to shift their support to more promising prospects.

Considered as a source of information, the balloting indicates whether a candidate is gaining or falling behind. One strategy sometimes used in this connection is to "hide" a few votes on early ballots by giving them to others and reclaiming them little by little to show a steady increase.[75] Or a candidate may decide to bide his time and delay making his bid. In that case a weak initial total of votes is not likely to be commented upon because the front runner occupies the center of attention. Later, a dark horse may occasion surprise by his rapid climb and may hope that most delegates will decide to hitch their wagons to a rising star.

The importance of indicators of uncertainty in contested conventions has been empirically validated. Eugene B. McGregor, Jr., proves that "the candidate making the largest gain from the first to the second ballot went on to win the nomination . . . in . . . eight out of the ten most recent multi-ballot conventions . . . held since 1892. . . ." The exceptions, such as the 103-ballot Democratic convention in 1924, are the result of such "extreme ideological divisions" as urban, Catholic "wets" (who opposed prohibition of alcoholic drinks) versus rural, Protestant "drys" (who favored Prohibition) at that time.[76]

Aspirants sometimes combine their voting strength in the convention in order to prevent a front-running candidate from gaining a majority. They will then negotiate the nomination among themselves. If the front runner's victory promises other aspirants insufficient access, they may defeat him by preventing a bandwagon in his favor. An apparently successful case of combining against the front runner occurred in 1920 when Harry Daugherty, Harding's manager, realizing that General Leonard Wood had to be defeated to give Harding a chance, offered to lend Illinois Governor Frank Lowden every vote he could spare until the governor passed Wood in the balloting. Then the alliance would be terminated. "Certainly you couldn't make a fairer proposition," Lowden responded, and the agreement was consummated.[77] The good old days of "lending" votes may be no more, however, because under the primary rules governing the obligations of delegates, candidates will be unable to exercise this kind of control over them.

The rational aspirant who leads but lacks a majority will bargain and promise access to leaders representing the requisite number of votes if he believes that no bandwagon will develop without stimulation. He may offer the vice-presidential nomination to one or more leaders of important states; he may hint at cabinet posts, patronage, or preferred treatment; he may explore concessions on policy. But before he can bargain, the candidate must know with whom to bargain. And among those delegations or caucuses that might be swayed he must find the ones amenable to what he can offer. This promises to be either very difficult or absurdly simple. If almost all delegates are pledged, the remaining few should be easy to find. If there is a multiballot convention, however, and if the delegates released do not give their allegiance to others who can dispose of their votes, many individual delegates will have to be reached. The importance of maintaining an apparatus for obtaining this information was evident in the past, but if there is ever a multiballot convention in the future, such an information-gathering capability will become indispensable because there will be so many more "bits" of data to keep in mind.

The front runner may reasonably expect to win without cost (that is, without making promises) unless leaders of opposing factions reach agreement on a ticket and appear likely to combine against him. Early front runners often win nominations precisely because they face a divided opposition. The case of the Democrats in 1960 is a perfect example of this. In the preconvention maneuvering, Adlai Stevenson might have cut into John Kennedy's liberal and labor support had he made himself available as a candidate. Many party regulars from the urban political machines and, in particular, ex-President Truman had no special liking for Kennedy, and Senator Lyndon Johnson of Texas could have drawn on a rather substantial reservoir of strength from southern delegations who were determined not to walk out even though they knew they would not approve of the civil rights plank of the platform. These groups could not get together and settle on a candidate who was more satisfactory to all of them than the front runner, Senator Kennedy. Labor clearly would accept no one to the right of Kennedy; the Southerners could abide nobody to the left of him. Adlai Stevenson was perhaps the leading candidate whose ideological location, prominence in the party, and public record could pass muster with all these groups, but he had alienated Truman and in any case refused to go to work in his own behalf. And so Kennedy's opposition stayed divided.

If a candidate thinks he can win on his own, he may be reluctant to risk sacrificing his ambition by "making a deal" to combine against a front runner. Yet if he hesitates too long, he may lose all. This apparently is what happened to Thomas E. Dewey in the 1940 Republican convention. As Senator Arthur Vandenberg recorded in his diary, "I offered to flip a coin with Dewey to see which side of the ticket each would take. Dewey never saw me again until the final voting. But it was too late. He missed the boat when he clung to his own first place ambitions. Between us we could have controlled the convention if it had been done in the first instance."[78]

The candidate who wishes to get support must show that he already has some to begin with. This is particularly the case when one contender is considering throwing his support to another in order to assure the latter's nomination. There would be no point in sacrificing one's chances in favor of another candidate who would then not have enough votes to win. This kind of situation occurred around the time of the fiftieth ballot at the 1924 Democratic convention. Al Smith informed Senator Oscar Underwood of Alabama that if two more southern states would give Underwood their support, Smith would also give the senator his support. The Underwood forces accepted the offer, but they were unable to find other southern states that would support their candidate and the scheme fell through.[79]

The bargaining process itself may be an excellent source of information on what delegates are likely to do under a variety of circumstances. Candidate organizations may carry out a series of probing actions to discover what delegates want, what they will take, what they will give in return. Out of the negotiations may emerge the beginnings of a commonly held picture of the shape of events to come.

Bargains may be tacit rather than explicit, made through intermediaries rather than by principals. Exactly what was promised may not be entirely clear or may be distorted later on. The delegate who wishes to collect what he believes to be his due may have trouble securing effective guarantees. Thomas Dewey never quite had the same understanding that Representative Charles Halleck of Indiana did about an offer of the vice-presidency in return for support in the Republican convention of 1948.[80] One delegate to the 1960 Democratic convention told reporters that he was the nineteenth person to be offered the vice-presidency by the Kennedy forces. Under the circumstances, he allowed as how he would take cash.[81] Proffering positions in return for support has declined of late, possibly because contested conventions have also declined. Despite the distaste with which these deals are regarded, they may rise again; in case bargaining is necessary, what else will candidates have to bargain with?

It is possible that much less material reward for support comes out of the convention than is commonly supposed. An incoming president, for example, may well decide to handle patronage through the dominant party faction in a state rather than suffer the disabilities of supporting a weak dissident faction that helped him at a convention. Nevertheless, if delegates believe that rewards are likely to follow support, as many apparently do, their actions will conform to this belief. Since politics plays an important part in the lives of many delegates, moreover, ability to identify with the nominee may confer an important sense of political identity (as a Reaganaut or a Kennedyite) that is valued in and of itself.

One by one the leading candidates try their luck. Timing is of the essence. Each candidate seeks the strategic moment to push his candidacy. A miscalculation, a decision, perhaps, to move ahead before sufficient support is available for the final push, may prove fatal to a candidate's chances. In a closely contested convention the prize may go to the candidate with sufficient information about others' intentions to make the successful move.

Whispering campaigns say, "Candidate X is certain to win; get on the bandwagon while you still have a chance." Rumors arise that a crucial delegation will swing to a particular candidate. The balloting may remain substantially unchanged and reveal no secrets. It is difficult to know what to believe. No mass meeting of thousands of delegates can hope to find out who is acceptable to most of them. It is up to the leaders to assert control.

In the absence of quick agreement at the convention, the demonstrations and adjournments give party leaders, if there are any, time to meet to try to find a candidate who can receive a majority of votes. This is the "smoke-filled room" of convention lore. Its inhabitants try to work out an agreement that will meet their desires, but they are severely limited in their choice by their estimate of what the people will accept at the polls and what the other delegates will stand for. Delegates have independent influence and different interests and there may be only a limited range of agreement among them.

The essential trick is to convince others that one's preferred view of what will happen is the correct one. This is apparently what took place in the 1920 Republican convention, when Harry Daugherty succeeded in convincing party leaders that a deadlock was inevitable and that only Harding could break it. Much the same kind of thing occurred in 1844 when Gideon Pillow and George Bancroft spread the word that Lewis Cass, John C. Calhoun, or Martin Van Buren could not possibly win, but that James Polk would carry the day.[82]

In order to break a deadlock, it is necessary to convince some delegates that the candidate they prefer cannot win and that they would be well advised to switch to one who can. The leaders at the 1920 Republican convention decided to communicate this point convincingly by calling for several additional ballots during which nothing changed.[83] This also helped to assure losing party factions that their candidates had had a fair chance. At the 1924 Democratic convention, however, which went to 103 ballots, the lengthy voting apparently did not communicate the hopelessness of their cause to the leading candidates. Not only did incompatibility and intransigence block bargaining, but short-lived booms kept arising, an indication that the delegates shared no common view of future events.[84] The shock to loyal party members was so great that many years later John Nance Garner chose to submerge his own chances and throw the 1932 convention to Franklin Roosevelt rather than risk another agonizing stalemate.[85]

Most of this is now history; television and primary elections have shortened procedures, made demonstrations largely pointless, facilitated internal communications at conventions, and given delegates a lot less to communicate about.

☆ The Vice-presidential Nominee

When the convention finally selects its presidential candidate, it turns to the anticlimactic task of finding a running mate. Vice-presidential nominees are chosen to help the party achieve the presidency. Party nominees for president and vice-president always appear on the ballot together and are elected together. Since 1804, a vote for one has always been a vote for the other.

The vice-president occupies a post in the legislative branch of the government that is mostly honorific, and his powers and activities in the executive branch are determined by the president.[86] The electoral interdependence of the two offices gives politicians an opportunity to gather votes for the presidency. Therefore, the prescription for an "ideal" vice-presidential nominee is the same as for a presidential nominee, with two additions: he must possess those desirable qualities the presidential nominee lacks, and he must be acceptable to the presidential nominee.

The vice-presidency is the most frequent position from which presidents of the United States are drawn. Just under a third of our forty presidents were at one time vice-presidents. Four were later elected to the presidency in their own right; eight first took office upon the death of a president; and of course Mr. Ford succeeded because of President Nixon's resignation. American history has given us thirteen good reasons—one for each man who succeeded to the presidency—for inquiring into the qualifications of vice-presidents and for examining the criteria by which they are chosen.

The presidential candidate who has firm control over his nomination is in a position to use the vice-presidential slot to help win the election. This is what Abraham Lincoln did in 1864 when he chose a "War Democrat," Andrew Johnson, whom he hoped would add strength to the ticket. In the same way, John F. Kennedy chose Lyndon Johnson to help gather southern votes, especially in Texas; and Richard Nixon chose Henry Cabot Lodge of Massachusetts in 1960 to help offset the Democratic party advantage in the Northeast. In 1964 President Johnson chose a man who was helpful in unifying the party and maintaining its good electoral prospects. Johnson's own credentials as a liberal Democrat down through the years were not strong; when Kennedy picked him as vice-president he was opposed on these grounds by many labor leaders and by leaders from several of the most important urban Democratic strongholds. In choosing Senator Hubert Humphrey of Minnesota, a longtime liberal leader, President Johnson adhered to the familiar strategy of ticket balancing. President Ford, with his midwestern and congressional background, may have had the same thing in mind when he chose a more liberal eastern establishment figure, Nelson Rockefeller, to be his nominee for vice-president; threats from the right wing of the Republican party to his own nomination chances caused him to switch away from Rockefeller by the next convention. Carter, meanwhile, chose a popular senator, Walter Mondale, in part to make up for his own lack of "insider" qualifications. And Ronald Reagan, more securely tied to the Republican right wing than Ford, leaned toward the moderate side of his own party in picking George Bush.

Recent vice-presidential candidates sometimes have been distinguished men who had a great deal to recommend them. But the help they could offer their parties was undoubtedly an important consideration. Spiro Agnew was chosen in 1968 because, with the Democrats badly divided and Nixon assured of the nomination, it was important to find a running mate who was not (at least not then) hated by anyone. Nixon had seen the results of a poll indicating that all of the leading candidates for the vice-presidency would hurt his chances of election more than they would help him. Agnew was little known outside his home state of Maryland, had been a Rockefeller supporter, had defeated a Democratic segregationist in his gubernatorial race, was a member of one of the "newer" ethnic groups (Greek-American), and impressed Nixon with his personal qualities. At the time of his selection, he was, as he himself said, not exactly a household word. No one suspected that he would later become one—as the first vice-president to resign in disgrace in return for avoiding a criminal indictment.[87]

Sometimes a presidential candidate will try to help heal a breach in the party by offering the vice-presidential nomination to a leader of a defeated party faction. Or the presidential candidate may try to improve his relationships with Congress by finding a running mate who has friends there. Franklin Roosevelt chose Harry Truman for both these reasons. Humphrey balanced his ticket in 1968 by choosing Senator Edmund Muskie, a quietly eloquent, moderate man, a member of an ethnic group (Polish-Americans) concentrated in the cities of the eastern seaboard, to balance his own Midwest populist background and fast-talking style.

A Republican presidential candidate from the East will try to pick a vice-president from the Midwest or Far West. It has been thought desirable, as in the case of Reagan and Bush, for both to reside in large, two-party "swing" states. With the mode of delegate selection among Democrats biased in favor of one-party states (owing to the abolition of the unit rule and the winner-take-all primary), however, this tendency may no longer prevail. A liberal Democrat running for president will try to find a more conservative running mate—unless the idea is to emphasize the differences between the parties, in which case the vice-presidential nominee should be more extreme in his or her views than the main contender. If it is impossible to find one person who combines within his heritage, personality, and experience all the virtues allegedly cherished by American voters, the parties console themselves by attempting to confect out of two running mates a composite image of forward-looking-conservative, rural-urban, energetic-wise leadership that evokes hometown, ethnic, and party loyalties among a maximum number of voters. That, at least, is the theory behind the balanced ticket.

There have been times when a president has insisted on having his personal choice selected as vice-president. Andrew Jackson was adamant about running with Martin Van Buren, and Franklin Roosevelt went so far as to write out a refusal to accept the Democratic nomination in 1940 when party leaders balked at the thought of Henry Wallace. The presidential nominee clearly is expected to have a lot to say about his running mate. More and more in recent years the expectation has been that the presidential candidate himself makes the choice after due consultation with party leaders. Indeed, failure to act decisively may well be regarded now as a sign of weakness. Yet there have been times when presidential candidates have not wished to become involved in internal party battles and have let the convention decide. William Jennings Bryan would not even allow his own Nebraska delegation to signal his preferences by voting on the vice-presidential nomination at the 1896 Democratic convention, and Adlai Stevenson preferred to let Estes Kefauver and John F. Kennedy fight it out for the prize in 1956. Had George McGovern let the delegates decide in 1972, he could have avoided responsibility for selecting Senator Thomas Eagleton of Missouri, who had to leave the ticket in mid-campaign after it was disclosed that he had once been hospitalized and treated for severe depression. If the delegates had picked Eagleton, McGovern could have supported him by reminding the news media that Democrats were supposed to be liberal and it would go against liberal principles to treat a temporary mental illness as a permanent disability.

When especially able men have appeared in the vice-presidential office from time to time, this may have been more because of the blessings of Providence than because of wise actions on anyone's part. If good results require noble intentions, then the criteria for choosing vice-presidents may leave much to be desired. Why should the great parties, we might ask, not set out deliberately to choose the candidate best able to act as president in case of need? Should ticket balancing and similar considerations be condemned as political chicanery?

In a speech to the Harvard Law School Forum in 1956, former Vice-president Henry A. Wallace declared: "The greatest danger is that the man just nominated for President will try desperately to heal the wounds and placate the dissidents in his party. . . . My battle cry would be—no more deals —no more balancing of the ticket." In 1964, the Republican party evidently also endorsed this view. The selection of the 1964 Republican nominee, Representative William Miller of upstate New York, was intended to violate criteria used in the past for balancing the ticket. Although he came from a region different from Barry Goldwater and was a Catholic, Miller was chosen primarily because of his ideological affinity with the presidential candidate. The special style of Goldwater and his supporters required that consistency of views, opposition to the other party on as many issues as possible, and refusal to bargain prevail over the traditional political demands for compromise, flexibility, and popularity.[88] This was also apparently the sentiment of many Republicans in 1976. Yet, surprisingly, the standard bearer of the purist wing of the party, Ronald Reagan, said he would choose as his running mate a liberal Easterner, Senator Richard Schweiker of Pennsylvania. This was his last-ditch attempt to win the nomination, and it was a gamble he lost. But it was consistent with Mr. Reagan's views four years later, when he said:

> There are some people who think that you should, on principle, jump off the cliff with the flag flying if you can't have everything you want. . . .
> If I found when I was governor that I could not get 100 percent of what I asked for, I took 80 percent.[89]

From the standpoint of the electoral success of candidates, balancing the ticket seems only prudent. But there are other reasons for ordinary citizens to prefer that candidates make an effort in this direction. One of the chief assets of the American party system in the past has been its ability (with the exception of the Civil War period) to reduce conflict by enforcing compromise within the major factions of each party. A refusal to heal the wounds and placate dissidents is nothing less than a declaration of internal war. It can only lead to increased conflict within the party. Willingness to bargain and make concessions to opponents is part of the price for maintaining unity in a party sufficiently large and varied to be able to appeal successfully to a population divided on economic, sectional, racial, religious, ethnic, and perhaps also ideological grounds. To refuse entirely to balance the ticket would be to risk changing our large, heterogeneous parties into a multiplicity of small sects of "true believers" who care more about maintaining their internal purity than about winning public office by pleasing the people.

This is not to suggest that the president and vice-president must be worlds apart in their policy preferences in order to please everyone. There is obvious good sense in providing for a basic continuity in policy in case a president should die or be disabled. But this need not mean that the two should be identical in every respect, even if that were possible. Within the broad outlines of agreement on the basic principles of the nation's foreign policy and of the government's role in the economy, for example, a president would have no great difficulty in finding a variety of running mates who were somewhat more or less liberal than himself, who appealed to somewhat different groups, or who differed in other salient ways. To go this far to promote party unity, factional conciliation, and popular preference should not discomfort anyone who realizes the costs of failing to balance the ticket.

Actually there is no evidence whatsoever to suggest that vice-presidents add to or detract from the popularity of presidential candidates with the voters. By helping unite the party, however, and by giving diverse party leaders another focus of identification with the ticket, a vice-presidential nominee with the right characteristics can help assure greater effort by party workers, and this may bring results at election time. Even if balancing the ticket does not help the party at the polls, it may indirectly help the people. It may aid our political parties in maintaining unity within diversity and thereby in performing their historic function of bringing our varied population closer together.

☆ The Future of National Conventions

One of the lessons of recent presidential elections is that national conventions are declining in importance as decision-making bodies.[90] They are not now taken seriously as decision-making instruments of the party of an incumbent president. The turnover of delegates from convention to convention is very high, averaging about 64 percent.[91] This suggests the introduction of large numbers of delegates who are recruited by national candidates rather than by local parties. The successes of John Kennedy in 1960, Barry Goldwater in 1964, Richard Nixon in 1968, George McGovern in 1972, Jimmy Carter in 1976, and Ronald Reagan in 1980, as well as the new rules in the Democratic party, make it plausible that increasingly commitments are being made earlier and earlier in the nomination process, even when the nomination of the party out of office is being contested among several factions.

The large number of first-ballot nominations in recent years shows that important things are happening in the "out" party before the convention meets. Nationwide television coverage of the primaries gives early candidates a head start on the free publicity of the election year.[92] Private polls (as well as those published in the newspapers) put more information about the comparative popularity of candidates in the hands of party leaders earlier than before. The proliferation of primaries sends national candidates into more and more states in search of committed delegates. Thus the pressures upon state party leaders to decide what they want to do seem to be urging them to make decisions earlier in the election year—before national publicity creates a rush of sentiment in one direction or another that takes matters wholly out of their hands. When one or a few party leaders come to feel the need for early decisions, soon the others must follow suit or lose their own room for maneuvering. These early decisions must, perforce, take place at widely separate places on the map. This enhances the bargaining power of candidates who can deal with party leaders piecemeal under these circumstances, rather than having to face them en masse at a convention, where they can wheel and deal with one another.

If this tendency is correctly identified, it leads to the further conclusion that over the long run, as mass media continue or possibly increase their saturation coverage of early events in the election year, and as early primary elections become more and more important, successful candidates (at least of the party out of office) increasingly will have to have access to large sums of money apart from the resources generally available to the party, a large personal organization, and an extra measure of skill and attractiveness on the hustings and over television. In these circumstances, other resources—such as the high regard of party leaders—would come to be less important. Thus, early candidacy, opulent private financing (preferably gathered by a mail campaign that pulls in small contributions fully matchable by the federal subsidy), good, early personal publicity and strong personal organizations, such as characterized the Kennedy, Goldwater, Nixon, McGovern, Carter,

Table 3.4
Number of Presidential Ballots in National Party Conventions 1928–1980*

Year	Democrats	Republicans
1928	1	1
1932	4	(1)
1936	(1)	1
1940	(1)	8
1944	(1)	1
1948	(1)	3
1952	3	1
1956	1	(1)
1960	1	1
1964	(1)	1
1968	1	1
1972	1	(1)
1976	1	(1)
1980	(1)	1
First-ballot total:	12/14	12/14
	(6 incumbents)	(4 incumbents)

Combined (Democrats and Republicans) first-ballot nominations:
Nonincumbents: 14/18
Incumbents: 10/10

*Nominations won by incumbents are in parentheses.

and Reagan preconvention campaigns, can overcome strong misgivings on the part of party leaders, whose main concern is winning elections. If "out" party candidates in the future follow similar strategies, the national convention as a decision-making body may go into total eclipse.

There are a few countervailing tendencies. The predominance of proportional and districting rules in Democratic party primaries plus the federal financial incentives that will surely entice candidates of middling promise into the primaries decrease the probability that one candidate will have a clear majority before the convention. If a candidate does not win big and early, the chances are he or she will not make it large and late. A bare victory in the last big primary that produces a bumper crop of delegates under a winner-take-all rule, like the one that carried McGovern in, will, with the abolition of the winner-take-all rule, no longer be possible. After all, Jimmy Carter won his great victory at the 1976 convention with only a little more than one-third of the delegates pledged to him. It may be that, current history to the contrary notwithstanding, at some future time one-third or so will not be enough to stampede a convention.

The same trends that might at some time make it harder to win decisively before the convention also would make bargaining difficult once there. Proportional and district primaries give the advantage to the more extreme tendencies because they place a premium on the intense commitments of candidate enthusiasts; so does the weakness of party organization and the proclivity of educated activists with time on their hands to be stylistically purist and ideologically distant from voters. In part this problem can be mitigated by the 1982 decision of the Democrats to admit public office holders to the convention as unpledged delegates. Up to 15 percent of the 1984 convention will be constituted in this fashion.

How do these forces balance out? Differently, we surmise, in different years. In 1976 it appeared that the efforts of party leaders to write rules that would breathe new life into national conventions were effectively nullified by the mass media. The media gave such overwhelming publicity to early events in the election year, thus boosting early front runner Jimmy Carter, that party leaders were stampeded well before the convention. Had Carter been less "vague" about the issues, or had his opponents realized how crucial early primaries and conventions had become, conceivably the outcome would have been different. Carter's success illustrates the overwhelming benefits of early activity.

The dilemmas of a centrist candidate were well exemplified in 1972 by Senator Muskie of Maine, who had to compete for the votes of party moderates with Senators Humphrey and Jackson. Because Wallace and McGovern supporters were more intense in their convictions earlier on, they were able to build grass-roots organizations. Had Wallace's people caught on to the rules of the primary process in time, they might well have done a lot better. When Wallace became active, he took the right with him. When former New York Mayor John Lindsay dropped out after the Florida primary and former Senator Eugene McCarthy after the Illinois primary, McGovern had the left pretty much to himself. He could count on a plurality over his rivals. By the time Humphrey emerged as the strongest center candidate, McGovern was barely able to beat him out. And that may have been appropriate. Within the Democratic party, the left liberals may have a small majority among those who turn out at primaries, but that is not the same, as McGovern discovered, as a national majority.

A healthy political party requires activists as well as voters. So long as the policy preferences and group identifications of these two populations are reasonably compatible, their differing interests can be reconciled by bargaining. Once they grow far apart, however, the tension between them may become unbearable until one or another leaves its ancestral party. In Europe this tension frequently takes the form of a clash between the militant party cadres and the moderate parliamentarians interested in winning elections. Since it is the parliamentarians who elect the party leaders in parliament, including the prime minister, they have real resources with which to combat the militants. The separate elections of senators and congressmen and the federal system in the United States, however, take the presidential nomination outside of normal politics. Congressional and gubernatorial candidates rarely run on as radical or conservative a basis as the rhetoric of their activist supporters might suggest, and they participate less than they used to in picking the presidential nominee. Thus, these elected officials have much less of a stake in the presidency. On the Democratic side the party leaders who used to guard that stake increasingly are weak or absent. This sufficiently alarmed the Democrats so that their Hunt Commission of 1982 provided that a large number of members of Congress should be welcomed as unpledged delegates.

What is remarkable, when one thinks of it, is that special arrangements should have to be made to bring party officeholders back into the conventions or to allow the people who probably know most about the candidates to support whomever they think best. Leaving out the politicians who have to appeal to the electorate is a poor way to choose candidates for the greatest national office.

Just as the news media have interacted with political forces to produce the ratifying rather than the deciding convention, so the two have combined to give the conventions their electoral meaning. Deprived of their decision-making role, the conventions become more amenable to use in the campaign. Not having to worry about winning the nomination, candidates can more carefully consider how they want to manage the presentation of their party for advertising purposes. Asked to appraise the importance of national conventions, we would have to say that they have changed from being the big guns of the nominating process to the first shots of the election campaign.

Now the candidates may want their delegates to look presentable to television viewers, but they are not in a position to do much about it. They can, as we have seen, assure the presence of delegates pledged to them, making sure the delegates do their duty by voting for them. So far, from the candidate's viewpoint, so good. While the delegates have mostly pledged their votes, however, they have not hocked their souls. They may turn against their candidate on platform issues. As Jimmy Carter discovered in 1980, these issues were all the more important to delegates by virtue of the fact that they had no other decision to make. What is more, delegates who have come to the convention to express support for their varied lifestyles can do that simply by being who they are and showing up on television. Young or old, black or white, male or female, straight or gay, liberated or conventional, the delegates make a statement about what they stand for simply by being there.

To appear before the public, of course, delegates must get on television. What gets across to the voter is what television journalists choose to put on. Aside from the few obligatory famous names, the usual principles apply— controversy and deviance make better copy than straight gestures of support. Whatever the delegates appear to be, television accentuates that pattern at its leading edges, stressing differences rather than similarities to the past. Should voters look in and say (to themselves and friends and neighbors) that these delegates are not "my kind of people," candidates may find that their ability to project a certain image is overwhelmed by contrary notions that voters have gathered for themselves.

Chapter 4

The Campaign

Once the conventions are over, the two presidential candidates traditionally "relax" for a few weeks until Labor Day, when they ordinarily begin their official campaigning. From that day onward they confront the voters directly, each carrying the banner of his political party. How do the candidates behave? Why do they act the way they do? And what kind of impact do their activities have on the electorate?

For the small minority of people who are party workers, campaigns serve as a signal to get to work. How hard they work depends in part on whether the candidates' political opinions, slogans, personalities, and visits spark their enthusiasm. The workers may "sit on their hands," or they may pursue their generally unrewarding jobs—checking voting lists, mailing campaign flyers, ringing doorbells—with something approaching fervor. They cannot be taken for granted; activating them and imbuing them with purpose and ardor is perhaps the first task of the candidate.

For the rest of the population, most of whom are normally uninterested in politics, campaigns call attention to the advent of an election. Some excitement may be generated and some diversion (as well as annoyance) provided for those who turn on the TV to find that their favorite program has been preempted by a political speech. The campaign is a great spectacle.

Talk about politics increases, and a small percentage of citizens may even become intensely involved as they get caught up in campaign oratory.

For the vast majority of citizens in America, campaigns do not function so much to change minds as to reinforce previous convictions. As the campaign wears on, the underlying party identification of most people rises ever more powerfully to the surface. Republican and Democratic identifiers are split further apart—polarized—as their increased awareness of party strife emphasizes the things that divide them.[1]

The Center for Political Studies at the University of Michigan has found repeatedly that about three-quarters of those in its samples who are eligible to vote claimed a party identification; of these, three-fifths were Democrats.[2] Thus the outstanding strategic problem for Democratic politicians is to get their adherents to turn out to vote for Democratic candidates. No need to worry about Republicans or independents if Democrats can do this basic job. Democrats therefore stress appeals to the faithful. They try to raise in their supporters the old party spirit. One of their major problems, as we have seen, is that most citizens who identify with them are found at the lower end of the socioeconomic scale and are less likely to turn out to vote than those with Republican leanings. So the Democrats put on mobilization drives and seek in every way to get as large a turnout as possible. If they are well organized, they scour the lower-income areas. They provide baby-sitters, cars to get the elderly and infirm to the polls, and occasionally, inducements of a less savory kind to reinforce the party loyalty of the faithful. The seemingly neutral campaigns put on by radio, TV, and newspapers to stress the civic obligation to vote, if they have any effect at all, probably help the Democrats more than the Republicans.[3]

For Republicans involved in presidential nominating politics, the most important fact of life is that their party is without question the minority party in the United States. What is more, the Republican minority has shrunk somewhat over the past twenty-five years. In presidential elections in which considerations of party are foremost, and allowing for the greater propensity of Republicans to turn out to vote, it has been plausibly argued that the Democrats could expect to win with around 53 or 54 percent of the vote.[4] This is close enough to kindle hope in Republican breasts. Despite the clear Democratic majority in this country, it must be assumed that either major party can win a presidential election. But over the past thirty years it has generally been necessary for the Republicans to devise a strategy that could help them not only win, but win from behind.

The decline in party identification from something over three-quarters to

Table 4.1
Party Identification of Adults

	Republican	Democratic	Other
1940	38%	42%	20%
1950	33	45	22
1960	30	47	23
1964	25	53	22
1968	27	46	27
1972	28	43	29
1974	23	44	33
1976	22	45	33
1977	20	49	31
1978	23	48	29
1979	22	46	32
1980	26	43	31
1981	27	43	30

SOURCE: *Gallup Monthly Index* (July 1974, Nov.–Dec. 1975, Dec. 1977, Dec. 1981).

just above two-thirds of the adult population may lead to questions about the continuing importance of party identification. It is doubtful that independent voters are or will soon become the decisive voters in presidential elections. For one thing, about two-thirds of all independents have leanings; scratch an independent and underneath you are likely to find an almost-Republican or a near-Democrat, and those who are left are least likely to turn out. This is no mere artifact of the way a survey question is asked; the voting behavior in presidential elections of independents who lean one way or another much more closely resembles that of either Democrats or Republicans than it does other independents. The likelihood of "independent" voters coalescing into a meaningful mass and becoming a cohesive force in national politics is thus fairly remote.[5]

☆ Three Underdog Strategies

With the handwriting so plainly on the wall, the strategic alternatives available to Republicans can hardly be regarded as secret. They can be boiled down to three possibilities. First, Republicans can attempt to deemphasize the impact of party habit as a component of electoral choice by capitalizing upon a more compelling cue to action. The nomination of General Eisen-hower, the most popular hero of World War II, overrode party considera-tions and is a clear example of the efficacy of this strategy.[6] Efforts to play upon popular dissatisfaction in a variety of issue areas also exemplify this strategy, but these dissatisfactions must preexist in the population and must be widespread and intense before they will produce the desired effect. When issues do come to the fore in a compelling way, the payoff to the advantaged party is sometimes enormous, because these are the circumstances under which new party loyalties can be created. Or the Republican candidate can do as Ronald Reagan did in 1980 and concentrate on looking benign while hoping his opponent's personal unpopularity will keep enough Democratic voters at home to make a Republican victory possible. This involves the cooperation of an obligingly self-destructive Democratic party.

Another possible Republican strategy, similar in some ways to the first, also seeks to depress the salience of party in voters' minds by blurring the differences between the parties, by seeking to efface certain of the stigmata that have been attached to the party over the years as stereotypes having general currency (e.g., "party of the rich").[7] This strategy gives full recogni-tion to the arithmetic of Democratic superiority and also to the unit rule of the Electoral College, which weighs disproportionately votes cast in the large states that so often contain the heaviest concentrations of traditional allies of the Democratic party.[8] It has been used by Republican nominees such as Willkie, Dewey, and Nixon, with results that have often fallen short—some-times barely short—of victory; in consequence this "me-too" strategy has over the years intermittently been controversial among Republicans. The fact that no Republican candidate has actually been able to gain a majority vote with it has created doubts about its efficacy.[9] The "me-too" strategy may entail the advocacy of policies generally favored by most American voters, but this approach apparently does not mirror correctly the political senti-ments of Republican activists.[10] Critics of the "me-too" approach have ar-gued that this strategy merely alienates potential Republican voters while failing to attract sufficient Democrats. Alienated Republicans, so goes this argument, seeing no difference between the policies espoused by the major parties, withdraw from politics into apathy.[11]

Thus, a third strategy, whose claim of victory is based upon the presuppo-sition of a hidden Republican vote, can be identified. This was the strategy pursued by the Goldwater forces in 1964. Its main characteristic is the attempt to sharpen rather than blur party lines on matters of substantive policy. Goldwater supporters argued that he could win, basing their case upon the possibility that he could put together a coalition in the Electoral College of southern and western states and, in particular, upon the notion of a hidden vote. But did this hidden vote exist, or was it a misperception by those who believed it and supported Goldwater, thinking he could win?

The resulting disastrous consequences for the Republican party at the congressional and state levels[12] invite the exercise of hindsight on the question of the hidden Republican vote. But, for once, hindsight merely confirms foresight. It was apparent both before and after the 1964 election that there was little evidence of a hidden Republican vote waiting to be tapped by an unequivocally conservative candidate.

In examining the evidence we must first ask where the Republican vote that this strategy seeks to tap could be hidden. Presumably not among Democrats, at least outside the South, since this approach relies so heavily upon sharpening the cleavage between the two parties. Nor can there be much of a hidden vote among disaffected conservative Republicans who fail to turn out, since the best knowledge we have of Republicans is that they do turn out and vote Republican.[13]

The only other possible location for the hidden vote is among those who profess no regular party affiliation—roughly 33 percent of the potential electorate. What do we know about these people that might lead us to conclude that they can be moved to vote Republican by a highly ideological appeal based on conservative and right-wing doctrines?

There is, in fact, no reason at all to suspect that these people can be reached in this way. All the information we have on true independents indicates that they are much less interested, less informed, less likely to seek information about politics, and less likely to vote than are regular partisans. Nonaffiliates are relatively unconcerned about issues and are only dimly aware of political events.[14] Efforts to reach this population are likely to fail. Attempts to outline issue positions to them, to engage their support in behalf of any self-consistent philosophical and political position, seem on a par with the famous campaign to sell refrigerators to Eskimos.

There is a well-known suspicion, voiced from time to time by imaginative writers, that conservative elements of the population are in fact alienated from politics and sit in the wings, frustrated, immobilized, and without party loyalties, until someone pursuing a Goldwater-like strategy gives them the "choice" they are looking for. This is probably a canard. What fragments of evidence we have point to the probability that the dedicated conservatives and right-wing ideologues who are sufficiently interested in politics to hold strong opinions about public policy do in fact belong to political parties and participate actively in them. These people are almost all Republicans. Thus, the hidden votes that Goldwater hoped to attract probably were hidden inside the votes Richard Nixon received in 1960.[15]

Another assumption underlying the hidden-vote theory is that in 1964 it would have been possible to attract this mythical vote in substantial numbers without losing the allegiance of large numbers of more moderate people who supported the almost-successful candidacy of Richard Nixon in 1960.

In fact, this proved impossible to accomplish. An enormous number— probably around 20 percent—of Nixon's 1960 supporters voted for Lyndon Johnson in 1964.[16] But this outcome might have been extrapolated from poll and primary election data in the preconvention period which showed that, even among Republican voters, Goldwater enjoyed far from overwhelming support.[17]

In addition, he aroused great antipathy among the general population. According to the Gallup poll in mid-September, 38.3 percent of respondents expressed definite hostility to Goldwater (including 14.7 percent expressing the most extreme hostility on an eleven-point scale), while only 8.1 percent expressed any antipathy at all toward President Johnson.[18] Likewise, on a number of issues, Louis Harris surveys found that sizable majorities in the general population defined themselves as opposed to positions that they believed Senator Goldwater held.[19]

☆ The Strategies in Application: 1964 to 1980

The election of 1964, as a result of the Goldwater nomination and the campaign strategy he pursued, was an extremely good test of the hidden-vote hypothesis and also, by indirection, of the "me-too" Republican strategy, which was closer to the strategy of Richard Nixon in 1968. Nixon's main tactic was to avoid antagonizing voters, to avoid direct confrontations with the opposition or with the press, and to avoid saying anything controversial about Vietnam.[20]

Because of Nixon's hairbreadth plurality over Humphrey in 1968, a conclusive explanation for his victory cannot be given. It is clear, though, that he won back almost all of the Republicans who had deserted their party in the Goldwater election four years before. He also won over many Democrats who had voted for Johnson. Indeed, "a full 40 percent of Nixon's vote came from citizens who had supported Lyndon Johnson in 1964!"[21] Votes received by the Democratic party dropped from 61 percent in 1964 to something less than 43 percent in 1968, a total loss of 19 percent. The vote for the Republican presidential candidate rose a comparatively small 4 percent from 39 to 43. The third-party candidacy of George Wallace made up the difference. Insofar as the matter can be determined at all, almost all of Wallace's votes came from people who nominally considered themselves Democrats but who, in his absence, would have given more of their votes to Nixon than to Humphrey. The primary effect of the Wallace candidacy, therefore, was to decrease slightly Nixon's margin of victory.[22]

Despite the unusually severe defections in 1968 from the Democratic party at the presidential level, the party label continued to exert its customary force at state and local levels. The result in elections for the House of Representatives was virtually a standoff. The *Congressional Quarterly* shows that where the Democrats had occupied 57.7 percent of the legislative seats in the state capitols throughout the nation before the election, afterwards they retained virtually the same proportion despite the fact that there were contests of some kind in forty-three states.[23] While there is ample evidence that people defected from the Democratic candidate in large numbers, it was premature—and in fact probably incorrect—to say that they had abandoned their party for good.

The strong Democratic recovery in the 1970 election bore this out. In the Senate, the very large Democratic class of 1958—first elected in a Republican recession and reelected in the Goldwater landslide—finally faced a reasonably normal electoral situation. They sustained a net loss of only two seats. Meanwhile, in the House, the Democrats picked up nine seats. They might have done better, but Nixon's 1968 coattails were nonexistent, and it is presidential coattail victories every four years that more than any other factor produces the decline in House seats held by the president's party in the next midterm election. In 1970 Democrats also registered dramatic gains in state elections, gaining eleven governors.

In the face of a Republican presidential victory of overwhelming proportions in 1972, the Democrats nearly held their own in Congress, actually gaining two Senate seats and losing only twelve House seats—including six in the South, where party alignments have been changing. In the 1974 midterm election, with the Watergate scandals of the Nixon administration much in the air, and without McGovern at the top of the ticket to stave off a landslide, Democrats won an enormous victory, gaining forty-three seats in the House, five governor's seats, and four Senate seats. The Democratic party has won victories of this range and depth fairly frequently over the past two decades, in 1958, 1964, and 1974. Democratic landslides defeat Republicans all up and down the ticket. Republican landslides, on the other hand, when they occur, appear to be more highly particularized to a single race. Eisenhower can overwhelm Stevenson as in 1956, Nixon can defeat McGovern as in 1972, but these results do not carry over to help the Republican party generally, and any gains frequently are obliterated by the very next election. This is a chronic difficulty of the minority party, even in a reasonably competitive two-party system.

In 1980, the Republicans did so well in electing Ronald Reagan over Jimmy Carter that it was widely assumed that at long last a party realignment was about to occur.[24] This assessment proved to be quite wrong, but it was understandable that such an idea should have arisen. After all, virtually every presidential election brings with it something anomalous, unusual, novel, and hence interesting in the way events sort themselves out. Afterward, pundits and political analysts set about patting and palpating the body politic, trying to discover what, if anything, has really changed. Usually, the correct answer is not much. The political habits of voting Americans, while subject to mood swings, are pretty stable on the whole. The same old parties—Democrats and Republicans since 1860—divide up most of the political offices. Every once in a great while, however—the 1860s, the 1890s, and the 1930s are examples—for one reason or another the very terrain shifts and recontours itself under the political parties, and we have a significant party realignment: new, more or less permanent, majorities and minorities, a new sort of ideological consensus, new participants in politics, or all three.

Partisan realignments are such intellectually stimulating events that it is no wonder that political observers are awaiting the next one with some impatience. And so, of course, are hopeful beneficiaries of the new dispensation. So it should come as no surprise even to the most casual follower of American politics that the 1980 election, like so many of its predecessors, would provoke at least a few political analysts to announce a party realignment, and that the definitive demise of the party system dominated by the New Deal coalition was finally at hand. All those doomsaying prophets who hoisted their umbrellas in vain way back during the Eisenhower years, waiting for the sky to fall on the Democrats, could at long last hear the pitter-patter of something or other just above their heads.

An elected incumbent president, for the first time since Herbert Hoover in 1932, had been defeated for a second term of office. And, even more surprisingly, the Senate, after twenty-six years, had a Republican majority. "For the first time in a generation," David Broder wrote in the *Washington*

Post, "it is sensible to ask whether we might be entering a new political era
—an era of Republican dominance."[25]

The sort of answer one might give to such a question is not wholly devoid
of significance in the world of partisan politics. If it can plausibly be argued
that a realignment has taken place, then presumably it can be claimed that
the legislative program of the president is, as an attempt to fulfill an electoral
mandate, the most accurate available translation into law and public policy
of an authentic majority sentiment among the people at large. This programmatic mandate is something grander and more impressive than merely the
entitlement to hold office: that sort of entitlement is something a president
gets by winning the election, by whatever margin, in the Electoral College.
The winner of a programmatic mandate, on the other hand, has a talking
point of considerable weight in the continuing process of persuasion that goes
on as the president interacts with the people whose cooperation he needs to
accomplish his goals. Armed with a mandate, a president can speak with a
stronger voice in setting the terms for the consideration of legislative alternatives. Without a secure mandate, presidents must give ground to other elected
officials, to the claims of tradition, of expertise, of political expediency.

So the discussion of party realignment in the 1980 election carried some
political freight along with it and was no mere academic exercise. The beliefs
of political actors about the proper interpretation of the electoral results will
color the ways in which they treat one another in Washington. The impressive legislative victories won by President Reagan during his first year in
office suggested that more than a few politicians were convinced that the 1980
elections had indeed produced what the president's poll taker, Richard
Wirthlin, labeled "a political Mount Saint Helens."[26] Steven V. Roberts of
the *New York Times* located the legislative successes of President Reagan's
first year in his "overwhelming electoral victory, and the outpouring of public
support for his policies generated by a politically savvy White House."[27]

The evidence for party realignment or for the emergence of a new majority backing the president's program was, however, extremely thin. It was
based on, at most, four considerations: (1) the size of Mr. Reagan's victory,
(2) the unexpectedness of Mr. Reagan's margin of victory, (3) the results in
the Senate, and (4) the results in the House of Representatives. None of these
could stand much scrutiny as a basis for believing that the 1980 election
caused a realignment within the electorate.

While it is true that Governor Reagan defeated President Carter for the
presidency by an overwhelming landslide in the Electoral College, 489 votes
to 49, the actual numbers of voters for the two candidates—43.9 million to

35.5 million—were much closer, or, as percentages of the two-party vote, 55 percent to 45 percent. The electoral vote landslide was the third biggest in the twentieth century, but in percentage of the two-party vote ten other twentieth-century presidential elections gave their winners more impressive majorities.

Up until election day, most public opinion analysts were declaring the 1980 presidential election too close to call. Thus the size of Reagan's margin of victory was undoubtedly surprising to some observers, leading them to exaggerate its magnitude, and to mistrust their own grasp of the contours of public opinion. There were, however, perfectly plausible explanations for the discrepancy between poll results a week before the election and results of the election itself. Two such explanations were (1) that as has been true periodically in the past (as, for example, in 1976 or 1948) some larger-than-usual number of voters and hence poll respondents could have made up their minds relatively late in the campaign,[28] and (2) that predictions by poll analysts of the actual turnout of their respondents were flawed because they failed to register the extent to which voters on one side—supporters of President Carter—would eventually decide not to vote.[29]

In the end, 46 percent of the age-eligible population did not vote for president, a percentage of stay-at-homes larger than in any election since 1948. And, of course, there was a sizable third-party vote, constituting 4.4 percent of the age-eligible population, or 5.7 million votes.

Thus, as a proportion of all age-eligible voters, 27 percent voted for Ronald Reagan for president, while 73 percent did not. This impaired President Reagan's right to govern not one whit, but it did, of course, bear significantly on the resources of popularity on which he might expect to draw. It is well known that a president's popularity is ordinarily a wasting asset, and thus where a president begins his inexorable downward slide plays a part in determining how popular he is at any later stage.[30] President Reagan began with a modest 51 percent of respondents approving of his conduct of the presidency. By the fourteenth month of his presidency, 46 percent of the voters believed he was doing a satisfactory job, as compared with at least 50 percent for each of his five most recent elected predecessors. As compared with other presidents, Mr. Reagan has maintained a relatively unfavorable position throughout his term of office, despite claims that his talent at explaining his views over television was unusually advantageous to him, and even more remarkably, in spite of whatever sympathetic surge of good will was generated by the attempt on his life on March 30, 1981.[31]

The next ground for the belief that the 1980 election constituted a significant break with the past was the fact that the United States Senate changed hands and brought in a Republican majority. Because Republican presidential landslides have generally failed to resonate farther down the ticket, as in 1972 and 1956, the fact that at the senatorial level the Republicans did well in 1980 takes on significance. Nine Democratic incumbents lost in the general election to Republicans, and no Republican incumbents lost to Democrats. Out of nine open seats, seven went Republican. There was a Republican gain in the Senate of twelve seats, for an overall majority of 53 to 47 seats.

Some of the defeated senators were well-known liberals: Church of Idaho, Bayh of Indiana, Culver of Iowa, McGovern of South Dakota, and Nelson of Wisconsin were all beaten by conservative Republican members of the House running strongly conservative campaigns. This led David Broder to comment:

> The election was plainly more than a repudiation of Jimmy Carter. . . . [W]as there an ideological message in the 1980 vote? There sure was . . . you had to be dense to miss . . . a flat-out repudiation of basic economic, diplomatic, and social policies of the reigning Democratic liberalism.[32]

The electoral results were actually more mixed ideologically. While the Republican gains were remarkable, seven liberal Democratic senators were reelected, some of them by very wide margins. Some conservatives—notably Barry Goldwater in Arizona—experienced great difficulty in holding their seats. Some incoming Republicans—Rudman of New Hampshire, Gorton of Washington—while quite possibly not as liberal as the Democrats they replaced, campaigned not as conservatives but as moderates. In Pennsylvania, the Republican senatorial candidate was more liberal than the Democratic one. And for two open Senate seats, in Illinois and Connecticut, Democrats running as liberals beat more conservative Republicans.

More important for the underlying argument is the fact that the change in the ideological and party balance of the Senate indicated no great surge at the level of voters. By aggregating the vote totals for thirty-three Senate seats, and excluding the vote for Democratic incumbent Russell Long of Louisiana, who ran unopposed, we discover that 3 million more votes were cast for Democratic than Republican candidates.

How can this have happened? Senatorial electorates, following state boundaries, are of greatly unequal size. On the whole, Republicans won the closely contested races, and won in some very small states—New Hampshire,

Idaho, Utah, the Dakotas, Nevada—while Democrats won most of the senatorial landslides, notably in California, where Alan Cranston was reelected by a margin of 1.6 million votes. Of the fifteen races where the winner received 55 percent of the vote or more, eight were won by Democrats. In the eighteen close races where the winner got less than 55 percent of the vote, fifteen were won by Republicans.

The Reagan landslide failed to overturn the Democratic majority in the House of Representatives, but it did reduce that majority by thirty-three seats, from 276 Democrats to 243 out of 435 seats. The party balance in the House reverted to the identical number—243 Democrats to 192 Republicans —as occurred after the Nixon hairbreadth 1968 victory over Hubert Humphrey, which nobody mistook for a realignment. That was just one Democratic seat less than was produced by the 1972 Nixon landslide against McGovern, which was also not a realignment. In the midterm elections of 1970 and 1974, the Democrats picked up twelve and forty-seven seats, respectively. In the next presidential election, the old New Deal coalition elected Jimmy Carter president and 292 Democrats to the House. As Robert Axelrod's research showed:

> For the Democrats, the New Deal Coalition made a comeback in 1976. For the first time since the Johnson landslide of 1964, the Democrats got a majority of the votes from each of the six diverse majorities which make up their traditional coalition: the poor, blacks, union families, Catholics, southerners, and city dwellers.[33]

In the context of the previous few elections, what the House electoral results of 1980 showed was a set of outcomes well within normal expectations, not anything remotely approaching a realignment.

We have so far considered evidence allegedly favoring the proposition that the 1980 election was the occasion of a fundamental party realignment in which President Reagan received a programmatic mandate. We must conclude that this evidence is weak if not contradictory to that argument.

A fair amount of other evidence also weighs heavily against the realignment hypothesis. This is information gathered from public opinion surveys about such matters as (1) policy agreement of the electorate with conservative positions espoused by President Reagan, (2) reasons given by Reagan voters for their presidential choice, (3) patterns of voting defection by nonvoters, (4) trends in general party identification, and (5) the voting behavior of new voters. All five of these indicators pointed in the direction of no realignment.

Table 4.2
Senate Seats by Margin of Victory, 1980 Election

	Democrats	Republicans	Winner's Percent of Vote
1	Inouye* (H.)		78%
2		Garn* (Utah)	74
3	Hollings* (S.C.)		72
4		Andrews (N.D.)	71
5	Glenn* (Ohio)		71
6		Mathias* (Md.)	66
7	Ford* (Ky.)		65
8		Dole* (Kans.)	64
9	Cranston* (Ca.)		59
10	Bumpers* (Ark.)		59
11		Laxalt* (Nev.)	58
12		Abdnor (S.D.)	58
13	Dodd (Conn.)		57
14	Dixon (Ill.)		56
15		Murkowski (Alas.)	55
16		Quayle (Ind.)	54
17		Grassley (Iowa)	54
18		Gorton (Wash.)	54
19		Nickles (Ok.)	52
20		Packwood* (Or.)	52
21	Eagleton* (Mo.)		52
22		Rudman (N.H.)	52
23		Denton (Ala.)	51
24		Spector (Pa.)	51
25	Hart* (Col.)		51
26		Hawkins (Fl.)	51
27		Mattingly (Ga.)	51
28	Leahy* (Vt.)		51
29		Kasten (Wisc.)	51
30		Goldwater* (Az.)	50
31		Symms (Id.)	50
32		East (N.C.)	50
33		D'Amato (N.Y.)	45

*indicates incumbent

They deserve to be taken with especial seriousness because they reflect results from many different surveys done under a variety of auspices, both commercial and academic.

Since 1937 or thereabouts, public opinion polls have been asking voters about their party affiliations. The long-term stability of the responses has been notable. There seems to be no room for doubt that over the four-and-a-half-decade period for which such figures exist, persons claiming identification with the Democrats have outnumbered Republicans in the general population, and by large numbers. This would surprise nobody who has been attentive to election results over this same stretch of years. Only twice in the entire generation since Franklin Roosevelt's first election in 1932—after the elections of 1946 and 1952—have the Republicans controlled both houses of Congress. When landslides have favored Democrats—for example, in 1934, 1936, 1958, 1964, and 1974—massive Democratic majorities have resulted in Congress, and shock waves have been felt farther down on the ticket; for example, in state assemblies. After the 1980 elections, however, looking at the system from the bottom up, the Republicans got no such advantage. Although Republicans gained some seats, the Democrats were still comfortably ahead, with 4,497 state legislature seats, compared with 2,918 for the Republicans. And Democrats controlled sixty-three state assemblies, compared with thirty-four controlled by Republicans.

A short time after the election, party identifications seemed to be leaning toward the Republicans. The effect proved to be short-lived, more likely than not the result of respondents making a momentary choice to join what the newspapers were telling them was a 1980 bandwagon. This phenomenon was similar to the striking effect of President Kennedy's assassination on voters' recollections of the way they had voted in the 1960 election. In any event, by November 1981 the readings on party identification were back to about the way they had been all along: 45 percent Democrats, 27 percent Republicans, the rest undecided or independent.

If the presidential mandate is interpreted not as a partisan but as an ideological matter, then presumably the relevant attitudes in the population at large would have less to do with party affiliation than with matters of public policy—government spending, in particular—though conceivably various "life-style" issues might also play a part in causing a party realignment. Once again the available numbers sustained no such interpretation. To the contrary, in the first survey by Louis Harris and ABC News after President Reagan won the election, there were majorities for the anti-Reagan position on such social issues as abortion, affirmative action, handgun registration, and the Equal Rights Amendment. On government spending, one particularly thoroughgoing National Opinion Research Center poll near to the election, reported by Everett Ladd, illustrates what many surveys showed: a structure of public attitudes in and around 1980 similar to those visible for many years.[34] This means attitudes sympathetic to defense spending, negative on welfare and foreign aid, and generally supportive of high levels of government activity in other areas. No evidence of realignment there.

☆ Party Realignment and the 1980 Election

Theory about party realignment is sufficiently well developed in political science to have produced at least two contending schools of thought about the dynamics of change in the general population when realignments occur.

Table 4.3
Public Opinion on Public Spending, 1980

Majorities say we are spending

Too little on		Too little or about the right amount on		Too much on	
Halting crime	(72%)	Halting crime	(94%)	Foreign aid	(74%)
Drug addiction	(65%)	Drug addiction	(92%)	Welfare	(59%)
Defense	(60%)	Health	(92%)		
Health	(57%)	Education	(89%)		
Education	(55%)	Defense	(88%)		
The environment	(51%)	The environment	(84%)		
		Big cities	(76%)		
		Blacks	(74%)		
		Space exploration	(57%)		

QUESTION: "We are faced with many problems in this country, none of which can be solved easily or inexpensively. I'm going to name some of these problems, and for each one I'd like you to tell me whether you think we're spending too much money on it, too little money, or about the right amount. First [an item is read], are we spending too much, too little, or about the right amount on [the item]? (A) Space exploration program (B) Improving and protecting the environment (C) Improving and protecting the nation's health (D) Solving the problems of the big cities (E) Halting the rising crime rate (F) Dealing with drug addiction (G) Improving the nation's education system (H) Improving the conditions of Blacks (I) The military, armaments and defense (J) Foreign aid (K) Welfare."

SOURCE: 1980 General Social Survey, National Opinion Research Center, University of Chicago, Chicago, Ill.

One school, which seems to have the weaker argument, says that party realignments are caused by voters changing their minds, and, over time, their party affiliations come into conformity with their commitments on issues.[35] According to this school, a 1980 realignment ought to have been visible in the defections of conservative Democrats who made a down payment on what in due course would have been a conversion to regular Republican loyalty.

In order for this argument to work with 1980 data, it ought to be possible to show a fair amount of ideologically motivated voting. In light of the Reagan victory, and the overall figures on party identification, it should not be difficult to uncover a sizable population of Democratic defectors on the presidential vote. But the question remains: why did they defect?

A large CBS-*New York Times* exit poll on election day provided some information. Almost 13,000 voters were asked as they left their polling places why they had voted as they had voted. Reasons given by Reagan voters did not make them sound like right-wing ideologues: only 11 percent said they voted for Reagan because he was conservative.[36]

The more thorough Michigan survey does suggest, however, that self-identified conservative Democrats were more likely to vote for Reagan than those who said they were liberals.[37] This makes sense: Reagan was, after all, the more conservative candidate. But it remained to be seen whether Reagan could make permanent converts of them.

Another theory of party realignment emphasizes not conversion of voters from one party to another but mobilization of previously quiescent nonvoters.[38] On the face of it, any election in which there is low turnout, as was the case in 1980, is an unlikely realigning election through the workings of this theory, simply because it is large numbers of new voters who are supposed to do the realigning of the parties. Nevertheless, it is worth a look at new voters to see whether they were overwhelmingly Reagan voters. The short answer is that evidently they were not.

The national sample survey that we use for this analysis—the best one available for this purpose—is the one executed by the University of Michigan for a nationwide consortium of academic users. It gives no consolidated picture of first-time voters, but such a picture can be constructed out of three different partial indicators: (1) respondents who voted for the first time by reason of age; (2) respondents who recalled that they did not vote in the last election; and (3) respondents who recalled not voting in any previous elections.

The distribution of the presidential votes of these 1980 voters when viewed alone certainly does not look like a basis for realignment: mildly Democratic voting with a strong John Anderson showing among young voters, mildly Republican voting among the rest. It is useful in addition to compare these voting distributions with figures from like populations in three other years: 1972, when Richard Nixon beat George McGovern in a landslide that nobody interpreted as a realignment: 1976, a Democratic year in which the New Deal coalition reemerged; and 1964, the last Democratic landslide year, which gives us a glimpse of what a real landslide looks like in figures of this sort. We know that 1972 was not the harbinger of a realignment. The 1980 figures rather resemble the 1972 figures. In 1976, no landslide year, the Democrats did rather better with first-time voters than the Republicans did in either of their landslides. And compared with Johnson's victory over Goldwater in 1964, the 1980 figures on first-time presidential voting do not even look like a landslide, never mind a realignment.

Table 4.4
Presidential Race

1. First-time voters (age)

	1980	1976	1972	1964
Republican	38.2%	41.7%	49.3%	22.4%
Democratic	41.8	50.0	50.2	77.6
(Anderson	18.2)			

2. Didn't vote in previous election

	1980	1976	1972	1964
Republican	50.0%	25.7%	51.4%	22.1%
Democratic	43.2	66.1	45.9	77.9
(Anderson	4.5)			

3. Didn't vote in previous elections

	1980	1976	1972	1964
Republican	45.7%	35.3%	53.5%	12.5%
Democratic	34.3	62.7	43.7	87.5
(Anderson	11.4)			

QUESTION: Who did you vote for in the election for President?

SOURCE: 1980 American National Election Study, Center for Political Studies, University of Michigan.

So what did happen in the 1980 election? If it was not a realignment, why did the voters elect Ronald Reagan? Republican voters, no doubt, voted for him because he was a Republican, and in many cases because they agreed with him about politics. As the party identification figures show, Republicans alone normally do not field enough voters to elect anybody president. Of the Reagan voters who gave reasons at the exit poll, 38 percent, by far the largest number, could best be interpreted as unhappy with the presidency of Jimmy Carter. As William Schneider pointed out, only 37 percent of the voters who voted for Carter in 1976 voted for him again in 1980.[39] By comparison, Reagan got 67 percent of all those who voted for Gerald Ford in 1976. A huge number—28 percent of those voting for Carter in 1976—stayed home in 1980 and did not vote for president at all.

Thus the best short answer to what happened in 1980, for those who like short answers, was that it was a referendum not on Ronald Reagan or his campaign promises, but on Jimmy Carter. The evidence for a conservative mandate, or for a party realignment, cannot be squeezed out of the best available evidence.

In the twenty years since the first edition of *Presidential Elections,* far more changes have taken place in the life-styles of Americans than many observers have appreciated. And these changes are bound to have political effects. Consider, for example, the civil rights movement, women's liberation, widespread concern over technological danger, or the decline in the effectiveness of large-scale institutions from trade unions to the big churches to political parties. The allegiances of the past, like party identification, as well as the necessary limits to the choices that mass electorates can make, have dampened the political effects of social change. Thus it is especially worthwhile to speculate about developments that may have considerable future importance but have not yet manifested themselves with sufficient force or clarity to command general assent.

In a book in progress, Samuel Popkin gives special attention to changes in the political attitudes of women and young people. Once upon a time women were more Republican than men, a phenomenon casually attributed to their concern with conservative family values and their supposed deference to authority. Young people were presumed to be liberal and to become progressively more conservative as they grew older. Do these relationships still hold true?

During Dwight D. Eisenhower's presidency women voted a good 5 percent more Republican than men. They gave Richard Nixon 6 percent more of their votes than they gave to John Kennedy, his Democratic opponent in

1960. Since then, however, they have voted progressively more Democratic, to the point that, in 1980, Popkin argues there were two elections: one in which Reagan beat Carter fifty-six to thirty-six among men and a much closer election among women that Reagan won 48 percent to 43 percent, five versus twenty points. Indeed, Gerald Ford and Richard Nixon did better with women than Reagan did. Why?

Popkin finds evidence that women cared more about certain issues than men. One was war and peace in which Reagan was seen as more likely to be militant. Some other issues, according to Popkin, are " 'eco-fear' . . . radiation, cancer, . . . additives, contaminants, hazardous waste. . . ." The gender gap on this complex of concerns, he thinks, is as large as 20 percent in various polls. And, he continues,

> The third aspect of this long term reorientation of women and men to the political parties is that women are personally much more concerned than men about the social budget. This heightened concern reflects changes in women's lives over the last 20 years. The proportion of women in the labor force has doubled since 1960. Today a majority of American women are working part time or full time, and over their lifespan, virtually all young women today expect to be part of the labor force either before or after they have their children. Women are much more concerned about the working poor; many of the working poor are women who are left with the children after the divorce.
>
> Further, . . . women are concerned about the small job that could be easily automated and are feeling particularly vulnerable today to technological innovation. Thus, women in general are a little more concerned about the budget cuts than men as working poor and as workers worried that technology could cost them their job.[40]

In 1952 one out of seven voters was over sixty-five. Today the ratio is down to one out of five and narrowing. Concern over Social Security and other aid to the elderly, Popkin believes, will impel this age group to vote more Democratic. But young people are cross-pressured. On one side, they are fiscally conservative, seeing themselves as paying for these programs. Those who pay and those who receive have different interests. On the other side, they would like to share in the governmental largesse with programs like tuition loans at low rates of interest. Candidates who are socially liberal and fiscally conservative, like John Anderson or Jerry Brown, or proponents of a minimum state, should, Popkin thinks, appeal to the young.[41]

Among the more interesting signs of change has been what Ladd calls the "dealignment" of the American electorate, a phenomenon signifying that the ethnic, economic class, and regional tendencies of voters since the New Deal period of the 1930s, from which analysts are used to taking their bearings, have shifted markedly. Voters of Irish and Italian ancestry who used to go Democratic and those of German and English stock who tended to be Republican now are much closer together in their preferences for presidential candidates. Whereas Protestants used to vote from 15 to 20 percent more Republican than Democratic, the difference narrowed to 11 percent in 1976 and 7 percent in 1980. During the post-New Deal era manual workers and business and professional people were about 18 to 20 points apart in their Democratic and Republican proclivities. In 1980, the difference had shrunk to 8 percent, with business and professional voters just 5 percent more and manual workers merely 3 percent less for Reagan than the rest of the country. One looks in vain for regional differences in 1980. Support for the Democratic party among white voters around the country ranged from a low of 32 percent in the West to a high of 36 percent in the North Central states. Only the racial-ethnic cleavage, notably among blacks and Hispanics, remains strong and possibly growing. The difference between a realignment and a dealignment is that in the former new cleavages arise to replace the old, but in the latter past cleavages are diminished without new ones necessarily taking their place.[42] This can be a good sign: people are no longer voting their class, region, or religion but are taking a more reasoned look at the parties and candidates. This can be bad; politicians can no longer count on stable support from different parts of the electorate. To govern presidents need to form and maintain coalitions, but if they have to do this on an ad hoc basis, they are less likely to be successful. This can be confusing in that both observers and politicians may be missing the trends that will prove important in the future.

The different positions of black and Hispanic voters pose interesting dilemmas for these groups and for the major political parties. Black people are largely Democratic in their vote, though their turnout is still low. This makes them vitally important to the Democratic party. However, if black voters, as the political phrase has it, "have nowhere to go," their bargaining power is reduced. That is why talk is heard about running a black candidate for president, not in the expectation of victory, but as a means of putting pressure on Democrats in Congress and on Democratic candidates for the presidential nomination to undertake appropriate actions and pledges so that the "black vote" will no longer be taken for granted. Aside from the evident divisiveness of running a racially based candidate, this strategy may backfire; black voters might actually face a choice between one of their own, whom some would want to support lest their threat be perceived as hollow, and taking responsibility for the defeat of a Democratic candidate. Such a defeat would indeed make their threat good, but it would also perpetuate Republican rule with consequences presumably detrimental to their economic interests.

Republican party leaders would very much like greater black support. A party that wants to win and to govern must draw support from all sectors of the population. Yet the policy preferences of black leaders for higher federal spending on social welfare conflict with the minimal government stance of the Republican party. There are two possible routes to accommodation: one is that Republicans convince some black voters that they will be better off with policies that emphasize growth of the private sector; the other is that the Republican party moderate its position at the cost of alienating some of its present supporters. It cannot be desirable for the nation to have party differences reinforce racial cleavages.

The position of Hispanics is especially delicate. Shall they play the part of an aggrieved ethnic group, competing with black groups for, if this is not a contradiction in terms, the position of favored oppressed minority? Or shall they seek to join the mainstream, dividing their loyalties, much as Samuel Gompers advised labor early in this century, by trying to reward their friends and punish their enemies? Hispanics are the fastest growing ethnic group, adding to their population by high birth rates and a considerable "undocumented" immigration from Mexico in particular and Latin America in general. They could become 20 percent of the potential electorate, and their choice may well be a fateful one.

And not only for them. For the Republicans to get less than 10 or 15 percent of the black vote is bad enough; for the same situation to repeat itself with Hispanics would be catastrophic. If the party could still win the presidency under these circumstances, which would be most unlikely, it would have divided the nation on racial-ethnic grounds.[43] More likely, however, this is a losing strategy.

☆ Theory and Action

The contents of election campaigns appear to be largely opportunistic. The swiftly changing nature of events makes it unwise for candidates to lay down all-embracing rules for campaigning which cannot meet special situations as they arise. A candidate may prepare for battle on one front and discover that the movement of events forces him to fight on another. Yet on closer examination, it is evident that the political strategist has to rely on some sort of theory about the probable behavior of large groups of voters under a few likely conditions. For there are too many millions of voters and too many thousands of possible events to deal with each as a separate category. Keynes pointed out years ago, quite rightly, that those among us, including politicians, who most loudly proclaim their avoidance of theory are generally the victims of some long-dead economist or philosopher whose assumptions they have unknowingly assimilated. The candidates must simplify their picture of the political world or its full complexity will paralyze them; the only question is whether or not their theories, both explicit and implicit, will prove helpful to them.

What kind of organization shall they use or construct? Where shall they campaign? How much time shall they allocate to the various regions and states? What kinds of appeals shall they make to what voting groups? How specific shall they be in their policy proposals? What kind of personal impression shall they seek to create or reinforce? How far should they go in castigating the opposition? These are the kinds of strategic questions for which presidential candidates need answers—answers that necessarily vary depending on their party affiliations, their personal attributes, whether they are in or out of office, and on targets of opportunity that come up in the course of current events. Let us take up each of these questions in turn, taking care to specify the different problems faced by "ins" and "outs" and by Democrats and Republicans. For purposes of illustration, we shall turn often to the past few elections.

☆ "Ins" and "Outs"

While the incumbent may have disadvantages to offset some of his advantages, as we saw in Chapter 2, the challenger faces his own set of problems. He may not be well known and may find that much of his effort must be devoted to publicizing himself. All the while, the president is getting reams of free publicity and is in a position to create major news by the things he does—a tariff on imported oil, proposals for lowering taxes, impounding and/or releasing billions for highways and public works.[44] Or the incumbent may play president for the press without risking exposure on issues. Gerald

Ford's chief of staff in 1976 admitted this made things easy for his candidate. "Let's face it," he said, "we played to television's problems. We knew that their measure of fair treatment was equal time. So we would go out in the Rose Garden and say nothing—just sign a bill—and we'd get the coverage."[45]

The candidate aspiring to office may find that he lacks information, which puts him at a disadvantage in discussing foreign policy and defense issues. Frequently, the president offers as a matter of courtesy, or strategy, to supply both party nominees, or his opponent, with regular briefings. The out-party candidate may deliberately keep from finding out too much, however, for fear that he be held back in his criticism by an implied pledge not to use information the president has furnished to him. Perhaps the major advantage the challenger possesses is his ability to criticize policies freely and sometimes in exaggerated terms, whereas the incumbent is often restrained by his current official responsibilities from talking too much about them. Obligations to other nations, for example, may restrain a president from talking about changes in foreign policy or from tipping his hand in situations like Vietnam or the Middle East. Knowing too much is not necessarily helpful if inside information leads one to lose the forest for the trees. Ordinary citizens would have no difficulty telling a national television audience that the Soviet Union has armed forces in and exerts considerable control over Poland. President Ford, with other relevant but confidential things on his mind when he debated Jimmy Carter, answered differently and caused a furor.[46]

☆ Organizations and Accidents

While the incumbent has a going organization, molded and tested through his years in office, the challenger has to build one piecemeal as he goes along in the frantic days of the campaign when there is never enough time to do everything that has to be done. Should he have an executive of his own run the show without much of a nod to the professionals of the state parties or the national committee? They may resist, if not sabotage, his efforts. And, if he gets into trouble later, as Nixon discovered, they may abandon him who scorned them. Should he enlist the cooperation of the old party workers, knowing that he may thereby lose some control over his campaign? Should there be two centers of campaigning with the inevitable duplication and problems of coordination? There is apparently no costless solution to this problem. There always seems to be grumbling from party professionals and the candidate's own people about their relationship.

All candidates seek special volunteer organizations to help attract voters who prefer not to associate themselves with the party organizations. The distaste with which some middle- and upper-class people regard party organizations is difficult to overcome. It is easier to construct new organizations in which they can feel ennobled by direct attachment to the candidate rather than (as they may feel) associating with a group of vulgar politicians. The danger here is that the volunteer organizations will take on lives of their own and attempt to dictate strategy and policy to the candidates. The candidates need the volunteers, but it is advisable for candidates to follow the lead set by John Kennedy in keeping tight reins on them, thus assuring reasonable coordination of efforts and avoiding the possibility of capture.

The mechanics of electioneering are no simple matter; they cannot be entrusted wholly to amateurs. Not only must the candidate get to his various speaking engagements on time, but he also needs to have some good idea of the audience he is addressing and what kind of approach to take. In the hurly-burly of the campaign, where issues and plans may change from day to day, where yesterday's ideas may have to make room for today's problems, where changes of schedule are made in response to the opportunities and dangers suggested by private and public polls, a poor organization can be severely damaging. The troubles of Adlai Stevenson present a case in point. His apparent distaste for the niceties of organization in 1956 hurt him badly. He was excessively rushed going from one place to another and thus lost the valuable assets of composure and thoughtfulness which should have been his stock-in-trade. If he continually made speeches that were inappropriate for his audiences, it may have been because he was badly informed about who his audience would be, not because he was talking "over people's heads." For instance, once during the 1956 campaign he made a speech in New Haven redolent with allusions to Yale and Princeton, with punch lines depending on knowledge of what the "subjunctive" was, to an audience that happened to be composed largely of old-time Democratic party workers from around Connecticut.[47] In 1976, Republican vice-presidential candidate Bob Dole did especially badly in his debate with Walter Mondale because he was too aware of his immediate audience—a mixed group of savvy partisans who enjoyed his inside jokes and partisan jibes—and forgot that his main impression, the one that counted, would be made to the relatively unsophisticated television audience.

In 1972, because George McGovern and his staff were tired, and busy preparing for the challenge to their California delegates, they did not check as carefully as they might have into their vice-presidential nominee's background. To be sure, some mix-ups, if not a few outright fiascoes, are inevitable given the frantic pace and the pressure of time. Resilience is not the least qualification of a presidential candidate.

An example of the risks and rewards of a special campaign organization are illustrated by President Nixon's decision in 1972 to bypass entirely the Republican party in setting up his Committee to Reelect the President. This comported with Nixon's desire to insulate himself as much as possible from the fortunes of the Republican party. On behalf of an incumbent president, Maurice Stans, Herbert Kalmbach, and others had no difficulty raising enormous amounts of money. Some estimates of the total take range up to $60 million.[48] Since 1972, businessmen whose firms are in regulated industries have testified that they gave campaign contributions in part to protect themselves and their companies against adverse decisions of the government, and some of them pleaded guilty to charges of illegally contributing to Nixon's campaign chest as an ordinary corporate expense. At the Committee to Reelect the President (CREEP), meanwhile, persons of low character and no common sense devised plans to spend the gross surpluses the President's fundraisers were supplying. One such plan has become famous, since it entailed bugging the headquarters of the Democratic National Committee, the botching of which led to the President's near-impeachment and to the unraveling of the Nixon presidency.

Two little-noticed facts about the CREEP operation deserve mention here. The first is that by raising money in this fashion, President Nixon starved many other Republican candidates who had to rely on many of the same sources for cash. The second is that apparently the President and his employees had no intention of sharing the proceeds with other Republicans. Yet when Nixon's downfall came, he dragged numerous Republicans down with him, at a minimum by spoiling the party's chances at the next election. This illustrates the profound stake political parties have in the caliber of their presidential candidates.

☆ Where to Campaign

In deciding where to campaign, the candidates are aided by distinctive features of the national political structure that go a long way toward giving them guidance. They know that it is not votes as such that matter but rather electoral votes, which are counted on a state-by-state basis. The candidate who wins by a small plurality in a state gains all of that state's electoral votes.

The candidates realize that a huge margin of victory in a state with a handful of electoral votes will not do them nearly as much good as a bare plurality in states like New York and California, with large numbers of electoral votes. So their first guideline is evident: campaign in states with large electoral votes. There is not much point, however, in campaigning in states where they know they are bound to win or to lose. Thus, states that almost always go for a particular party receive less attention. Hence, the original guideline may be modified to read: campaign in states with large electoral votes which are doubtful. In practice, a "doubtful" state is one where there is a good chance for either party to capture the state. Politicians usually gauge this chance by the extent to which the state has delivered victories to both parties within recent memory. Candidates of both parties thus spend more time in New York, Ohio, Illinois, Pennsylvania, Texas, and California than they do elsewhere. Even if one or two one-party states should change in one election, the likelihood of such an event is too slim and the payoff in terms of electoral votes too meager to justify extensive campaigning when time might better be spent elsewhere. As the campaign wears on, the candidates take soundings from the opinion polls and are likely to redouble their efforts in states where they believe a personal visit might turn the tide.

In 1976 Hamilton Jordan had these matters worked out to mathematical extremes—awarding points to states based on these sorts of considerations, and then allocating campaign days to each of them for his candidate, Jimmy Carter, the vice-presidential candidate, and members of the Carter family.[49]

Here we once again come across the pervasive problem of uncertainty. No one really knows how much value in changed votes or turnout is gained by personal visits to a particular state. By the time the campaign is under way, most voters have made up their minds.[50] Opponents of the candidate are unlikely to go to see him anyway and one wonders what a glimpse in a motorcade will do to influence a potential voter. Yet no one is absolutely certain that whistle-stop methods produce no useful result. Visiting various localities may serve to increase publicity because many of the media of communication are geared to "local" events. It also provides an opportunity to stress issues like energy or unemployment that may be of special significance to citizens in a given region. Party activists may be energized by a look at or a handshake with the candidate. New alliances, such as the one that emerged in 1964 between Goldwater and many long-time Democratic sectors of the Deep South, can be solidified. So rather than let the opportunity pass, the candidates usually decide to take no chances and get out on the hustings. They hedge against uncertainty by doing all they can.

Consider the case of John Kennedy in Ohio. He traversed that pivotal state several times in the 1960 campaign and exerted great physical effort in getting himself seen traveling there. But when the votes were counted, he found himself on the short end. The future president professed to be annoyed and stumped at why this happened. An analysis of the voting returns showed that Kennedy's vote was correlated with the percentage of Catholic population in the various counties.[51] Kennedy made a considerable improvement over the Democratic showing in 1956, but that was not enough to win. Despite evidence of this kind, which suggests that personal appearances may well be overwhelmed by other factors, visits to localities will undoubtedly continue. Who can say, to take a contrary instance, that Kennedy's visit to Illinois did not provide the bare margin of a few thousand votes necessary for victory?

There was a time when presidential nominees faced the serious choice of whether to conduct a "front porch" campaign or to get out and meet the people. A candidate like Warren Harding, who his sponsors felt would put his foot in his mouth every time he spoke, was well advised to stay home. More hardy souls, like William Jennings Bryan, took off in all directions only to discover that to be seen was not necessarily to be loved. An underdog, like Harry Truman in 1948, goes out to meet the people because he is so far behind. A favored candidate, like Thomas Dewey in 1948, goes out to meet the people to avoid being accused of complacency. Everybody does it because it is the fashion, and the spectacle of seeing one's opponent run around the country at a furious pace without following suit is too nerve-wracking to contemplate. It is beside the point that no one knows whether all this does any good. Richard Nixon seems to have learned from his enervating experience in 1960, when he pledged to visit each and every state and then had to follow through, despite a severe illness. In 1968 he ran a different kind of campaign, taking account of the fact that radio and television made it possible to reach millions without leaving the big metropolitan areas. Nixon did a small amount of traditional campaigning, which was faithfully chronicled by the press corps that followed him around the country. But more basic to his strategy was the technique of fixing upon regional centers and making major appearances and speeches in these places, followed by elaborate, regionally oriented television commercials that reached the voters directly—"over the heads," so to speak, of the news media that were covering and interpreting only the part of the campaign they could see—which did not include Nixon's television programs.[52]

In 1972 Nixon had even more reason to pursue the same tactics. As the incumbent, he did not have to worry about establishing personal visibility or name recognition. And he was blessed with an opponent who made well-publicized mistakes. Among the worst of these was announcing a series of detailed policy proposals early in the campaign. For a time it almost seemed as if McGovern were the incumbent and that Nixon was running against McGovern's "record."

In President Carter's famous 1976 *Playboy* interview, in which he spoke of having lusted in his heart, he also said that "the national news media have absolutely no interest in issues at all. . . . The travelling press have zero interest in any issues unless it's a matter of making a mistake. . . . There's nobody in the back of this plane who would ask an issue question unless he thought he could trick me into some crazy statement."[53] Whether or not the specific charge was true, the general idea has some cogency. The campaign is about choosing a president. Since most issues are complex, and most voters aren't interested, the media seek issues that do double duty, illuminating an area of interest and displaying a candidate's fitness to govern. Unfortunately, a candidate's mistakes can fall in this category, though what counts as a mistake depends on what doubts about the candidate exist in voters' minds. President Ford's advisors told him, based on considerable interviewing, that many voters who otherwise liked him thought he was "not smart enough" or sufficiently competent or commanding.[54] His remark about Poland not being under Soviet domination, which he kept repeating because he did not want to seem to be acquiescing to the fact on behalf of the United States, was a serious mistake and hurt him so much because it hit him where he was vulnerable. His opponent, Jimmy Carter, was vulnerable to charges of being arrogant and devious.[55] This is why his *Playboy* interview hurt him. "It demonstrated," Carter told an interviewer, "a confirmation of Ford's proposal to the American people that I was not quite to be trusted. . . ." And that was not all. At the end of the *Playboy* piece, Carter, thinking the tape was off, appeared to disparage Lyndon Johnson. Asked about this in Texas, Jimmy Carter seemed to say not that he had been mistaken but that someone else had misrepresented what he said.[56] This put a further strain on his credibility.

In order to avoid making mistakes, Carter tended to repeat the same prepared speeches. His chief policy planner, Stuart Eizenstat, repeatedly urged him to vary the menu. After he delivered speeches, however, the future president answered questions from the audience, saying what he believed, because that, he thought, was the way to be open and honest. This would invite reporters to attend to Carter's extemporaneous comments rather than to the particular points a speech was supposed to make. Thus Carter got into trouble on such "issues" as his criticisms of the head of the Federal Bureau of Investigation, seeming to say he would increase taxes on middle-income people, and appearing to approve of "ethnic purity." In this context, it is not surprising that dealing with issues fell from favor in the Carter camp. Hamilton Jordan, Carter's chief of staff, confessed, "I don't care if we ever have another issues speech."[57]

For Ford, "issues" as they are normally conceived were beside the point. His numerous vetoes of popular spending programs were well known. His problem was to establish his personal competence and credibility. That is why his staff, in a section of their strategy paper called "Establish Leadership Qualities," included such advice as "Avoid self-deprecating remarks (Ford not a Lincoln) and acts (being photographed with a cowboy hat)."[58] Ford's difficulties arose not because of where he stood on one or another issue but by failing to appear decisive. When his secretary of agriculture, Earl Butz, told a gross story that was a slur on black people, for example, Ford's failure to fire Butz on the spot hurt his candidacy. His best media appearances were the interviews with a sports announcer, Joe Garagiola, who, by contrast, made Gerald Ford look taller, more hirsute, and more intelligent.[59]

☆ Domestic Issues

On the broad range of domestic affairs and "pocketbook" issues, the Democrats are highly favored as the party most voters believe will best meet their needs. Statements like "The Democrats are best for the workingman" and "We have better times under the Democrats" abound when people are asked to state how they feel about the Democratic party. The Republicans, on the other hand, are viewed as the party of depression under whose administration jobs are scarce and times are bad. A campaign in which the salient issues are economic, therefore, is more likely to aid the Democrats than the Republicans.[60] Of course, if the incumbent president is Democratic and the economy is faltering, emphasizing economic issues may not do him much good.

Economic policy thus occasions little difficulty for the Democratic party. The Democratic party's historic task has been to be liberal in several senses of that word. It promises something for everyone. There are extensions of social welfare programs financed by the federal government, increased minimum wages for the underpaid, medical insurance for new groups of people, better prices for the farmer, irrigation for arid areas, flood protection and power dams for river basins, and so on. No one is left out, not even business-men, who are promised prosperity. The fact that most, if not all of these goals are incompatible with fighting inflation is not of overwhelming importance; Democrats can promise to be against inflation too. But should the issue switch to "excessive spending," Democrats would be at a disadvantage.

Republicans are clearly on the defensive in the realm of domestic policy, a situation stemming from the fact that they were in office when the Great Depression took place, and during two sizable but shorter depressions more recently (1970–1971, 1982–1983). They try to play down domestic issues. They do best when emphasizing foreign policy ("Bring the boys back from Korea"; "End the war in Vietnam"); general management of government ("We can do it better"); inflation ("We're for sound money, not like those spendthrift Democrats"); or an outstanding personality ("I like Ike"). When domestic issues are debated, a Republican candidate following the "me-too" underdog strategy takes care to stress that, whatever else he may say, he is in favor of social programs. And he adds that he is in favor of helping farmers, laborers, old people, pensioners, teachers, and other worthy folk to extend their gains. That he will do this better and cheaper becomes his refrain and the major point of difference with his opponent. He is understandably upset at Democratic insinuations that he and his party have not become fully reconciled to Social Security. This is especially true as the financing of the Social Security system becomes more precarious. Over and over again such a candidate insists that he and his opponent agree on goals of domestic policy, and that the only difference separating them is the minor matter of means.[61] For if the gulf between the parties is thought to be wide on "pocketbook" issues, a majority of voters would unhesitatingly choose the Democrats.

Both parties, of course, have some difficulty in reconciling their presiden-tial and congressional wings, but in the realm of domestic policy the Demo-crats have an easier task. The crucial electoral votes come from large states where the labor union and minority group interests reinforce the Democratic presidential aspirant's demand for liberal policies. Democratic conservatives, who are in a minority even in Congress, can be and largely are increasingly ignored. Since Franklin D. Roosevelt, all Democratic presidential candidates have decided that they can win without the South but not without the large states in other sections of the country. Television and radio make the old practice of saying different things in different parts of the country rather more dangerous than it used to be, although a further technological development, personalized direct mail, may have given candidates back some options that television took away.

The Republicans face much more difficult problems of internal dissension. Their congressional contingent is largely cohesive and generally conservative. The result is that Republican presidential candidates more often than not ignore the preferences of their congressional brethren. Party conservatives do not like the "me-too" implications of the stands taken by their conciliatory presidential candidates. In the past they have felt their candidate ought to hit harder at what they regard as Democratic statism and looseness with the public purse. But the number of strategically placed voters, or the groups from whom they take their cues, who disagree with this approach is too great for Republican candidates to ignore. Though at times he can "talk tough" in remarks directed to selected Republican audiences, he usually must "say more or less the same thing, regardless of his audience." With the exception of Barry Goldwater in 1964, all Republican candidates since 1936 evidently have concluded that there are not enough adherents of minimal government to elect a Republican president, and that since they have no place else to go, the Republican candidate will get their votes anyhow. It is permissible for lesser lights, such conservatives as vice-presidential candidates Spiro Agnew and Robert Dole, to go out on the hustings to mollify the right wing. But ordinarily it is political suicide to make wholesale attacks on the Democratic party and its domestic policies. Candidate Ronald Reagan would attack big government but he wouldn't, until he assumed office, get too specific about it. Republican candidates must claim that the Republicans too are for a better environment, worker safety, and good health care, but that they will accomplish these things for less money and with less bureaucracy than the Democrats.

☆ Foreign Affairs

In the realm of foreign affairs, the Republicans traditionally have the advantage. The fact that the Democrats occupied the presidency during the First and Second World Wars, the Korean War, and the initial stages of heavy American involvement in Vietnam has apparently convinced most voters that Democrats tend to lead the country to war. Republicans have on the whole escaped this stigma and are known as the party of peace, a position underscored by Senator Dole in the 1976 vice-presidential debate when he said: "I figured up the other day, if we added up the killed and wounded in Democrat wars in this century, it would be about 1.6 million Americans, enough to fill the city of Detroit."[62] Whether this impression of Democrats is any more

useful or valid than that of Republicans as the party of depression is beside
the point for present purposes. We are after the strategic implications, which
are interesting. For if foreign affairs issues can be made sufficiently important
to enough voters, the Republicans stand a better chance of winning. Republicans generally do best by building up foreign affairs and playing on the fear
that Democrats are not competent in this field. Since Ronald Reagan and his
party wanted to increase preparedness in defense, their tack was to say that
this would help prevent war. Democrats have the choice of deemphasizing
foreign policy, something that has become increasingly difficult to do, or
trying to show somehow that they are more peace-loving than Republicans,
or, in recent times, aping the Republican argument on domestic policy—we
can do it better and cheaper.

How this used to work in practice can be seen in Richard Nixon's 1960
campaign, in which the lamb of domestic controversy turned into the lion of
foreign affairs. Nixon sought to differentiate himself as much as possible from
Kennedy in the field of foreign policy. He suggested that he was capable of
securing peace (i.e., the absence of armed conflict anywhere in the world, a
tall order) without surrender and that Kennedy was not. He tried to
strengthen the prevailing impression of the Democratic party as the party of
war. He implied alternatively that Kennedy would permit the Communists
to make unwarranted advances (for example, in Matsu and Quemoy), and
that the Democrats would make rash moves (Cuba). Even Nixon's espousal
of an aggressive line, such as he took regarding Matsu and Quemoy, helped
him because in foreign affairs voters trusted the Republicans. On the other
hand, Kennedy's equally aggressive stand toward Cuba in his speeches did
not help him.[63]

All this may appear paradoxical, but it is perfectly understandable in the
light of our knowledge of voting behavior. Kennedy did not succeed in
convincing most voters that issues of foreign policy were more important
than domestic concerns. He won on his party affiliation, on domestic issues,
and on his appeal to Catholics.[64] Had he succeeded in alerting voters to the
importance of foreign affairs, there is every reason to believe he would have
lost support, since voters, in line with their previous inclinations, would
have decided that the perilous times called for a Republican in the White
House.

The 1960 television debates reflected this. Those viewers of the debates
who were especially attentive to foreign policy issues were more likely to be
pro-Nixon than pro-Kennedy, just the reverse of the situation in domestic
affairs. A summary of public opinion surveys on the debates concludes, "The

evidence suggests that foreign affairs was the paramount issue during the entire campaign and . . . since Nixon was generally conceded to be the more expert and experienced in foreign affairs—he was far ahead of Kennedy in perceived ability at 'handling the Russians' and 'keeping the peace'—the focus on foreign affairs was clearly to Nixon's advantage."[65]

Foreign affairs also helped Nixon in the 1968 campaign. He managed to combine peace with toughness without saying exactly how he would bring peace or where he would get tough. Democratic dissension on the Vietnam war issue did not hide the fact that Democratic presidents were in office when the war expanded and were unable to end it. Nothing Nixon said could have added to that, and anything more specific would have gotten him into trouble with one side or the other in a campaign in which his major strategy was to anger as few people as possible.

In 1972, foreign policy proved to be a sizable problem to Senator McGovern. His strong dovelike position on American participation in the Vietnam war especially commended him to the vocal, active Democrats who did so much to help him win the nomination. But once he faced President Nixon in the general election, McGovern's avowed willingness to sponsor a quick withdrawal of American troops, to cut defense spending, to "beg" Hanoi for the release of American prisoners, and to refuse future military aid to South Vietnam all were seen in a context in which voters were used to trusting Republicans, not Democrats. Thus the issue that may have been McGovern's trump card in winning the nomination could only do him harm if it remained salient in the general election.[66] In 1980, Jimmy Carter's perceived weakness in dealing with the Iranian hostage crisis undoubtedly forced his hand in ordering a dramatic rescue mission, which, by failing, doubled his political losses.[67]

The distinction between domestic and foreign policy has always been a bit artificial. It has been maintained because of the ability of the United States to insulate its domestic economy from international forces. Today that ability is diminishing. The decline of the dollar in foreign exchange compelled the Carter administration to pursue a deflationary policy—cutting spending, advocating less monetary expansion, selling bonds tied to foreign currencies. Energy prices, which obviously affect everyone, are set by the international market or by OPEC, not by the United States government. The Reagan administration would like to reduce trade barriers to serve its foreign policy, but it is having a hard time beating back protectionist forces worried about domestic unemployment. The high value of the dollar has led to much higher levels of imports and lower levels of exports than the administration would

like, but an effort to devalue the American dollar would have immensely
adverse international repercussions.

☆ Social Issues

If, on the whole, foreign affairs and war and peace are Republican issues, and
domestic welfare and the economy are Democratic issues, what about the
third great cluster of "social issue" problems, variously labeled (and understood) as law and order, domestic violence, and race relations? As Richard
Scammon and Ben Wattenberg point out, this issue has grown enormously
in prominence to voters over the past few years: "Suddenly, some time in the
1960s, 'crime' and 'race' and 'lawlessness' and 'civil rights' became the most
important domestic issues in America."[68] It is too early to tell whether this
cluster of issues works consistently for or against a particular political party.
More likely, over the short run, it works against incumbents. After all,
everyone is against crime. Since crime tends to increase, incumbents must
have failed to do whatever ought to be done to make things better. The
officeholder may say, as Governor Reagan of California did in 1970, that he
is needed even more because of the very fact that conditions are deteriorating.
But this argument is unlikely to carry much weight.

A fourth array of issues—also social issues, like abortion, ecology, and
gun control—involve life-styles as well as distributions of benefits. The fierce
passions aroused by these issues have led the national political parties per se
to avoid taking stands. No one knows whether this can continue until these
issues lose their relevance, or whether what are now single-issue groups will
seek electoral expression in the form of new parties as, in a minor way, has
happened on abortion with the appearance of right-to-life candidates. In
Germany, with its inviting system of proportional representation in Parliament, a so-called Green Party has organized around ecology.

Concern about damage to human life and the natural environment from
technology evokes different passions than does gun control or abortion. The
right to bear arms invokes norms of free choice and resistance to coercion.
The right-to-life movement invokes moral standards. Differences between
right and wrong are to be maintained and enforced by government. The clean
air and pure food groups want government to prevent contamination by, as
congressmen keep calling them, "corporate polluters." Thus there are conflicts between pro- and anti-free-market principles as well as support for and
opposition to government intervention in private life.

These differences may help explain President Reagan's views. While the president has supported anti-gun control and anti-abortion forces (without, it should be said, allowing them to get in the way of his other programs), he has not done the same in regard to environmental concerns. Indeed, by regarding them as interference with free-market principles, and by appointing people such as Secretary of the Interior James Watt, to whom environmentalists are bitterly opposed, Reagan may be on his way to making "the environment" a partisan issue.

☆ Presentation of Self

Another set of strategic problems concerns the personal impression made by the candidates. A candidate is helped by being thought of as trustworthy, reliable, mature, kind but firm, a devoted family man, and in every way normal and presentable. No amount of expostulation about the irrelevance of all this ordinariness as qualification for an extraordinary office wipes out the fact that candidates must try to conform to the public stereotype of goodness, a standard that is typically far more demanding of politicians than of ordinary mortals. It would be an excruciating process for a candidate to remodel his entire personality along the indicated lines. And, to be fair, most candidates are not so far from the mark as to make this drastic expedient necessary or they would not have been nominated in the first place. What the candidates actually try to do is to smooth off the rough edges, to counter what they believe are the most unfavorable impressions of specific aspects of their public image. Kennedy, who was accused of being young and immature, hardly cracked a smile in his debates with Nixon, while the latter, who was said to be stiff and frightening, beamed with friendliness. Kennedy restyled his youthful shock of hair, and Nixon thinned his eyebrows to look less threatening. Jimmy Carter made intimate revelations to show he was not cold and calculating but serious and sincere. Gerald Ford was photographed a lot around the White House to show he was in command. Ronald Reagan smiled and ducked ("There you go again") when Jimmy Carter tried to portray him as dangerous. And just as Kennedy made it possible for Roman Catholics to be considered for the presidency, Reagan broke the taboo on divorce.

The little things that some people don't like may be interpreted favorably by other people. Hubert Humphrey was alleged to be a man who could not stop talking. His garrulousness, however, was just another side of his encyclopedic and detailed knowledge of the widest variety of public policies. He might have talked too much to suit some, but the fact that he knew a lot pleased others. Was George McGovern kindly and compassionate? Or just wishy-washy? Is Ronald Reagan amiable and charming or is that a vacuous expression on his face?

The political folklore of previous campaigns provides candidates with helpful homilies about how to conduct themselves. Typical bits of advice include the following: always carry the attack to your opponent; the best defense is offense; separate the other candidate from his party; when in doubt as to the course that will produce the most votes, do what you believe is right; guard against acts that can hurt you because they are more significant than acts that can help you; avoid making personal attacks that may gain sympathy for the opposition. Unfortunately for the politicians in search of a guide, these bits of folk wisdom do not contain detailed instructions about the conditions under which they should and should not be applied.

The case of Adlai Stevenson suggests a familiar dilemma for candidates. Shall they write (or have written for them) new speeches for most occasions, or shall they rest content to hammer home a few themes, embroidering just a little here and there? No one really knows which is better. Stevenson is famous for the care he took with his speeches and the originality he sought to impart to his efforts. Had he won office he might have established a trend. As it is, most candidates are likely to follow Kennedy and Nixon, Johnson and Goldwater, and Carter and Ford in using just a few set speeches. Ronald Reagan's virtuoso shuffling of his well-worn index cards, with their anecdotes of questionable accuracy, seems to have served him well enough. In view of the pervasive inattention to public affairs and political talk in our society, this approach may have the advantage of driving points home (as well as driving mad the newsmen who must listen to the same thing all the time).[69] Newspaper people and television journalists who cover the campaigns complain quite a lot about the repetitiousness of presidential candidates, as though the campaign should be designed mostly to amuse them. This ranks high on the list of unsolved (and no doubt unsolvable) problems of American democracy: how to appeal to the relatively inattentive American people without totally alienating the superattentive mandarins of the news media through whom a candidate must reach the rank-and-file voter.

More important, perhaps, is the desirability of appearing comfortable in delivery. Televised speeches are the major opportunities for a candidate to be seen and evaluated by large numbers of people. Eisenhower's ability to project a radiant appearance helped him; Stevenson's obvious discomfort before the camera hurt him. On this point we have evidence that those who listened to Stevenson's delivery over radio were more favorably impressed with him than those who watched him on TV.[70] In 1968, Richard Nixon used regional television appearances as a means of reaching voters directly and making an end run around what he feared would be hostile press coverage of his campaign.[71] With television occupying an important place in American life, ability to make a good appearance is not a trivial matter. If people are judged by the company they keep, the scruffy, countercultural, hippie appearance of many delegates to the 1972 Democratic convention did not help their nominee. The reaction throughout the nation was negative—these were not "folks like us." Viewers were uneasy with what, on the screen, seemed like visible evidence of a culture that was indeed counter to their own. Jimmy Carter's "paste-on" smile and rigid bearing contrasted poorly with Ronald Reagan's easy grin and relaxed manner, though these surface indicators, like Gerald Ford's alleged clumsiness, may have nothing to do with performance in office.

The major difficulty with the strategic principles we have been discussing is not that they are too theoretical, but that they do not really tell the candidates what to do in case they are mutually incompatible. Like proverbs, one can often find principles to justify opposing courses of action. ("Look before you leap," but "He who hesitates is lost.") Nixon in 1960 could not take full advantage of international affairs without hitting so hard as to reinforce the unfavorable impression of himself as being harsh and unprincipled. Kennedy could hardly capitalize on the Rooseveltian image of the vigorous leader without attacking the foreign policy of a popular president. The result is that the candidates must take calculated risks when existing knowledge about the consequences of alternative courses of action is inadequate. Hunch, intuition, and temperament necessarily play important roles in choosing among competing alternatives.

☆ Television Debates

The famous TV debates of 1960 between Nixon and Kennedy provide an excellent illustration of the difficulty of choosing between competing considerations in the absence of knowledge of the most likely results. With the benefit of hindsight, many observers now suggest that Nixon was obviously foolish to engage in the debates. Let us try to look at the situation from the perspective of each of the presidential aspirants at the time.

Kennedy issued a challenge to debate on television. The possible advantages from his point of view were many. He could use a refusal to debate to accuse Nixon of running away and depriving the people of a unique opportunity to judge the candidates. Among Kennedy's greatest handicaps in the campaign were his youth and the inevitable charges of inexperience. Television debates could and did help to overcome these difficulties by showing the audience not so much that Kennedy was superior in knowledge but that there was not that much difference in the information, age, and general stature of the two men. Whatever administrative skills or inside information Nixon might have had would not show up on the screen as the candidates necessarily confined themselves to broad discussions of issues known to all politically literate people. Kennedy could only guess but he could not know that Nixon would not stump him in an embarrassing way in front of millions of viewers. But Kennedy understood that despite the reams of publicity he had received, he was unknown to many voters, much less known than the vice-president. Here was a golden opportunity to increase his visibility in a sudden and dramatic way. And his good looks would not hurt him with those who like to judge the appearance of a man.[72]

Nixon was in a more difficult position. To say no would not have been a neutral decision; it would have subjected him to being called a man who was afraid to face his opposition. Saying yes had a number of possible advantages. One stemmed from the numerical disadvantage of the Republican party. Normally, most people do not pay very much attention to the opposition candidate, making it difficult to win them over. Televised debates would provide a unique instance in which huge numbers of people attracted to both parties could be expected to tune in attentively. Nixon had good reason for believing that if he made a favorable impression he would be in a position to convince more of the people he needed to convince (the Democratic identifiers) than would Kennedy. The risk that Kennedy might use the opportunity to solidify the support of those attracted to a Democrat simply had to be taken. Another potential advantage that might have accrued to Nixon arose from his previous political life. He had been labeled by some people as "tricky Dick," an immoral and vindictive man. This picture might have been supplanted on television by the new Nixon of smiling visage and magnanimous gesture who had it all over his opponent in knowledge of public affairs. Nixon had to judge whether his handicap was serious or whether it was confined to confirmed liberals whose numbers were insignificant and who would never have voted for him in any event. He also had to guess whether it would be worthwhile to overcome this handicap, even if it also meant giving Kennedy an opportunity to overcome his own disabilities.[73]

Perhaps a record of success in debate situations going back to high school was not irrelevant in guiding Nixon to his eventual decision to go on television with his opponent.[74] Surveys taken after the event suggest that Nixon miscalculated.[75] But if he had won the election instead of losing it by a wafer-thin margin, he would hardly have been reminded of any error on his part, and there would probably have been discussions of what a brilliant move it was for him to go on TV.

The election of 1964 presented an entirely different set of circumstances. President Johnson, an incumbent enjoying enormous personal popularity at the head of the majority party, had nothing to gain and everything to lose by debating his rival. And so, despite strenuous efforts by Senator Goldwater and his allies to involve the President in debates, none were held.

By 1968, observers were beginning to question whether candidates would ever again seek an epic confrontation with one another on the 1960 model. What seems to be required before the likely occurrence of such a debate is two major candidates equally eager for such a battle. If one is an incumbent, or feels himself securely in the lead, there is little incentive to debate. Hubert Humphrey pursued Richard Nixon fiercely on this point in 1968, but Nixon prudently refrained from a debate that would needlessly have risked his chances of victory. His excuse in 1972 was that a president in office could not tell all he knew.

Because inertia had begun to work against the idea of debates, the fact that they occurred again in 1976 was somewhat surprising. Neither candidate had been elected to the presidency, but Gerald Ford, the less articulate of the two, was the incumbent president. Although the Democrats did not do especially well in the debates, Ford's side, the Republicans, which had the most to lose by debating, undoubtedly lost ground twice. One time was when Ford left the impression that in his opinion Eastern Europe was not under Soviet domination, an occasion for a week's worth of "clarifications." The other was when Senator Robert Dole, his vice-presidential running mate, misjudged the audience entirely and bounced partisan one-liners ineffectually off the beatific brow of Senator Walter Mondale, thus spoiling one of the few chances the Republicans had to woo Democratic voters.[76]

The strategy of participation in presidential debates was well illustrated in the 1980 Democratic party primaries. In the fall of 1979 President Carter's public popularity was exceedingly low, Senator Kennedy's was exceedingly high, and Governor Brown of California was struggling for recognition as a serious candidate. Thus, every candidate had an interest in participation: the President needed it because he was way behind; Senator Kennedy needed it because he was still a challenger; and Governor Brown needed it most of all because he considered himself a good debater and hoped to show that he could hold his own with the front runners. Then the Iranian seizure of American hostages served almost instantly to raise the President's popularity. Senator Kennedy's popularity plummeted after he gave an embarrassingly bad television interview to Roger Mudd and had difficulty explaining the Chappaquiddick incident. Thus, the situation changed. President Carter no longer stood to gain a lead but to lose one, so he bowed out of the debates on the grounds that it would be inappropriate to campaign while the hostages were being held, a circumstance that might continue almost indefinitely. The Senator and the Governor protested in vain. Hurt worst of all, Brown lost the chance to share the limelight with the President, which, at that stage, might have given him the public prominence he needed.

In 1980 there were problems in deciding what to do about including the major independent candidate, John Anderson, in debates. President Carter refused to publicize Anderson, and so in the end only one debate took place instead of a series, and it was held very late in the campaign only between Carter and his Republican challenger, Ronald Reagan. On balance it seems to have helped Reagan, who may have lost on high-school debate rules but projected a benignity that was helpfully at odds with the picture of a dangerously radical opponent that Jimmy Carter was trying to paint.[77] So Carter became another incumbent who lost ground by submitting to a staged debate.

The strategic imperatives surrounding debates seem to be emerging with some clarity. Debates can hurt incumbents. Challengers have far less to lose, and may gain simply by keeping their countenance and appearing on the same stage with the holder of high public office. Opinion makers and the custodians of the flame of disinterested public spiritedness seem agreed that debates are wonderful exercises in public enlightenment. This scarcely seems credible to minimally intelligent viewers of the actual debates we have had, but this sentiment nevertheless exists, and may tempt candidates to engage in public debates against their better strategic judgment.[78]

☆ Getting a Good Press

Although we have seen that newspapers—whether in editorials or news stories—do not markedly influence reader opinion, it is still important for a candidate to get the most favorable coverage possible. It usually does not pay to try to line up support from publishers who have already made up their minds before the campaign has officially started. But the candidates can and do assiduously court the newspaper, periodical, and television journalists assigned to them.[79] Not only do candidates throw parties for press and staff, but they follow their coverage and complain about it. Strong feeling within the Carter camp in 1976 that Ford was being let off too easily on issues but that Carter was being hard-pressed, for example, led Carter to call a meeting at which he discussed his grievances with the press.[80] Ford's pollsters felt that media coverage of the debates reinforced the image of him as a bumbler from which they had been trying to escape. And in 1980 Carter complained about but could not counter the journalistic view of Reagan as a good guy.

The space a candidate gets in the paper, his time on television, and the slant of the story may depend to some extent on how the reporters regard him. If they find it difficult to get material, if they find the candidate suspicious and uncommunicative, this, too, may affect how much and what gets on the air or published. Little things, such as phasing news to meet the requirements of both morning newspapers and the evening network news shows, or supplying reporters with human-interest material, are helpful to the candidate. The personality of the candidate, his ability to command the respect of the rather cynical men and women assigned to cover him, may count heavily. Democratic candidates probably have to work a little harder at cultivating good relations in order to help counteract the editorial slant of most papers. But Republicans have to work a little harder to win the sympathies of reporters of liberal tendency who dominate the national press corps.[81] Both also must make the most of their opportunities in public appearances or radio and TV speeches. If what they say and do "makes news," and their press secretaries help promote the stories, they may get space through the desire of the newspapers to sell copies.

Thus far, we have spoken of the news media as if they were a monolithic entity. But there are all sorts of news outlets with differing biases, needs, and audiences. A great deal of a candidate's attention is devoted to stories destined for the racial, religious, and ethnic interest-group press. The circulations of these publications may not be huge, but it is assumed that they have readers who are concerned with topics of special interest to smaller and more attentive constituencies. A story on religion in politics in a religious journal may do more to convince people than much greater coverage in the daily press.

Finally, there is the overwhelming importance of staging the daily bit of news for the nightly television programs of the networks. Candidates know they will be on these programs every night: but doing and saying what? In order to seize control of the situation they stage little dramas: an announce-ment in front of the Statue of Liberty or in the midst of a picturesque slum; a walk through a series of ethnic shops, delicatessens, farms, factories and shopping centers. If the backdrop is right, the candidate thinks, the coverage may be too. And sometimes it is.

☆ Mud-Slinging and Heckling

In the closing days of what appears to be a close race, there may be a temptation for the parties, now thoroughly engrossed in the heat of battle, to loose a stream of invective at the other side. How much of this they do and how often they do it is partially determined by the kind of people they are. In the long run, however, the standards of the voting population deter-mine the standards of the candidates. Should it happen that vituperation is rewarded, we can expect to see it occur again. Should it prove to be the case, however, as in the Scandinavian countries, that departures from proper deportment are severely punished at the polls, candidates can be expected to take the hint. One of the results of the Watergate scandals is said to be the advent in the populace at large of a "post-Watergate morality" in which failure to abide by rules of common decency can be expected to be strongly disfavored. This does not necessarily provide much in the way of guidance to candidates, however. It may, in fact, be a gross violation of common decency, as elites understand such matters, to hurl an accusation of immoral-ity at an opponent that forces him into a complex explanation which few people will understand. Yet it may be winning politics to indulge in such smear tactics under the incentives set up by post-Watergate morality. For example, there are frequently adequate and legitimate reasons of public policy for congressmen to travel abroad on public funds, even if they have a good time doing it. But woe betide the congressman who for one reason or another is forced to defend this case before an aroused electorate.

Many observers claim that Senator Edmund Muskie fatally injured his campaign for the 1972 Democratic nomination by showing too much emo-tion in response to a Republican smear that branded him a racist. Muskie, it is true, had in many prior campaigns managed with enormous success to show indignation at the moral lapses of opponents who attacked him,[82] but this time something went wrong, and he was widely criticized for showing the wrong demeanor.

Perhaps on this one occasion he should have taken a leaf from the book of Franklin Delano Roosevelt, who paid no attention to most accusations about him but seized on an attack involving his dog, Fala, to rib his opponents unmercifully for impugning a dog that could not reply.[83] If all else fails, it is always possible to take the advice attributed to a Chicago politician who said that in politics, as in poker, the way to meet scandalous charges is to "call 'em and raise 'em. If you are denounced as a fool, call your opponent a damned fool; if he says you are a crook, call him a robber; if he intimates that you are careless with the truth, tell your audience that he is a pathological liar."

Why, we may wonder, are candidates supposed to behave in a more exalted fashion in politics and in the midst of a passionately fought contest than we would expect of them in other areas of life? Successful public officials, like successful business executives, union leaders, and people in other walks of life, deal with people as they are, not as they would wish them to be. Campaigning is concerned primarily with winning support; any secondary effects it may have, such as educating the public, are (unfortunately) incidental. If we wonder at the level of appeals made to us in elections, we need look only as far as our own qualities to get the answer. There are occasions when we might be thankful that our politicians do not fully reflect the ethical standards actually practiced in society. Knowledge of our own character may explain the wish and expose the fallacy of expecting politicians to be better than we are.[84]

However, the standards of the voting population do not necessarily determine the actions of organized hecklers and mischief makers. Heckling has probably always been a part of any politics in which votes are publicly solicited, though Americans have never indulged in the practice to the degree that it exists in Great Britain. The heckling in the 1968 campaign was different in scope from that of recent American politics. Both Hubert Humphrey and George Wallace had to face frequent, deliberate, disruptive activities by groups of young people whose aim was to prohibit them from speaking at all, rather than to "score points" on them through clever interruptions. If a rule of thumb were to be developed from this, it would seem to be that extreme conservatives and moderate liberals were most likely to face such activity, while moderate conservatives (e.g., Richard Nixon) and extreme liberals (e.g., various peace-and-freedom types) would escape. To the degree that such heckling had any impact, in the end it probably gained a little sympathy for the candidate under fire. Unlike mud-slinging, however, in which a campaign that boomerangs is usually quickly squelched by party leaders, the disruptive forms of heckling in 1968 were less easy to control.

The hecklers had no candidate who might have lost votes by being identified with them and, in any event, their purpose was to show contempt for the electoral process rather than for any single candidate.

Both Carter and Ford eschewed opportunities for mud-slinging. When it looked like his fortunes were in decline, Carter was urged to link Ford explicitly to Watergate through his pardon of Nixon. Carter refused, saying, "It will rip our country apart."[85] Presented with an opportunity to accuse Carter of corruption in regard to the family peanut business, Ford squelched the matter.[86]

It is ironic that President Nixon and his campaign managers should have sought, in 1972, to adapt the tactics they attributed to the far-out left to their own uses. The contempt of insiders for a political system that nurtures them is a far more serious phenomenon than the antics of dissidents. Yet it appears that the Nixon campaign hired people to fake evidence tending to discredit former Democratic presidents and to harass Democratic presidential candidates by playing "dirty tricks" on them (such as ordering huge numbers of pizzas in their name). Presumably the passage of laws prohibiting such behavior in the future will be of some help, but the fact that the reelection campaign of a president of the United States sheltered such disgusting behavior is a shameful blot upon our history.[87]

In the United States we seem to be in a middle position in regard to mud-slinging. It is not everyday practice, but neither is it a rarity. A glance at the history of presidential campaigns suggests that vituperation is largely irrelevant to the outcomes of campaigns and that its benefits are problematical. Thomas Jefferson was accused of seducing a highborn Virginia maiden, fathering a brood of mulattoes, and being an atheist. Andrew Jackson was called a murderer, a gambler, and an adulterer. Lincoln was charged with being a vulgar village politician and fourth-rate lawyer. Grover Cleveland was accused of fathering an illegitimate child, and though he was not certain of its paternity, he admitted responsibility. His opponents taunted him with the chant:

> Ma, Ma, where's my Pa?
> Gone to the White House
> Ha! Ha! Ha!

The point is, however, that all these men won office, as have many others who have been subject to similar aspersions.

Even more instructive is the case of William Henry Harrison, whom

Democratic politicians derogated with the remark that he would be content to spend the rest of his life in a log cabin drinking hard cider. His party seized on this to make him into a symbol of the common man and drowned out all attempts to discuss issues with cries about humble living in log cabins. Van Buren, the Democratic candidate, was crushed with doggerel like this:

> Let Van from his coolers of silver drink wine
> And lounge on his cushioned settee;
> Our man on his buckeye bench can recline
> Content with hard cider is he.[88]

☆ Feedback

As the campaign progresses, the candidates attempt to take soundings from various sources and to modify their behavior to make the most of opportunities as they arise. But this process presents tremendous problems in the chaotic atmosphere of a campaign. Even under conditions of comparative tranquillity, who knows what the world is like? In our everyday lives we make assumptions that simplify reality tremendously in order to make decisions. Consider, then, the poor candidate who must try to take hold of a complicated universe in which the actions and the reactions of millions of voters, his own staff, his opponents, party workers, the press, and other relevant publics have to be taken into account under widely varying conditions. There is, of course, hardly any time to think about these matters. The strategies adopted by the candidates surely depend on some notions about what the consequences of these strategies will be. In turn, it is necessary to make assumptions about how people are going to act in response to one's own actions. Yet no one can be certain that the simple picture of the world in his mind corresponds to the complex reality.

The candidate evolves an organization and a staff whose purpose in part is to inform him of the state of the political world. But he comes to know soon enough that it is unwise to trust his closest associates completely. Their fortunes are identified with his, their future prospects may depend on his, and their very battles for him may warp their judgment. Will they come to think that bad news should be withheld lest it sap his will to win? Will their hopes and fears color their judgment? Will the fact that they, in turn, depend upon other "loyalists" mean that those they trust are also unreliable? It is clear that the candidate has to place some sort of discount on the reports of his advisors. But it is not clear how much of a discount should be taken.

In trying to get a more objective estimate of the political situation, a candidate has a number of devices available—polls, the mass media, audience reaction—which are better than nothing but which are ambiguous and difficult to interpret. The first question about a poll is whether or not to believe it. Candidates now as a matter of course have analysts to tell them what their surveys mean, but they could be wrong. Perhaps the apparent findings are more an artifact of the way the questions are phrased and the kind of people who administer them than of any objective reality. The questions asked may be the important ones to the pollster but not necessarily to the voter.[89] The increasing professionalism of surveys, their quick access to respondents via random-access telephone dialing, and the sophistication of pretested questionnaires and computer-aided analyses make it more and more likely, however, that candidates will have timely and accurate knowledge of public opinion. In addition, they may attend to the mass media. If newspapers happen to be on a candidate's side, he risks the distortions of favoritism; if they are against him, he risks the distortions of malice. If they are neutral, he may wonder if they know any more about what is going on than he does. Yet he ignores what they say at his peril. The candidate cannot possibly read all the papers or listen to all the commentators; he requires summaries. Here again appears the risk of unconscious distortion by his eager staff.

Closest to the candidate's experience in the mad rush of the campaign are the audiences he addresses, and he may anxiously scan their response. At the beginning of the campaign, he is likely to try out different approaches on audiences composed of the party faithful. As a result, he may conclude that what the "people" want are the kinds of traditional cries that rally those who are already disposed to vote for him; but this, at least for a Republican, may not reach the voters he needs to convince, and for a Democrat may not activate enough people to go to the polls. The Republican candidate discovers that the people want an end to disastrous government spending, and the Democratic standard-bearer learns that they want more welfare programs. As the campaign progresses, candidates begin to believe that the crowds are no longer so one-sided, and their varying size and enthusiasm may be read as significant portents. There are, however, many possible reasons to explain why crowds turn out: curiosity, desire to heckle, nothing else to do, a look at a glamorous figure, as well as the desire to support a particular candidate. A large crowd may mean many things. It may mean that the candidate's managers have picked their spot wisely (such as market day at a farm distribution center) and have brought their man to a crowd rather than a crowd to him. Or a large crowd may mean that the candidate has succeeded in gaining intense support from the strongest party identifiers, but their enthusiasm may tell him nothing about his general prospects or the appeals he needs to make. In 1960, the disparity between the roaring crowds and the vote in a state like Ohio may have brought home the reality of this kind of misperception to the Kennedy forces.[90]

The feedback a candidate gets can hurt him if it reinforces and amplifies negative soundings that lead to pessimistic interpretations of his chances. Consider the plight of Vice-president Humphrey in 1968. He emerged from the Democratic convention with his party in disarray and his own image tarnished because he could not condemn, condone, or control events in the streets of Chicago or on the convention floor. Before he could pull his party together, he received indications that his campaign was falling apart. In the first few weeks the crowds (compared with those for Nixon) were poor wherever he went. Although a candidate normally rises in the estimation of the people after he has received exposure during his nomination, Humphrey's public opinion poll rating stayed low after the convention. His chances seemed pitifully small. An immediate result was that financial contributions did not come in as expected. Consequently he did not have enough money to go on TV in the early days of his campaign, when it might have helped him most, and he had to spend a considerable portion of his first month raising the necessary funds. In those days Humphrey was pyramiding his liabilities and discovering why it is hard to start on your way up when everyone tells you you are already too far down. Nowadays, with major party campaigns paid for by the public finance of elections, the financial consequences of a candidate's unpopularity are not so serious.

While the candidate is making his assessment as best he can, others in his organization are doing the same. The party organizer, for example, may gauge the trend of the campaign by the number of people who show up at party headquarters willing to do some work. This may be as good an index as any. Like the mass meeting, however, attendance at headquarters may be an unreliable indicator of success. Party headquarters may be attracting a special, limited segment of the public that is attracted to a man like the candidate or lonely people who find this a good way to meet others. The reports of workers in the various states may or may not be more useful. Although they may be wholly accurate, they are subject to the usual biases and may be representative only of narrow portions of the public rather than a good sample of the electorate. After an election it may be amusing to note that an activity like Les Biffle's nationwide tour masquerading as a chicken farmer proved more reliable for Harry Truman than the polls of 1948.[91]

During the campaign, however, this was just one among a number of cues.

One hears much about campaign blunders, as if there really were objective assurance that another course of action would have turned out better for the unfortunate candidate. The most famous of these in recent years was Thomas E. Dewey's decision in 1948 to mute the issues, which was said to have snatched defeat from the jaws of victory.[92] A vigorous campaign on his part, it was said, would have taken steam out of Harry Truman's charges and would thus have brought victory to Dewey. Perhaps. What we know of the 1948 election suggests that it provoked a higher degree of voting on the basis of economic class than any of the elections that have succeeded it.[93] A slashing attack by Dewey, therefore, might have polarized the voters even further. This would have increased Truman's margin, since there are many more people with low than with high incomes. Had the election gone the other way—and a handful of votes in a few states would have done it—we would have heard much less about Dewey's blunder and much more about how unpopular Truman was supposed to have been in 1948.

A whole series of "mistakes" have been attributed to Richard Nixon in 1960, the year he lost the election by such a small margin. Here are two, culled from a best-selling book on the 1960 campaign. On the civil rights plank of the Republican platform:

> The original draft plank prepared by the Platform Committee was a moderate one. . . . This plank, as written, would almost certainly have carried the Southern states for Nixon and, it seems in retrospect, might have given him victory. . . . On Monday, July 25th, it is almost certain, it lay in Nixon's power to reorient the Republican Party toward an axis of Northern-Southern conservatives. His alone was the choice. . . . Nixon insisted that the Platform Committee substitute for the moderate position in civil rights (which probably would have won him the election) the advanced Rockefeller position on civil rights. . . .[94]

On Nixon's failure to protest the imprisonment of Martin Luther King during the campaign:

> He had made the political decision at Chicago to court the Negro vote in the North, only now, apparently, he felt it quite possible that Texas, South Carolina, and Louisiana might all be won to him by the white vote and he did not wish to offend that vote. So he did not act—there was no whole philosophy of politics to instruct him.[95]

Hindsight is capable of converting every act of a losing candidate into a blunder. Victory can have the same effect in reverse. Consider the situation of Richard Nixon, 1968 version, as he dealt with the same southern white-northern black dilemma—in the same way. Theodore White reports:

> Nixon had laid it down, at the Mission Bay gathering, that none of his people, North or South, were to out-Wallace Wallace. He insisted, as he was to insist to the end of the campaign, that he would not divide the country; he wanted a campaign that would unify a nation so he could govern it. To compete with Wallace in the South on any civilized level was impossible. . . . Instead, Nixon would challenge Wallace in the peripheral states—Florida, North Carolina, Virginia, Tennessee, South Carolina. . . . It was only later that the trap within this strategy became evident—for, to enlarge his base in the Northern industrial states, Nixon would have to reach across from the rock-solid Republican base there, across center, to the independents, the disenchanted Democrats, to the ghettos. But to do that would be to shake the peripheral strategy in the new South. And to hold to the course he had set for the peripheral strategy limited his call in the North.[96]

Nixon's strategy was aimed, in both years, at chipping off the "peripheral" southern states while not taking such a strong anti-civil rights position as to bring northern black voters to the polls in great numbers and to turn northern suburban whites against him.

In 1968, of course, he won; his margin over 1960 consisted of North Carolina, South Carolina, Illinois, and New Jersey. Would it have been a gain for him to "out-Wallace Wallace"? Not likely, in view of the heavy margins Wallace piled up in the states he did carry and his inability to do very well elsewhere. Would it have been a gain for Nixon to repudiate all possible anti-civil rights votes? Not likely, in view of the near unanimity against him of the black vote and probably of most strongly pro-civil rights white liberals. In short, did his strategy of equivocation almost win or almost lose the presidency for Richard M. Nixon in 1960 and/or 1968? Absent the opportunity to rerun these elections with different strategies, no one can say.

We have previously dealt with Nixon's decision to engage in television debates with Kennedy. Let us take a look at his decision on timing the 1960 campaign. Nixon calculated that the election was going to be very close because the Democrats were the majority party in the country and the

Republicans lacked Eisenhower. Nixon reasoned, therefore, that the candidate who closed his campaign with the strongest spurt would be the winner.[97]
Consequently, he held his fire somewhat until the latter part of October,
hoping thereby to peak his campaign while Kennedy's was falling off. This
is precisely what he did, and Kennedy's supporters were worried that
Kennedy had lost and Nixon had gained impetus in the last two weeks.
Nevertheless, Kennedy won. What lesson might a future candidate derive
from this experience? Nixon's strategy of timing has a common-sense ring to
it. Yet it is really difficult to say whether it had meaning. Would he have done
better to come to a peak earlier? Might the general public not have gotten
tired of a full-blast effort straight through? There is no way of knowing. It
is possible that Nixon lost because of his strategy, that he gained, though not
enough, or that the strategy had no effect whatsoever. It would have been
possible to use a successive survey of the same voters to check on whether
votes were changed in his favor during the period he put on the steam, but
other factors could also affect the outcome of such a study. Furthermore,
there is no way of measuring how well he might have done had he pursued
a different strategy.

How should George McGovern have treated the Eagleton affair of 1972?
Had he failed to remove Senator Eagleton as vice-presidential nominee, the
campaign might have revolved around charges, ill-founded or not, that Eagleton was psychologically unfit to succeed to the presidency if and when that
became necessary. McGovern, moreover, felt that he had been taken in by
Eagleton's failure to mention his past psychiatric treatment. Had McGovern
kept Eagleton on the Democratic ticket, however, on the grounds that past
illness should not disqualify for future activity, positive use might have been
made of the events. If the Democrats were indeed the party of the people who
needed help, this was certainly a good time to demonstrate it. Punitive
Republicans might have been compared with compassionate Democrats. But
there is reason to believe that McGovern activists threatened to abandon his
campaign if he did not dump his running mate. These activists were apparently outraged at the thought that their issue preferences would be subor-
dinated to discussion of mental illness. They were, of course, beaten before
the race began, so they had nothing to lose by sticking to principle; but they
did not know that then.

Some perceptions of political reality are so overwhelming that everyone
accepts them as true. According to Reagan strategist Richard Wirthlin,
commenting on the 1980 campaign, "there was no question, in our own
minds . . . that if we could make this campaign a referendum on the perform-

ance of Jimmy Carter, we would win the election." Patrick Caddell, who performed a similar role in the Carter campaign, agreed that "There was no way, looking at the perceptions that people had about the President, that we could survive either a primary or general election . . . if we allowed it to become a referendum on the first three years of the Carter administration. . . . We had to keep the campaign on the candidates and we had to try to keep it on the future—a movie about the future, as one of our analysts said —as opposed to a movie about the past. We would lose the latter flat out; we knew that." Once the Carter campaign failed to convict Ronald Reagan of being too dangerous to elect, the contest was over. Still, it could have ended differently. As Everett Ladd concludes,

> In the end the 1980 election became what the Republicans had hoped and the Democrats had feared—a referendum on the Carter adminis- tration. Some observers think it could not have been otherwise, in view of the depths of the public rejection of the Carter administra- tion's performance. I do not accept this view. In my judgment it unfairly minimizes the impact of Reagan's campaign and insuffi- ciently appreciates the importance of both the Republican candidate's performance and the strategic choices he made—including Reagan's impressive handling of his October 28 debate with Carter. In any case, what had been a close contest through September and October be- came an electoral landslide for the GOP, as the electorate resolved its indecision and voted no on the Carter administration.[98]

Should the candidate arrive at a coherent strategy that fits reasonably well with what is known of the political world, he still will find that the party organization has an inertia in favor of its accustomed ways of doing things. The party workers, upon whom he is dependent to some extent, have their own ways of interpreting the world, and he disregards their point of view at some risk. Should the candidate fail to appear in a particular locality as others have done, the party workers may feel slighted. More important, they may interpret this as a sign that the candidate has written off that area and they may slacken their own efforts. Suppose the candidate decides (as now, with expenditure limitations under the federal subsidy, all candidates must) to divert funds from campaign buttons and stickers to polls and television or transportation? He may be right in his belief that the campaign methods he prefers may bring more return from the funds that are spent. But let the party faithful interpret this as a sign that he is losing—where, oh where, are those familiar indications of his popularity?—and their low morale may encourage a result that bears out this dire prophecy. An innovation in policy may shock the loyal followers of the party. It may seem to go against time-honored precepts that are not easily unlearned. Could a Republican convince his party that a balanced budget is not sacred? Or a Democrat that it is? A selling job may have to be done on the rank and file; otherwise they may sit on their hands during the campaign. It may make better political sense (if less intellectual sense) to phrase the new in old terms and make the departure seem less extreme than it might actually be. The value of the issue in the campaign may thus be blunted. The forces of inertia and tradition may be overcome by strong and persuasive candidates; the parties are greatly dependent on their candidates and have little choice but to follow them, even if haltingly. But in the absence of a special effort, in the presence of enormous uncertainties and the inevitable insecurities, the forces of tradition may do more to shape a campaign than the overt decisions of the candidates possibly can.

Appendix

Forecasting the Outcome

As the time for voting draws closer, more and more interest focuses on attempts to forecast the outcome. This process of forecasting elections is not at all mysterious; it depends on well-settled findings about the behavior of American electorates, many of which have already been discussed. But it may be useful for citizens to understand how the "experts" go about picking the winner.

There are several ways to do it. One way, popularized by journalists Joseph Alsop and Samuel Lubell, is to interview the residents of neighborhoods where there are people who in the past have voted with great stability in one pattern or another. There are neighborhoods, for example, that always vote for the Republicans by a margin of 90 percent or better. Let us say that the interviewer finds that only 50 percent of the people he talks to tell him they are going to vote for the Republicans this time, but when he visits areas voting heavily Democratic, respondents continue to support the Democratic nominee heavily. A finding such as this permits the reporter to make a forecast, even though it is based on only a very small number of interviews that may represent not at all the opinions of most voters.

Reporters who use this technique very rarely make firm predictions about election outcomes. Instead, they concentrate on telling about the clues they have picked up: what they learned in heavily black areas, what the people in Catholic areas said, what midwestern farmers say, what people from localities that always vote with the winner report, and so on.[99] This technique is impressive because it digs into some of the dynamic properties of what goes into voting decisions. It reports which issues seem to be on people's minds. It examines the different ways in which members of different subgroups see the candidates and the campaign. It is also a technique that can be executed at relatively low cost. But it is unsystematic, in that people are not polled in proportions reflecting the distributions of their characteristics in the population (so many men, so many women, so many white, so many black, and so forth). Thus the results of this technique would be regarded as unreliable in a scientific sense, even though they may enhance people's intuitive grasp of what is going on. The results are also unreliable in the sense that two different journalists using this method may come to drastically different conclusions, and there is no certain way of resolving the disagreement; nor is there any prescribed method for choosing between their conflicting interpretations.

A second technique was used most extensively in its pristine form by the economist and statistician Louis Bean and does not rely on interviews at all.[100] Bean, it will be remembered, contradicted all the polls and predicted that President Truman would be reelected in 1948. The Bean method relies principally upon assumptions about (1) the stability of voting habits, (2) the stability of the relationship between turnout and the two-party vote, (3) the stability of the relationship between the two-party distribution of the vote in one area and the two-party distribution of the vote in another, and (4) the continuation of voting trends in whatever direction they may be heading. Some of these assumptions are quite dubious, as we shall see, and Bean customarily hedged his predictions by claiming that they would hold unless some issue or another interceded to upset them. His method does not provide a way for the impact of issues to be examined, and, in fact, Bean did not demonstrate how the effects of issues sustained or failed to sustain his predictions.

The basic material out of which Bean constructed his forecasts is a historical record of two-party voting. Let us suppose the Democratic percentage of the two-party vote has risen in each of the past five elections. The Bean technique continues the line on the graph in a simple extrapolation. Even when the percentage of the two-party vote does not describe a straight line on a graph, it is possible to make an extrapolation by assuming that the historical pattern of fluctuation will be followed in the future.

Another type of analysis done by Bean made use of the September election results in Maine. This became unusable when Maine moved its election day from September to November, thus bringing it into line with practice in the rest of the country. But for many years it was possible to make a forecast based on the Maine results. Maine's distribution of the two-party vote, Bean said, bore a historically consistent relation to the national two-party vote distribution, rising and falling at about the same rate, but always somewhat below the nation on the Democratic graph and above the nation on the Republican graph. And so it was possible to forecast the outcome nationwide, or in any state, by noting the two-party ratio in the early Maine results and correcting it for two-party voting habits in the area whose result he wanted to predict.

The strength of forecasting from historical voting statistics arises out of the marvelous stability of American voting habits. But the weakness of such a technique is also manifest. Sometimes gross changes in population through immigration, or changes in the appeals of the parties to different voting groups, will throw the historical two-party vote ratios in the sample area out of joint. When a forecast made with this technique is wrong, it is usually quite difficult to tell whether transitory or lasting causes are at the root of it. This limits the usefulness of the forecast greatly, since, in the end, it rests on assumptions that have only partial validity in any one election, and nobody can say precisely how or where or to what extent they may be valid.

A third technique is a variant of the two foregoing types of analyses and is used by electronic computers at the radio and television networks on election night. The basic principle of these machines, for our purposes, can be described simply. They are given information about the past voting history of various locales. As these locales report their returns on election night, the machine compares this year's result with the information about previous years and arrives at a prediction of how this year's election will turn out when all the votes are counted. The system is exactly the same as we have already described for Alsop and Lubell, only the machine can be loaded with historical information about many localities—precincts, wards, and so on—and then the machine compares this historical information, not with voting *intentions* as expressed by a few interviewees, but by voting *results* as expressed by the whole voting population of the area. The method the machine uses to predict the outcome early in the evening is roughly the same as Louis Bean's technique, only, once again, instead of the Maine election, the machine has results from a great many early reporting areas and can therefore correct discrepancies arising out of one or two purely local situations. Networks now supplement this information with the results of exit polls, statements about voting behavior collected as voters leave the polling place. These findings can be fed into the computer very rapidly—well before votes are officially counted—and give the networks an early feel for what is going on. They do not tell us why nonvoters fail to vote, of course, and this may be important in the end in understanding a given election.

Interestingly enough, at least one of the network machines on election night in 1960 was not programmed to compare the votes in key precincts in previous elections with 1960 results. The IBM system set up for CBS began election night in 1960 with the erroneous prediction that Richard Nixon would win the presidency—a prediction that was later corrected as more and more returns came in.[101] It is useful to pause for a moment to look at this mistake, because it demonstrates clearly that these machines, like any other tools, are only as good as the people who use them.

The IBM computer was fed information based not on the geographic locale of the vote, but rather on the order in which the vote was reported to election headquarters. Thus, all the machine knew in 1960 was how many Democratic votes and how many Republican votes had been reported at 7:00 P.M. in previous elections, at 7:15, and so on. But it did not know *where* these votes had come from. The introduction of a faster method of vote-counting in Kansas between 1956 and 1960 was the reason for the IBM computer's early mistake. A flood of Kansas Republican votes arrived earlier than ever before. The computer, not knowing where they came from, compared them with the early returns in 1956, which were from the "swing" state of Connecticut, and drew a false conclusion.

Since the order in which states report their vote varies quite a bit more than the voting habits of people living in specific early reporting places, it seems likely that all the computers in the future will be working on geographic assumptions. It will in all probability be almost impossible to find out what assumptions the computers are using during election-night coverage, however, because of the hot competition among networks to hold viewers. This makes it very difficult to get complicated information on the air, no matter how significant.

The final method for predicting elections is the most controversial and by all odds the most famous: polls. These are based on a few simple assumptions that have been found to be quite correct over the years. One is that people generally will tell you the truth if you ask them how they are going to vote. Another is that it is not necessary to ask everyone what he is going to do in order to get as accurate a forecast as if you had asked nearly everyone.

The polls are commercial operations and, these days, they are big businesses. In addition to the publicly available polls, such as the Gallup and Harris newspaper reports, politicians commission private polls. They are expensive. They entail writing up a list of questions and asking them all, and all in the same way, to several thousand people spread all over the country; collecting the answers; and figuring out what it all means. Each of these phases of the operation—writing questions, selecting the sample of the total population to be interviewed, interviewing, organizing the answers, and interpreting the results—requires skill and training. This expertise is what commercial polling organizations provide.

In the past, regrettably, some of these organizations have treated the technical aspects of their operation as trade secrets (which they are not) and have left the impression that their forecasts are the result of a particularly efficacious kind of magic. Since the fiasco of 1948, when pollsters were so sure of the result that they became professionally careless, there has been less ballyhoo. But the general reader will do well to keep a sharp eye on the following points as the polls begin reporting early in the campaign.[102]

1. How big is the population that is reported to be "undecided"? In some elections, members of this group cast the crucial ballots. In reporting their results pollsters have a rule that says: "If the undecided people were to cast their ballots in the same proportion as those who have made up their minds. . . ." But wait. If those people *were* like the decided, they too would have made up their minds. Sometimes they *do* vote like early deciders, but sometimes they don't. Unfortunately, not enough is known about when they do and when they don't; the best advice we can give is to pay close attention to what the pollster says he is doing about them, and if they are more than 10 to 15 percent of the population sampled, then place little confidence in the reliability of the reported outcome. Until these people make up their minds, it is too early to tell about the outcome.

2. How stable is general sentiment in the population? Very often the polls will report wide swings of sentiment from week to week. In 1960, the Gallup organization began averaging one week's totals with the previous week's part way through the campaign—without telling its readers.[103] This tended to depress the extent of an apparent shift of sympathy from Nixon to Kennedy, and it also tended to make the figures appear a great deal more stable and settled than they actually were. In general, wide swings of sentiment from week to week mean that opinions have not crystallized sufficiently for a reliable prediction to be made. Hence the

rush to Reagan in the last week of the 1980 election led to a much stronger showing for him than any of the major polling organizations predicted.

3. Remember that the polls are based on a gross, overall, nationwide sample, but that presidential elections are decided by the distribution of votes in the Electoral College. Thus a really reliable prediction would have to include a state-by-state breakdown. This is prohibitively expensive, and so it is not done. If it were done, it would be possible to detect situations like the following: Candidate A has 49 percent of the popular vote in polls taken in all the populous states and 75 percent of the popular vote in sparsely settled states. He loses badly to Candidate B in the Electoral College, although it looks like it was going the other way. Pollsters generally caution that they are trying only to forecast the percentage distributions in the popular vote. Here again, if the result is closely divided at around 50 percent, then the poll may be quite close to being perfectly accurate but still forecast the wrong winner.

4. Some people never show up to vote on election day; these tend to be undecideds and Democrats (in that order) more often than Republicans, but in any event some sort of grain of salt has to be taken with results in order to account for the phenomenon of differential turnout. Most experienced polling organizations do build some sort of correction into their results based on assumptions about how many people in their sample will actually vote. It is important to know precisely what this assumption is and what the resulting corrections are.

5. Many people feel that the samples used by pollsters—of 2,000 to 5,000 people—are inadequate to represent the feelings of the millions of Americans whose voting they are supposed to represent. This, by and large, is a false issue. Experience has shown that very few of the errors one makes with a sample of 3,000 are correctable with a sample of 15,000 or 20,000, although the expense of polling such a population rises steeply.[104]

Generally, it is not a sampling error that is at fault nowadays when pollsters' predictions go awry, but illicit "cooking" of the data or incompetent interpretations of findings. One famous instance of a sampling error occurred when polling was in its most rudimentary stages. In 1936 the *Literary Digest* predicted a landslide victory for the Republican Alfred Landon.[105] When Franklin D. Roosevelt won overwhelmingly, the *Digest* became a laughing-stock and soon thereafter went out of business. What had happened was simple enough. The magazine had sent out millions of postcards to telephone subscribers asking them how they intended to vote. The returns showed a huge Republican triumph. Surely, the *Digest* must have thought, we cannot possibly be wrong when our total response is so large and so one-sided. But, of course, something was terribly wrong. And that stemmed from the fact that only 2.3 million people responded out of 10 million recipients of the cards, and these were all voluntary respondents. So the *Digest* got its returns from a group in the population more likely to vote Republican and completely ignored the larger number of poorer people who were going to vote Democratic. There is a much greater tendency for people of wealth and education to return mail questionnaires so that the bias in favor of people likely to vote Republican was further enhanced.[106]

In 1948, a whole series of errors were made, but none of them seem to have been connected with the size of the sample. In that year, the Gallup, Roper, and Crossley polls all predicted that Governor Dewey would unseat President Truman. Among the problems with the polls that year, the following were uncovered by a committee of social scientists after the event.[107]

1. The pollsters were so sure of the outcome that they stopped taking polls early in the campaign, assuming that the large population of undecideds would vote, if they voted, in the same way as those who had made up their minds early in the campaign.

2. The undecideds voted in just the reverse proportions.

3. Many instances were revealed where polling organization analysts, disbelieving pro-Truman results, arbitrarily "corrected" them in favor of Dewey. The methods of analysis employed were not traced in any systematic way, however, because they could not systematically be reconstructed from records of the polling organizations.

4. Sampling error occurred not because of the size of the samples, but because respondents were selected by methods that gave interviewers too much leeway to introduce biases into the sample. The so-called quota-control method (which instructs interviewers, for example, out of twenty interviews to pick ten men, ten women; fifteen Protestants, four Catholics, one Jew; seventeen whites and three blacks, and so on) has been replaced with "stratified random samples," in which geographic areas are picked randomly, and neighborhoods and houses within neighborhoods are selected randomly with controls so that areas representing a variety of

economic levels are sure to be selected. This gives the people in charge of the poll greater control over who is going to be in their sample and prevents interviewers from asking only people who live near them or who are conveniently accessible in some other way and are likely to be similar to them in social standing and political outlook. Today, when virtually all American households have telephones (far more than in 1936) telephone surveys using sophisticated methods of randomization have been developed. Because they are much cheaper than door-to-door sampling, larger numbers of respondents can be contacted.

Predicting presidential elections is largely a matter of satisfying curiosity. It is a great game to guess who will win, and we look to the polls for indications of the signs of the times. But the importance of this kind of prediction is not great. After all, we get to know who has won very soon after election day with much greater detail and accuracy than the polls can supply. The bare prediction of the outcome, even if it is reasonably correct, tells us little about how the result came to occur. More may be learned if it is possible to break down the figures to see what kinds of groups—ethnic, racial, economic, regional—voted to what degree for which candidates. Yet our enlightenment at this point is still not great. Suppose we know that in one election Catholics voted Democratic 60 percent of the time and in another election this percentage was reduced to 53. Surely this is interesting; but unless we have some good idea about why Catholics have switched their allegiance, our knowledge has hardly advanced. The polls often tell us "what" but seldom "why." There is, however, no reason why polling techniques in the future cannot be used to answer "why" questions.[108]

The usual polling technique consists of talking to samples of the population at various points in time. The samples may be perfectly adequate, but different people constitute each successive sample as the interviewers seek out people who meet their specifications. It is difficult to discover with any reliability why particular individuals or classes of people are changing their minds because interviewers ordinarily do not go back to the same people who gave their original preferences. A panel survey is used to overcome this difficulty.[109] In a panel survey, a sample of the voting population is obtained and the very same people are interviewed at various intervals before election day and perhaps afterwards. This technique makes it possible to isolate the people who make up their minds early and those who decide late. These groups can be reinterviewed and examined for other distinguishing characteristics. More important, perhaps, those voters who change their minds during the campaign can be identified and studied. If a panel of respondents can be reinterviewed over a number of years and a series of elections, it may become possible to discover directly why some people change their voting habits from election to election.

Chapter 5

Reform

In 1968 the Democratic party endured a season of turmoil: its incumbent president withdrew his candidacy to succeed himself, a leading candidate to succeed him was assassinated, and its national convention was conducted amidst extraordinary uproar. In the aftermath of that convention, a party commission on reform of the nomination process—the McGovern-Fraser Commission as it was called—was constituted, and a year later brought in some proposals for changing presidential nominations. These were adopted by the Democratic party.

After every national nominating convention since then, the Democrats have had such a commission. Table 5.1 gives pertinent facts about their leadership and their main effects. It is fair to say that for the past fifteen years reform has been in the air. Even Republicans have been affected, since in some cases state laws have had to be enacted to comply with Democratic party regulations.

Previous chapters have incorporated the results of these reforms into the description of the process we have given so far, concentrating on features of the presidential nomination process as it presently exists and on the political consequences that flow from our system as it is now organized. Some of these features have been part of the landscape of American politics for a generation

Table 5.1

Reform Commissions of the Democratic Party, 1969–1982

Name	Duration	Leadership	Main Effects
McGovern-Fraser	1969–72	Senator George McGovern (S.D.); Representative Donald M. Fraser (Minn.)	Established guidelines for the selection of delegates; outlawed two systems of delegate selection
Mikulski	1972–73	Barbara A. Mikulski, Baltimore City Councilwoman	Banned open cross-over primaries; replaced stringent quotas on blacks, women, and youths with nonmandatory affirmative action programs
Winograd	1975–80	Morley Winograd, former chairman of Michigan Dem. Party	Eliminated loophole primary; shortened delegate selection season; increased size of delegations to accommodate state party and elected officials; maintained ban on cross-over primaries; required primary states to set filing deadlines for candidates 30 to 90 days before the voting
Hunt	1980–82	Governor James B. Hunt, Jr. (North Carolina)	Provided uncommitted delegate spots for major party and elected officials; relaxed proportional representation; ended ban on loophole primary; shortened primary and caucus season to a 3-month-window; weakened delegate binding rule; maintained candidate's right to approve delegates; maintained affirmative action and equal division rule; maintained ban on cross-over primary

Adapted from William Crotty, *Party Reform* (New York, 1983), pp. 40–43. Additional sources: Adam Clymer, "Democrats Adopt Nominating Rules for '80 Campaign," *New York Times*, June 10, 1978; Clymer, "Democrats Alter Delegate Rules, Giving Top Officials More Power," *New York Times*, March 27, 1982; and Rhodes Cook, "Democrats' Rules Weaken Representation," *Congressional Quarterly Weekly Report*, April 3, 1982, p. 750.

or more; others are new, and the changes they may bring about lie mostly in the future. Nevertheless, if there is one certainty about presidential elections, it is that this process is subject to continuous pressure for change.

In this chapter we review a number of proposals for future change of the American party system and its nomination and election processes. Because of the rapid reforms of the past few years, some of the impetus behind suggestions for further reform has no doubt slackened. As past solutions lead to future problems, however, new proposals enter the agenda and old ones depart.

These new proposals for change stem on the whole from two camps, which for purposes of discussion we wish to treat as distinct entities. One camp urges "openness" and "participation" in the political process and has advocated weakening party organizations and strengthening candidates, factions, and their ideological concerns. The other group urges strengthened parties, but not as the focus of organizational loyalties so much as the vehicles for the promulgation of policy. Thus, while both sets of reformers ostensibly disagree about whether they want parties to be strong or weak, this comes down to a difference in predictions about the outcome of the application of the same remedy, for both in the end prescribe the same thing: more ideology as the tie that binds voters to elected officials, and less organizational loyalty.

☆ The Political Theory of Policy Government

The first branch of the party reform movement has its antecedents in the writings of Woodrow Wilson, James Bryce, and other passionate constitutional tinkerers who founded and breathed life into the academic study of political science. The descendants of these thinkers have through the years elaborated a series of proposals that are embodied in a coherent general political theory. This theory contains a conception of the proper function of the political party, evaluates the legitimacy and the roles of Congress and the president, and enshrines a particular definition of the public interest. Different advocates of reform have stated this theory with greater or less elaboration; some reformers leave out certain features of it, and some are disinclined to face squarely the implications of the measures they espouse. We shall try here to reproduce correctly a style of argument that, though it ignores the slight differences separating these party reformers one from another, gives a coherent statement of their party reform theory and contrasts it with the political theory that critics of their position advance.[1]

This group of party reformers suggests that democratic government requires political parties that (1) make policy commitments to the electorate, (2) are willing and able to carry them out when in office, (3) develop alternatives to government policies when out of office, and (4) differ sufficiently to "provide the electorate with a proper range of choice between alternatives of action."[2] They thus come to define a political party as "an association of broadly like-minded voters seeking to carry out common objectives through their elected representatives."[3] In a word, party should be based on policy.

Virtually all significant party relationships are, for these reformers, mediated by policy considerations. The electorate is assumed to be policy motivated and mandate conscious. Policy discussion among party members is expected to create widespread agreement upon which party discipline will then be based. Pressure groups are to be resisted and accommodated only as the overall policy commitments of party permit. The weaknesses of parties and the disabilities of governments are seen as stemming from failure to develop and support satisfactory policy programs. Hence it seems sensible to refer to this theory of party reform as a theory of "policy government." This theory suggests "that the choices provided by the two-party system are valuable to the American people in proportion to their definition in terms of public policy."[4] It differs from the participatory brand of party reform in that policy reformers believe they are revitalizing party organizations, whereas participatory democrats are likely to be indifferent to party organization.

Opponents of party reform believe that democratic government in the United States requires the minimization of conflict between contending interests and social forces.[5] Their ideal political party is a mechanism for accomplishing and reinforcing adjustment and compromise among the various interests in society to prevent severe social conflict. Where reformers desire parties that operate "not as mere brokers between different groups and interests but as agencies of the electorate," their critics see the party as an "agency for compromise." Opponents of party reform and policy government hold that "the general welfare is achieved by harmonizing and adjusting group interests."[6] In fact, they sometimes go so far as to suggest that "the contribution that parties make to policy is inconsequential so long as they maintain conditions for adjustment."[7] Thus, the theory of the political party upheld by critics of the party reform position is rooted in a notion of "consensus government."

A basic cleavage between advocates of policy government and consensus government may be observed in their radically opposed conceptions of the public interest. For advocates of consensus government, the public interest is defined as whatever emerges from the negotiations, adjustments, and compromises made in fair fights or bargains among conflicting interest groups. They suggest no external criteria by which policies can be measured in order to determine whether or not they are in the public interest. So long as the process by which decisions are made consists of intergroup bargaining, within certain specified democratic "rules of the game," they regard the outcomes as being in the public interest.

For advocates of policy government, the public interest is a discoverable set of policies that represents "something more than the mathematical result of the claims of all the pressure groups."[8] While they suggest that there are ways of judging whether a policy is in the public interest, apart from the procedural test applied by supporters of consensus government, these methods are never identified. This lack of concrete criteria spelling out the public interest would not present great difficulties if policy government advocates did not demand that an authoritative determination of party policy be made and that party members be held to it. Information about the policy preferences of members is supposed to flow upward, and orders establishing and enforcing final policy decisions are supposed to flow downward in a greatly strengthened pyramid of party authority. Without criteria of the public interest clearly in mind, however, party leaders can define the public interest in any terms they find convenient.

If we were to have parties that resembled the ideal of the party reformers, what would they be like? They would be coherent in their policies, reliable in carrying them out, accountable to the people, sharply differentiated and in conflict with each other, disciplined and hierarchical internally. Let us see, then, what it would take to create a party system of this kind.

For the parties to carry out the promises they make, the people responsible for making promises would have to be the same as (or in control of) the people responsible for carrying them out. This means, logically, one of two alternatives. Either the people who controlled party performance all year round would have to write the party platforms at the national conventions, or the people who wrote the platforms would have to be put in charge of party performance. In the first case, the party platforms would have to be written by leaders such as the congressmen who at present refrain from enacting laws favored by both national conventions. State and local political leaders would write their respective platforms. Under such an arrangement, very little formal, overall coordination or policy coherence seems likely to emerge. Since logically coherent, unified policy is the main point of policy government, making possible rational choices by voters, we must reject the first alternative as a way to fulfill the demands of party reformers.

In fact, it is the second alternative that is most often recommended by advocates of policy government. National conventions must make policy that will be enforced on national, state, and local levels by means of party discipline, and the people who write the convention platforms must be put in charge. This arrangement also has a fatal defect: It ignores the power of the people who do not write the platforms. How are independently elected congressmen to be bypassed? Will present-day sectional and state party leaders acquiesce in this rearrangement of power and subject themselves to discipline from a newly constituted outside source? Party reform has already gone some distance toward reducing the influence of these people in the presidential nomination process. Will they give up their independent capacity as public officials to make policy as well? Generally, we assume they will not.

One reformer says: "As for the clash of personal political ambitions in the United States, they are being completely submerged by the international and domestic concerns of the American public. War and peace, inflation and depression are both personal and universal issues; tariff, taxes, foreign aid, military spending, federal reserve policies, and hosts of other national policies affect local economic activities across the land. Politicians who wish to become statesmen must be able to talk intelligently about issues that concern people in all constituencies. . . ."[9]

But is it necessarily the case, as party reformers suggest, that the increasing importance of national issues will inevitably lead to placing greater power in the hands of party leaders with national (that is to say, presidential) constituencies? There is no necessary connection between political power in the national arena and the national scope of issues. National political power may rest upon local control of nomination, alliances with local interest groups, and many other bases. Even if national issues become more important, as they well may, this may only enhance the powers of the local interests best able to influence national policy—such as, for example, the people in the congressional districts that elect influential members of the House of Representatives. So far, the nationalization of policy has been accompanied by the rule of single-issue strengthened groups rather than interpretive national institutions.

The people who have the most to lose from policy government are the leaders of Congress. As of now, the major electoral risks facing national legislators are local. This does not mean that they will necessarily be parochial in their attitudes and policy commitments. But it does mean that they are not necessarily bound to support the president or national party leadership on issues of high local saliency. In order to impose discipline successfully, the national party must be able either to control sanctions presently important to legislators, such as nomination to office, or to impose still more severe ones upon them. At the moment, our system provides for control of congressional, state, and local nominations and elections by geographically localized electorates and party leaders. Presidents are not totally helpless in affecting the outcomes of these local decisions, but their influence is in most cases quite marginal.[10]

In the light of this, one obvious electoral prerequisite of disciplined parties is that local voters must be so strongly tied to national party issues that they will reward their local representatives for supporting national policy pronouncements, even at the expense of local advantage. To a certain extent, with the growing influence of national news media and the rising educational level of the electorate, as well as some increase in the general propensity to be ideologically purist, this condition is being met. The issues on which the national party makes its appeal must either unify a large number of constituencies in favor of the party or appeal at least to some substantial segment of opinion everywhere. But even if this could be accomplished, it would be strategically unwise for parties to attempt to discipline members who lived in areas that are strongly against national party policy. This would mean reading the offending area out of the party. Therefore, reformers must show how they intend to contribute to the national character of political parties by enforcing national policies upon members of Congress whose local constituencies are drastically opposed to national party policy, or whose constituents do not pay attention to issues but care more for the personality or the services of their congressman.[11] Insofar as leeway exists, let us say, for Republicans in the Northeast—nowadays called "gypsy moths"—to support liberal programs and for Southern Democrats—"boll weevils"—to oppose them, the parties shall, in fact, have retained their old, "undisciplined," "irresponsible" shapes. Insofar as this leeway does not exist, splinter groups of various kinds are encouraged to split off from the established parties. This is a consequence regarded as undesirable by most party reformers.

A second method for reducing the independent power over policy of independently elected congressional leaders has begun to have an effect in national politics. This method addresses not the prospects for nomination and election of congressional leaders but rather their capacity to lead in Congress. Adherence to the conservatism of the majority of Republicans in

Congress has in general been a prerequisite of leadership within the Republican party. Among congressional Democrats, however, consistently the majority party in Congress and in the nation, more leeway has existed for congressional leaders—at any rate for committee chairmen, who in the past have been selected by seniority—to take whatever policy positions they pleased.

Since the mid-1950s, sentiment has grown in Congress that conservative Democratic committee chairmen should be more responsive to the policy preferences of the majority of the majority party, and in recent years the Democratic caucus of the House of Representatives has acted to remove committee chairmen they have regarded as unresponsive. This has not, however, proceeded strictly along ideological lines. One of the first chairmen to be removed, Wright Patman of Texas, was as liberal as any Democrat in the House, including his replacement, Henry Reuss of Wisconsin. Another chairman, Edward Hebert of the Armed Services Committee, was replaced by a leader ideologically indistinguishable from him on matters coming before the committee. So, despite the unlimbering of a new weapon that has the potential of encouraging party responsibility in Congress, it has not been used consistently quite in this way, and concerns related to the management of Congress itself have thus far been more significant than the shaping or enforcement of party policy in the activities of the reactivated Democratic caucus.

☆ The Evolution of a Second Branch of Party Reform

It should be obvious that party reforms are generally not politically neutral. They are designed almost entirely to strengthen the president and to weaken Congress, especially as Congress is presently constituted. Reforms of the party system are in general also designed to help Democrats and weaken Republicans. The reasoning is this: Republican presidents represent a party generally unsympathetic to increased activity by the federal government. Hence, they will be inclined to ask less of Congress, and thus they run less risk of being stymied on matters of policy by a recalcitrant Congress. Democratic presidents, on the other hand, on behalf of the more liberal, more activist, and more innovative party, ask much more of Congress and customarily have to settle for much less of what they ask for.

It seems to us quite understandable that agitation for party reform, which during the late 1940s so excited the liberal academicians who are its chief proponents, died away to a whisper during the Eisenhower decade. In the early 1960s frustrated liberals took up their cudgels in the cause of party "responsibility" and presidential prerogative. The underlying aim, it seems to us, was to speed up the social changes that they desired by trying to rig the rules of the game more in favor of that political institution, the presidency, which shared their policy preferences.

The close connection between the desire for party reform and the policy preferences of reformers was again illustrated in the late 1960s. Reformers could no longer complain about the failure of a conservative Congress to enact New Deal-type welfare measures; the Eighty-ninth Congress had taken care of that. Their attention now became focused on foreign policy because they were outraged by America's continued involvement in the war in Vietnam. It turned out that presidents were, if anything, more in favor of military involvement in Vietnam than were many congressmen. The frustrations of reformers were centered on the inability of senators who favored an antiwar policy to persuade the president to withdraw American troops and commitments as fast as they would have liked. Hence, it was no longer feasible to advocate reforms that would enable presidents to pursue presidential foreign policies despite the reluctance of congressmen. Instead, reformers began to entertain notions of limitations on presidential prerogatives. It is, unfortunately, exceedingly difficult to stop presidents from doing things one doesn't like (such as, for example, fighting a war in Indochina) without also preventing them from taking actions of which one approves (such as, for instance, fighting inflation or unemployment). Since liberals want a strong presidency in domestic affairs and conservatives want a strong presidency in foreign affairs, the result is a phenomenon we all observe, namely, ambivalence about the power of the presidency.

Because it is not feasible to limit the damage presidents can do without also limiting the good they can do, the attention of many current party reformers has focused on making the presidential selection procedure more responsive to their preferences without regard to the strengthening of parties. They believe that if the nomination procedure were opened up to more party voters in primaries and to party activists in district and state conventions, they would have a better chance of nominating a candidate they prefer. Their immediate cause for complaint was the 1968 Democratic convention, in which they believed the fortunes of nominees like Eugene McCarthy and George McGovern were damaged by undemocratic modes of delegate selection. In view of the commanding margin of victory at the convention for Hubert Humphrey, it seems doubtful that different procedures, even if they had been enforced at the time, would have changed enough delegate votes to make a difference in the 1968 outcome. But it was strongly thought so at the time, and at that convention rules changes were begun that changed the face of politics in the Democratic party.[12] The assumption behind the views of new reformers, who represent generally left-wing policy positions within the Democratic party, is that if the people are given a choice they will support candidates with policy preferences more like their own.

☆ Reform by Means of Participatory Democracy: An Appraisal

The efforts of purists who advocate participatory democracy and who have attempted to make the Democratic party the vehicle of this approach to government have met with considerable success over the past few years. Here we wish to contemplate the theory of politics that underlies this position. Ordinarily, participatory democrats criticize the American political system in two respects. First, they argue that elections have insufficient impact on policy outcomes of the government. These critics see no direct link between public policy and the desires of electoral majorities. Second, there is the critique of the electoral process itself, which argues that policy does not represent what majorities want because elected representatives are not responsive to majority desires. These criticisms are simple-minded in one sense and cogent in another. They are simple-minded in that they ignore the immense problems that would have to be overcome if we were truly serious about transforming America or any large diverse population into a participatory democracy. They are cogent in that responsiveness to majorities on questions of policy is a fundamental value that gives legitimacy to democratic government. The connection between such criticism and the legitimacy of government makes it important to deal at least briefly with some of the issues and problems that should be raised (and usually are not) by judgments of this fundamental nature.

The first and obvious question to ask is whether the criticisms are based on fact. Is the American system unresponsive to the policy desires of a majority of its citizens? Unfortunately, there is no unambiguous way to answer this question. If we focus our attention, for example, on the mechanics of the policy process, we find what appears to be government by minorities. In some policy areas a great number of people and interests, organized and unorganized, may have both a say in open hearings and some influence on the final product. But fewer individuals may be involved in areas dealing with other problems and policies, some of which will be of a specialized nature, of limited interest, and so on. Certainly it is true that even members of Congress do not have equal or high influence over every decision: committee jurisdictions, seniority, special knowledge, party, individual reputation—all combine to weigh the influence of each member on a different scale for each issue.

So we must conclude that if we adopt direct participation in and equal influence over the policy decisions of our government (the decisions that "affect our lives") as the single criterion of democracy, then our system surely fails the test. So, we might note, does every government known to us— possibly excepting two or three rural Swiss cantons.

Another approach might focus on public opinion as an index of majority desires. Using this standard a quite different picture emerges. The vast majority of policy decisions made by the government have the support of popular majorities. In cases where this is not true, the lack of "responsiveness" may have several causes, not all of them curable: (1) conflicts between majority desires and intractable situations in the world (for example, the desire to transform, peaceably, the Soviet Union into a liberal democratic ally); or (2) public attitudes favoring certain sets of policies that are mutually incompatible (such as the desires for a very high rate of employment and very low rates of inflation); or (3) clear, consistent, and feasible majority desires that are ignored by the government because the desires are unconstitutional or antithetical to enduring values of the political system, to which leaders are more sensitive than popular majorities. Surveys, for example, have from time to time revealed majorities in favor of constitutionally questionable repressive measures against dissenters and the press.

Criticisms of presidential elections are more difficult to assess. American politics does respond to the application of resources that are arguably nondemocratic and that cause the influence of different actors to be weighed unequally. In a truly democratic system, it could be argued, each person would count for one and no person would count for more than one: the system would respond to numbers and only numbers. As we have indicated, however, money, incumbency, energy and enthusiasm, popularity, name recognition, ability, and experience are all valuable assets within the structure of American politics. Should the system be condemned for this? Should we attempt to eradicate the influence of these resources? Before joining a campaign in behalf of this cause, it may be wise to consider for a moment why these nondemocratic resources are useful.

Possession of the relevant political resources could increase an individual's influence because candidates seek the support of such people. They do so because a contender needs money to publicize himself and his cause and because he needs experienced and able allies to help him convey his image effectively to the voter. Political resources and the people who possess them are important, in short, because campaigns are important. And campaigns are important because the general public needs to be alerted to the fact that an election is near. Partisans must be mobilized, the uncommitted convinced, perhaps even a few minds changed. Resources other than votes are important because—and only because—numerical majorities must be mobilized.

American politics responds to nondemocratic resources because many, if not most, citizens are politically apathetic. If nearly everyone participated, no other resources would be necessary. Why is political apathy widespread? There are several alternative explanations. Perhaps it is because the system presents the citizenry with no real alternatives from which to choose. However, in the election of 1964, there was at least a partial test of this "hidden vote" theory, and the evidence is negative. And in 1972, another year when there was an unambiguous choice, nonvoting hit a high for elections up to then. Perhaps it is because the public has been imbued with a "false consciousness" that blinds them to their "real" desires and interests. This explanation is traditionally seized upon by the enlightened few to deny value to the preferences of the ignorant many. The people, we are told, are easily fooled; this testifies to their credulity. They do not know what is good for them; this makes them childlike. But when the people cannot trust their own feelings, when their desires are alleged to be unworthy, when their policy preferences should be ignored because they are not "genuine" or "authentic," they are being deprived of their humanity as well. What is left for the people if they are deprived of judgment, wisdom, feeling, desire, and preference? Such an argument would offer little hope for democracy of any sort, for it introduces the most blatant form of inequality as a political "given": a structured, ascribed difference between those who know what is "good" for themselves and those who must be "told." No doubt it is true that much of the time we do not know (without the advantage of perfect foresight) what is best for us. But that is not to say that others know better, that our consciousness is false but theirs is true. Persons who make this argument do not believe in democracy.

A more hopeful and less self-contradictory explanation of political apathy might note that throughout American history a substantial number of citizens have not wished to concern themselves continually with the problems and actions of government. Many citizens prefer to participate on their own terms, involving themselves with a particular issue area or problem. These citizens' participation is necessarily sporadic and narrower than that of the voter interested in all public problems and actively involved in general political life. Many other citizens (surely a majority) are more interested in their own personal problems than in any issue of public policy.[13] This, we would suggest, is the real "silent majority": citizens who meet their public obligations by going to the polls at fairly regular intervals, making their selections on the basis of their own criteria, and then supporting the actions and policies of the winners—whether they are their first choices or not. In the intervals, unless they themselves are personally affected by some policy proposal, most of these citizens simply wish to be left alone.

Recently a number of studies have shown unfavorable citizen attitudes toward the political system, what is sometimes called "alienation." These attitudes do not explain low rates of voting participation, however; persons who score high in these attitudes evidently participate at about the same rate as the nonalienated.[14] So we surmise that most citizens do not vote because they are concerned with other things important to them, like earning a living or painting a picture or cultivating a garden, and not because they feel it is so difficult to influence outcomes. They simply do not take much time and effort to become informed enough to want to vote. But, given the peripheral importance of politics in many peoples' lives, even a little bit of extra effort at making it easier to vote does make a difference in turnout. Were this not so, laws making it easier to register and to vote would not be as successful as they are in increasing voter participation.

Consider a society in which all citizens were as concerned about public matters as the most active of our party volunteers. Such a society would not require mobilization: all who were able to would vote. The hoopla and gimmickry associated with our contemporary (and past) political campaigns would have little effect: this citizenry would know the record of the party and the candidate and, presumably, would make their reasoned choice on this basis. Should such an active society be the goal of those whose political philosophy is democratic? This question should not and cannot be answered without first addressing the problem of how such a society could be achieved.

Without attempting to be comprehensive, a few difficulties do merit some specific comment. First and foremost, political participation—as Aristotle made clear several thousand years ago—takes a great deal of time. For this reason (among others) a large population of slaves was felt to be a necessary concomitant of participatory government: it freed Athenian citizens from the cares of maintaining life and thus provided them the leisure time that made their political activity possible. But having rejected some hundred years ago this ingenious solution to the problems related to relatively large-scale participation, we must deal with the fact that the vast majority of our citizens must work for a living. Most Americans lack the disposable time that permits professionals and students and other privileged people to choose their working hours. Most citizens lack the time, even if they had the temperament and training, to engage continually in politics. To the degree that representative institutions—political parties, legislatures, elected executives—are denigrated in favor of more direct modes of activity, the majority of the people will be without the means of participation through which they can most effectively make their will felt. In short, to impose requirements of direct participation on those desiring a voice in decisions would be to ensure that the incessant few rather than the sporadic many would rule: thus the 1960s' slogan "power to the people" really proposed to replace a representative few, who are elected, with an unrepresentative few, who are self-appointed. And this, as we have indicated, is precisely the effect that changes in the rules governing nominations in the Democratic party are having.

There is an alternative explanation for the decline in participation that deserves consideration. If government is perceived to be the source of difficulty rather than the solution to problems, it would not be surprising if fewer people thought it worthwhile contributing to the selection of those who would invariably do more harm than good. Whoever wins, the slogan would be, the people lose. Surprising as it may seem, both major parties have contributed to disparagement of government. In olden times, when parties still helped structure conflict, way back to the mid-1960s, the overarching issues were all too obvious: Conservatives (including most Republicans) who had to pay taxes for other people's programs were generally against expansion of the public sector, and liberals (including most Democrats) who spent other people's money on behalf of their constituencies were mostly in favor of them. Then simplicity began to give way to complexity. As the legitimacy of the political process came under attack by opponents of the Vietnam War, a disposition strengthened by the civil rights movement and the Watergate affair, spokesmen for beneficiaries began to attack social welfare policies as grossly inadequate and unfair, too little and too late, and tainted by the corruption of the system from which they stemmed. At the same time, as the system's capacity to detect failure by making sophisticated policy evaluations leaped ahead of its ability to deliver policy success, former liberals became "neo-conservatives" who attacked many governmental policies and the disrepute their failures brought upon government.

If it were true, as was alleged on the left, that welfare programs were a form of domination over poor people, harming instead of helping them, then Ronald Reagan should have been regarded as their savior, for he certainly promised and provided less of this domination. If it were the avowed aim of conservatives to rebuild respect for authority, denigration of the federal government is a poor way to prove their point. Why, to take a current controversy, should President Reagan be trusted to spend an increased defense budget wisely when he and his colleagues doubt the ability of the rest of the government to achieve desirable results? And since effective government depends on a high-caliber civil service, why should all concerned think to gain by castigating public servants? This is no method for recruiting talented young people to serve in government, or for retaining the services of talented older people.

Thus there are difficulties with a theory that demands high levels of political participation. We raise this issue not because we are opposed in principle to the idea of an active, participatory, democratic society. By persuasion and political education the majority of our citizens might indeed be convinced that the quality of our shared existence could and should be improved through more continuous devotion to public activity. But this is quite different from arguing that the rules of the game should be changed to disenfranchise those who presently lack the opportunity or desire to be active in this sense. We do not favor efforts to implement ideal goals when the preconditions and the means of achieving these goals do not exist. We do not favor actions that in the name of democracy (or under any other guise) restrict the ability of most of the people to have their political say. We do favor nomination processes that blend solutions to the problem of getting into office with solutions to the problems of governing thereafter.

☆ Three Specific Reforms

Comprehensive reform of the party system rides in on tides of strong feeling. Until such feelings exist among party activists, rational advocacy looking toward reform is wasted; once such feeling exists, rational advocacy is superfluous. So the type of analysis we undertake here is bound to be uninfluential. We attempt it only because thoughtful citizens outside the mainstream of political life may find it instructive to consider the consequences of the best-laid plans. Once these consequences have had an opportunity to manifest themselves, however, a new generation of reform may be in order. After all, practically everything that reformers object to now was once somebody's favorite reform.

We suspect that the achievement of many—not all—of the specific objectives of party reformers would be detrimental to their aims and to those of most thoughtful citizens. Let us consider, for example, three specific reforms of governmental machinery that are commonly advocated to make the parties more responsive to popular will and more democratic. Party reformers often advocate a variety of changes in the nomination process, simplification of the process of registering voters, and modification or abolition of the Electoral College. Two of these reforms might well have the exactly opposite effects.

☆ An Appraisal of the Nomination Process

In order to evaluate the nominating process, it would be helpful to suggest a set of goals that most Americans would accept as desirable and important.[15] The following seven standards appear to meet this test: any method for nominating presidents should (1) aid in preserving the two-party system, (2) help secure vigorous competition between the parties, (3) maintain some degree of cohesion and agreement within the parties, (4) produce candidates who have a likelihood of winning voter support, (5) lead to the choice of candidates who are reasonably well qualified, (6) lead to the acceptance of candidates as legitimate, and (7) result in officeholders who are capable of generating support for public policies they intend to pursue. We first look at some suggested alternatives to a system that relies heavily upon decision making by party leaders at national conventions.

A national direct primary has often been suggested. Many people took heart in 1968 from the way in which the piecemeal primaries around the country facilitated the expression of antiwar sentiment, and they noted that nonprimary states were less responsive to persons whose participation in party activities was largely precipitated by strong feelings about the war. This led to a conclusion that primaries were rather a good thing and that, therefore, a national primary was in order.

We believe this would have serious disadvantages. First of all, it would have been self-defeating as far as the professed goals of many antiwar people who advocated it were concerned. By contesting primaries one at a time in

1968, Senator Eugene McCarthy, and later Senator Robert Kennedy, were able to construct "test cases." We doubt that McCarthy, given the limitations of his resources before New Hampshire, could have even entered a national primary.

This merely points to a more general problem of financing national primary elections. It is quite probable that many candidates—perhaps as many as ten of them—might obtain enough signatures on nominating petitions or qualify by some other device to get on the ballot. Imagine a crowd of challengers hustling all over the United States campaigning in a national primary. It would take, of course, enormous amounts of money. The parties could hardly be expected to show favoritism and so could not finance these candidates. Although government financing would no doubt be made available, this would have to depend upon demonstrated ability to raise money previously in order to discourage frivolous candidates. The preprimary campaign, therefore, would assume enormous importance and would be exceedingly expensive. Nationwide challengers would have to have access to very large amounts of money. It would also help if they were already well known. They would also have to be quite sturdy physically. It is not hard to forecast that nobody would win a clear majority in a primary with a large number of contenders. Since all contenders would be wearing the same party label, it is hard to see how voters could differentiate among candidates except by already knowing one or two of their names in favorable or unfavorable contexts, by liking or not liking their looks, by identifying or not identifying with their ethnic or racial characteristics, by attending to their treatment in the press and by television news reports, or by some other means of differentiation having nothing whatever to do with ability or inclination to do the job, or even with their policy positions. Since patents on policy positions are not available, it is reasonable to suppose that more than one candidate would adopt roughly the same set of positions. Or they might, for the purpose of the primary, falsely portray themselves as disagreeing. Thus, voters would be fortunate if the intellectual content of the campaign consisted of quibbling about who proposed what first and, more relevantly, who could deliver better.

Suppose, then, that the primary vote was divided among several candidates. Suppose, as is the case for gubernatorial elections in some southern states, that ten or twelve aspirants divided the votes. One possibility is that the party nominee would be the candidate with the highest number of votes, say, 19 percent of those cast, a much less democratic choice than we now have. Another possibility would be for the two highest candidates to contest a fifty-state runoff after the first primary and before the general election in a campaign that would begin to remind observers who can remember that far back of a marathon jitterbug contest. The party might end up with a good candidate, of course, if there was anything left of him to give to his party in the *real* election campaign, which would follow. Then if the poor fellow were elected he would have to find the energy to govern. By following this procedure, the United States might have to restrict its presidential candidates to wealthy athletes.

It is also possible that the parties would emerge with candidates no better on the average than those picked in smoke-filled rooms to run for high office. And perhaps they would be worse on the average, because the national primary provides for no consideration of the criteria of fitness to hold office, which can best be applied by those who actually know the candidates, who have themselves a heavy investment of time and energy in making the government work, and who know that they may have to live at close quarters with the results of their deliberations. It is difficult to persuade those who participate only casually in politics, and those who tend to do so when moved by a great issue of the day, that the intensity of their feelings does not confer a sweeping mandate. These feelings, no matter how worthy, do not make occasional participants more worthy than steady participants. They do not confer a special moral status upon latecomers to politics as compared with people who are already active. Party activists or even party leaders cannot always be excluded on grounds of moral inferiority from decision making in the presidential nomination process. The great virtue of primaries is, of course, that they provide a means—increasingly supplemented by polls—of gauging the popularity of various candidates and their effectiveness in public speaking under adverse circumstances. On the other hand, the virtue of conventions and state caucus systems (when they are allowed to operate) is that by living at closer quarters than ordinary citizens with the results of the collective choice, party leaders may bring to the choosing greater knowledge and even, sometimes, a higher sense of responsibility.

It is generally conceded that Adlai Stevenson would have made a better president than Estes Kefauver, who ran and won in most of the primaries in 1952. Stevenson, for his entire career in elective office, was the product of selection by party leaders—in some cases even by "bosses"—who were knowledgeable and continuously involved in the political process, acquainted with what governing demanded and with the personal capabilities of the politicians among whom they chose. Walter Mondale, who withdrew from the 1976 preprimary sweepstakes because of a reluctance to spend a year in various motels around the country, is not a conspicuously worse—indeed by some standards he is a better—public servant than some of those who leaped joyfully into the fray. Mondale first served in the Senate by appointment and was picked by Jimmy Carter to be his running mate without the sanctification of an election. Yet nobody supposes Mondale was picked without regard for democratic constraints. Now that Mondale has decided either that motels have improved or he has become more ambitious, we will see whether his ability to hurdle the campaign obstacle course makes him a better candidate.

Giving politicians some rights to influence political choices is not per se an evil system. Unchecked by the ultimate necessity to appeal for votes it would no doubt degenerate. Political leaders certainly would not run a system that responded easily to short-run opinions of high intensity in the electorate, but sometimes this sort of system will pick a popular candidate over a candidate in whose personal capacities the delegates have more faith. This, we think, is what delegates to the Republican convention of 1952 did when they nominated Dwight Eisenhower over Robert A. Taft. Still, conventions and caucuses of party leaders can invoke criteria of judgment unavailable to mass electorates.

In short, we believe that as long as there are many things we demand of a president—intelligence as well as popularity, integrity as well as speaking ability, private virtue as well as public presentability—we ought to foster a selection process that provides a mixture of devices for screening according to different criteria. The mixed system we advocate is not perfect, of course, but it is greatly superior to the unmixed nonblessing of the national primary.

We are not ready to give up at least some of the state primaries we now have, although it is now widely believed—and we agree—that we have too many. It is eminently desirable that it be possible in a number of states, separated geographically and in time, for test cases to be put to voters and for trial heats to be run among aspirants for high office. But a national primary would be like a steady diet consisting exclusively of dessert.

National primaries would also lead to the weakening of the party system. It is not unusual for a party to remain in office for a long period of time. If state experience with primaries is any guide, a prolonged period of victory for one party would result in a movement of interested voters into the primary of the winning party, where their votes would count for more.[16] As voters deserted the losing party, it would be largely the die-hards who were left. They would nominate candidates who pleased them but who could not win the election because they were unappealing to a majority in the nation. Eventually, the losing party would atrophy, seriously weakening the two-

party system and the prospects of competition among the parties. The winning party would soon show signs of internal weakness as a consequence of
the lack of opposition necessary to keep it unified. Since the long-run weakness of the Republican party in our system comes close to providing these
conditions already, we believe that the institution of a national primary
would in this respect be especially dangerous.

A national primary might also lead to the appearance of extremist candidates and demagogues who, unrestrained by allegiance to any permanent
party organization, would have little to lose by stirring up mass hatreds or
making absurd promises. On the whole, the convention system of the past
discouraged these extremists by placing responsibility in the hands of party
leaders who had a permanent stake in maintaining the good name and
integrity of their organization. Some insight into this problem may be had
by looking at the situation in several southern states, where most voters vote
only in the Democratic primary and where victory in that primary is tantamount to election. The result is a chaotic factional politics in which there
are few or no permanent party leaders; the distinctions between the "ins" and
"outs" become blurred; it is difficult to hold anyone responsible; and demagogues sometimes arise who make use of this situation by strident appeals.[17]
The fact that under some primary systems an extreme personality can take
the place of party in giving a kind of minimal structure to state politics should
give pause to the advocates of a national primary.

We believe, in short, that very widespread use of direct primaries weakens
the party system; it encourages prospective candidates to bypass regular
party organizations in favor of campaigns stressing personal publicity, and
it throws nominations entirely into the hands of persons whose stake in the
workings of the political process is not great enough to ensure that the
eventual nominee is qualified for the presidency by experience, qualities of
mind, or by virtue of political alliances with others professionally engaged in
political activity. The use of primaries at the state level has produced a variety
of anomalous experiences: totally unqualified candidates whose names have
resembled those of famous politicians have been nominated by innocent
voters; ethnic minorities concentrated in one party have defeated attempts by
party leaders to offer "balanced tickets," thus dooming to defeat their entire
ticket in the general election; and palpable demagogues have defeated responsible candidates. All of these consequences may not persuade reformers that
an increase in the use of direct primaries is not a good idea, but they must
be faced. If we value political parties, which reformers often profess to do,
then we must hesitate to cut them off from the process of selecting candidates

for public office, to deprive them of incentives to organize, and to set them prematurely at the mercy of masses of people whose information at the primary stage is especially poor.

This is not, we suggest, an elitist doctrine. Responsible political analysts and advocates must face the fact that party identification for most people provides the safe cognitive anchorage around which political preferences are organized. Set adrift from this anchorage, as they are when faced with an intraparty primary election, most voters have little or nothing to guide their choices. Chance familiarity with a famous name or stray feelings of ethnic kinship under these circumstances seem to provide many voters with the only clues to choice.[18] Given the conditions of popular interest and participation that prevail, we question throwing the future of the party system entirely and precipitously into the hands of primary electorates.

So long as the relevant choice is between a mixed system and a national primary, our choice lies with diversity. Suppose, however, that the number of state primaries, already overly large by our standards, grows still further. Might not a national primary be better than a series of state primaries? It might.

Stretching our primaries seriatim over the election year has the advantage of permitting knowledge of candidates to develop over time. This approach also allows candidates who might otherwise be passed over to get exposure. Money, moreover, can be raised as one goes along instead of all at once. A small band of devotees, finally, may go further and last longer if, like Antaeus, who gained strength when he touched the earth, they can replenish themselves after each primary. These virtues are counterweighted by vices.

Candidates of purely local appeal and regional leaders would not do as well if there were a national primary. Corps of activists, purists and politicians alike, will matter less and the media and their managers more, for the need to reach large numbers of people in a short time will require use of the mass media in preference to individual or small-scale efforts at persuasion. The ability to capture party meetings will not matter because there will be no meetings worth capturing. Candidates of prior national reputation, whether in politics or in some less likely sphere, such as sports or the movies, will have the advantage, as will the rich, who can spend their money on their own behalf. As their purpose in entering the primary will be to win the election, candidates will cater more to the people and less to party purists. Indeed, a national primary, contested through the national media, might enable candidates to lessen their dependence on activists because they can enter directly into relationships with voters in the mass.

The great disadvantage of national primaries is that they weaken the main intermediaries between the people and their government—political parties. But if the existing and evolving presidential nominating process also weakens parties, and if it, in addition, enthrones purists over politicians, then given this unfortunate choice, a more direct relationship between candidates and their countrymen might be the lesser evil.

Regional primaries, about which there is much talk but (as yet) little action, have apparent appeal as a halfway house between a single national primary and a multitude of state primaries. There are basically three "degrees" of regional primary that have been proposed thus far. The mildest form merely requires that all states holding presidential primaries schedule them for one of four sanctioned dates, spaced a month apart, and that all candidates on a list prepared by the Federal Election Commission appear on the ballot. A second type of proposal would group states into geographic regions. All states within a given region that choose to have a primary would be required to hold it on the same day, on the second Tuesday of a month between March and July. Further down the slippery slope is plan to make primaries mandatory for all states.[19]

Under the regional primary system candidates would not have to campaign in as many distant places at nearly the same time; this would save them money and effort. Since each election would encompass a larger geographic area, however, the need to campaign earlier, to be better known at the start, and to have more money with which to begin would be greater than it is now. It also seems likely that regional primaries would, in effect, push all states to hold primaries, thereby increasing the territory a candidate must cover and the consequent cost of campaigning. The major advantage of regional primaries, assuming they were spaced about one month apart as in one plan, would be that both politicians and people could reconsider their earlier choices in the light of the latest information. Yet if delegates were pledged to candidates, the flexibility of bargainers at the national conventions would still be diminished, and if delegates were selected by congressional district, or on a proportional basis, activist voters and their candidates would still have an enormous advantage. In addition, the predilection of the media to simplify complex phenomena would mean that voters in states given later dates would have their choices severely constrained because of the results of earlier primaries. It is possible that conflicts among states may doom the entire enterprise. If not, regional primaries, which create an opportunity to reconsider the rules of voting, may be more interesting as an effort to turn back in the guise of going forward than they are in and of themselves.

Of late, there has been a noticeable change in elite opinion. Nowadays the avowed purpose of reforming the primaries is to strengthen the party system. As usual, opinion is divided about which change will lead to what consequences and whether the purpose is to give artificial advantages to the existing major parties or to facilitate the emergence of better (as well as stronger) parties. One idea is called the "window plan" because it would drastically limit the time (to three months) during which primaries can be held. Presumably, clumping states together would confuse the media so that premature identifications of a front runner would be more difficult to make. Maybe. But perhaps, examining the entrails of whatever suited their purpose, media journalists would declare winners anyway. No doubt "Lone Rangers" like Eugene McCarthy in 1968 and Jimmy Carter in 1976 would find it more difficult to burst out ahead of the pack because there would be no Iowa or New Hampshire primaries standing alone to permit that. This would help better-known candidates. But more money earlier and more time to prepare would also be necessary because so much was being crowded into so short a time. This would enhance the roles of media and money. With four or five primaries, conventions or caucuses a week, the importance of a state would depend on how many delegates it was entitled to (based on population and its electoral support for the party) as well as how early its primary took place.

Compressing the time of the preconvention period would also reduce the number of candidates who could run and increase their need to appeal to a broad audience. This would either make candidates similar and innocuous or winnow out those who lacked widespread appeal or both. In one respect, voter choice would be easier because they would be able to choose among the smaller number of candidates who had sufficient resources to make the race. In another respect, voters would be deprived of a full spectrum of candidates. There is no need to go further as the "window" plan is again but a way-station toward a national primary.

In order to escape from domination by primaries, it has been proposed that they be considerably reduced in number and replaced by party caucuses. This might be construed as a desire for a return to rule by party "bosses," if one could still find people exercising that role. On the part of many of their present-day supporters, however, caucuses represent not a retreat but an advance toward a kind of communitarian political culture, one in which the mediating role of party activists is reinvigorated as an alternative to the dominance of mass culture through the media. As Wilson Carey McWilliams puts it, "the media specialists who shape campaigns have no ties to particular publics (or . . . parties); they are part of the mass with which they deal,

faceless and unaccountable." Rejecting plebiscitary politics and nationalization of parties through governmental legislation, McWilliams bids the modern parties look to "the private order for [their] vitality."[20] James M. Burns,
in *Party Renewal in America*, set out a similar vision of a town-hall party
democracy:

> The caucus would help restore a sense of place, of home, of neighbor-
> hood, within the parties; could help restore a world of small publics
> and local politics; could help realize, perhaps, Jefferson's splendid
> vision of a ward system that, in McWilliams' words, could combine
> the warm if parochial patriotism of local communities with the
> broader, more enlightened perspectives of central regimes.[21]

Fearing that national conventions will either wither on the vine or be
replaced by congressional imposition of a national primary, Everett Ladd
(together with Austin Ranney and Thomas Mann) has proposed that candidate eligibility to run in a primary depend on certification by a party national
committee or on getting a large number of signatures on petitions from at
least twelve states. Party conventions would also have to make room for office
holders, numbering one-third of the delegates, who would make the difference if the primaries were not decisive.[22] Pope McCorkle and Joel Fleishman
argue that involving Congress in maintaining the institutional status of the
major parties in the nominating process amounts to "a form of 'political
protectionism' for the two-party system."[23]

Our view is that there is a limit to force-feeding. State parties should have
maximum autonomy to realize their potential. Though parties would be
strengthened by closed primaries, we are, on this ground, opposed to forcing
them, as is happening in Wisconsin, to abandon practices they feel are best.
And though we feel that there are too many primaries and we would prefer
to see some of them replaced by conventions or caucuses, that change, if it
is to be desirable, must come from party members in the states and not be
imposed by congressional or national committee directives. Otherwise, every
few years, we would, no doubt on grounds of high principle, be urging some
other course of action.

In some respects, owing to actions of the Democratic party to restrict the
number of days on which primary elections can be held, all the disadvantages
of a national primary are coming into being: decision making by the badly
informed, early elections dominating the choices available in later ones,
rewards for demagogic behavior, penalties for coalition building as compared

with factional mobilization. Willy-nilly, the United States is being turned into a social laboratory in which party reformers can conduct experiments at the expense of the American people.

Another alternative of historical interest is presidential nomination by one of the branches of Congress. This, though, would be out of the question. The caucus system of nomination has been rejected since Andrew Jackson's time, because it did not give sufficient representation to the large population groups whose votes were decisive in the election.[24] Furthermore, the large fluctuations of party membership in Congress would lead to serious difficulties. If a party happened to do very poorly for a few years in several sections of the country, the representation in Congress from those areas would be small and they would, in effect, be deprived of a voice in nominating a presidential candidate for that party. This nominating procedure could advertise itself as being national in scope, but it would be far more likely than the present system to produce candidates with a limited sectional appeal. The attempts of leaders in areas where the party is weak to strengthen themselves by nominating a candidate who might help increase their vote would be stymied.

Perhaps, it may be argued, what is required is not some radically new method of nominating candidates, but reform of some of the more obnoxious practices of the present system. High on the list of objectionable practices would be the secret gathering of party leaders in the smoke-filled room. Some liken this to a political opium den where a few irresponsible men, hidden from public view, stealthily determine the destiny of the nation.[25] Yet it is difficult to see who, other than the party's leaders, should be entrusted with the delicate task of finding a candidate to meet the majority preference. If head-on clashes of strength on the convention floor do not resolve the question, the only alternative would be continued deadlock, anarchy among scores of leaderless delegates splitting the party into rival factions, or some process of accommodation.

Let us suppose that the smoke-filled room were abolished and with it all behind-the-scenes negotiations. All parleys would then be held in public, before the delegates and millions of television viewers. As a result, the participants would spend their time scoring points against each other in order to impress the folks back home. Bargaining would not be taking place since the participants would not really be communicating with one another. No compromises would be possible; leaders would be accused by their followers of selling out to the other side. Once a stalemate existed, breaking it would be practically impossible, and the party would probably disintegrate into warring factions.

An extensive system of state primaries in which delegates are legally compelled to vote for the candidate who wins in the state has led to the eclipse of the smoke-filled room without any formal action of a convention. Since delegates cannot change their positions except by direction of the candidate to whom they are pledged, there is little point in bringing party leaders together for private conferences. Sharply increasing the number of pledged delegates introduces great rigidity into the convention because under conditions of stalemate no one is in a position to switch his support.

This more or less is coming to resemble the situation of the Democratic party today. The Democratic party, through its current rule changes, has managed to embody the following contradiction: by fragmenting delegations it has increased the chances of a contested convention, and by giving preference to pledged delegates it has decreased the likelihood that delegates will be able to bargain with one another. These conditions have been masked by the overriding influence of primaries and television which, by forcing earlier and earlier decisions, has spared the party so far the consequences of a meaningful convention under conditions of extreme fragmentation. Failure to arrive at a decision to nominate a candidate acceptable to all could conceivably lead to withdrawal of the defeated factions from the party. Since the national party is unified, if at all, only by the choice of a presidential candidate, inability to bargain out an agreement invites serious party fragmentation. The resulting party realignment would then depend on what happened in the Republican party.

Situational factors are of critical importance. If the Republicans nominated a staunch conservative and the Democrats a near-radical, the incentives would increase for liberal Republicans and moderate Democrats to bolt their respective parties and even, conceivably, to join in a new-old Democratic-Republican party. The old two-party system would be gone. In its place, as in France and Japan, would be a center party that usually governs, with occasional challenges from right and left. The peripheral parties would be cohesive but unable to govern. The moderate center party would govern but, being heterogeneous, find agreement difficult. Instead of party competition under a two-party system, there would be factional competition within the major party of a multiparty system. We leave it to the reader to decide if the choice available to the public under such circumstances would be greater or better than it is now.

Much criticism has been leveled at the raucousness of demonstrations that take place on the convention floor while candidates are being nominated.[26] Criticism of demonstrations on the grounds that they are unseemly and vulgar seems to us to be trivial. There is no evidence to substantiate a claim that the final decision would be better in some way if demonstrations were banned. Undoubtedly, the demonstrations have been overdone and might be cut short. This task can safely be left to the requirements of television. As the conventions of the past few years have shown, television dictates briefer demonstrations to retain the attention of the vast audience that the party would like very much to influence in its favor.

The television coverage of the 1968 national conventions raised a number of questions concerning their future management. We wonder if all the things that went wrong at the Democratic convention of that year were the result of willful mismanagement or whether at least some of the difficulty can be attributed to the increasing unwieldiness of the convention. Delegates complained of an inability to attract the attention of the chair. The microphones allocated to each delegation on the floor were turned on and off at the rostrum, so it was impossible to use them to get the chair's attention. Attempts to telephone the chair from the floor were often ignored. Attempts to approach the rostrum were repulsed by security guards. Attempts to signal the chair were defeated by the noise and movement in the hall.

It is hard to see how such a huge and chaotic organization can conduct itself as a parliamentary body. In fact, plenary sessions of the convention have two functions—ceremonial and business. We think it is time to consider a separation of these functions. Ceremonial activities can take place in an amphitheater or a stadium. The general public can be invited. On such occasions there are two classes of people: performers and spectators.

When the convention is conducting its business, however, a different division of labor is involved, and a different decorum should prevail. If it is not possible for a convention to conduct itself as a parliamentary body when all 2,000 or 3,000 members are present, perhaps some democratic and equitable means could be found to restrict the number of official delegates so as to make communication among them feasible. In fact, one effect of reforms designed to increase the representativeness of delegations has been to increase the size of each state delegation. Quotas, whether implicit or explicit, have, according to this perspective, not only increased the numbers of delegates, but also decreased the probability that they could deliberate as a body. If, let us say, 1,000 delegates met at business meetings, much of the paraphernalia associated with meetings of 10,000 could be dispensed with. The number of guards and security officers could be cut. The business of keeping order could be placed where it belongs—in the hands of the chair, who directs sergeants-at-arms publicly, rather than in the hands of an anonymous functionary, who in 1968 at Chicago apparently felt free to dispatch security officers to harass delegates on the floor.

A smaller number of people on the floor, the possibility of spontaneous communication with the chair and with other members, and parliamentary decorum would unquestionably facilitate and properly dignify the business of the convention. It would also provide a warrant for the reexamination of the role of television cameras at national conventions.

We believe television and other news media should continue to cover national party conventions with all the care and energy they have always used. But we question the propriety of wandering television and newspaper reporters on the floor of a convention. To be sure, so long as conventions continue in their present overblown form, reporters may as well be on the floor, since everyone else is. But if conventions were reduced in size and, for business purposes, maintained parliamentary decorum, perhaps it would be possible to consider the problems created by news media representatives at national conventions. Neither Democrats nor Republicans alone will take the lead in grappling with this problem, because both fear the wrath of the media. Thus, academic observers are ideally situated to open this discussion.

We want to increase respect for presidential nominations by having them conducted in a serious atmosphere conducive to mature deliberation. The presence of hordes of correspondents on the convention floor introduces a discordant note somewhere between individual breast-beating and mass hysteria. The very presence of numerous reporters, with their microphones and television cameras, creates a carnival atmosphere. No one would ordinarily make an important decision surrounded by people hurriedly throwing questions. No one would take seriously a decision made by people constantly distracted from the main proceedings by side conversations.

A superabundance of TV cameras on the convention floor plays up to the worst instincts of the politicians gathered there. It is hard for ordinary mortals to resist publicity; it is asking too much of politicians to forego an opportunity for national exposure. Yet the purpose of the convention (if it were again to become a decision-making body) is not to make the delegates look good at home, but for them to make a wise choice where they are.

The mass media not only report events; they create news. They are always after sensational stories. If conflict and controversy is not inherent in a situation, they will seek to create it. A momentary misunderstanding on the floor might be cleared up later on, but reporters will jump in immediately to widen the breach. In 1980, for example, we could see television reporters leaving the floor of Madison Square Garden in hot pursuit of a small rump group of Alaskans; these few delegates wanted to distract television coverage with their boycott of the Democratic keynote address of Morris Udall, who as chairman of a House of Representatives Interior Committee subcommittee had in some way offended them.

Imagine what football games would be like if they were reported as national conventions presently are. Imagine that a quarterback is getting clobbered in the next Super Bowl. His line is weak and defenders are pouring all over him. After the fifth interception, he receives a fearful blow. Before he can pick up his shattered bones a dozen TV reporters stick their microphones and cameras in his face, shouting questions at him. "Did you get good protection today?" "Anybody let you down, hey?" A few answers on the spot and the team might never be able to work together again.

Is it asking too much for nominations of future presidents to be conducted with at least the same dignity as presently obtains at football games? The press, radio, and TV can broadcast the proceedings and report events from booths above the convention floor. No one but delegates and frail, elderly, unthreatening sergeants-at-arms should be allowed on the floor while the convention is at work. Ample interview facilities should be provided just off the floor. When a delegate is wanted for an interview, a page should be sent to fetch him just as is done in Congress. "Mr. Smith," the page might say, "a network wants to harass you in room nine," and if Mr. Smith wants to be harassed he can walk off the floor to accomplish that mission.[27] The American people deserve full reporting of the national conventions; no one wants to limit the media in any legitimate coverage. But improving the conduct of national conventions and increasing public respect for their decisions are reasons enough to ask the media to pay a small cost for a large public benefit.

The convention, as we have said, normally aids party unity in a variety of ways. It provides a forum in which initially disunited fragments of the national party can come together and find common ground as well as a common nominee. The platform aids in performing this function. In order to gain a majority of electoral votes, a party must appeal to most major population groups. Since these interests do not always want the same thing, it is necessary to compromise and, sometimes, to evade issues that would lead to drastic losses of support. And since the parties must contain somewhat conflicting interests, internal accommodation is essential to avoid splits. A perfectly clear, unequivocal, consistent platform on all major issues presupposes an electorate and a party system divided neatly and more or less evenly along ideological lines, and that is not the case in this country.

Reformers' concern with party platforms stems primarily from two assumptions: first, that there is a significant demand in the electorate for more clear-cut differences on policy; second, that elections are likely to be a significant source of guidance on individual issues to policy makers. Yet both these assumptions are either false or highly dubious. On a wide range of issues leaders in both parties are much further apart than are ordinary citizens who, in fact, are separated by rather small differences.[28] To the often considerable degree that party platforms spell out clear and important differences on policy, this probably results far more from a desire of party leaders to please themselves or from misinformation about what the voters desire than from any supposed demand from the electorate. It is, of course, possible for a party to meet at least three of the four prerequisites for policy government reform (making policy commitments to the electorate, developing alternatives to governmental policy when out of office, and differing sufficiently to provide "a choice, not an echo") if a large enough majority of its own activists so desire. We have argued that such activists are unlikely to be victorious if they force one major party far away from the other on a great number of issues at the same time and then campaign vigorously on this new position. The Republican experience of 1964 and the Democratic experience of 1972 make it clear that such a strategy can be pursued, but the outcomes of those elections stand as a warning to political activists who entertain such notions again. In any event, it is exceedingly difficult (if not impossible) to discover just what an election means in terms of the policy preferences of a majority. About all that one can expect from a platform is an indication of the general direction in which a candidate and the dominant factions in his party intend to go, and the present party platforms do reasonably well in this respect.

Some critics objected to the traditional convention's stress on picking a winner rather than the "best candidate," regardless of his popularity. This objection is not compatible with the democratic notion that voters should decide who is best for them and communicate this decision in an election. Only in dictatorial countries does a set of leaders arrogate unto themselves the right to determine who is best regardless of popular preferences. An unpopular candidate can hardly win a free election. An unpopular president can hardly secure the support he needs to accomplish his goals. Popularity can be regarded as a necessary element for obtaining consent in democratic politics.

Although popularity is normally a necessary condition for nomination, it should not be the only condition. The guideline for purposes of nomination should be to nominate the best of the popular candidates. But "best" is a slippery word. A great deal of what we mean by "best" in politics is "best for us" or "best represents our policy preferences," and this can hardly be held up as an objective criterion. What is meant by "best" in this context are such personal qualities as experience, intelligence, and decisiveness. Nevertheless, it is not at all clear that an extreme conservative would prefer a highly intelligent liberal to a moderately intelligent candidate who shared his conservative policy preferences. Personal qualities clearly are subject to discount based on the compatibility of interests between voter and candidate.

One alternative—taking the nomination away from activists and giving it directly to at least some of the voters through a national primary—has previously been considered. Another—stacking party rules against purists—has been rejected so far. In fact, the rules of the Democratic party have in general moved in the opposite direction, toward more primaries, more pledged delegates, and fewer uncommitted delegates responsive to party leaders. The Hunt Commission on party reform suggested, and the national committee adopted, a rule providing delegate seats to party office holders—county chairmen, state committee people, congressmen, minority and majority leaders in state legislatures—but the numbers involved will be small: only about 15 percent of the membership of the convention. In addition, the Democrats have shortened the primary period from six to three months. Both these acts are intended to damp down the influence of purists on the ultimate decision of the convention, but it remains to be seen if they will. Unpledged party leaders seem unlikely to oppose the preferences of the 85 percent of the delegates who come to the convention already pledged, but perhaps the 15 percent will serve as an incentive for state parties to try to select other unpledged delegates on their own. The principal effect of squeezing the primary season from six to three months seems to us likely to be a net benefit for front-running candidates, who are best organized and equipped to run everywhere, and a corresponding decline in the fortunes of dark horses, already an endangered species.[29] The timing of elections could be changed so that governors, mayors, and other elected officials would be up for election at the same time, thus increasing their incentive to influence the choice of a popular president. If state parties were permitted to pick their delegations unmolested by national rules, the national convention would then be a convocation of party leaders tempered by primary preferences, and not a collection of candidate enthusiasts who appear in an election year in order to represent themselves rather than the electorate.

Whatever our preferences might be, structural changes that may be made will not affect social currents, such as the vast increase in formally educated people, that have produced purism. Although the present rules magnify purism, they do not create it. Purists do not have to win all intraparty battles; politicians could contest them. Why, then, are politicians of late so weak and purists so powerful?

Reform, which one might think would strengthen parties, has in recent years tended to weaken them. Once a candidate gets financial support from the government, he has less use not only for fat cat financiers but also for party politicians. Recent provisions for midterm party conferences and conventions stress expression at the expense of election.

Parties may be weak, but why should their regulars be weaklings? Why should the extremes be more passionate than the middle of the party spectrum? To put the question that way is to answer it: moderate beliefs tend to be moderately pursued. But why should moderates, who are most numerous in the population, be least in evidence in party meetings and primaries? Because they are inattentive, preoccupied, or satisfied, and their opponents are not. Should conditions change so that large numbers of people feel they are suffering, as in a depression, larger numbers of moderates will appear. For this phenomenon—known to Marxists as the "overmobilization" of the masses—to be long-lasting, the nation would have to be in a constant state of turmoil, hardly a desirable prescription to cure the ills of party.

The conclusion we would draw is that a mixed system—primaries together with other methods of delegate selection that give predominance to party regulars—provides a reasonable balance between popularity and other important considerations. Without denying an element of popular participation, the decision is ultimately thrown into the hands of the people who ought to make it if we want a strong party system—party leaders.

For some critics the defect of conventions lies not only in their poor performance in nominating candidates, but also in their failure to become a sort of "superlegislature," enforcing the policy views of the platform upon party members in the executive branch and Congress. We have previously indicated that such enforcement is most unlikely to be achieved. Let us suppose for the purposes of argument that the conventions could somehow become much more influential on matters of national policy. How could either party retain a semblance of unity if the stakes of convention deliberations were vastly increased by converting the platform into an unbreakable promise of national policy? If one believes that an increase in heated discussion necessarily increases agreement, then the problem solves itself. Experience warns us, however, that airing sharp differences, particularly when the stakes are high, is likely to decrease agreement. At the 1964 Republican convention, for example, black delegates, bitter about the defeat of Governor Scranton's proposed amendment on civil rights to the GOP education plank, held a protest march around the Cow Palace and, when Goldwater was nominated, announced that they would sit out the campaign.[30] This could not have helped Goldwater's chances of election. The fact that platforms are not binding permits a degree of unity necessary for the delegates to stay put long enough to agree on a nominee. By vastly increasing the number of delegates who would bitterly oppose platform decisions and would probably leave the convention, the proposed change would jeopardize the legitimacy of its nominating function. Paradoxically, in such circumstances it would be difficult to resist the temptation to make the platform utterly innocuous in order to give offense to no one.

Even so, platforms do have a far from negligible impact on public opinion. Platform planks are enacted as governmental policy slightly more than half the time.[31] And programs favored by the public, according to opinion polls, are twice as likely to be enacted if they also appear in party platforms.[32] When large majorities favor programs, both parties are likely to put them in their platforms; when the public is somewhat more divided and important constituencies object, however, the parties are likely to go against popular majorities. Thus Republican platform planks on welfare and economic issues and Democratic provisions on labor unions and social issues tend to run counter to majority opinion.[33] The question of who the parties are for, special or general constituencies, is resolved by going for the majority when it is substantial, and modifying that position when it conflicts with special party concerns.

There are good reasons for opposing the desires of those who love the conventions so much that they like to see them convene every year or two. For without a presidential candidate to nominate, conventions have little to do. If the purpose of these meetings is to give free advice, there would seem to be little point to them. Congressmen are likely to pay as little attention to convention talk as they would to the pronouncements of any advisory committee that does not appreciate the context within which they operate. After all, congressmen are subject to different risks and sanctions than are most delegates, get little help from the national party in securing nomination and election, and have no reason to be beholden to it for suggesting policies that may get them into trouble. The notion of getting delegates together under circumstances where their disagreements are certain to come out merely for the purpose of making recommendations does not seem promising.

The 1974 midterm conference in Kansas City of the Democratic party was notable not for its accomplishments, because there weren't any, but because it barely avoided a damaging party split over demographic quotas. Party activists returned from Kansas City bathed in good feeling—or was it sweat?—because they managed to avert outright catastrophe there. The Memphis Democratic conclave of 1978 provided only one high spot—an opportunity for Senator Edward Kennedy to upstage President Carter by advocating a popular but costly medical insurance scheme that the administration had put on the back burner. In 1982 nothing happened at the Philadelphia Democratic midterm convention. This was hailed as a great work of political engineering by Chairman Charles Manatt.

Especially now that they are an endangered species, the superiority of the traditional national conventions to the available alternatives is clear. Only the convention permits us to realize in large measure all of the seven goals—maintenance of the two-party system, party competition, some degree of internal cohesion, candidates attractive to voters, qualified candidates, acceptance of nominees as legitimate, and a connection between winning the nomination and governing later on—that we postulated earlier would commonly be accepted as desirable.

☆ An Appraisal of Permanent Voting Enrollment

One reform that has received increasing attention and that presumably would have at least marginal effects on all stages of presidential elections without directly altering either the means of nominating candidates or the ways in which they campaign is universal automatic voter enrollment. A distinguishing feature of American national elections is the low share of the potential electorate that actually votes. In 1972 the number of age-eligible nonvoters (61,924,000) was one and one-half times the number of votes cast for McGovern and one and one-third times the number cast for Nixon. In 1976 the showing was slightly worse: 68,485,000 age-eligible people did not vote, as compared with the 39,000,000 who voted for Ford and 40,800,000 who voted for Carter. And in 1980, 77,866,000 age-eligible people did not vote, while only 35,484,000 voted for Carter and 43,904,000 voted for Reagan.

One study suggests that the American system of voter registration may be responsible. It shows that the level of voter registration is easily the greatest influence (accounting for 80 percent of the variance) on the percentage of the population that actually votes, far greater than any other single factor usually cited in studies of voting by those registered and, in fact, greater than all such factors put together.[34]

Unlike the citizens of foreign democracies wherein the government takes responsibility for registration, the American must prepare for the eventual vote by registering before the election, at a time when political information and interest are at a low point.[35] Since interest and information are the important factors, the level of registration can be advanced or retarded by altering the time of year when voter registration rolls are closed or the physical ease of reaching a registration point, and practicing political leaders are well aware of this.[36] As Stanley Kelley and his collaborators observe, "Local differences in the turnout for elections are to a large extent related to local differences in rates of registration, and these in turn reflect to a considerable degree local differences in the rules governing, and the arrangements for handling, the registration of voters."[37]

Proposals for universal automatic voter enrollment differ according to administrative arrangements for enrollment, the time when it would occur, the duration of enrollment, and the level of government to which it would apply. The basic idea, however, is that the United States would be divided into election districts, and deputy registrars within them would go door to door, enrolling every citizen who did not refuse to be registered.[38]

Some areas of the United States use universal automatic enrollment already. They get striking results; the state of Idaho makes an aggressive search for new registrants, and as Table 5.2 shows, the consequences for voting turnout are impressive. Table 5.2 also compares U.S. national figures with those in Great Britain, and it is apparent that the percentage registered is strongly associated with the percentage of the potential electorate voting.

While the rest of the United States now lags behind the Idaho performance, there was once a time, in an era when the impact of the president was remote, mass communication absent, and electronic voting equipment unheard of, when more than 70 percent of *potential* (not just registered) voters turned out in presidential elections; in the election of 1876, 82 percent of the possible voters turned out for the nation as a whole. Soon thereafter, however, harsh registration restrictions were introduced, cloaked in rhetoric about stopping corruption but aimed at keeping down the vote of "undesirable

Table 5.2

The Important Influence of Rules for Registration on the Proportion of the Electorate That Actually Votes

	All U.S. (1968)	Idaho (1968)	Great Britain (1970)	Great Britain (1966)
Persons of Voting Age (thousands)	120,773	400	40,778	36,936
Percent Registered	74.5	91.8	91.5	97.4
Percent Registered Who Vote	81.3	79.4	72.0	75.8
Percent Persons of Voting Age Who Vote	60.6	72.8	69.5	73.8

elements" (immigrants and black voters)—which they did. As Kelley et al. observe:

> turnout in presidential elections in the U.S. may have declined and then risen again, not because of changes in the interest of voters in elections, but because of changes in the interest demanded of them. . . . [Not] only . . . [are] electorates . . . much more the product of political forces than many have appreciated, but also . . . to a considerable extent, they can be *political artifacts*. Within limits, they can be constructed to a size and composition deemed desirable by those in power.[39]

The effect of universal automatic enrollment on presidential politics seems relatively straightforward. We know that those who are disenfranchised by current practices are generally those with lower levels of political information and interest, and these are traditionally the young, the less well-educated, those lower in income, and black citizens.[40] We also know how these groups behave politically; they are much more Democratic than Republican, but far less stable in all aspects of their participation than other groups in the electorate. Their effective entry into politics would intensify the need for the parties to follow the presidential strategies we have already outlined. Democrats could afford even more to try to emphasize party identification through partisan appeals, while Republicans would be forced even more to follow "me-too" strategies, obscure party lines, claim they could better deal with domestic problems on which the Democrats focus, and emphasize foreign affairs.

Whether this expanded electorate would have any direct effect on primaries and delegate selection would depend on the particular enrollment plan adopted. At one extreme, if enrollment were held every four years in October and provided for continuation on the rolls only if the registrant voted in each election held in the district—state and municipal elections, as well as federal —the reform would have little direct effect. If the canvass occurred in the spring, however, and registrants had to vote only once every four years to stay on the rolls, there would be a significant addition to the presidential electorate. Some have argued that this portends new strength for nonparty-organization activists, since this new group would be far less tied to any political organizations than the already enfranchised groups.

Both black and white former nonvoters are likely to favor increased expenditures on policies designed to benefit lower-income people. But on questions of political style—protest, demonstrations, and the like—most newly registered voters, including young voters, will undoubtedly favor more traditional standards of seemly behavior.[41]

While universal automatic voter enrollment deals with the means by which the share of the potential electorate that gets to the polls can be changed, there are a whole series of lesser reforms that deal with changes in the size of the potential electorate itself. The major limiting factors on this potential electorate are legal requirements concerning residence, age, literacy, criminal conviction, mental incompetence, and U.S. citizenship.

The most notorious of these restrictions has been the residence requirement. In a nation noted for the geographic mobility of its population, a majority of states required, as recently as 1972, one year within the state, three months within the county, and thirty days within the precinct to vote in any election, including presidential. In 1972 the Supreme Court ruled in *Dunn* v. *Blumstein,* 405 U.S. 330, that thirty days was an ample period of time for the State of Tennessee to register its voters and declared its existing six-month state residency requirement an unconstitutional denial of equal protection. In two subsequent per curiam decisions, *Marston* v. *Lewis,* 410 U.S. 759 (1973), and *Burns* v. *Forston,* 410 U.S. 686 (1972), the court held that an extension to fifty days was permissible under certain conditions, but that this time period represented the absolute limit.

What might the consequences be of this sort of change in the rules? American Institute of Public Opinion surveys suggest that those previously disenfranchised by lengthy residence requirements are disproportionately in the twenty-one-to-thirty age group.[42] We know that voters in this age group are more Democratic than Republican but less identified with any party than are older voters, that they have less political information and are less interested, and that they participate less in all forms of political activity.

Wolfinger and Rosenstone find that the effect of registration laws has been to depress voting turnout in national elections by approximately 9 percent. Yet even if relaxation of voter registration restrictions brought about a corresponding expansion in the electorate, they conclude that the impact on electoral outcomes would be "wholly insignificant," since "the ideological composition of the expanded electorate would be virtually identical to that of the actual electorate in 1972."[43]

The same can, of course, be said for a group which has gotten the most recent attention—eighteen-, nineteen-, and twenty-year-olds. They could be expected to behave much as twenty-one- to thirty-year-olds, only less. In 1970 the Supreme Court upheld the right of this group to vote in national elections, but left it for individual states to decide the age requirements in state elections.[44]

There are four other major groups currently kept out of the potential presidential electorate:

1. Travelers and the ill. William Andrews estimates that while 3,400,000 absentee ballots were cast in 1960, another 3,600,000 voters could not vote because they had departed or become ill too late to receive an absentee ballot.[45] People who vote by absentee ballot are of higher socio-economic status than the electorate as a whole. Hence the Republican party has recently paid more attention to them. In the 1982 gubernatorial election in California, for instance, absentee ballots made the difference in the Republican victory.[46]

2. Aliens. In 1960 aliens who could not vote totaled 2,800,000.

3. Ex-felons. Convicted felons are permanently stripped of voting rights in most states, and there were 1,400,000 such persons in 1960.[47]

4. Illiterates. Of the 3,400,000 illiterates in 1960, 1,500,000 were literate but not in English.

The analysis of whether or not such groups should be allowed to become part of the electorate must be much the same as that for nonregistrants. To the degree that voting is a means to distribute the political goods of a society, they presumably have as much (perhaps more) of a stake in its outcome as do other groups, and while some of them may be low in general political information, this would not be an adequate reason, in our view, to deprive them of the vote.

☆ An Appraisal of the Electoral College

Close presidential elections, those in which the new president has only a narrow margin in the total popular vote, always lead to renewed public discussion of the merits of the Electoral College, since close elections remind people of the mathematical possibility that the candidate with a plurality of all the votes will not necessarily become president. Reform interest surges even higher when a regionally based third party, such as the party George Wallace led in 1968, becomes strong enough conceivably to prevent any candidate from having an electoral vote majority. This would drive the decision into the U.S. House of Representatives, which under the Constitution decides such matters when the Electoral College cannot.

The number of reform plans generated in the aftermath of the 1968 elections was legion. There were, however, three basic alternatives proposed to the present system, and the rest were variations. One would abolish the Electoral College outright and weigh votes equally everywhere. The net effect of such a proposal would be to undermine slightly the current strategic advantage enjoyed by populous, two-party, urbanized states. It might also have some long-run effects on the two-party system itself, but these would depend on other changes in the social situation within the country. The second proposal would retain the apportionment of the Electoral College (which gives numerical advantage to the smaller, rural states) but abolish the unit-rule electoral vote (which operates strongly in favor of populous states). This proposal is quite extreme in its import, which would be to confer an additional political bonus upon states traditionally overrepresented in positions of congressional power. A third, quite similar, proposal also retains the apportionment of the Electoral College but distributes an Electoral College vote for the plurality vote winner in each congressional district and two additional electoral votes for the winner in each state. Since this system maximizes the strength of one-party states and of those forces that are most important in the U.S. House of Representatives, it could in fact realign the presidential coalition in fundamental ways.[48]

The Constitution provides that each state, regardless of its population, shall be represented in the Senate by an equal number of senators. This means that the eight largest states, with just under 50 percent of the votes in 1980, have just sixteen senators. In the course of legislative proceedings, these senators' votes can be canceled by the sixteen votes of the senators from the eight least populous states, with 2 percent of the voters in the 1976 presidential election. Before the series of Supreme Court decisions beginning with *Baker* v. *Carr* and extending through *Wesberry* v. *Sanders* and *Reynolds* v. *Sims*, [49] the less populous, more rural states had been similarly favored in the distribution of seats in the House of Representatives. At one point in the early 1960s an average vote in Nevada was worth eighty-five times as much as an average vote in New York in elections for the House. The requirement that each state have at least one representative still gives the smaller states a slight edge over the big states in congressmen per capita (about 505,000 per congressman in the smaller states, and about 520,000 in the large states). The imbalance is comparatively far less than it was as recently as ten years ago; it roughly corresponds to the advantage that more populous, urbanized, two-party states enjoy in the Electoral College, and thus in access to the presidency.

The present Electoral College system, with its votes apportioned according to the total of Senate and House seats a state has, awarded on a "winner-take-all" basis, does provide a clear advantage to two groups of states. It yields a secondary advantage to the smallest states, since their overrepresentation in the Senate and the House guarantees them overrepresentation in the Electoral College; in 1980, all six states with three electoral votes each had a ratio of 260,000 or fewer citizens per electoral vote, while every state with thirteen or more electoral votes had a ratio of 410,000 or more citizens per electoral vote. But it is primarily the larger states, through the unit-rule principle, who benefit from the Electoral College. A candidate who can get a narrow majority in California can get almost as many electoral votes (forty-seven) as he could by carrying all of the sixteen smallest states (sixty-one); he can, mathematically, carry California by one vote and not receive any votes in those sixteen states and do just as well. This fact alone suggests that a presidential candidate should spend his energy in the larger states and tailor his programs to appeal to voters there, provided that energy expended there is likely to yield results. In fact, the larger states are usually quite close in their division of the major party vote, while the smaller states are more nearly "sure" for one party or the other. In 1980 the average share of the vote for the winner in the sixteen smallest states gave the winner a 25 percentage point margin of victory; in the eight largest states, on the other hand, the average share of the vote for the winner was 51 percent, and none of them gave the winner more than a 17 percentage point margin. In fact, the average margin of victory in these eight largest states was only 10 percent. The large states are the home of many organized minorities, especially racial and ethnic minorities, and this has traditionally meant that both presidential candidates have had to pitch their appeals to attract these groups, or at least not to drive them off. This is a major reason why U.S. presidents, Republicans as well as Democrats, have frequently been more activist, welfare-oriented, minority-oriented—in a word, more liberal—than their congressional party counterparts. Some of the critics of the current system have pointed to this advantage for the larger states, and especially their urban minorities, as a drawback of that system, to be reformed out of existence,[50] but most have concentrated their fire on the possibility of the "wrong winner," and the "undemocratic" nature of the unit rule.

Allowing a majority (or plurality) of voters to choose a president has a great deal to commend it. This is the simplest method of all; it would be most easily understood by the greatest number of people; it is the plan favored by the majority of Americans; and it comes closest to reflecting intuitive notions of direct popular sovereignty through majority rule. But to end the matter there would be too simpleminded. There is more than one political lesson to be learned by a closer examination of the Electoral College and available alternatives to it.

The outright abolition of the Electoral College, and the substitution of the direct election of the president, would certainly reduce the importance of the larger states. It would mean that the popular vote margin that a state could provide, not the number of electoral votes, would determine its importance. For example, under the present system a candidate who carries California by 144,100 votes (as Reagan did in 1980) has garnered one-sixth of the support he needs to win, while under the direct-vote system states like Massachusetts or Alabama can sometimes generate three and four times that much margin. In the two-party states, in which category most of the larger states fall, voters are cross-pressured in many ways, and a candidate can seldom count on defeating his opponent by a very large margin. The reason, then, that the large states lose influence is that this system switches influence from the close states to one-party states; in some states where one party's organization is weak, large majorities for the other party are easier to turn out at election time, and special rewards would be forthcoming for party leaders who could provide a large margin of victory for their candidate. As candidates currently look with favor on those who can bring them support in the large states, because this spells victory, so might they be expected to look with favor on those who can bring them large popular margins in the one-party states, should that become the criterion. The emphasis would not be on which candidate was going to win the state, already a foregone conclusion, but by how many votes he was going to win. The small states do not gain, however, because even when they are one-party, they are not large enough to generate substantial voting margins. Direct election thus changes the advantage from the biggest and the smallest two-party states to the medium-sized one-party states, and these, in the United States, happen most commonly to be located in the South.[51]

Table 5.3 lists all states having more than fourteen electoral votes and all

Table 5.3
Comparison of Popular Vote Margin with Electoral Vote Margin, 1976

| | *Popular Vote Margin, 1976* | | |
	Small (less than 100,000)		*Large (more than 100,000)*
	Md.	Va.	12-Ga. (495,666)
	Kt.	Vt.	10-Minn. (251,045)
	Id.	N.D.	6-Ark. (230,701)
	La.	Miss.	10-Tenn. (191,910)
	Kan.	Okla.	13-N.C. (185,405)
	Ct.	Iowa	13-Ind. (169,244)
Small	Mo.	Del.	4-Utah (155,798)
(13 or	Wash.	N.M.	9-Ala. (155,100)
fewer)	R.I.	Nev.	5-Neb. (126,013)
	N.H.	Ha.	7-Colo. (124,014)
	Wis.	S.D.	6-Ariz. (123,040)
	Wyo.	Me.	6-W. Va. (121,154)
Electoral	Alaska	Ore.	8-S.C. (104,658)
	Mont.		3-D.C. (109,945)
Vote			
	26-Ill. (92,974)		14-Mass. (399,199)
Margin	17-N.J. (65,035)		41-N.Y. (288,767)
	25-Ohio (11,116)		21-Mich. (197,028)
			17-Fla. (166,469)
Large			45-Cal. (139,960)
(14 or			26-Tex. (129,019)
more)			27-Penn. (123,073)

NOTE: No popular vote margins or electoral vote margins are given for states in the upper left quadrant (states with fewer than 13 electoral votes and popular vote margins of less than 100,000). For all other states, the number preceding the state is its number of electoral votes and the number following the state is its popular vote margin.

states having more than a margin of 100,000 votes for the winner in 1976, the last close election. It shows clearly that the major gainers under a direct-election system would be southern states, for six out of the eleven southern states that were not "big states" on an electoral vote basis are now "big states" because of their vote margin (along with eight other randomly assorted states); conversely, three of the ten "big states" by the Electoral College standard are now "small," and all of the ten lag behind Georgia in their importance to a presidential candidate.

This does not, of course, settle the matter, for one of the reasons that direct election is touted is that third parties cannot deadlock the process. In fact, those southern states with the largest 1968 margins were not powerful but weak, for they did not contribute to a winner but to a third-place loser.

How one feels about this situation depends on (1) how one still feels about the diminution of large-state influence and the gain by sundry other smaller states, (2) how much of a plurality one feels a newly elected president should have, and (3) how this plurality limit will affect others in the system.

Clearly, third-party votes under a direct-election system are wasted if the candidate with a plurality wins, no matter how small that plurality; if this is how the system is made to work, it is quite possible that future "Dixiecrat"-type movements will disappear or will merge into Southern Republicanism. At best, voters could express only their anger by voting for third-party candidates and this would be at the cost of foregoing the chance to decide an election. We suspect, however, that most Americans would feel uncomfortable with a president who, even though he won a plurality, was elected by, say, only 35 percent of the voters. One of the virtues of the present electoral vote system is that it magnifies the margin of a presidential victory (as, for instance, in 1980, Reagan's 10 percent victory margin gave him 91 percent of the electoral vote), presumably conferring added legitimacy and with it acceptance of the new president's responsibility to govern in fact as well as in title. Any system of direct election would almost have to eliminate the majority principle in favor of some plurality, or it would clearly lead to much more, not less, deadlock; in three out of our past eight presidential elections, the winning candidate was without an absolute majority.

Reformers have generally agreed, though, that the winner must win by at least a substantial plurality; consequently the Electoral College reform amendment that passed the House in late 1969 provided for a runoff between the top two candidates if no one secured as much as 40 percent of the popular vote in the initial election.[52] The first effect of this provision would be to hand back influence to third parties; if one's candidate is going to have a second

chance to win the office anyway, there is an incentive for any sizable organized minority to contest the first election on its own. That the runoff would
likely be used if it were provided is suggested by the 1968 figures, when there
was a fairly strong third-party candidate in the race. A fourth candidate,
perhaps a peace advocate, would have needed to pull only 6 or 7 percent of
the national total to keep either candidate from having the required 40
percent (Nixon won with only 43.4 percent, although he had 56.2 percent of
the electoral vote); a large enough minority was sufficiently concerned about
this one issue to make this a real possibility.[53] Once this becomes even a
plausible expectation, there is no reason for other intense minorities not to
do likewise and visions of a segregationist party, a black party, a labor party,
a peace party, an ecology party, even a right-to-life party, a farmers' party,
and so on, appear. Whereas one of the strong points of the present system
is that it enforces a compromise by penalizing all minorities that will not
come to terms, the direct-election system could well encourage a Continental
European model, in which numerous groups contest the first election and
then recombine for the second; at the very least, severe changes would be
worked on the present convention system.[54] Should such a result have occurred in 1968, or should it occur in the future, the simplicity, ease of
comprehension, and inherent majoritarian rightness of the direct-election
solution would quickly disappear.

The direct-election plan passed by the House received a warmer reception
in the Senate than the previous time it appeared there—in 1956 it was voted
down 66 to 17—but there were, not surprisingly, two major opposition
groups. The first was the bloc of liberal senators from the biggest states, who
had most to lose. The second was composed of some of the conservative
senators from the smallest states, whom we have named as the group deriving
second-greatest benefits from the current system. They argued that direct
election would be a complete breach of the federalism underlying our Constitution, since it would de facto abolish state boundaries for presidential elections.[55]

Another proposal, once embodied in the unsuccessful Lodge-Gossett
Resolution, is seen by some reformers as an acceptable "compromise" between outright abolition of the Electoral College and its retention.[56] In this
scheme, the electoral vote in each state is split between the candidates according to their proportion of the state's popular vote. This may seem to be a
procedural compromise, but it is a rather extreme reform in political terms.
As Table 5.4 shows, the large, urban, two-party states would have been nearly
eclipsed in 1976, in a way that direct election could not do. Seven out of the

Table 5.4

Comparison of Actual Electoral Vote Margin with
Proportional Electoral Vote Margin, 1976

Electoral Vote Margin	Proportional Electoral Vote Margin		
	Small (1.00 or less)	Large (1.00 or more)	
(13 or fewer)	All other states	9-Ala. (1.2) 6-Ariz. (1.0) 6-Ark. (1.8) 12-Ga. (4.0) 13-Ind. (1.0) 10-Minn. (1.3) 5-Neb. (1.1)	13-N.C. (1.5) 8-S.C. (1.1) 10-Tenn. (1.3) 4-Utah (1.2) 6-W.Va. (1.0) 3-D.C. (1.9)
(14 or more)	45-Cal. (0.8) 17-Fla. (0.9) 26-Ill. (0.5) 17-N.J. (0.4) 25-Ohio (0.0) 27-Penn. (0.7) 26-Tex. (0.8)	15-Mass. (2.2) 21-Mich. (1.2) 41-N.Y. (1.8)	

NOTE: The number preceding the state is its actual number of electoral votes; the number following the state is its electoral vote margin under the reformed, proportional system.

ten largest states would not in 1976 have been able to provide their winner with even one full electoral vote margin, while thirteen other states would have been able to do so. Using 1980 figures, large states under Lodge-Gossett are congruent with large states in reality, but usually there are sharper disparities between the two groups.

The bargaining position of the large states at national conventions would be drastically reduced, and presidential nominees would have to follow a different strategy in their campaigns, giving special attention to those states in which they felt a large difference in electoral votes could be attained. Once again, the proposed reform emphasizes the amount of difference within the state between the winner and the loser. In this case, however, the electoral votes of the states are divided rather than the popular votes. This effectively cancels out the advantage of the large states entirely. The fact that the Electoral College underrepresents the large states in the first place even further reduces their influence. The beneficiaries are again the one-party states, as well as the smaller states, since in any particular election West Virginia and Arizona, for example, may have more to contribute to the difference in electoral votes than Illinois, New Jersey, Ohio, or Texas.

There are two versions of this plan, one that divides electoral votes to the nearest vote and one that divides them to the nearest tenth of a vote. Most proponents favor the plan to divide them to the nearest tenth, since the nearest whole vote in many cases still would understate the closeness of the vote in a large number of states, especially those with five or fewer electoral votes to divide, and "representativeness" is the primary theoretical advantage of the plan. Since preventing deadlock is supposed to be one of the goals of Electoral College reform, it is interesting to note that with the majority vote victory required by proponents of both plans, either the whole or the tenth-vote system would have thrown the 1968 election into the House of Representatives (Nixon 235, Humphrey 221, Wallace 74; or Nixon 233.8, Humphrey 223.2, Wallace 78.8, others 2.2); and the system allotting electoral votes to the nearest tenth would have deadlocked the election of 1960 (Kennedy 264.8, Nixon 263.5, others 7.7).

The reduction in influence suffered by the large states under this proportional proposal might mean, in effect, that the already overrepresented sparsely populated and one-party states in the Congress would entirely dominate the national lawmaking process, unchecked by a president obliged to cultivate urban and two-party constituencies. It is perhaps gratuitous to point out that the same plurality problem is present if the deadlock is dealt with by letting the plurality candidate win. Even with a plurality provision, splintering is facilitated under this plan because a party need only pull a fraction of a percentage point of a major state's total vote in order to get some electoral votes. The present system at least cuts off splinter groups without a strong regional base.

A third plan, the district plan, has been proposed as still another "political compromise" between the other two major reform proposals, on the grounds that since thirty-eight states must ratify a Constitutional amendment on electoral reform, the fifteen states with three or four electoral votes are not likely to support either of the first two proposals because each dilutes their current strength. The district plan would give a presidential candidate one electoral vote for every congressional district he carried, plus two more for every state. It has been pushed largely by conservative senators; it is clearly the most radical of all the reform proposals in its effect on the U.S. political system, and it is least advantageous to the big states. This system would have given Nixon victory in 1968 (289–192–57), but if it had already

Table 5.5
Electoral Outcomes under Various Plans

	Present Plan	Direct Plan	Proportion Plan	District Plan
1980	Reagan Wins	Reagan Wins	Reagan Wins	Reagan Wins
	Reagan 489	Reagan 50.7	Reagan 272.9	Reagan 396
	Carter 49	Carter 41.0	Carter 220.9	Carter 142
		Anderson 6.6	Others 44.2	
		Others 1.6		
1976	Carter Wins	Nobody Wins	Nobody Wins	Winner unclear
	Carter 297	Carter 50.1	Carter 269.5	Carter 259
	Ford 240	Ford 48.0	Ford 258.0	Ford 257
	Others 1	Others 1.9	Others 10.5	Unknown 27*
1968	Nixon Wins	Nixon Wins	Nixon Wins	Nixon Wins
	Nixon 301	Nixon 43.4	Nixon 233.8	Nixon 289
	Humphrey 191	Humphrey 42.7	Humphrey 223.2	Humphrey 192
	Wallace 46	Wallace 13.5	Wallace 78.8	Wallace 57
1960	Kennedy Wins	Kennedy Wins	Nobody Wins	Nixon Wins
	Kennedy 303	Kennedy 49.7	Kennedy 264.8	Kennedy 245
	Nixon 219	Nixon 49.6	Nixon 263.5	Nixon 278
	Others 15	Others .7	Others 7.7	Others 15

*Because several states did not have complete figures for presidential vote compiled by congressional district, we could not determine which candidate would have received those electoral votes.

been in effect he probably would not have been running, since he would have won the election of 1960 (Nixon 278, Kennedy 245). Since the goals of electoral reform are supposedly to prevent the wrong man from winning, to avoid deadlock, and to do away with winner-take-all arrangements, it is hard to see what is offered by a system that would have given the less popular man victory, provides no more guarantee against deadlock than the present system (Wallace in 1968 got forty-five electoral votes under the actual system, but would have received fifty-seven under this one), uses a winner-take-all principle, and has the incidental feature of ending the activist character of the American presidency and giving policy control to one-party areas for the foreseeable future.[57]

Under the present Electoral College system, there has been no time since 1876 when any splinter group has been able to make good its threat to throw the election into the House, and in fact this is quite unlikely to occur since it requires all of the Deep South (Louisiana, Arkansas, Mississippi, Alabama,

Georgia, South Carolina, North Carolina) to vote for a third party, plus a very even division in nonsouthern votes. Even in 1948 Harry Truman won an Electoral College majority despite threats from both a third and a fourth party. In spite of the mathematical possibilities, not once in this century has the loser of the popular vote become president. On the other hand a direct-election plan that required a 40 percent plurality might well have forced a runoff in 1968 and 1976. Both the proportional and district plans would have created deadlocks in recent elections. In view of this analysis of the effect of electoral reforms, it is curious that many liberal reformers support changes in the Electoral College.

Underlying all of these arguments, of course, is the premise that most structural reforms "tend" to shift influences in certain ways. There may well be situations of social polarization that electoral system alternatives by themselves cannot paper over. But while we have argued that there is no better system than the current one, from the standpoint of the professed goals of most reformers, there is one minor change that would aid them. Under the present plan the electors who make up the Electoral College are in fact free to vote for whomever they wish. As an almost invariable rule, they vote for the winner in their state, but abuses are possible, and two within recent memory come to mind:

1. The unpledged electors chosen by citizens in Mississippi and Alabama in 1960 decided for whom they would vote only after the election. This clearly thwarts any popular control.

2. This liberty allowed George Wallace to hope that he could run for president, create an electoral deadlock, and then bargain with one of the other candidates for policy concessions in exchange for his electors.

An amendment making the casting of electoral votes automatic would dispel both of these possibilities.

We have argued that there is no serious reason to quarrel with the major features of the present system, since in our form of government "majority rule" does not operate in a vacuum but within a system of "checks and balances." The president, for example, holds a veto power over Congress, which, if exercised, requires a two-thirds vote of each house to be overridden. Treaties must be ratified by two-thirds of the Senate, and amendments to the Constitution must be proposed by two-thirds of Congress or of the state legislatures and ratified by three-fourths of the states. Presidential appointments, in most important cases, must receive senatorial approval. The Supreme Court passes upon the constitutionality of legislative and executive actions. Involved in these political arrangements is the hope that the power of one branch of government will be counterbalanced by certain "checks" from another, the result being an approximate "balance" of forces. In our view, it is not necessarily a loss to have slightly different majorities preponderant in different institutions, but it is definitely a loss to have the same majority preponderant in several branches while other majorities are frozen out. In the past the Electoral College had its place within this system. Originally designed to check popular majorities from choosing presidents unwisely, the Electoral College later on provided a "check" on the overrepresentation of rural states in the legislative branch by giving extra weight to the big state constituencies of the president.

Majority rule should be placed in proper perspective by considering other aspects of democratic government, such as the principle of political equality or the need for effective government. It would not help majorities, for instance, to so fractionalize the electoral or popular vote that all presidents would be rendered ineffective. Overrepresentation of rural interests in Congress has in the past inhibited political equality. To check this inequality we either had to alter the circumstances that promoted it or provide some other means of preventing rural interests from dominating the political system. Now that the method of determining the composition of Congress has undergone change, owing to fair reapportionment, we can consider abolishing the Electoral College and turn to majority (or plurality) voting in electing presidents. Other things being equal, a simpler and more direct method would be preferable to a device as complex in operation and as difficult to understand as the Electoral College. But the probable defects and equivalent complexities of alternatives to the Electoral College thus far proposed make us skeptical that the day has yet arrived when we can say that other things are in fact equal.

☆ Party Differences and Political Stability

The case for the desirability of party reform often rests on the assumption that American political parties are identical, that this is confusing and frustrating to American voters, and that it is undesirable to have a political system where parties do not disagree sharply.

We would suggest rather, that there are enough differences between the political parties to give voters a choice, but that many wide policy differences between the parties would be undesirable from the standpoint of the stability of the political system. The parties could well be somewhat further apart on a few issues, however, without necessarily decreasing the stability of the system. Our conceptual tools are too rough to say much about these small departures from the existing situation; let us consider only extreme changes of the kind advocated by the proponents of policy government.

Imagine for a moment that the two parties were in total and extreme disagreement on every major point of public policy. One group would appease the USSR; the other would court nuclear war. One group would stop Social Security; the other would expand it drastically. One group would raise tariffs; the other would abolish them. Obviously one consequence of having clear-cut parties with strong policy positions would be that the costs of losing an election would skyrocket. If parties were forced to formulate coherent, full-dress programs and were forced to carry them out "responsibly," and in full, then people who did not favor these programs would have little recourse. Clearly their confidence in a government whose policies were not to their liking would suffer, and, indeed, they might feel strongly enough about preventing these policies from being enacted to do something drastic, like leaving the country, or not complying with governmental regulations, or, in an extreme case, seeking to change the political system by force.

In fact, we have a political system that is kind to losers. Why? Because both presidential parties usually agree on a wide variety of issues; because people other than the president have to pass on policies before they are enacted into law, and these people are not bound by the presidential platform. This is, we suggest, not necessarily a bad thing. Suppose that each major political party were composed solely of people who supported it because, and only because, it represented their views on a wide range of policies. The surface attractiveness of this idea diminishes rapidly once we consider the consequences. The most immediate results would be extraordinary instability in the party system. For as soon as people changed their minds or the party changed its position, vast numbers of its adherents would leave. Great swings in party strength might take place, leaving the minority party on occasion virtually without representation. Or, alternatively, fearing great unpopularity, parties would never change their views about anything. Who, then, would take on the burdens of party opposition? Who would take the lead in introducing rival policies to compete for public favor?

The existence of a one-party system would be the least of our troubles. What would be the point in building up a party organization if it were doomed to come tumbling down with every significant change of opinion? None at all. So the function of nominating and electing candidates would become a matter for shifting groups of individuals, varying from issue to issue and place to place. Naturally, those groups with the best temporary organizations, the most money, and the greatest interest in the policies of the day would predominate. No longer would it be possible to use party identification as a shortcut, as a means of reducing costs of acquiring information about candidates. Unless voters spent most of their time finding out precisely what officeholders were doing, they would have little idea how to vote. Nevertheless, their votes might be more important to them because the dizzying alternation of policy would have created such political chaos that normal patterns of life would be disrupted. We need go no further to make the point that the existence of a hard core of party adherents who do not easily switch party allegiance from year to year provides an element of stability for the party system and thus for the whole political system as well. Paradoxically, the attempt to make issues all-important as a means of increasing the rationality of public decisions greatly decreases the chances for making any sort of meaningful decisions at all.

Party platforms written by the presidential parties should be understood not as ends in themselves but as means to obtaining and holding public office. It would be strange indeed if a party found policies like Social Security and unemployment compensation to be enormously popular and yet refused to incorporate them into its platform.[58] This would have to be a party of ideologues who cared everything about their pet ideas and nothing about winning elections. Nor would it profit them much since they would never get elected and never be in a position to do something about their ideas. Eventually, ideologues have to make the choice between pleasing themselves and winning elections.

Actually, party platforms do change over a period of time in a cyclical movement. The differences between the parties may be great for one or two elections, until innovations made by one party are picked up by the other. The net change from one decade to the next, however, is substantial. Let us begin when platforms are more or less alike. Their similarity begins to give way as it appears that certain demands in society are not being met. The minority party of the period senses an opportunity to gain votes by articulating and promising to meet these demands. The majority party, reluctant to let go of a winning combination, resists. In one or two elections the minority party makes its bid and makes the appropriate changes in its platforms. Then, in the ensuing elections, if the party that has changed its platform loses, it drops the innovation. If it wins, however, and wins big, the other party then seeks to take over what seem to be its most popular planks, and the platforms become more and more alike again.

We can see this cycle clearly in the New Deal period. The 1932 Democratic platform, though hinting at change, was much like the Republican one, especially in its emphasis on balancing the budget. A great difference in platforms could be noted in 1936 as the Democrats made a bid to consolidate the New Deal and the Republicans stood pat. The spectacular Democratic triumph signaled the end of widely divergent platforms. By 1940 the Republicans had concluded that they could not continue to oppose the welfare state wholesale if they ever wished to win again. By 1952 the parties had come much closer to each other as the Republicans adopted most of the New Deal. Though the platforms of the major parties were similar to each other in both 1932 and 1952, the differences between 1932 and 1952 for either party were enormous.[59]

Sometimes reformers deplore what they regard as an excessive amount of mud-slinging in campaigns, but they also ask that differences among the major parties be sharply increased in order to give the voters a clear choice. The two ideas are incompatible to some extent. It would be surprising if the parties disagreed more sharply about more and more subjects in an increasingly gentlemanly way. A far more likely outcome would be an increase in vituperation as the stakes of campaigns increased, passions rose, tempers flared, and the consequences of victory for the other side appeared much more threatening than had heretofore been the case.

Those who claim American elections are a fraud and wish to see great things decided in these contests often point to Great Britain as a shining example of the right way to do things. There, in that wiser country, where the fires of class warfare are held (fortunately) to burn more fiercely, the voters have real choices. They vote a government in or out, and the victorious party goes about making great changes in order to carry out its mandate.

This tale may be a pretty one, according to one's taste for conflict, but it is exaggerated. The truth is that drastic changes occur every once in a great while, much as American party platforms present sharp and profound differences about that often. Such was the case in 1945 when the Labour party staged its great bid to bring the full welfare state to Britain and to nationalize what it could. The overwhelming Labour victory did its work. The Conservatives soon decided to adopt all the most popular parts of the Labour party program—medicare, increased pensions—and left Labour holding the unpopular bag of nationalization. By 1955 the two major parties in Britain were presenting much the same program. By 1958 the only difference we could find was that Labour offered sixpence more on the pension. Most of the time, in fact, in Britain as in the United States, the great parties lean toward the middle.[60]

When they do not, as when in the late 1970s and early 1980s the Labour party moved significantly to the left, a number of predictable consequences ensue. One is that party splits occur, in this case giving rise to the new, more centrist, Social Democratic party. Another is that this split permits the other major party, the Conservatives, to move further to the right without paying an electoral penalty.

☆ Is Party Reform Relevant?

Even if reform were successful and the political system did not suffer detrimental effects such as we have outlined, many of the problems at which reform is aimed still would not be closer to solution. Thus, it can be argued that the achievement of party government is beside the point.

Can we say, for example, that the present system causes widespread party incoherence in Congress? This is perhaps an overstated problem for, in fact, on roll-call voting and in many other matters party allegiance is the strongest cohesive force in Congress. It has been demonstrated that party is stronger than other bases of allegiance, stronger than sectionalism, rural versus urban, native-born versus foreign-born.[61] Party cohesion depends, to be sure, on the nature of the issue. On the organization of Congress itself and on patronage matters, each party is aligned 100 percent against the other. On a significant number of issues there is widespread agreement among members of both parties, a situation that, because it limits and focuses conflict, is usually regarded as desirable. Some issues, such as race relations, may split each of the parties down the middle. On the economic and welfare issues, where the general label of "liberal" is commonly attributed to Democrats and "conservative" to Republicans, cohesion, while not perfect, is high; the labels make sense. If we look over the years at votes on medical care for the aged, aid to cities, regulation of oil and gas prices, budget and tax issues, and so on, we can discover that a preponderant majority of both parties takes opposing views. Cohesion does exist and it is important. Since it is not perfect, however, and one party rarely has an overwhelming advantage, it is often necessary to gain some votes from the opposing party in order to make up a majority. Party, therefore, cannot properly be viewed as a drag on unified policy making. It is most often a force making for greater cohesion than would be the case without it. By itself, it does not supply all the agreement necessary for policy making, but party supplies much of the means for mobilizing lawmaking majorities. In the American context of separated and fragmented powers, based on a population divided along many lines, this is no small accomplishment.

Party is also important in a sense that has been neglected. The cohesion of House Republicans and the disunity of Democrats is largely a function of their relative size. Were the House of Representatives to become more evenly divided among the parties, Republicans could afford to show less cohesion because they would be appealing to broader constituencies, but Democrats would find it easier to get together. Competition is the key.

Consider now the realm of foreign policy, where decisions made at any moment literally involve our survival and possibly that of the human race. How would policy government help us? The answer, presumably, is that the United States government would be able to follow more consistent, less internally contradictory policies and that these would lead to happier results. This assumes first that inconsistent policies are, in themselves, undesirable, a proposition that has never been convincingly demonstrated. In fact, inconsistency, "imbalance," and incoherence may in many instances be beneficial because of the necessity for satisfying diverse interests both at home and abroad through various policies of the government. By pursuing inconsistency in its policies the government often gains the legitimacy and support that are necessary to govern at all. A second assumption of the reformers is that the lack of party cohesion has been a major problem in foreign affairs. But this is simply not the case. In fact, it appears that virtually every major policy initiative of a president in the past twenty years—the blockade of Cuba, the Marshall Plan, NATO, the Eisenhower Doctrine, nonintervention in Indochina in 1954, the Gulf of Tonkin Resolution, intervention in Korea and Vietnam, the Panama Canal Treaty—has been supported by Congress, in most cases promptly and enthusiastically. When dissent appears, as it did in regard to policy toward Southeast Asia, it is a manifestation of a pervasive lack of trust between president and people, not merely between members of the same party. Dissent, moreover, comes as often from members of the president's own party as from the opposition; therefore dissent on foreign affairs is not a consequence of the party system, unless reformers seriously contemplate a system where foreign policy dissent from within the president's party is forbidden. Resolution of the differences over the size of the defense budget (there is consensus that it should be increased but not by how much) will be facilitated by the fact that many Republican congressmen think the president's figures are too high. It appears to us that dissent on foreign affairs —even by members of a president's own party—is not as unpopular with liberal reformers as it once was.

The difficulties facing the United States may be traced to causes for which the party system cannot be blamed. The rise of the Soviet Union as a great power generally hostile to America, the problems of our foreign policy in West Europe owing to contradictions between the desire of Europeans to be defended by America and their fear of the possible consequences, the breakup of colonialism, the creation of weapons of unparalleled destructiveness—all these developments have neither been hastened nor delayed by the character of our party system. American makers of foreign policy have found that they could not solve problems associated with these global issues primarily because of the enormous difficulties involved, not because Congress refused to accept the correct policies. Presidents and secretaries of state today find that the world is intractable; there are so many things they can do little or nothing about. They have to deal with a worldwide range of problems, make decisions of enormous technical complexity, gain consent of allies with differing interests, and take account of huge forces arrayed against them, all largely outside the help or the hindrance the party system can give them.[62]

Perhaps the most significant area with impact on foreign policy in which some internal contradiction among party policies appears is tariffs.[63] The United States seeks the stability of nations like Japan, on the one hand, and contemplates setting up tariff barriers which may help undermine this stability on the other. Interests that find themselves disadvantaged seek a sympathetic hearing in Congress, whose members are less attuned to global foreign policy considerations than is the president. As the competitiveness of American industry decreases, adding to already high unemployment, renewed efforts to protect industry (and the workers it employs) have occurred. These efforts are not especially concentrated along party lines, however.

It would not, in any event, be surprising if governments were concerned about protecting the interests of domestic industries to some extent. Looking at nations like Britain, France, and Germany, whose governments can usually command automatic support in their parliaments, we find that they also are interested in protecting their domestic industries and the workers who depend on them. The continued negotiations on the European Common Market budget make this abundantly clear. If party government, let us say, on the British model were suddenly to appear in the United States, there would still be the necessity of bargaining with interests within the majority party, and no one doubts that the impact of tariff levels on industry would have to be considered.

When we turn to Great Britain, where policy government has long been established, we do not find that ability to command a certain majority in the House of Commons helps prime ministers solve foreign policy problems better than presidents. In fact, the most notorious example of failure of democratic leadership in modern history comes not from the United States but from Great Britain. There, in the 1930s, Stanley Baldwin and Neville Chamberlain led their country to the brink of ruin when they failed to inform the people of the growing danger of Nazi Germany, partly because they thought their people were profoundly pacifist and would defeat them at the polls. These men were patriots who wished their country well; they had devoted their lifetimes to its service. Had they realized the full implications of their failure to act, they undoubtedly would have done otherwise. Uncertain of the course of events and prone to underestimate the danger of their foes abroad, they allowed themselves to be swayed by the notion that the people would not stand for the truth, no matter how essential that truth was. Surely the existence of a cohesive party system, with sharp policy differences between the parties, did nothing to avoid this disaster. If anything, party cohesion permitted Baldwin and Chamberlain to proceed with impunity despite attacks leveled by Churchill and others who vainly sought to alert the nation. So strong was party unity that it took the calamitous events of 1940, which threatened the very existence of the nation, to bring about a change in government.

Policy government is not, however, irrelevant for purposes of domestic politics, and we will want to define more precisely its likely impact. But before we proceed, it is necessary to modify the policy government proposals so that they are more defensible. For so long as proponents of policy government insist that the parties be both responsive to popular will and extremely far apart on many policies, the contradictions in this approach do grave damage to the consistency and validity of their proposals. Let us modify the reformers' proposals by stating that the major presidential parties should be able to propose coherent policies to the electorate and to carry them out after they assume office, regardless of whether their policies are similar.

Now we are in a position to write a sort of profit-and-loss statement on what would be involved in domestic politics if policy government were instituted. The benefits would accrue almost entirely to left-wing liberals and right-wing conservatives (and the interests they represent) with superior access to a president, who would have a better chance of securing the enactment of the measures they prefer. Moderate congressmen would stand to lose their power and their policy preferences as their congressional bastions were weakened if not rendered useless. Congressional liberals and conservatives would gain more of their preferred policies, but their power as congressmen would suffer as Congress lost power. Where the present system enables them to maintain their power as congressmen while achieving some of their policies, they would have to choose between power and their other preferences under policy government. People who prefer more or fewer welfare programs and a traditionally powerful Congress would have to weigh their competing preferences carefully. Beyond this point we see dimly at best. In order to achieve somewhat greater party cohesion on domestic affairs we would risk an unspecified increase in social conflict and a somewhat greater likelihood of producing splinter parties. What the citizen has to decide is whether the benefits are worth the costs.

We think that the supporters of policy government overestimate by far the magnitude of the problem from their own viewpoint. It is not true that the parties are basically lacking in cohesion and certainly not true that no welfare legislation is passed by Congress. On the contrary, more has been done than anyone dreamed was possible as late as the 1950s. In 1960, defense expenditures accounted for about 45 percent of the national government's budget and welfare accounted for under 20 percent. Today the proportions are nearly reversed. It seems excessive to us to contemplate far-reaching changes in the party system, changes which are exceedingly difficult to achieve and whose desirability is at least questionable when there are much less drastic and much more desirable means available for securing the kinds of legislation the proponents of policy government want so badly. If there has been difficulty the past several years, it surely has not resulted from a lack of policy, but rather from inadequate implementation. The old consensus parties were able to pass the laws reformers wanted, but newly reformed parties have not helped to generate support for the policies that have been enacted. And a determined effort by a conservative president was able to garner sufficient support in Congress to effect a sizable rollback. This gives added credence to the idea that wholesale party reform is not a prerequisite to legislative change.

A basic difficulty is that policy-government advocates have been so enchanted with the mystique of the presidency, and so annoyed with Congress, that they do not perceive the excellent opportunities available to them for altering the pattern of legislation. Let us consider some of the activities that have brought results:

1. Apportionment is now equitable, at least in terms of population, and consequently metropolitan areas have received greater representation in Congress.

2. Liberal strongholds in the cities have begun to supply congressional candidates who are making careers out of service in Congress, rather than regarding their service as a stepping-stone toward a judgeship or some other such position. Progress in this direction since 1958 has meant that conservatives no longer enjoy their former superiority of seniority, skill, and dedication.

3. Party leaders have paid more attention to the distribution of congressional committee positions, and congressional rules have changed so that liberal majorities on crucial committees may be more readily achieved. In the past decade, the start of nearly every Congress has provided important examples of this process at work.

No doubt it seems easier to talk blithely about a revolution in the party system than actually to do something to increase the support that the mass of people give to legislation presumed to benefit them. Action in any one or all of these directions, in our opinion, does more to secure "liberal" legislation than talking about policy government or taking actions that are bound to be futile. Knowing what we know, now we can well understand why the clamor for congressional party reform died down after the Eighty-ninth Congress passed an enormous amount of the legislation that liberals had tried so hard to get in the 1940s and 1950s. The major reason these bills passed was that the Democrats were able to elect an extraordinary majority (particularly in the House) in 1964. Indirectly, of course, Barry Goldwater's candidacy was responsible for putting enough liberal Democrats in Congress to complete virtually the entire New Deal. It should also be said, however, that years of effort, begun half a decade before, had altered the composition of crucial congressional committees and were also important in securing this result.

The presidency of Republican Ronald Reagan may give pause to liberal reformers. Though his campaign rhetoric was too general to suit them, he has certainly played the part of the responsible party president who proposed and attempted to carry out a wide-ranging program designed to modify (if not to undo) the efforts of his Democratic predecessors. There was no mistaking his thrust—less domestic government and more for defense. Indeed, if any president has performed according to the "responsible government" model, it is Ronald Reagan, who tried (and to some extent succeeded, at least in his first year) to carry out his campaign promises. If the results are not to everyone's liking, no one can say they were not forewarned as to the direction the candidate would take in the event he were elected. And if some citizens prefer more moderation and compromise, they should then consider whether they really want parties and candidates to carry out their pledges. Is the argument for party reform that the nation needs more Reagans, whether of the right or left? Evidently, given favorable political conditions in Lyndon Johnson's first term and Ronald Reagan's first year, cohesive presidential programs enacted en masse by Congress are possible without the party changes we have been considering. Or shall we now hear about a second generation of reforms designed to prevent the possibilities, now realized, of the first generation of reforms?

Most of the reforms suggested by students of the party system have been, we believe, designed to give greater power to liberal presidents to enact their domestic programs and to diminish, correspondingly, the power of Congress. For the conduct of foreign affairs these changes would be largely irrelevant. With respect to the stability and inclusiveness of the two major parties themselves, the reforms might well be detrimental, because of the encouragement they would give to splinter parties. And finally, we observe that the case for party government has certainly not been made. The enunciation of large national problems does not in and of itself demonstrate the linkage of these problems to the party system. The prescription of reforms does not in and of itself provide the strategy or the power or the inducements to carry them out.

It is evident that the condition of American political parties has changed greatly over the past twenty years. Today the influence of parties on government is extremely weak as a result of successful efforts to centralize national parties and spread participation toward candidate activists and away from party regulars. Reform has weakened parties. We suspect that more reform will weaken them still further.

Chapter 6

American Parties
and Democracy

Over a relatively short period of time, a new sort of American political system is coming into being. Among its features are high degrees of mass participation in hitherto elite processes, the replacement of political parties with the news and publicity media as primary organizers of citizen action and legitimizers of public decisions, the rise in the influence of media-approved and media-sustained interest groups, and the decline of interest groups linked to party organizations. Certain sorts of decision making are easy in a system structured in this way: simple voting, for example, in which alternatives are few and clear-cut. Complex decision making, in which various alternatives are compared one after the other, contingencies are weighed and tested tentatively, second and third choices are probed for hidden consensuses, or special weight is given to intensity of likes and dislikes, is extremely difficult in such a system. Therefore, much influence flows into the hands of those who structure alternatives in the first place—candidates and media stars.

But the job of the parties continues even as the party organizations decline in influence. For presidential elections, we have observed the replacement of the convention with primary elections as the most significant part of the

267

process, and the nomination of candidates whose links to party and to their leading fellow partisans are weak or even antagonistic.

Because the American political system is moving toward a role for political parties that stresses their activities as policy advocates, it seems to us important to discuss at length the implications of this trend for democratic government. Our argument makes two main points. The first is that it is necessary for parties of advocacy in a democracy to receive mandates on public policy from majorities of convinced believers in their programs, but that this condition is not met in America because of the ways in which electorates actually participate in elections and conceive of public policy.

Our second point is that in view of the actual disposition of attitudes toward public policy in the electorate as compared with party elites, the fact that we are moving toward parties of advocacy poses some significant and largely unmet problems for American democracy. This is because it is not the policy preferences of the electorate that are being advocated. Moreover, the implementation of policy requires the sort of institutional support that parties can orchestrate only if they have some permanency and are not required to give birth to themselves anew every four years, nominate a candidate, and then wither away.

☆ Elections and Public Policy

No doubt uncoerced and competitive elections aid in making the political system open and responsive to a great variety of people and groups in the population. But it would not be correct to say that our elections transmit unerringly the policy preferences of electorates to leaders or confer mandates upon leaders with regard to specific policies. Consider the presidential landslide of 1972, which resulted in a Republican president but also in a Democratic Congress that was bound to disagree with him. Or the Democratic landslide of 1964, when the two major presidential candidates also had sharply divergent, consistent policy differences. Two years later, in the election of 1966, the Republicans regained much of the ground in Congress that they had lost. In 1980, Ronald Reagan won comfortably; by 1982, the Democrats had recouped. Even in a landslide the mandate is at best a temporary, equivocal matter. And in any case elections that are even as clear-cut as these are rare.

It is easy to be cynical and expect too little from elections or to be euphoric and expect too much from them. A cynical view would hold that the United States was ruled by a power elite—a small group outside the democratic process. Under these circumstances the ballot would be a sham and a delusion. What difference can it make how voting is carried on or who wins if the nation is actually governed by other means? On the other hand, a euphoric view, holding that the United States is ruled as a mass democracy with equal control over decisions by all or most citizens, would enormously magnify the importance of the ballot. Through the act of casting a ballot, it could be argued, a majority of citizens would determine major national policies. What happens at the polls would not only decide who occupies public office; it also would determine the content of specific policy decisions. In a way, public office would then be a sham because the power of decision in important matters would be removed from the hands of public officials. A third type of political system, in which numerous minorities compete for shares in policy making within broad limits provided by free elections, has more complex implications. It suggests that balloting is important but that it does not often determine individual policy decisions. The ballot both guides and constrains public officials, who are free to act within fairly broad limits subject to their anticipations of the responses of the voters and to the desires of other active participants.

It is evident that the American political system is of this third type. Public officials do make major policy decisions, but elections matter in that they determine which of two competing parties holds public office. In a competitive two-party situation such as exists in American presidential politics, the lively possibility of change provides an effective incentive for political leaders to remain in touch with followers.

But it would be inaccurate to suggest that voters in presidential elections transmit their policy preferences to elected officials with a high degree of reliability. There are few clear mandates in our political system because elections are fought on so many issues and in so many incompletely overlapping constituencies. Often the same voters elect candidates to Congress and to the presidency who disagree on public policies. Thus, mandates are not only impossible to identify, but even if they could be identified they might well be impossible to enact because of inconsistency in the instructions issued to officials who must agree on legislation.[1]

Presidential elections are not referenda. The relationship between presidential elections and policies is a great deal subtler than the relations between the outcomes of referenda and the policies to which they pertain. In theory, the American political system is designed to work like this: Two teams of politicians, one in office, the other seeking office, both attempt to get enough votes to win elections. In order to win, they go to various groups of voters and, by offering to pursue policies favored by these groups, hope to attract their votes. If there were only one office-seeking team, their incentive to respond to the policy preferences of groups in the population would diminish; if there were many such teams, the chances that any one of them could achieve a sufficient number of backers to govern would diminish. Hence the two-party system is regarded as a kind of compromise between the goals of responsiveness and effectiveness.

The proponents of a different theory would say that elections give the winning party a mandate to carry out the policies proposed during the campaign. Only in this way, they maintain, is popular rule through the ballot meaningful. A basic assumption in this argument is that the voters (or at least a majority of them) approve of all or most of the policies presented by the victorious candidate. No doubt this is plausible, but not in the sense intended because, as we have seen, a vote for a presidential candidate is usually merely an expression of a party habit: particular policy directions are not necessarily implied in the vote. Most voters in the United States are not ideologically oriented. That is, they do not see or make connections among issues. They do not seek to create or to adopt coherent systems of thought in which issues are related to one another in some logical pattern. If this is the case, then voters can hardly be said to transmit preferences for particular policies by electing candidates to public office.

Other basic objections to the idea that our elections are designed to confer mandates on specific public policies may also be raised. First, the issues debated in the campaign may not be the ones in which most voters are interested. These issues may be ones that interest the candidates, that they want to stress, or that interest segments of the press; but there is no clear reason to believe that any particular issue is of great concern to voters just because it gets publicity. Time and again, voting studies have demonstrated that what appear to be the major issues of a campaign turn out not to be significant for most of the electorate. In 1952, for example, three great Republican themes were communism, Korea, and corruption. It turned out that the communism issue, given perhaps the most publicity, had virtually no impact. Democrats simply would not believe that their party was the party of treason, and Republicans did not need that issue to make them vote the way they usually did. Korea and corruption were noticeable issues.[2] Yet how could anyone know, in the absence of a public opinion poll, which of the three issues was important to the voters and which constituted a mandate? There were, in any event, no significant policy differences between the parties on these issues—Democrats were also against communism and corruption and also wanted an end to the war in Korea. A broadly similar story can be told, as we have done, for more recent elections.[3]

A second reason why voting for a candidate does not necessarily signify approval of his policies is that candidates pursue many policy interests at any one time with widely varying intensity, so that they may collect support from some voters on one issue and from other voters on another. It is possible for a candidate to get 100 percent of the votes and still have every voter opposed to most of his policies, as well as having every one of his policies opposed by most of the voters.

Assume that there are four major issues in a campaign. Make the further, quite reasonable, assumption that the voting population is distributed in such a way that those people who care intensely about one major issue support the victorious candidate for that reason alone, although they differ with him mildly on the other three issues. Thus, voters who are deeply concerned about the problem of nuclear defense may vote for candidate Jones, who prefers a minimum deterrence position, rather than Smith, who espouses a doctrine that requires huge retaliatory forces. This particular group of voters disagrees with Jones on farm price supports, on the size of government, and on national health insurance, but they do not feel strongly about any of these matters. Another group, meanwhile, believes that farmers, the noble yeomanry, are the backbone of the nation, and that if they are prosperous and strong, everything else will turn out all right. So they vote for Jones, too, although they prefer a large defense budget and disagree with Jones's other policies. And so on for other groups of voters. Jones ends up with all the votes, yet each of his policies is preferred by less than a majority of the electorate. Since this is possible in any political system where many issues are debated at election time, it is hard to argue that our presidential elections give unequivocal mandates on specific policies to the candidates who win.[4]

People vote for many reasons not directly connected with issues. They may vote on the basis of party identification alone. Party habits may be joined with a general feeling that Democrats are better for the common man or that Republicans will keep us safe—feelings too diffuse to tell us much about specific issues. Some people vote on the basis of a candidate's personality, or his "image." Others follow a friend's recommendation. Still others may be thinking about policy issues but may be all wrong in their perception of where the candidates stand. It would be difficult to distinguish the votes of these people from those who know, care, and differentiate among the candidates on the basis of issues. We do know, however, that issue-oriented persons are usually in a minority, while those who cast their ballots with other things in mind are generally in the majority. When voters want to move government in a more liberal or conservative direction, their desire is one of degree, not of kind.

Even if there is good reason to believe that a majority of voters do approve of specific policies supported by the victorious candidate, the mandate may be difficult or impossible to carry out. A candidate may get elected for a policy he pursued or preferred in the past that has no reference to present circumstances. One could have voted Republican in 1952 because Dwight Eisenhower got rid of the rascals in the Truman administration, or Democratic in 1976 in response to Watergate; but this did not point to any future policy that was currently in the realm of presidential discretion. "Corruption" in 1952 was a kind of issue on which there was really no way of carrying out a supposed mandate other than determining to be honest, a course of action we may be pardoned for believing that Adlai Stevenson would have followed as well. John F. Kennedy promised in 1960 to get the nation moving. This was broad enough to cover a multitude of vague hopes and aspirations. More specifically, as president, Kennedy may dearly have wished to make good this promise by increasing the rate of growth in the national economy, but no one was quite sure how to do this. Lyndon Johnson was able to make good many of his 1964 campaign promises on domestic policy, but observers after the election were hard put to distinguish his subsequent Vietnam policies from those promised by Barry Goldwater. Both Ronald Reagan and Jimmy Carter promised to reduce inflation and unemployment, but it would have taken more foresight than anyone possesses to know how or to what degree or for what length of time.

Leaving aside all the difficulties about the content of a mandate, there is no accepted definition of what size electoral victory gives a president special popular sanction to pursue any particular policy. Would a 60 percent victory be sufficient? What about 51 percent or 52 percent, however, or the cases in which the winner receives less than half of the votes cast? And is it right to ignore the multitudes who do not vote and whose preferences are not directly registered? One might ignore the nonvoters for the purpose of this analysis if they divided in their preferences between candidates in nearly the same proportions as those who do vote. But they often do not. In practice, this problem is easily solved. Whoever wins the election is allowed to pursue whatever policies he pleases, within the very important constraints imposed by the checks and balances of the rest of the political system. This, in the end, is all that a "mandate" is in American politics.

Opinion polls may help the politician gauge policy preferences, but there are always lingering doubts as to the polls' reliability. It is not certain in any event that they tell the political leader what he needs to know. People who really have no opinion may give one just to satisfy the interviewer. People who have an opinion but who care little may be counted equally with those who are intensely concerned. Many people giving opinions may have no intention of voting for some politicians who heed them, no matter what. The result may be that the politician will get no visible support from a majority that agrees with him, but instead he will get complaints from an intense minority that disagrees. The people who agree with him may not vote, while those who differ may—as single-issue interest groups are reported to do—attempt retribution at the ballot box. Those who are pleased may be the ones who would have voted for the public official anyway. And unless the poll is carefully done, it may leave out important groups of voters, overrepresent some, underrepresent others, and otherwise give a misleading impression. The correlations that are made—say, support comes disproportionately from certain economic or social groups—do not explain why some people, often a substantial minority, possessing these self-same characteristics act in the opposite way.

Let us turn the question around for a moment. Suppose a candidate loses office. What does this tell him about the policies he should have preferred? If there were one or two key issues widely debated and universally understood, the election may tell him a great deal. But this is seldom the case. More likely there were many issues and it was difficult to separate out those that did from those that did not garner support for his opponent. Perhaps the election was decided on the basis of personal images or some events in the economic cycle or a military engagement—points that were not debated in the campaign and that may not have been within anyone's control. The losing candidate may always feel that if he continues to educate the public to favor the policies he prefers, he will eventually win. Should he lose a series of elections, however, his party would undoubtedly try to change something—policies, candidates, organization, maybe all three—in an effort to improve its fortunes.

Let us suppose that a candidate wins an election. What does this event tell him and his party about the policies he should prefer when in office? Can he take it on faith that the policies he proposed during the campaign are the popular ones? Some undoubtedly were rather vague, and specific applications of them may turn out quite differently from what the campaign suggested. Others may founder on the rock of practicality; they sounded fine but they simply cannot be carried out. Conditions change and policies that seemed appropriate but a few months before turn out to be irrelevant. As the time for putting policies into practice draws near, the new officeholder may discover that they generate a lot more opposition than when they were merely campaign oratory. And those policies he pursues to the end may have to be compromised considerably in order to get the support of other participants in the policy-making process. Nevertheless, if he has even a minimal policy orientation, the newly elected candidate can try to carry out a few of his campaign proposals, seeking to maintain a general direction consonant with the approach that may—he cannot be entirely certain—have contributed to his election.

The practical impossibility in our political system of ascertaining mandates is one important reason why it is so difficult for parties to emphasize their function as policy advocates. It is, however, entirely possible for parties to adopt mandates that have little or no support in the general population. It is to the exploration of this trend that we now turn.

☆ Parties of Advocacy versus Parties of Intermediation

The presidential election process in the United States is in transition. It was only a short time ago—1952—that a president of the United States could, and with good reason, dismiss a prospective Estes Kefauver victory in the New Hampshire primary as "eye-wash." Now primaries select most convention delegates, and combined with the effects of the media, have an overwhelming impact on the outcome of the nomination process.[5]

Behind the shift in the role of primary elections lie shifts in the roles of political activists, both candidate enthusiasts and party regulars, and changes in the powers and the significance of the news media. We believe that these changes and other changes that we have discussed—the shift to public financing not only of the general election, for example, but also of primary elections, the vast increase in the number of primaries, and the new rules for converting votes into delegates—add up to a fundamental redefinition of the place of the national political parties in our public life. One way to characterize this redefinition is that the conception of parties as agents of policy government has begun to prevail, and the conception of parties as agents of consensus government has begun to fade.

Purists are favored as never before by the rules of the game, and politicians disfavored. In the early days of preprimary activity, the people who become most active are apt to be those who have the most spare time, the most ideological commitment, and the most enthusiasm for one candidate above all others. Since the rules are now written to encourage activity at an earlier and earlier date, as a basis for federal subsidies during the primaries, it follows that purists will have more to say about the eventual outcome of the nomination process. Party regulars, on the other hand, who tend to wait until they can see a majority forming and who dislike the wasted resources and effort of kamikaze candidacies, are systematically disfavored by the new rules of the game. By the time their peculiar skills and interests in majority building are desperately needed—notably at the convention—it is too late for them to get into the process: most of the seats will have been taken by the enthusiasts for particular candidates who won in the various primaries and state conventions.

Building upon these thoughts for a moment, we can ask how the emerging structure of presidential election politics helps and hinders political parties in performing the tasks customarily allotted to them in the complex scheme of American democracy. In essence, we would argue that the parties have been greatly strengthened in their capacities to provide advocacy and weakened in their abilities to provide intermediation or facilitate implementation in the political system.

Advocacy is strengthened because the rules of the game offer incentives to those party leaders able to attract personal followings on an ideological basis. This much is clear. What is lost, in our view, is a capacity to deliberate, weigh competing demands, and compromise so that a variety of differing interests each gain a little. This loss would not be so great if the promise of policy government—to select efficacious programs and implement them successfully—were likely to be fulfilled in performance. But, on the record so far, this is doubly doubtful.

It is doubtful because for many of the problems that form the basis of political campaign discussion—crime, racism, hostility abroad—there are no known, surefire solutions. And second, even if we knew what to do about more of our problems, it is unclear that, given the ways in which various forces in our society are arranged, presidents alone could deliver on their promises.

This last dilemma is especially poignant in the case of a candidate like George McGovern, who spoke to a very wide spectrum of issues. Yet he could not prevent serious errors from creeping into his discussion of defense spending, and there were contradictory implications in his social programs when they were considered in the light of total spending and hence inflation and taxation. These programs, as offered by McGovern, moreover, were apparently very unpopular. Yet gaining public acceptability is part of making policies work. Policy government might enhance the legitimacy of government by increasing the effectiveness of programs, but the insensitivity of its advocates to the needs for consensus makes that unlikely. Hence neither policy nor consensus, advocacy nor intermediation, is likely to be served.

Two factors account for the decline in the vital function of intermediation by parties. First, candidates have far fewer incentives than heretofore to deal with interest groups organized on traditional lines, or with state and local party leaders. These leaders and groups have in the past provided links between national politicians and the people and have focused the hopes and energies of countless citizens upon the party organizations as meaningful entities in the nomination process. Nowadays, as we have been told by politicans as varied as Eugene McCarthy and Richard Nixon, a candidate for the presidency need no longer build up a mosaic of alliances with interest groups and party leaders. Now, through the miracle of the mass media (especially television), through mass mailings to appeal for money, and through federal subsidy if these mass mailings are successful, presidential candidates can reach every home and touch every heart and claim the allegiance of followers based on symbolic appeals rather than concrete bargains.

This is the first sense in which parties have been diminished in their capacity to mediate between the desires of ordinary citizens and the policies of government: candidates act as though they no longer need parties to reach voters. In a second sense parties have lost the capacity to mediate between leaders and followers because the formal properties of plebiscitary decision making, such as occurs in primary elections, leave little room for a bargaining process to occur. Contingent choices are impossible to express straightforwardly through the ballot box. Thus a candidate who is acceptable to a sizable majority but is the first choice of only a few systematically loses out under the new rules to candidates who are unacceptable to most but secure in their control over a middle-sized fraction (20 to 30 percent, depending on how many play the game) of first-choice votes.

It is in this powerful sense that we can say that "participatory" democracy, as the American party system has begun to practice it, is inimical to "deliberative" democracy. As more (and different) people have won the right to participate in the nomination process, the kinds of communication they have been able to send to one another have become impoverished. They can vote, but they cannot bargain. They can make speeches, but they cannot deliberate.

Let us see what happens when a free spirit like George McGovern breaks through the network of old politicians and gets nominated for president. A piece of bad luck afflicts his campaign: his vice-presidential candidate has concealed a medical history that may weaken the ticket. The *New York Times* writes, "Dump Eagleton." The *Washington Post* writes, "Dump Eagleton."

What does an "old" politics candidate do? Presumably he gets on the telephone and asks around among interest-group leaders and state and local party bosses. "Can we stand the flak?" "What do the party workers think?" "What do *you* think?" "Here's what *I* think."

What does a "new" politics candidate do? Well, what choice has he? To whom can he place a telephone call other than the farflung members of his immediate family? There is no negotiating with the editorial board of the *New York Times* in a smoke-filled room. There is no give-and-take with the moderator of "Meet the Press." The moderator gives. Politicians take.

We have no way of knowing whether the paradox of participation swallowing up deliberation has had the net effect of turning citizens away from political parties. It is in any event the case that by a variety of measures—nonvoting, propensity of voters to decline to identify with a political party, direct expressions of disapproval of parties—political parties have, like so many other institutions of American society, suffered substantial losses in public confidence. In our view, the most promising way for them to regain public confidence is to avoid extremist candidates and to make an effort to become more deliberatively democratic in their internal processes.

What's wrong with policy government? What could be wrong with so intuitively attractive an idea? Governments must make policies. Candidates must be judged, in part at least, on their policy preferences as well as on indications of their ability to perform when in office. Has there not been, in the recent past, too much obfuscation of issues and too little candor in speaking one's mind? Obviously our society needs more rather than less discussion of issues, greater rather than less clarification of alternatives. It is equally evident that mere lust for office, pandering to the popular whims of the moment, is no qualification. Getting people together may be worse than keeping them apart if they agree on the wrong thing or, as it turns out, on nothing substantial at all.

What is wrong is that the premises upon which policy government is based are false. Most people do not want parties that make extreme appeals by taking issue positions far from the desires of the bulk of the citizenry.[6] Perhaps people feel safer if their parties give them a choice but if losing is not a catastrophe. The idea that the American people are waiting for a consistent line of policy that differs greatly from what they are getting has now been conclusively refuted. The Goldwater election should have destroyed the myth of the "hidden" Republican vote, and if any Democrats neglected to vote in 1972, they were McGovern's opponents, not his supporters.

Untenable, also, is the assumption that when the parties focus on their issue differences there is more intelligent debate, thus helping citizens make wiser choices. What actually happens, as exemplified by the Goldwater-Johnson election of 1964 and the Nixon-McGovern election of 1972, is that the farther apart the candidates are on the issues, the less discussion and the more emotion there will be. Apparently, when the distance is too large to be bridged, the candidates shout at (rather than speak to) each other. When one of them is quickly defined as outré by most people, his opponent need not reply to his arguments in a serious way. No one will ever know how much the country suffered by failing to have a serious debate on foreign policy in 1964. Charging that Goldwater would bring atomic war didn't answer the question of what the government should do in Vietnam. And in 1972 discussing the unsuitability of George McGovern was not quite the same as contemplating the fitness of Richard Nixon.

Adherents of issue expression have so far managed to control only one presidential nominating convention at a time; but suppose they manage in the future to face off a right-wing Republican against a left-wing Democrat? The trends now misperceived as a product of consensus government—alienation, nonvoting—as likely as not would show an alarming increase as the vast majority of citizens discover that their preferences have been disregarded and that they have nowhere to turn. Indeed, it may well be that the vastly increased participation of purists has, by making campaigns distasteful to the majority, led to the very decline in participation they deplore.

It is one thing to say that policy options have been insufficiently articulated and quite another to create conflict and develop disagreements where these did not exist before. Political activists in the United States for a while were more ideological and polarized than at any time since studies were first conducted in the 1930s, and possibly since the 1890s or even the Civil War. Should ordinary citizens be compelled to choose from policy alternatives that appeal to purists, or are they entitled to select from a menu closer to their tastes? The question is not whether there will be issues, for inevitably there must be, but who will set the agenda for discussion and whether this agenda will primarily reflect differences in the population or among elites. Although a full range of experience is lacking in the United

States, modern French history shows that it is possible for a nation to be kept in turmoil by differences that, though real to certain elites, have little resonance in the population as a whole.

"What's wrong with a party of advocacy" is that it conceals a justification for rule by elites who act to impose preferences largely opposed by the great majority of people. Policy government does not lead to participatory democracy, because participation does not in fact increase uniformly. It decreases in the population as a whole and increases among certain selected elites, drawn from the upper-middle and upper classes, who have the time and inclination to engage in bouts of intense political activity.

Thus, the rationale behind parties of advocacy leads to plebiscitary democracy. If it is not only desirable for all citizens to vote in general elections but also for them to choose candidates through preelection primaries, it must be even more desirable for them to select governmental policies directly through referenda. Instead of rule by special interests or cliques of congressmen, the public's interest would supposedly be expressed by the public. Experience with referenda in California, however, suggests that this is not quite how things work in practice. Without measures for limiting the number of referenda, citizens are swamped by the necessity of voting on dozens of items. Elites, not the people, participate in the selection and wording of referenda. And how they are worded is of course extremely important. Money—to arrange for signing petitions to get on the ballot—becomes more meaningful than ever. The public is faced with a bewildering array of proposals, all sponsored by special interests that want a way around the legislature. To learn what is involved in a single seemingly innocuous proposal to raise somebody's salary or issue bonds takes hours of study. To understand twenty or more is unduly onerous. Is the citizen better off guessing or following the advice of the local newspaper rather than trying to choose a legislator or a party to represent his interests? Are citizens or legislators better qualified to understand that Proposition 13 in California would not only keep property taxes down, which it was supposed to do, but would also, by depriving localities of resources, centralize control over many areas of public policy, which no one wanted?

After a decade of severe internal difficulty, when confidence in virtually all national institutions suffered repeated blows, the need for consensus-building parties seems clear. Political purism might be desirable for a people homogeneous in all ways except the economic; but can a multiracial, multiethnic, multireligious, multiregional, multiclass nation like the United States sustain itself when its main agents of political action—the parties—

strive to exclude rather than include, to sharpen rather than dull the edge of controversy?

It is even doubtful that the rise of parties of advocacy leads to a more principled politics. If principles are precepts that must not be violated, when contrary principles are firmly embedded in the programs of opposing parties, one man's principles necessarily become another's fighting words. A few principles, such as those enshrined in the Bill of Rights, may be helpful in establishing boundaries beyond which governmental action may not go. A plethora of principles inevitably stakes out competing sovereignties whose jurisdictions can only be violated at great peril. The principle of having opposing principles is the worst of all hypocrisies: a declaration of war under protestations of peace, viciousness parading as virtue.

Compromise, of course, can also be a curse. If everything were bargainable, including basic liberties, no one would feel safe and, indeed, no one would be. Similarly, if candidates cared everything about winning and nothing about how they win, if they were not restrained by internal norms or enforceable external expectations, elections would become outrages.

Without the desire to win elections, not at any cost but as a leading motive, however, there is no reason for politicians to pay attention to the people who vote. Winning, moreover, requires a widespread appeal. Thus the desire to win results in moderation, in appeals to diverse groups in the electorate, and in efforts to bring many varied interests together. This is why we prefer politicians to purists, and parties of intermediation to parties of advocacy. In addition, parties of advocacy do not sustain themselves well in government. Thus they fail to assist political leaders in mobilizing consent for the policies they adopt, and this widens the gap between campaign promises and the performance of government.

The quality and not only the quantity of party support is what matters. Presidential primaries may be diluted by party caucuses. But if purists dominate the caucuses, all we would get is a worse equivalent of primaries except that they would, given the relatively small size of caucuses, be even more unrepresentative of the population as a whole. Should parties become vehicles for purists, as happened recently to the British Labour party, the nation would have to rely on holders of public office for responsiveness. Without party ties, or with such ties pushing parties further from voters, we would have a situation common in parliamentary democracies but unusual in the United States: congressional parties seeking to escape domination by parties outside the legislature on the grounds that they, the elected officials, are in closer touch with popular preferences.

Despite significant changes in recent years leading to advocacy as a central activity of the most active participants in presidential election politics, it remains uncertain whether this tendency has as yet become firmly rooted in the orientations of ordinary citizens toward politics or in their voting habits. Politics is contingent; events that have every right to occur may be forestalled by others no one can predict. Who, from the campaign and platform of 1932, could have foretold what Franklin D. Roosevelt would become? Trends that appear irresistible to us now may fade away like the snows of yesteryear. Because so many of the rules of presidential election politics are changing, it is impossible for us to say with a high degree of assurance how parties, candidates, and voters will adapt to the new incentives and disabilities that have been enacted into law. We are confident only in asserting that the adaptations they make will be of enormous consequence in determining the ultimate capacity of the American political system to sustain the fascinating and noble experiment in self-government begun two hundred years ago.

Notes

☆ Preface

1. "Seeking Legal Relief from Excessive Regulation of California's Parties" (mimeo, July 1982). The committee describes itself as "an organization of scholars, political practitioners, and other citizens interested in strengthening our political parties. . . ."

☆ Introduction

1. See Paul T. David, Ralph M. Goldman, and Richard C. Bain, *The Politics of National Party Conventions* (New York, 1964), for a lengthy treatment of the history of the national party conventions.

2. An excellent statement discussing signs of party strength may be found in Gerald M. Pomper, ed., *Party Renewal in America: Theory and Practice* (New York, 1980).

☆ Chapter 1: The Strategic Environment: Participants

1. In his major work on public opinion, V. O. Key, Jr., states, "For most Americans issues of politics are not of central concern. . . ." At another point Key summarizes the literature as follows: "In analysis after analysis of opinions on specific issues, sizable proportions of persons have been shown to lack an opinion" (*Public Opinion and American Democracy* [New York, 1961], pp. 47, 185). When asked, "What things are you most concerned with these days?" two out of three people in a representative sample of registered voters in New Haven, Connecticut, spoke of such personal matters as jobs, health, and children. Only one out of five cited local, state, national, or international affairs (Robert A. Dahl, *Who Governs?* [New Haven, 1961], p. 279). Further supporting evidence may be found in Julian L. Woodward and Elmo Roper, "Political Activity of American Citizens," *American Political Science Review* 44 (December 1950), pp. 872–875; and Samuel Stouffer, *Communism, Conformity and Civil Liberties* (Garden City, N.Y., 1955), Chapter 3. Stouffer, in his 1954 survey, found that "the number of people who said they were worried either about the threat of Communists in the U.S. or about civil liberties was, even by the most generous interpretation of occasionally ambiguous responses, *less than 1 percent.* Even world problems, including the shadow of war, did not evoke a spontaneous answer from more than 8 percent" (p. 59). Using data from the University of Michigan's Center for Political Studies, Philip E. Converse estimates that those who have consistent and elaborately worked out political views on a variety of topics number about 3.5 percent of the voting population, and those who have some of these attributes number no more than 12 percent. He finds that 17.5 percent of the population have attitudes with no issue content whatsoever. See his article "The Nature of Belief Systems in Mass Politics," in David E. Apter, ed., *Ideology and Discontent* (New York, 1964), pp. 206–261, especially the table and commentary on p. 218. The elections of the 1960s and 1970s caused many political scientists to reexamine theories regarding the level of ideology among voters. Norman H. Nie and Kristi Andersen, in their article "Mass Belief Systems Revisited: Political Change and Attitude Structure," *Journal of Politics* 36, 3 (August 1974), pp. 540–591, argue that later data contradicted Converse's conclusions. Norman H. Nie, Sidney Verba, and John R. Petrocik take the argument one step further in *The Changing American Voter* (Cambridge, Mass., 1976), especially Chapter 10. There they argue that voters not only have developed more consistent attitude structures but are able to assess the proximity of their attitudes to those of one candidate as compared with another, thereby enabling issue voting on a large scale.

These arguments have been attacked on methodological grounds. See John L. Sullivan, James E. Pierson, and George E. Marcus, "Ideological Constraints in the Mass Public: A Methodological Critique and Some New Findings," *American Journal of Political Science* 22 (May 1978), pp. 250–269, and Eric R. A. N. Smith, "The

Levels of Conceptualization: False Measures of Ideological Sophistication," *American Political Science Review* 74 (September 1980), pp. 685–696, with comments by Paul R. Abramson, Nie, Verba and Petrocik and Smith himself in *American Political Science Review* 75 (March 1981), pp. 146–155. Additional criticisms have been made by David Repass, who suggests that voters' issue positions may be rationalizations after the fact ("Issue Salience and Party Choice," *American Political Science Review* 65 [June 1971], pp. 389–400). Philip E. Converse and Gregory B. Markus argue that issue voting has not increased in *"Plus Ça Change . . .* The New CPS Election Study Panel," *American Political Science Review* 73 (March 1979), pp. 32–49. Finally, John L. Pierce and Paul R. Haynes have repeated Converse's original analysis for all presidential elections from 1956 through 1976. In "Conceptualization and Party Identification: 1956–1976," *American Journal of Political Science* 26 (May 1982), pp. 377–387, they conclude that the amount of issue voting done by citizens has not changed much over a twenty-year period.

2. See Angus Campbell, Philip E. Converse, Warren E. Miller, and Donald E. Stokes, *The American Voter* (New York, 1960), pp. 89–115. Writing of the 1956 presidential election, for example, the authors say that "the rate of turnout among persons of high interest exceeded that among persons of low interest by nearly 30 percent. . . ." (p. 102). See also Gordon M. Connelly and Harry M. Field, "The Non-Voter—Who He Is, What He Thinks," *Public Opinion Quarterly* 8 (Summer 1944), pp. 175–187. The work of the late Angus Campbell and his associates at the University of Michigan's Survey Research Center (later known as the Center for Political Studies), to which we will refer frequently, is based on numerous sample surveys of the entire American voting population. These studies, which have been going on since 1948, have through the years increased in breadth and sophistication and at the moment represent the largest pool of data we have on the political attitudes of Americans. The work of the late Paul Lazarsfeld, Bernard Berelson, and their associates at the Columbia Bureau of Applied Social Research has been going on since 1940. Rather than national sample surveys, the BASR group has collected data of a more focused kind, often limited to a single community. The BASR group pioneered in the use of panel surveys, which consist of series of reinterviews with the same respondents. For a description and critique of these and other materials we shall be using, see Peter H. Rossi, "Four Landmarks in Voting Research," in Eugene Burdick and Arthur J. Brodbeck, eds., *American Voting Behavior* (Glencoe, Ill., 1959), Chapter 1, and Peter B. Natchez, "Images of Voting: The Social Psychologists," *Public Policy* 17 (Summer 1970), pp. 553–588.

3. The most comprehensive current study of voting participation—based on very large U.S. census surveys—is Raymond E. Wolfinger and Steven J. Rosenstone, *Who Votes?* (New Haven, 1980). See also Bernard Berelson, Paul F. Lazarsfeld, and William N. McPhee, *Voting* (Chicago, 1954), p. 25; Campbell et al., *The American Voter*, pp. 475–483; and Key, *Public Opinion and American Democracy*, pp. 195–199.

For a detailed discussion of socioeconomic status and political participation, see Sidney Verba and Norman H. Nie, *Participation in America: Political Democracy and Social Equality* (New York, 1972), especially Chapter 8. For a sensitive but inconclusive discussion of the different forces influencing various types of participation, see Richard A. Brody, "The Puzzle of Political Participation in America" in Anthony King, ed., *The New American Political System* (Washington, D.C., 1978), pp. 287–324.

4. Campbell et al., *The American Voter,* pp. 120–145. Robert E. Lane concludes, "Over the long run party identification has more influence over a person's vote decision than any other single factor . . ." (*Political Life* [Glencoe, Ill., 1959], p. 300).

5. In general, as the table below shows, voters have become less likely to make up their minds during the primary campaigns or the conventions and slightly more likely to wait until the general election campaign to decide on a candidate.

Table 1.8

Timing of Voters' Decisions in Presidential Elections, 1948–1980

	1948	1952	1956	1960	1964	1968	1972	1976	1980
Before the nominating conventions (%)	37	34	57	30	40	33	43	33	40
During the conventions (%)	28	31	18	30	25	22	17	20	18
During the campaign (%)	25	31	21	36	33	38	35	45	40
Don't remember, not ascertained (%)	10	4	4	4	3	7	4	2	2

SOURCES: William H. Flanigan and Nancy H. Zingale, *Political Behavior of the American Electorate* (Boston, 1979), p. 171; Survey Research Center/Center for Political Studies election studies.

See pp. 5–21 for a more detailed discussion of party loyalty as opposed to "independence." Here we should note that, as Keith et al. show in the following table, "strong identifiers" are quite different from either "weak" identifiers or people who do not claim a party loyalty but will admit "leaning" to one or the other.

Table 1.9

Mean Democratic Vote, 1952–1980

Strong Democrats	84%	Strong Republicans	3%
Weak Democrats	63	Weak Republicans	12
Independent Democrats	66	Independent Republicans	12
	Pure Independents	34%	

See Bruce E. Keith, David B. Magleby, Candice F. Nelson, Elizabeth Orr, Mark Westlye, and Raymond E. Wolfinger, "The Myth of the Independent Voter" (paper delivered at the 1977 Annual Meeting of the American Political Science Association). Earlier research did not differentiate among the various sorts of independents and characterized the entire population of independents as comparatively uninvolved in politics, less interested, less concerned and less knowledgeable than are party identifiers. These generalizations hold better for the truly nonpartisan subset of "pure independents." See Campbell et al., p. 143 and Berelson, Lazarsfeld and McPhee, pp. 25–27. For a somewhat different treatment, see Robert Agger, "Independents and Party Identifiers," in Burdick and Brodbeck, etc. *American Voting Behavior,* Chapter 17. William H. Flanigan and Nancy H. Zingale use Michigan Center for Political Studies data to conclude, "In all recent elections the independents and weak partisans were more likely to make up their minds during the campaign, while the strong partisans characteristically make their decisions by the end of the conventions" (*Political Behavior of the American Electorate,* third ed. [Boston, 1979], p. 174).

6. Berelson, Lazarsfeld, and McPhee, *Voting,* pp. 215–233. George Belknap and Angus Campbell state that "for many people Democratic or Republican attitudes regarding foreign policy result from conscious or unconscious adherence to a perceived party line rather than from influences independent of party identification" ("Political Party Identification and Attitudes Toward Foreign Policy," *Public Opinion Quarterly* 15 [Winter 1951–1952], p. 623). There is an ongoing debate about what causes party loyalties to change. Is change the result of an influx of new voters to one party or the result of party switches by habitual voters? We think it more likely that what we perceive as change is actually a replacement of old voters by new. This process is strongly suggested for Canada by Richard Johnston in "Party Alignment and Realignment in Canada, 1911–1965," unpublished Ph.D. dissertation, Stanford University, 1976. V. O. Key also supported a mobilization-of-new-voters interpretation in "A Theory of Critical Elections," *Journal of Politics* 17 (February 1955), pp. 3–18. Arthur S. Goldberg's study of American data finds that children tend to defect from the party identification of their parents when the parents' party identification is atypical for their status and the children are relatively well educated ("Social Determinism and Rationality as Bases of Party Identification," *American Political Science Review* 63 [March 1969], pp. 5–25). And Kristi Andersen, in *The Creation of a Democratic Majority 1928–1936* (Chicago, 1979), p. 69, argues that "the surge in the Democratic vote in 1932 and 1936 came primarily from . . . newly mobilized groups": those who came of political age in the 1920s but did not vote until 1928, 1932, or 1936, and those who came of age between 1928 and 1936. On the other side, see the intriguing arguments for opinion change by individual voters in Robert S. Erikson and Kent L. Tedin, "The 1928–1936 Partisan Realignment: The Case for the Conversion Hypothesis," *American Political Science Review* 75 (December 1981), pp. 951–962.

7. Various voting studies previously cited contain substantial discussions of this subject. See Robert E. Lane, "Fathers and Sons: Foundations of Political Belief," *American Sociological Review* 24 (August 1959), pp. 502–511; Campbell et al., *The American Voter,* pp. 146–147; H. H. Remmers, "Early Socialization of Attitudes," in Burdick and Brodbeck, eds., *American Voting Behavior,* pp. 55–67. Key, *Public Opinion and American Democracy,* pp. 293–314, sums up in these words: "Children acquire early in life a feeling of party identification; they have sensitive antennae and since they are imitative animals, soon take on the political color of their family. . . ." (p. 294). See, especially, Fred I. Greenstein, *Children and Politics* (New Haven, 1965), Chapter 4. In a more recent work, Paul R. Abramson presents an interesting discussion of this familiar link and the forces that later play against it. See *Generational Change American Politics* (Lexington, Ky., 1975), especially Chapters 3 and 4.

8. ". . . People are more likely to associate with people like themselves—alike in political complexion as well as social position" (Berelson, Lazarsfeld, and McPhee, *Voting,* p. 83). See also Robert D. Putnam, "Political Attitudes and the Local Community," *American Political Science Review* 60 (September 1966), pp. 640–654, and more recently, Ada W. Finifter, "The Friendship Group as a Protective Environment for Political Deviants," *American Political Science Review* 68 (June 1974), pp. 607–626.

9. Paul Lazarsfeld, Bernard Berelson, and Hazel Gaudet, *The People's Choice* (New York, 1944), pp. 16–28.

10. Lazarsfeld, Berelson, and Gaudet, *The People's Choice;* Angus Campbell and Homer C. Cooper, *Group Differences in Attitudes and Votes* (Ann Arbor, 1956); Woodward and Roper, "Political Activity of American Citizens," pp. 872–875; Key, *Public Opinion and American Democracy,* pp. 99–120, 121–181; Berelson, Lazarsfeld, and McPhee, *Voting,* pp. 54–76; Robert Axelrod, "Where the Votes Come From: An Analysis of Electoral Coalitions, 1952–1968," *American Political Science Review* 66 (March 1972), "Communication," *American Political Science Review* 68 (June 1974), pp. 717–720; "Communication," *American Political Science Review* 72 (June 1978), pp. 622–624; and "Communication," *American Political Science Review* 76 (June 1982), pp. 393–396. The following table, reprinted from *National Journal,* is a summary of November and December 1982, and January 1983, Gallup polls, in which respondents were asked, "In politics, as of today, do you consider yourself a Republican, a Democrat or an Independent?"

11. V. O. Key, Jr., *Southern Politics* (New York, 1950), pp. 75–81, 223–228, 280–285. The South is becoming more evenly divided in its political loyalties because two trends have outweighed the effects of a third: the migration of Republicans into the South and the conversion of conservative Southerners to Republicanism have not been made up for by the increasing turnout of black people who vote overwhelmingly Democratic in presidential elections.

Table 1.10

	Republican	Democrat	Independent
Farmers	39%	31%	30%
Professional and business	33	35	32
Income $25,000 plus	30	37	33
In towns 2,500–50,000	30	37	33
Protestants	30	43	27
College educated	29	38	33
Whites	28	40	32
In towns under 2,500	28	42	30
Age 50 and older	28	51	21
Midwest	27	38	35
West	27	44	29
Clerical and sales	27	45	28
Non-union households	26	43	31
Men	25	42	33
Income $20,000–25,000	25	43	32
NATIONAL	25	45	30
Income $15,000–20,000	25	45	30
Women	25	47	28
Age 18–24	24	39	37
High school educated	24	45	31
East	24	46	30
Income $10,000–15,000	24	48	28
Non-labor force	24	52	24
Age 25–29	23	41	36
Cities 50,000–500,000	23	46	31
Skilled workers	22	43	35
South	22	52	26
Cities 500,000 to 1 million	21	46	33
Cities 1 million plus	21	54	25
Income $5,000–10,000	20	53	27
Catholics	19	50	31
Labor-union household	19	52	29
Grade school education	19	60	21
Jews	15	65	20
Income under $5,000	14	60	26
Blacks	6	77	17

SOURCE: *National Journal* (April 2, 1983), p. 720.

12. V. O. Key, Jr., "A Theory of Critical Elections," *The Journal of Politics* 17 (February 1955), pp. 3–18; Campbell et al., *The American Voter,* p. 160. See, more generally, James Q. Wilson, *Negro Politics* (Glencoe, Ill., 1960). Barry Goldwater's 1964 candidacy intensified the Democratic loyalties of black voters.

13. See Duane Lockard, *New England State Politics* (Princeton, 1959); Dahl, *Who Governs?,* pp. 33–51, 216–217; Elmer E. Cornwell, "Party Absorption of Ethnic Groups: The Case of Providence, R.I.," *Social Forces* 38 (March 1960), pp. 205–210; J. Joseph Huthmacher, *Massachusetts People and Politics* (Cambridge, Mass., 1959), pp. 118–126.

14. Samuel Lubell, *The Future of American Politics* (New York, 1951), pp. 129–157.

15. On Eisenhower see Campbell et al., *The American Voter,* pp. 55–57, 525–528, 537, and Herbert H. Hyman and Paul B. Sheatsley, "The Political Appeal of President Eisenhower," *Public Opinion Quarterly* 19 (Winter 1955–56), pp. 26–39. On McGovern, see Samuel L. Popkin, John W. Gorman, Charles Phillips, and Jeffrey A. Smith, "Comment: What Have You Done for Me Lately? Toward an Investment Theory of Voting," *American Political Science Review* 70 (June 1976), pp. 779–805.

16. The portions of this analysis that deal with voters and issues are taken from Chapter 8, "Public Policy and Political Preference," in Campbell et al, *The American Voter,* pp. 168–187.

17. See Hazel Gaudet Erskine, "The Polls: The Informed Public," *Public Opinion Quarterly* 26 (Winter 1962), pp. 669–677. This article summarizes questions asked since 1947 of national samples of Americans designed to ascertain their information on current news topics. Similar data for 1935–1946 are contained in Hadley Cantril and Mildred Strunk, *Public Opinion, 1935–46* (Princeton, 1951). In light of later work, Philip E. Converse is able to conclude and illustrate: "Surely the most familiar fact to arise from sample surveys in all countries is that popular levels of information about public affairs are, from the point of view of the informed observer, astonishingly low" ("Public Opinion and Voting Behavior," in F. I. Greenstein and N. W. Polsby, eds., *Handbook of Political Science,* Vol. IV [Reading, Mass., 1975], p. 79).

18. The data on which this conclusion is based refer to issues in rather general categories such as "economic aid to foreign countries," "influence of big business in government," and "aid to education" (Campbell et al, *The American Voter,* p. 182). It is highly probable that the proportion of people meeting the requirements of having an opinion and differentiating among the parties would be substantially reduced if precise and specific policies within these general issue categories formed the basis of questions in a survey. See Converse, "Public Opinion and Voting Behavior," for a recent discussion.

19. Campbell et al., in *The American Voter*, tentatively conclude that in the Eisenhower years, covered by their study, "people who paid little attention to politics were contributing very disproportionately to partisan change" (p. 264). Nie, Verba, and Petrocik argue that the American electorate has become more discerning in their electoral choices and that there has been an "increase in consistency among attitudes themselves, . . . increased relationship between attitudes and the vote, and [a] decreased relationship between party identification and the vote. The data suggest that the American public has been entering the electoral arena since 1964 with quite a different mental set than was the case in the late 1950's and early 1960's. They have become more concerned with issues and less tied to their parties" (*The Changing American Voter*, p. 166). Unresolved methodological problems cause us to regard these conclusions with some caution.

20. In the 1980 University of Michigan Center for Political Studies postelection survey, 35 percent of the respondents classified themselves as independents; of these respondents, only one-third did not further specify that they leaned toward the Democratic or Republican party.

21. Arthur H. Miller, Warren E. Miller, Alden S. Raine and Thad A. Brown, "A Majority Party in Disarray: Policy Polarization in the 1972 Election," *American Political Science Review* 70 (September 1976), p. 760. The issues studied include: Vietnam withdrawal, amnesty for draft dodgers, reducing military spending, government health insurance, guaranteed standard of living, urban unrest, campus unrest, protecting the rights of those accused of crime, government aid to minorities, equal rights for women, abortion, legalization of marijuana, busing, and a "liberal-conservative philosophic position." For similar findings, see Jeane J. Kirkpatrick, "Representation in the American National Conventions: The Case of 1972," *British Journal of Political Science* 5 (July 1975), pp. 265–322, and *The New Presidential Elite* (New York, 1976).

22. Philip E. Converse, "Information Flow and the Stability of Partisan Attitudes," *Public Opinion Quarterly* 26 (Winter 1962), pp. 578–599.

23. V. O. Key, Jr., with the assistance of Milton C. Cummings, Jr., *The Responsible Electorate: Rationality in Presidential Voting, 1936–1960* (Cambridge, Mass., 1966).

24. Campbell et al., *The American Voter*, pp. 153–160; Key, "A Theory of Critical Elections," pp. 3–18. Stouffer, *Communism, Conformity and Civil Liberties*, p. 87, says that Americans are concerned not with world problems, but with personal problems. He adds, "A 'business recession' finds a path into almost every home—whether it is that of a factory worker or that of a butcher who finds his sales of meat declining. It becomes a threat that is immediate and personal."

25. V. O. Key, Jr., *The Responsible Electorate*.

26. Key asserts that "as has been demonstrated, the citizen's identification with party tends to produce a tie consistent with his policy preferences" (*Public Opinion and American Democracy*, p. 460). See also Lazarsfeld, Berelson, and Gaudet, *The People's Choice*, Chapter 9.

27. See Converse, "The Nature of Belief Systems in Mass Politics"; and Morris P. Fiorina, *Retrospective Voting in American National Elections* (New Haven, 1981).

28. Richard A. Brody et al., "Vietnam, the Urban Crisis and the 1968 Presidential Election: A Preliminary Analysis" (paper delivered at the 1969 meeting of the American Sociological Association, San Francisco, California, September 1969). The authors polled four national samples of the electorate during the campaign and asked numerous questions about each issue. For a detailed interpretation of their Vietnam findings, see Benjamin I. Page and Richard A. Brody, "Policy Voting and the Electoral Process: The Vietnam War Issue," *American Political Science Review* 66 (September 1972), p. 979.

29. Page and Brody, "Policy Voting and the Electoral Process: The Vietnam War Issue."

30. Miller et al., "A Majority Party in Disarray," pp. 761–772.

31. This notion is developed by Anthony Downs, *An Economic Theory of Democracy* (New York, 1957).

32. Donald R. Kinder, "Enough Already About Ideology: The Many Bases of American Public Opinion" (paper delivered at the 1982 Annual Meeting of the American Political Science Association, Denver, Colorado, September 1982, pp. 23–27). Kinder reports that "between 1956 and 1976, Democratically-inclined Independents voted 70 percent, on the average, for the Democratic candidate (compared to 64 percent for Weak Democrats), while Independent Republicans gave an average of 88 percent of their votes to the Republican nominee (compared to 85 percent for Weak Republicans)" (p. 27). See also Keith et al., "The Myth of the Independent Voter."

33. Kinder, "Enough Already About Ideology . . . ," pp. 27–29.

34. Ibid., pp. 29–31.

35. Nelson W. Polsby, *Consequences of Party Reform* (New York, 1983), p. 87.

36. Fiorina, *Retrospective Voting in American National Elections.*

37. Donald R. Kinder and D. Roderick Kiewiet, "Sociotropic Politics: The American Case," *British Journal of Political Science* 11 (April 1981), pp. 129–161; and D. Rivers, "The Dynamics of Party Support in the American Electorate, 1952–1976" (paper delivered at the 1980 Annual Meeting of the American Political Science Association, Washington, D.C., August 28–31).

38. Converse, "The Nature of Belief Systems in Mass Politics"; and Converse and Markus, "Plus Ça Change . . . The New CPS Election Study Panel."

39. Kinder, "Enough Already About Ideology . . . ," pp. 31–32.

40. See, as one of many examples, William J. Crotty and Gary C. Jacobson, *American Parties in Decline* (Boston, 1980).

41. Herbert F. Weisberg, "A Multidimensional Conceptualization of Party Identification," *Political Behavior,* vol. 2 (1980), pp. 33–60. See also Keith et al., "The Myth of the Independent Voter."

42. See Arthur H. Miller and Martin P. Wattenberg, "Measuring Party Identification: Independent or No Partisan Preference," *American Journal of Political Science* 27 (February 1983), pp. 106–121.

43. U.S. Bureau of the Census, *Statistical Abstract of the United States 1981* (Washington, D.C., 1981), p. 496.

44. Paul E. Meehl, "The Selfish Voter Paradox and the Thrown-Away Vote Argument," *American Political Science Review* 71 (March 1977), pp. 11–30.

45. Campbell et al., *The American Voter.*

46. Paul R. Abramson and John H. Aldrich, in "The Decline of Electoral Participation in America," *American Political Science Review* 76 (September 1982), pp. 502–521, state that "the erosion of partisanship in the electorate can explain between 25 and 30 percent of the decline in participation in presidential elections and even more of the decline in off-year congressional elections."

47. For the first half of the argument, see Abramson and Aldrich, "The Decline . . ."; for the second, see Polsby, *Consequences of Party Reform.*

48. The theory of political behavior that takes as a major explanatory variable the social connectedness of actors is especially well explored in the work of Herbert McClosky and his students. See Jack Citrin, Herbert McClosky, J. Merrill Shanks and Paul M. Sniderman, "Personal and Political Sources of Alienation," *British Journal of Political Science* 5 (January 1975), pp. 1–31. See also Wolfinger and Rosenstone, *Who Votes?*

49. See Raymond A. Bauer, Ithiel de Sola Pool, and Lewis Anthony Dexter, *American Business and Public Policy* (New York, 1963), pp. 323–399, especially p. 373.

50. Jeffrey M. Berry, *Lobbying for the People: The Political Behavior of Public Interest Groups* (Princeton, 1977).

51. See Seymour M. Lipset, Paul F. Lazarsfeld, Allen H. Barton, and Juan Linz, "The Psychology of Voting: An Analysis of Political Behavior," in Gardner Lindzey, ed., *Handbook of Social Psychology* (Cambridge, Mass., 1954).

52. Axelrod, "Where the Votes Come From: An Analysis of Electoral Coalitions, 1952–1968"; and Axelrod, "Communication," *American Political Science Review* 76 (June 1980), p. 394.

53. Axelrod, "Communication," *American Political Science Review* 68 (June 1974), p. 720.

54. Axelrod, "Communication," *American Political Science Review* 76 (June 1982), p. 395.

55. Campbell et al., *The American Voter*, pp. 483–494.

56. CBS News/*New York Times* 1980 exit polls showed men voting 54 percent Reagan to 37 percent Carter and women 46 percent Reagan to 45 percent Carter (Everett Carll Ladd, "The Brittle Mandate: Electoral Dealignment and the 1980 Presidential Election," *Political Science Quarterly* 96 [Spring 1981], p. 16).

57. See Kathleen Frankovic, "Sex and Politics—New Alignments, Old Issues, *PS* 15 (Summer 1982), pp. 439–448; and *Public Opinion* 5 (April-May 1982), pp. 21–32.

58. Adam Clymer, "Polls Show a Married-Single Gap in Last Election," *The New York Times* (January 6, 1983).

59. See the data in Frankovic, "Sex and Politics . . ."

60. Celinda C. Lake, "Guns, Butter and Equality, the Women's Vote in 1980" (paper presented at the Annual Meeting of the Midwest Political Science Association, April 28–May 1, 1982).

61. Berry, *Lobbying for the People . . .* , p. 186.

62. Joseph E. Cantor, "PACs: Political Financers of the '80s," *Congressional Research Service Review* (February 1982), pp. 14–16.

63. "Corporate Political Action Committees Are Less Oriented to Republicans Than Expected," *Congressional Quarterly* (April 8, 1978), pp. 849–854.

64. Edwin M. Epstein, "Corporations and Labor Unions in Electoral Politics" in *Annals of the American Academy of Political and Social Science* 425 (May 1976), p. 49.

65. Ibid., p. 50. For more on PACs, see Crotty and Jacobson, *American Parties in Decline*, op cit., pp. 100–155. An especially complete recent account is Edwin M. Epstein, "PACs and the Modern Political Process" (paper delivered at the conference on "The Impact of the Modern Corporation," Columbia University, New York, 1982). See also Michael J. Malbin, ed., *Parties, Interest Groups, and Campaign Finance Laws* (Washington, D.C., 1980); and Elizabeth Drew, "Politics and Money," *The New Yorker* (December 6, 1982: pp. 54–149; December 13, 1982: pp. 57–111).

66. Frank J. Sorauf, "Parties and Political Action Committees in American Politics," in Kay Lawson and Peter Merkl, eds., *When Parties Fail* (forthcoming), p. 16.

67. Berry, *Lobbying for the People*, pp. 209–210.

68. Robert Cameron Mitchell, "National Environmental Lobbies and the Apparent Illogic of Collective Action," in Clifford S. Russell, ed., *Collective Decision Making: Applications from Public Choice Theory* (Baltimore/London, 1979), p. 100.

69. "Access" is the opportunity to press claims upon decision makers. This does not imply that those who have more access are more successful in pressing their claims, but it is generally supposed that claims have a better chance of realization when they are presented repeatedly and auspiciously to decision makers, and by "known" rather than "unknown" claimants. See David B. Truman, *The Governmental Process* (New York, 1951), pp. 264–270.

70. Our interpretation of parties is based largely on E. Pendleton Herring, *The Politics of Democracy* (New York, 1940); V. O. Key, Jr., *Politics, Parties and Pressure Groups*, 4th ed. (New York, 1958); David B. Truman, "Federalism and the Party System," in Arthur Macmahon, ed., *Federalism: Mature and Emergent* (New York, 1955), Chapter 8; Anthony Downs, *An Economic Theory of Democracy* (New York, 1957); and a burgeoning literature on state and local political party organizations. See especially Truman, *The Governmental Process*, pp. 262–287; and Sarah McCally Morehouse, *State Politics, Parties and Policy* (New York, 1981).

71. An acutely self-satiric evaluation of the purist mentality is contained in Richard M. Koster's "Surprise Party," *Harper's* (March 1975), p. 31: "Alan Baron, the sharpest of the young pros, who had coached the liberals brilliantly on the Mikulski and charter commissions, declared that, whatever happened, the conference was a success: we might lose organized labor, but we'd brought in God."

72. Herbert McClosky, Paul J. Hoffman, and Rosemary O'Hara, "Issue Conflict and Consensus Among Party Leaders and Followers," *American Political Science Review* 54 (June 1960), pp. 406–427.

73. Herring, *The Politics of Democracy*, especially pp. 272–287. Recent research suggests that political activists who are at one stage recruited to politics by their strong views on one or another set of policy issues or their attachment to a candidate may in time become party regulars with a well developed taste for winning elections. See, for example, Robert T. Nakamura and Denis G. Sullivan, "Neo-Conservatism and Presidential Nomination Reforms: A Critique," *Congress and the Presidency* 9 (Autumn 1982), pp. 79–97.

74. See John F. Bibby, "Party Renewal in the National Republican Party," in Gerald M. Pomper, ed., *Party Renewal in America* (New York, 1980), pp. 102–115; and

Cornelius P. Cotter and John F. Bibby, "Institutional Development of Parties and the Thesis of Party Decline," *Political Science Quarterly* 95 (Spring 1980), pp. 1–27.

75. William Prendergast, "Aspects of the Development of Republican State Organization" (paper delivered at the Annual Meeting of the American Political Science Association, St. Louis, 1961); Daniel M. Ogden, Jr., "Trends in Democratic State Party Organization" (paper delivered at the Annual Meeting of the American Political Science Association, St. Louis, 1961); Robert J. Huckshorn, *Party Leadership in the States* (Amherst, Mass., 1976), pp. 254–256; and Malcolm E. Jewell and David M. Olson, *American State Political Parties and Elections* (Homewood, Ill., 1978).

76. John F. Bibby, Robert J. Huckshorn, James L. Gibson, and Cornelius P. Cotter, "State Party Chairmen Role Orientations and Institutional Party Strength" (paper delivered at the 1981 Annual Meeting of the Western Political Science Association, Denver, Colorado, 1981).

77. Ibid.

78. Ibid.

79. The structure of American political parties is treated, among other places, in Key, *Politics, Parties and Pressure Groups.* The Supreme Court now gives the national convention the right to regulate standards for admission to it, even overriding enactments of state legislatures on the subject of primary elections, and in this important respect national standards can be imposed on state party organizations. See *Cousins v. Wigoda,* 419 U.S. 477 (1975) and *Democratic Party of the U.S. et al. v. LaFollette et al.* 450 U.S. 107. See also Everett Carll Ladd, Jr., with Charles D. Hadley, *Transformations of the American Party System* (New York, 1975); Austin Ranney, *Curing the Mischiefs of Faction: Party Reform in America* (Berkeley, 1975); William Crotty, *Party Reform* (New York, 1983); James Ceaser, *Reforming the Reforms* (Cambridge, Mass., 1982); and Polsby, *Consequences of Party Reform.*

80. If the federal government ends up subsidizing the national committees instead of individual candidates, the next phase of party reform could give the national parties much greater leverage.

81. Cotter and Bibby, "Institutional Development of Parties . . ."

82. See Warren E. Miller, "Presidential Coattails: A Study in Political Myth and Methodology," *Public Opinion Quarterly* 19 (Winter 1955–56), pp. 26–39.

83. William S. Livingston, "A Note on the Nature of Federalism," *Political Science Quarterly* 67 (March 1952), pp. 81–95.

84. Polsby, *Consequences of Party Reform,* passim.

85. See Robert R. Alford, *Party and Society* (Chicago, 1963), Chapter 6, "The Politics of Diversity." This reanalysis of a variety of surveys suggests that class-oriented

voting in the United States, while it exists, does not polarize voters to the extent that can be found in Great Britain or Australia. See also Axelrod, "Where the Votes Come From" and "Communication."

86. Party leaders may haggle over amounts, but they do not dispute the principle. Though the rhetoric occasionally spoke of a collapse of the Social Security system, for instance, the widespread understanding that a compromise settlement was essential has, in fact, produced one, at least for the next few years.

87. Herbert McClosky et al., "Issue Conflict and Consensus Among Party Leaders and Followers." The authors, who compared large samples of Democratic and Republican leaders on twenty-four major public issues, conclude that "the belief that the two American parties are identical in principle and doctrine has little foundation in fact. Examination of the opinions of Democratic and Republican leaders shows them to be distinct communities of co-believers who diverge sharply on many important issues." They add, "Little support was found for the belief that deep cleavages exist among the electorate but are ignored by the leaders. One might, indeed, more accurately assert the contrary, to wit: that the natural cleavages between the leaders are largely ignored by the voters" (pp. 425–426). McClosky et al. found that on most issues, the Democratic party elite held positions not only closer to the Democratic rank and file, but also closer to the Republican rank and file than those of the Republican elite. While the party elites still differed significantly from each other in 1972, the tables had turned and the "Republican elite held views that were more representative of the views and values of rank-and-file Democrats than were the views of Democratic delegates." Jeane Kirkpatrick, "Representation in the American National Conventions," p. 287.

88. Key, *Public Opinion and American Democracy,* p. 439, observes, "Of Democratic high participators . . . only 34 percent fall into white-collar occupations; of the Republican group comparable in political activity, 48 percent are from white-collar occupations. Substantially more Democratic than Republican high participators are blue-collar workers. Occupational differences between the party identifiers become more marked as level of political participation increases." See also Verba and Nie, *Participation in America,* especially Chapter 16.

89. Martin Schram, *Running for President: A Journal of the Carter Campaign* (New York, 1977), pp. 92, 93, 114, 150.

90. That such burdens exist as a routine demand on presidential candidates is argued in Nelson W. Polsby, *Political Innovation in America* (New Haven, 1984).

91. An excellent article by Everett C. Ladd, "The New Divisions in U.S. Politics," *Fortune* (March 26, 1979), pp. 88–96, illustrates these points with public opinion data comparing the clear-cut 1930s with the confused 1970s.

92. In 1960, for example, Minnesota Democrats split among delegates friendly to Senator Humphrey, to Governor Freeman, and to both. Freeman nominated John F. Kennedy for president. Senator Eugene McCarthy nominated Adlai Stevenson. And most of the delegation ended up voting for Humphrey.

93. Martin P. Wattenberg, "The Decline of Political Partisanship in the United States: Negativity or Neutrality?", *American Political Science Review* 75 (December 1981), pp. 941–950.

94. The unit rule is not prescribed in the Constitution or by federal law. Rather, it is the result of individual state action that provides, in all states except Maine, that electors for party nominees are grouped together and elected *en bloc* on a "general ticket" such that a vote for one elector is a vote for all the electors on that ticket, with the majority vote electing all electors for the state. Senator Thomas Hart Benton said in 1824, "The general ticket system . . . was the offspring of policy. . . . It was adopted by the leading men of [ten states] to enable them to consolidate the vote of the state. . . ."

Thomas Jefferson had earlier pointed out that ". . . while ten states choose either by legislatures or by a general ticket it is folly and worse than folly for the other states not to do it." In short, once a few states maximized their impact by using the unit rule, the others followed suit. See *Motion for Leave to File Complaint, Complaint and Brief, Delaware* v. *New York,* No. 28 Original, U.S. Supreme Court, October term, 1966; and Neal R. Peirce, "The Electoral College Goes to Court," *The Reporter,* October 6, 1966. In Maine the electoral votes of each Congressional district—of which there are two—are determined by the vote within the district, and the states' two electoral votes that it has by virtue of its senators are cast according to the overall vote in the state as a whole. Here is a summary of the law, taken from *Nomination and Election of the President and Vice President of the United States Including the Manner of Selecting Delegates to National Political Conventions* (Washington, D.C., 1980), p. 356: "Electors shall vote by separate ballot for one person for President and one person for Vice President. A presidential elector is elected from each congressional district and two at large. They shall convene in the Senate chamber in Augusta on the first Monday after the second Wednesday of December at 2:00 P.M. following their election. The presidential electors at large shall cast their ballots for President and Vice President of the political party which received the largest number of votes in the State. The presidential electors of each congressional district shall cast their ballots for the candidates for President and Vice President of the political party which received the largest number of votes in each congressional district."

95. Richard M. Scammon and Alice V. McGillivray, eds., *America Votes 1980* (Washington, D.C., 1981), pp. 48, 70, 278.

96. Further confirmation of this view is provided by Steven J. Brams and Morton D. Davis, "The 3/2's Rule in Presidential Campaigning," *American Political Science*

Review 68 (March 1974), pp. 113–134; Claude S. Colatoni, Terrence J. Levesque, and Peter D. Ordeshook, "Campaign Resource Allocations Under the Electoral College," *American Political Science Review* 69 (March 1975), pp. 141–152; and John A. Yunker and Lawrence D. Longley, "The Biases of the Electoral College: Who Is Really Advantaged?" in *Perspectives on Presidential Selection,* ed. Donald R. Matthews (Washington, D.C., 1973), pp. 172–203.

97. Schram, *Running for President,* p. 298.

☆ Chapter 2: The Strategic Environment: Resources

1. Our discussion of money in elections owes a great deal to the work of Herbert Alexander, who, over the years, has built up an unequaled store of knowledge on this subject. Recent legislation affecting money in politics includes the Federal Election Campaign Act Amendments of 1974, 2 USC 431, and the Federal Election Campaign Act of 1971. For a wide-ranging set of materials on election reform up to and including the 1971 act, see U.S. Senate Select Committee on Presidential Campaign Activities, *Election Reform: Basic References* (Washington, D.C., 1973). A compact summary of the state of the law as of 1975 is contained in U.S. Senate Subcommittee on Privileges and Elections of the Committee on Rules and Administration, *Federal Election Campaign Laws* (Washington, D.C., 1975). For a useful discussion of the new law's political implications, see the American Bar Association, *Symposium on Campaign Financing Regulation* (Chicago, 1975). Data about the 1980 election were supplied by Herbert Alexander from his *Financing the 1980 Election* (Lexington, Mass., 1983).

2. For 1960 figures, see Herbert E. Alexander, *Financing the 1960 Election* (Princeton, 1962), p. 10. Figures for 1964 are contained in Herbert E. Alexander and Harold B. Meyers, "The Switch in Campaign Giving," *Fortune* (November 1965), pp. 103–108. Figures for 1968 are contained in Herbert Alexander, "Financing Parties and Campaigns in 1968: A Preliminary Report" (mimeo, Citizens Research Foundation, Princeton, 1969). Figures for 1972, 1976, and 1980 are contained in Alexander, *Financing the 1980 Election,* p. 110, Table 4–6.

3. Alexander Heard, *The Costs of Democracy* (Chapel Hill, 1960), pp. 7–8; Herbert E. Alexander, "Financing the Parties and Campaigns," in Paul T. David, ed., *The Presidential Election and Transition, 1960–61* (Washington, D.C., 1961), pp. 116–118; Alexander and Meyers, "The Switch in Campaign Giving"; Alexander, "Financing Parties and Campaigns in 1968," p. 2; Alexander, *Financing the 1972 Election* (Lexington, Mass., 1976), pp. 77–78; Alexander, *Financing the 1976 Election* (Washington, D.C., 1979), p. 166; and Alexander, *Financing the 1980 Election,* p. 103.

4. See Edwin M. Epstein, "Corporations and Labor Unions in Electoral Politics," *Annals of the American Academy of Political and Social Science* 425 (May 1976), pp. 33–58.

5. Elizabeth Drew, conducting interviews during the Carter administration's first weeks in office, had this to report: "A man here said, '[Carter] spent so much time in the campaign saying that he didn't owe anybody anything that nobody thinks they owe him anything.' " "Our Far-Flung Correspondents: Settling In," *The New Yorker* (February 28, 1977), p. 87.

6. See Charles W. Hucker, "Political Party Finances: It's David vs. Goliath," *Congressional Quarterly* (June 24, 1978), pp. 1607–1613; Charles W. Hucker, "Campaign Consultants Portray Candidates as Fiscal Watchdogs," *Congressional Quarterly* (July 22, 1978), pp. 1857–1860; William J. Lanouette, "The Selling of the Candidates, 1978," *National Journal* (November 4, 1978), pp. 1772–1777; Edwin M. Epstein, "The PAC Phenomenon: An Overview," *Arizona Law Review* 22 (1980), pp. 355–372; Elizabeth Drew, "Politics and Money," *The New Yorker* (December 6, 1982: pp. 54–149; December 13, 1982: pp. 57–111); and Institute of Politics, John F. Kennedy School of Government, Harvard University, *An Analysis of the Impact of the Federal Election Campaign Act, 1972–1978,* prepared for the Committee on House Administration, U.S. House of Representatives (Washington, D.C., October 1979).

7. Heard, *The Costs of Democracy,* pp. 18–22, 39; Alexander, "Financing the Parties and Campaigns," p. 118; Alexander and Meyers, "The Switch in Campaign Giving"; Alexander, *Financing the 1972 Election.*

8. Alexander and Meyers, "The Switch in Campaign Giving."

9. Alexander, *Financing the 1972 Election.*

10. Heard, *The Costs of Democracy,* p. 6.

11. Ibid., p. 41; Herbert E. Alexander, *Financing the 1964 Election* (Princeton, 1966), pp. 68–69.

12. Heard, *The Costs of Democracy,* pp. 49–53.

13. For expenditure figures, see ibid., pp. 17–24, and, for 1956 on, see Alexander, *Financing the 1976 Election.* Table 2.1 is adapted from figures in both these books.
    On the state level, however, the story may be different. See Murray Levin and George Blackwood, *The Compleat Politician* (Indianapolis, 1962), pp. 227–243. In congressional elections the relationship is more complex: money both determines and reflects perceptions of the chances of a challenger, as funding is needed to overcome incumbents' advantages, while contributors do not want to fund likely losers. See Gary C. Jacobson, *Money in Congressional Elections* (New Haven and London, 1980).

14. Alexander, "Financing the Parties and Campaigns," p. 119.

Table 2.1

	Democratic Percentage of Two-Party Vote	Democratic Percentage of Two-Party Expenditures
1932	59	49
1936	62	41
1940	55	35
1944	52	42
1948	52	39
1952	44	45
1956	42	41
1960	50	51
1964	61	37
1968	49	35
1972	37	33
1976	50	47
1980	45	35

SOURCES: U.S. Bureau of the Census, *Statistical Abstract of the United States 1981* (Washington, D.C., 1981), p. 478; and Herbert E. Alexander, *Financing the 1980 Election* (Lexington, Mass., 1983), p. 109.

15. Alexander, *Financing the 1972 Election,* p. 98; and Alexander, *Financing the 1976 Election,* p. 169.

16. Alexander, *Financing the 1976 Election,* p. 246; Alexander, *Financing the 1980 Election; FEC Reports on Financial Activities 1979–1980, Final Report, Presidential Pre-nomination Campaign* (Washington, D.C., October 1981).

17. Alexander, "Financing Parties and Campaigns in 1968," p. 9.

18. Connally had so much private funding that he chose to refuse federal matching funds so as not to be bound by spending limits. He won one delegate.

19. Martin Schram, *Running for President: A Journal of the Carter Campaign* (New York), 1977, p. 55.

20. Ibid., p. 16.

21. See Theodore H. White, *The Making of the President, 1960* (New York, 1961), pp. 71–74.

22. See ibid., pp. 92–110, and Harry W. Ernst, *The Primary That Made a President: West Virginia, 1960* (New York, 1962), especially pp. 16–17, 29–31. Several factors appear to have contributed to Humphrey's difficulty in raising money. First and probably foremost, he had very little of his own to draw upon. Second, Adlai Steven-

son was being indecisive and refused to withdraw from contention. Thus, Stevenson's backers were encouraged to wait and see rather than switch monetary support to Humphrey. Had Stevenson not been in contention, Humphrey might have gotten more money. And third, Humphrey apparently was unwilling to do things that would severely alienate the other candidates or otherwise jeopardize his future associations in the party. He may, therefore, have been restrained from actions that would have aided him. A revealing passage in White, *The Making of the President, 1960* (pp. 109–110) indicates what may have been involved: "In New York, from which so much Stevenson money had originally come to Humphrey's coffers, [Connecticut] Governor Abraham Ribicoff, acting on Kennedy's instructions, warned all Stevensonians that if they continued to finance the hopeless campaign of Hubert Humphrey, Adlai Stevenson would not even be considered for Secretary of State. Where necessary, Kennedy lieutenants were even rougher; in Connecticut, Boss John Bailey informed former Connecticut Senator William Benton . . . that if he continued to finance Humphrey (Benton had already given Humphrey $5,000 earlier in the spring), he would never hold another elective or appointive job for Connecticut . . ." Benton disputes this story. "It was wholly out of character for John Bailey to say anything like the words Teddy White ascribed to him . . . John Bailey did get in touch with me, but what he said was this: 'Since you gave $5,000 to Hubert's campaign, I want you to even the account by giving $5,000 to Jack Kennedy's campaign.' I told John that if Jack was nominated for the presidency, I would give him $10,000, which I later did." Quoted in Sidney Hyman, *The Lives of William Benton* (Chicago, 1969), p. 529.

23. Quoted in Edwin M. Epstein, "PACs and the Modern Political Process" (paper delivered at a conference on The Impact of the Modern Corporation, Columbia University, November 1982), p. 16. For similar arguments see Elizabeth Drew, "Politics and Money" and William J. Crotty and Gary C. Jacobson, *American Parties in Decline* (Boston, 1980), pp. 100–155.

24. Quoted in Epstein, "PACs and the Modern Political Process," p. 17.

25. Quoted in Kay Lawson, "Building Stronger Political Parties in the Eighties: Accountability vs. Power" (Typescript, 1982).

26. Michael J. Malbin, "The Problem of PAC Journalism," *Public Opinion* 5 (December/January 1983), p. 16.

27. The sum was set at $20 million in the Federal Election Campaign Act Amendments of 1974. Using 1974 as the base year, this number is increased annually by a cost-of-living adjustment, calculated by the Department of Labor. The sum for 1983 is approximately $29.5 million.

28. Herbert E. Alexander and Brian A. Haggerty, *The Federal Election Campaign Act: After a Decade of Political Reform,* Report of a Conference Sponsored by Citi-

zens' Research Foundation, Washington, D.C., April 1981 (Los Angeles: Citizens' Research Foundation, University of Southern California, 1981), pp. 28–29.

29. Nixon Administration fund-raising scandals are discussed in Mark V. Nadel, *Corporations and Political Accountability* (Lexington, Mass., 1976), pp. 27–28, 30–37.

30. *1972 Congressional Campaign Finances,* 10 volumes (Washington, D.C., 1973).

31. *Buckley et al.* v. *Valeo et al.,* 424 U.S. 1 (1976). See also Daniel D. Polsby, *"Buckley v. Valeo:* The Special Nature of Political Speech," *Supreme Court Review* (1976), pp. 1–43.

32. Bill Keller and Irwin B. Arieff, "Special Report: Washington Fund Raisers," *Congressional Quarterly* (May 17, 1980), p. 1335.

33. In October 1968, for example, a multimillionaire named Stewart Mott offered to raise a million dollars for Hubert Humphrey, then in desperate need of cash. Mott "made it clear that the Presidential candidate would have to modify his views on Vietnam." Humphrey refused Mott's offer (Herbert Alexander and H. B. Meyers, "A Financial Landslide for the GOP," *Fortune* [March 1970], p. 187).

34. Quoted in Jasper B. Shannon, *Money and Politics* (New York, 1959), p. 35.

35. See Nadel, *Corporations and Political Accountability,* pp. 27–28, 32, on American Airlines' sense of being a victim of virtual extortion by the Nixon campaign.

36. Heard, *The Costs of Democracy,* pp. 249–258.

37. See ibid. and Shannon, *Money and Politics,* p. 59. On pp. 13–65, Shannon presents a colorful history of American experience in raising money for presidential campaigns.

38. Alexander and Meyers, "The Switch in Campaign Giving," pp. 103–108. In 1968, the Republican pattern of small giving continued, as it has since, augmented by the return to the fold of many large contributors who had defected to President Johnson in 1964. See Alexander, "Financing Parties and Campaigns in 1968."

39. Alexander, "Financing Parties and Campaigns in 1968," p. 64.

40. Alexander and Meyers, "The Switch in Campaign Giving," pp. 105, 186. Maurice Stans started an analogous "R. N. Associates" for candidate Nixon in 1968 (Jules Witcover, *The Resurrection of Richard Nixon* [New York, 1970], p. 239).

41. See Malbin, "The Problem of PAC Journalism." See also Tina Rosenberg, "Diminishing Returns: The False Promise of Direct Mail," *The Washington Monthly* (June 1983), pp. 32–38.

42. The provision of the Communications Act that focuses the attention of broadcasters so efficiently is section 315 which says, in part: "If any licensee shall permit any

person who is a legally qualified candidate for any public office to use a broadcasting station, he shall afford equal opportunities to all other such candidates for that office in the use of such broadcasting station." *U.S. Code Annotated,* Title 47, section 315. Television stations have few programs of news commentary and these are not usually overtly partisan. (To be sure, the wealthier party may buy more TV time for its candidate, but we have already discussed the limitations of this resource.) Radio news commentary is more ubiquitous, but only those who initially agree with the more highly opinionated commentators are likely to tune in regularly. Consider, however, the impact of television coverage of the 1968 convention in Chicago. Two incidents will suffice to give a sense of the options open to television news directors under special circumstances: "[San Francisco Mayor Joseph] Alioto rose on screen to nominate [Humphrey]; back and forth the cameras swung from Alioto to pudgy, cigar-smoking politicians, to Daley, with his undershot, angry jaw, painting visually without words the nomination of the Warrior of Joy as a puppet of the old machines. Carl Stokes, the black mayor of Cleveland, was next—to second Humphrey's nomination—and then, at 9:55, NBC's film of the bloodshed had finally been edited, and Stokes was wiped from the nation's vision to show the violence in living color.

"The Humphrey staff was furious—Stokes is their signature on the Humphrey civil-rights commitment; and Stokes' dark face is being wiped from the nation's view to show blood—Hubert Humphrey being nominated in a sea of blood." Theodore H. White, *The Making of the President,* 1968 (New York, 1969), pp. 300–302.

On the evening of August 28, 1968, according to Richard Pride and Barbara Richards, "NBC showed the same violent event, which lasted less than five minutes, from three different camera angles with three separate reporters and led viewers to believe it was one continuous battle lasting several hours" ("Denigration of Authority? Television News Coverage of the Student Movement," *Journal of Politics* 36 [August 1974], p. 640).

43. See Nathan B. Blumberg, *One-Party Press? Coverage of the 1952 Presidential Campaign in 35 Daily Newspapers* (Lincoln, Neb., 1954); Edwin Emery and Henry L. Smith, *The Press in America* (Englewood Cliffs, N.J., 1954), pp. 714 ff.; and Arthur Edward Rowse, *Slanted News: A Case Study of the Nixon and Stevenson Fund Stories* (Boston, 1957).

44. "411 Dailies Support Ford; 80 for Carter," *Editor and Publisher* (October 30, 1976), pp. 5, 12–13; and John Consoli, "Reagan Backed by 443 Dailies; Carter Trails with 126; Anderson with 40 and 439 Undecided," *Editor and Publisher* (November 1, 1980), pp. 9–13.

45. The classic formulation by A. J. Liebling, is: "With the years, the quantity of news in newspapers is bound to diminish from its present low. The proprietor, as Chairman of the Board, will increasingly often say that he would *like* to spend 75 cents now and then on news coverage, but that he must be fair to his shareholders" (*The Press*

[New York, 1961], p. 5). More recently, there is evidence of an improvement in the news coverage in some communities when the papers have been taken over by the more responsible chains. Cases in point would include Dallas, Philadelphia, San Jose and Oakland.

46. Bernard C. Cohen, in *The Press and Foreign Policy* (Princeton, 1963), presents figures from a variety of sources on foreign affairs news (Chapter 4). His conclusion: "The volume of coverage is low." See also Elie Abel, ed., *What's News, the Media in American Society* (San Francisco, 1981).

47. Here is an example, atypical but illuminating, of this aimlessness at work. Former House Speaker Joseph Martin in his memoirs describes the appearance of an editorial mildly critical of presidential candidate Thomas E. Dewey in Martin's own newspaper (Martin was nominally editor and publisher) on the day of Dewey's arrival in Martin's hometown during the 1948 campaign. "Behind all this fuss was a very simple explanation. Having a small staff, the *Evening Chronicle* bought 'boilerplate' editorials prepared by a syndicate. The day of Dewey's visit, the editorial in question happened to be on the top of the pile, and a man in the composing room slapped it into the paper. Ironically, he was one of the most ardent Dewey supporters in North Attleboro. As for myself, I never read the editorial until it was well on its way to fame" (Joseph W. Martin, Jr., *My First Fifty Years in Politics,* as told to Robert J. Donovan [New York, 1960], pp. 196–197).

48. This issue is carefully studied and evaluated by Edwin Bayley, *Joe McCarthy and the Press* (Madison, Wisconsin, 1981). See also Richard Rovere, *Senator Joe McCarthy* (New York, 1959), pp. 137, 162–69.

49. See Frank Luther Mott, *The News in America* (Cambridge, Mass., 1952), p. 110; and Emery and Smith, *The Press in America,* pp. 541 ff.

50. See William L. Rivers, "The Correspondents after 25 Years," *Columbia Journalism Review* 1 (Spring 1962). On p. 5 he says, "In 1960, 57 percent of the daily newspapers reporting to the *Editor and Publisher* poll supported Nixon, and 16 percent supported Kennedy. In contrast, there are more than three times as many Democrats as there are Republicans among the Washington newspaper correspondents; slightly more than 32 percent are Democrats, and fewer than 10 percent are Republicans. . . . More than 55 percent of the correspondents for newspapers consider themselves liberals; 26.9 percent consider themselves conservatives." More recently, see Stephen Hess, *The Washington Reporters* (Washington, D.C., 1981), pp. 87 ff; and S. Robert Lichter and Stanley Rothman, "Media and Business Elites," *Public Opinion* (October/November 1981), pp. 42–46, 59–60.

51. Michael Jay Robinson, "Just How Liberal is the News? 1980 Revisited," *Public Opinion* (February/March 1983), pp. 55–60.

52. See White, *The Making of the President,* 1960, pp. 333–338. Corroborative testimony is given by Benjamin C. Bradlee, *Conversations with Kennedy* (New York, 1975). On Barry Goldwater's press relations, see Charles Mohr, "Requiem for a Lightweight," *Esquire* (August 1968), pp. 67–71, 121–122.

53. Witcover, *The Resurrection of Richard Nixon,* p. 173. See also pp. 188–192.

54. Timothy Crouse, *The Boys on the Bus* (New York, 1972, 1973), pp. 189–190; Theodore H. White, *The Making of the President, 1972* (New York, 1973), pp. 251–268; Witcover, *The Resurrection of Richard Nixon;* and Joe McGinniss, *The Selling of the President, 1968* (New York, 1969).

55. Elmo Roper has observed that "on the civil rights issue [in 1948], Mr. Dewey draws the support of voters favoring exactly opposite things, and more than that, each side thinks Dewey agrees with them" (Hugh A. Bone, *American Politics and the Party System* [New York, 1955], p. 477). In 1968, the bulk of those voting for Eugene McCarthy in the New Hampshire primary were not Vietnam "doves," as McCarthy was, but were even more belligerent about the war than Lyndon Johnson. See Converse, "Public Opinion and Voting Behavior," p. 81.

56. When asked by the Gallup Poll in 1979 to gauge how much confidence they had in newspapers, among other American institutions, 51 percent of the respondents said "a great deal or quite alot," 47 percent said "some or very little," 1 percent said "none," and 1 percent had no opinion. The Gallup Poll, *Public Opinion 1979* (Wilmington, Delaware, 1980), p. 159. In 1980, only 42 percent said "a great deal or quite alot." *Public Opinion 1980* (Wilmington, Delaware, 1981), p. 247.

57. This paragraph summarizes the major findings of researchers on what has come to be called the "two-step flow" of information. See Elihu Katz and Paul F. Lazarsfeld, *Personal Influence* (Glencoe, Ill., 1955).

58. V. O. Key, Jr., *Public Opinion and American Democracy* (New York, 1961), p. 453.

59. Table 2.2 shows the growing preference for television over newspapers as a primary source of news.

60. Examples would be instances where candidates were not known to voters before the campaign or where they ran without benefit of party labels, as in local nonpartisan elections. See Charles R. Adrian, "Some General Characteristics of Nonpartisan Elections," *American Political Science Review* 46 (September 1952), pp. 766–776; Charles E. Gilbert and Christopher Clague, "Electoral Competition and Electoral Systems in Large Cities," *Journal of Politics* 24 (May 1962), pp. 323–349, especially p. 344; and Raymond E. Wolfinger and Fred I. Greenstein, "The Repeal of Fair Housing in California: An Analysis of Referendum Voting," *American Political Science Review* 62 (September 1968), pp. 753–769.

Table 2.2

Source of most news:	1959	1961	1963	1964	1967	1968	1971	1972	1974	1976	1978
Television	51%	52%	55%	58%	64%	59%	60%	64%	65%	64%	67%
Newspapers	57	57	53	56	55	49	48	50	47	49	49
Radio	34	34	29	26	28	25	23	21	21	19	20
Magazines	8	9	6	8	7	7	5	6	4	7	5
People	4	5	4	5	4	5	4	4	4	5	5
Don't know/ no answer	1	3	3	3	2	3	1	1	—	—	—

QUESTION: First, I'd like to ask you where you usually get most of your news about what's going on in the world today—from the newspapers or radio or television or magazines or talking to people or where?

SOURCE: *Public Opinion* (August/September 1979), p. 30.

61. Robert S. Ericson, "The Impact of Newspaper Endorsements on Presidential Elections" (paper delivered at the annual meeting of the American Political Science Association, 1974).

62. Angus Campbell, Philip E. Converse, Warren E. Miller, and Donald E. Stokes, *The American Voter* (New York, 1960), pp. 58, 530.

63. Gary C. Jacobson, "The Impact of Broadcast Campaigning on Electoral Outcomes," *Journal of Politics* 37 (August 1975), pp. 769–793.

64. Robinson, "Just How Liberal is the News? 1980 Revisited"; and Michael J. Robinson and Margaret H. Sheehan, *Over the Wire and on TV* (New York, 1983).

65. C. Anthony Broh, "Public Opinion, Polling and the Press: The Race for the Presidency" (working paper, Institute of Policy Sciences and Public Affairs, Duke University [1979]), p. 26.

66. See Richard L. Rubin, *Press, Party and Presidency* (New York, 1981), pp. 191–196. "Not only was [television journalists'] affirmation of primaries clear from the vastly disproportionate air time given primaries compared to other selection methods, but also numerous phrases attributing inherent democratic values to primaries appeared, sprinkled liberally throughout network news" (p. 193).

67. Nelson W. Polsby, *Consequences of Party Reform* (New York, 1983), passim.

68. For an early discussion of this phenomenon, see Stanley Kelley, *Professional Public Relations and Political Power* (Baltimore, 1956). See also Larry J. Sabato, *The Rise of Political Consultants: New Ways of Winning Elections* (New York, 1981).

69. See, for example, Jules Witcover's comments about reporters' attempts to deny Gerald Ford the advantage of the White House. Jules Witcover, *Marathon* (New York, 1977), pp. 528–556.

70. Nelson W. Polsby, "The Democratic Nomination," in Austin Ranney, ed., *The American Elections of 1980* (Washington, D.C., 1981), pp. 37–60; and The Gallup Opinion Index, Report #183 (December 1980), p. 51. Another example occurred during the 1964 campaign, when United States vessels in the Gulf of Tonkin were fired upon and President Johnson took to the airwaves to promise vigorous defensive measures. In late July, just before the incident, he received favorable ratings from 59 percent of the voters, to 31 percent for Goldwater; in early August, just after the incident, the president's score went up to 65 percent, and Goldwater's declined to 29 percent (American Institute of Public Opinion Survey, released October 18, 1964). For other examples, see Nelson W. Polsby, *Congress and the Presidency* (Englewood Cliffs, N.J., 1976), p. 66.

71. Witcover, *The Resurrection of Richard Nixon,* pp. 462–463.

72. Howard S. Bloom and H. Douglas Price, "Voter Response to Short-Run Economic Conditions: The Asymetric Effect of Prosperity and Recession," *American Political Science Review* 69 (December 1975), pp. 1240–1254.

73. A good indicator of whether or not people were better off in 1980 is real disposable income per capita, which, according to the following figures taken from *Survey of Current Business* increased by about 10 percent in constant dollars between 1976 and 1980:

Table 2.3
Disposable Personal Income per Capita

	1976	1980
Current Dollars	$5,477	$8,176
1972 Dollars	4,158	4,571

SOURCE: U. S. Department of Commerce, Bureau of Economic Analysis, *Survey of Current Business* 61 (March 1981), p. 10; *Survey of Current Business* 62 (July 1982), p. 37.

74. For Truman, see Harry S. Truman, *Years of Trial and Hope* (Garden City, N.Y., 1956), pp. 499–503, and Alben Barkley, *That Reminds Me* (Garden City, N.Y., 1954), pp. 225–232. For Johnson, see White, *The Making of the President, 1968,* passim.

75. See Samuel P. Huntington, *American Politics: The Promise of Disharmony* (Cambridge, Mass., 1981); Huntington, "The Democratic Distemper," *The Public Interest*

41 (Fall 1975), pp. 9–38; Aaron Wildavsky, "The Past and Future Presidency," *The Public Interest* 41 (Fall 1975), pp. 56–76; and Wildavsky, "Government and the People," *Commentary* 56 (August 1973), pp. 25–32.

76. Much of the material in this section is adapted from Nelson W. Polsby, *Political Promises: Essays and Commentary on American Politics* (New York, 1974), Chapter 5.

77. See Polsby, *Consequences of Party Reform;* and Byron E. Shafer, *Quiet Revolution: Reform Politics in the Democratic Party, 1968–1972* (New York, forthcoming).

☆ Chapter 3: The Nomination Process

1. Much of the discussion in this chapter is drawn from our own observations via the mass media of the nomination process, the personal observations of one of us who attended the Democratic National Conventions of 1960, 1968, 1972 and 1980 and the Republican National Conventions of 1964 and 1980, and from a set of basic texts on American parties and elections, including Moisei Ostrogorski, *Democracy and the Party System in the United States* (New York, 1910); C. E. Merriam and H. Gosnell, *The American Party System* (New York, 1929); Peter H. Odegard and E. A. Helms, *American Politics* (New York, 1938); Pendelton Herring, *The Politics of Democracy* (New York, 1940); E. E. Schattschneider, *Party Government* (New York, 1942); D. D. McKean, *Party and Pressure Politics* (Boston, 1949); V. O. Key, Jr., *Politics, Parties and Pressure Groups,* 4th ed. (New York, 1958); H. R. Penniman, *Sait's Parties and Elections* (New York, 1952); Hugh A. Bone, *American Politics and the Party System* (New York, 1955); Austin Ranney and Willmoore Kendall, *Democracy and the American Party System* (New York, 1956); William Goodman, *The Two-Party System in the United States* (Princeton, 1960); and Gerald Pomper, *Nominating the President: The Politics of Convention Choice,* 2nd ed. (New York, 1966).

We also found quite useful a more specialized literature on nominations, including Paul T. David, Malcolm C. Moos, and Ralph M. Goldman, *Presidential Nominating Politics in 1952,* Vols. 1–5 (Baltimore, 1954); Paul T. David, Ralph M. Goldman, and Richard C. Bain, *The Politics of National Party Conventions* (Washington, D.C., 1960); and Richard C. Bain, *Convention Decisions and Voting Records* (Washington, D.C., 1960).

2. Commission on Party Structure and Delegate Selection, *Mandate for Reform* (Washington, D.C., 1970), pp. 14–15.

3. See Democratic National Committee (Charles T. Manatt, Chairman), *Delegate Selection Rules for the 1984 Democratic National Convention* (Washington, D.C., March 26, 1982). For a discussion of some of the consequences of the rules, in the case of the 1980 convention, see Rhodes Cook, "Democrats Adopt New Rules for

Picking Nominee in 1980," *Congressional Quarterly Weekly Report* (June 17, 1978), pp. 1571–1572.

4. As the *New York Times* mused:

> Now, a full year before the first 1984 delegate selection, the competition for attention among hopefuls is so intense that a new device has been introduced into national politics: the announcement of the announcement.
>
> In mid-January, campaign planners for Senator Alan Cranston let it be known that the California Democrat would announce his candidacy Feb. 2. The result: a small story, followed by a bigger one—more prominence than would have resulted otherwise. Planners for Senator Gary Hart observed this gambit and promptly let it be known that he would announce Feb. 17. Planners for Walter F. Mondale said, not for attribution, that their man would do his thing on Feb. 21; off the record, they said, the event would be in St. Paul. Later they distributed a schedule confirming these rumors.
>
> Representative Morris K. Udall handled his different problem differently. His staff let it be known that he would announce his Presidential decision in a speech at the National Press Club last Wednesday. The day before, too late to affect attendance materially, a few reporters were told the Arizonan had reluctantly decided not to run after all.
>
> Planners for Senator John Glenn, who is generally regarded as a little slower off the mark than the other Democratic competitors, have been willing to say only that they will not have an announcement about his announcement until March or April. Come to think of it, maybe that's a story.

Phil Gailey and Warren Weaver, Jr., "The New Announcement," *New York Times* (February 14, 1983).

5. See William Cavala, "Changing the Rules Changes the Game: Party Reform and the 1972 California Delegation to the Democratic National Convention," *American Political Science Review* 68 (March 1974), p. 31, n. 20.

6. James Lengle and Byron Shafer, "Primary Rules, Political Power, and Social Change," *American Political Science Review* 70 (March 1976), pp. 25–40.

7. Stephen J. Wayne, *The Road to the White House: The Politics of Presidential Elections* (New York, 1981), p. 262.

8. See Harry W. Ernst, *The Primary That Made a President: West Virginia, 1960* (New York, 1962); Theodore H. White, *The Making of the President, 1960* (New York, 1961).

9. James Reston, "The Organized Disorder in California," *New York Times* (June 3, 1964), p. 30.

10. See Jules Witcover, *The Resurrection of Richard Nixon* (New York, 1970), Chapter 10.

11. Wayne, *The Road to the White House,* pp. 23, 265.

12. Charles O. Jones, "Nominating 'Carter's Favorite Opponent': The Republicans in 1980," in Austin Ranney, ed., *The American Elections of 1980* (Washington, D.C., 1981), pp. 61–98.

13. Elting E. Morison, *The Letters of Theodore Roosevelt* (Cambridge, Mass., 1954), p. 525. See also George E. Mowry, *Theodore Roosevelt and the Progressive Movement* (Madison, Wis., 1946).

14. See, for example, Jack Newfield, *Robert Kennedy: A Memoir* (New York, 1969), p. 293. For a different view, see Richard Scammon and Ben Wattenberg, *The Real Majority* (New York, 1970), Chapters 7–8.

15. Robert D. Novak, *The Agony of the G.O.P., 1964* (New York, 1965), p. 368. In the 1964 Nebraska Republican primary the results were:

Goldwater	67,369	49 percent
Nixon (write-in)	42,811	35 percent
Lodge (write-in)	22,113	16 percent

16. General Eisenhower's write-in vote of over 100,000 in Minnesota in 1952 is, of course, an example of what we have in mind. See David, Moos, and Goldman, *Presidential Nominating Politics in 1952,* Vol. 1, p. 32.

17. See Ernst, *The Primary That Made a President;* White, *The Making of the President, 1960.*

18. See Theodore H. White, *The Making of the President, 1968* (New York, 1969), p. 89; Lewis Chester, Godfrey Hodgson, and Bruce Page, *An American Melodrama* (New York, 1969), pp. 79–99; Arthur Herzog, *McCarthy for President* (New York, 1969), p. 97; Newfield, *Robert Kennedy,* p. 218.

19. Jack W. Germond and Jules Witcover, *Blue Smoke and Mirrors* (New York, 1981), p. 118.

20. Wayne, *The Road to the White House,* p. 264.

21. Further discussion will be found in F. Christopher Arterton, *Media Politics: The News Strategies of Presidential Campaigns,* manuscript in progress.

22. William H. Lucy, "Polls, Primaries, and Presidential Nominations," *Journal of Politics* 35 (November 1973), p. 843.

23. Ibid., p. 833.

24. Richard L. Rubin, *Press, Party, and Presidency* (New York, 1981), p. 194. The study cited is Thomas E. Patterson and Robert D. McClure, *The Unseeing Eye* (New York, 1976). See also Robert G. Kaiser, "T.V. on the Trail: A Three-Course Menu for Fluff," *Washington Post* (October 10, 1980).

25. Rubin, *Press, Party, and Presidency,* pp. 191–193.

26. See Austin Ranney, "Turnout and Representation in Presidential Primary Elections," *American Political Science Review* 66 (March 1972), pp. 21–37 for the period 1948 to 1968. The same held true in 1976, when turnout averaged 28 percent in the primaries versus 54 percent in the general election. See Austin Ranney, *Participation in American Presidential Nominations 1976* (Washington, D.C., 1977), p. 20, and James Lengle, *Representation and Presidential Primaries: The Democratic Party in the Post Reform Era* (Westport, Conn., 1981), p. 10. In 1980, the figures were 25 percent in primaries and 54 percent in the general election (Ranney, ed., *The American Elections of 1980,* pp. 353, 364).

27. For an interesting argument along these lines, see Malcolm E. Jewell, "A Caveat on the Expanding Use of Presidential Primaries," *Policy Studies Journal* 2 (Summer 1974), pp. 279–284.

28. Lengle and Shafer, "Primary Rules, Political Power, and Social Change."

29. Ibid.

30. Gerald Pomper, "New Rules and New Games in Presidential Nominations," *Journal of Politics* 41 (August 1979), pp. 784–805.

31. Of the eight new primary states, the southern ones, Texas, Arkansas, Kentucky, and Georgia had 250 delegates, while Idaho, Montana, Nevada and Connecticut combined had 95.

32. Larry M. Bartels, "Ideology and Momentum in Presidential Primaries" (paper delivered at the 1982 Annual Meeting of the American Political Science Association, Denver, Colorado, September 1982).

33. Richard Brody and Larry Rothenberg, "Participation in Presidential Primaries" (talk delivered at the Survey Research Center, University of California [Berkeley, March 15, 1983]).

34. Richard Reeves, *Convention* (New York, 1977), p. 180. Uncommitted delegates won 39 percent of the vote; Carter won 29 percent.

35. The Report of the McGovern Commission of the Democratic National Committee said: "A minority of the Rules Committee of the 1968 Democratic National Convention brought to the floor a proposal to further 'democratize' the selection of

delegates to future conventions. They proposed that the 1972 Convention shall require, in order to give all Democratic voters . . . full and timely opportunity to participate in nominating candidates, that (1) the unit rule be eliminated in all stages of the delegate selection process and (2) all feasible efforts [be] made to assure that delegates are selected through party primary, convention, or committee procedures open to public participation within the calendar year of the national convention. This minority report of the Rules Committee, subsequently passed by the delegates assembled in Chicago, carried an unquestionably stern mandate for procedural reform" (*Mandate for Reform,* a report of the Commission on Selection to the Democratic National Committee [Washington, DC, April 1970], p. 15).

36. Indeed, one possible candidate, Morris Udall, bowed out of the 1984 race in early February 1983, saying that it was already too late to mount a serious campaign. See "Mondale, Askew Join Oval Office Aspirants," *Congressional Quarterly Weekly Report* (February 26, 1983), p. 434; and Martin Schram, "Udall Won't Seek Presidency in '84," *Washington Post* (February 10, 1983).

37. James A. Farley, *Jim Farley's Story* (New York, 1948), pp. 11–13; and Farley's *Behind the Ballots* (New York, 1938), p. 70; see also John F. Carter, *The New Dealers* (New York, 1934), p. 34.

38. See Thomas M. Durbin and Michael V. Seitzinger, Congressional Research Service, under the direction of J. S. Kimmitt, Secretary of the Senate, *Nomination and Election of the President and Vice-President of the United States Including the Manner of Selecting Delegates to National Political Conventions* (Washington, D.C., 1980).

39. *Democratic Party of the U.S. et al.* v. *LaFollette et al.* 450 U.S. 107 (1981). In *LaFollette,* the national Democratic party sued the state of Wisconsin in order to defend the party's right to exclude from its national convention delegates selected in an open, cross-over primary. The Court held that Wisconsin could not "constitutionally compel the National Party to seat a delegation chosen in a way that violates the Party's rules" (p. 107).

40. See Nelson W. Polsby, "The Democratic Nomination," in Ranney, ed., *The American Elections of 1980,* pp. 37–60. "The Jordan memo," Martin Schram reports,

> outlined plans for using White House pressure and influence to encourage state officials to shift the dates of various primary elections and caucuses—to create a "preferred version" of the 1980 calendar that would benefit Carter's campaign.
> " . . . The easiest way to establish early momentum . . . is to win southern delegates by encouraging southern states to hold early caucuses and primaries. . . . It is in our interest to have states that we are likely to win scheduled on the same day with states that we might do poorly in."

Martin Schram, "Carter," in Richard Harwood, ed., *The Pursuit of the Presidency 1980* (New York, 1980), p. 84.

41. See Allan P. Sindler, "The Unsolid South," in Alan Westin, ed., *The Uses of Power* (New York, 1962), pp. 230–283. See also Abraham Holtzman, *The Loyalty Pledge Controversy in the Democratic Party*, Eagleton Series, no. 21 (New York, 1960). Another example is the seating of Texas delegates at the 1952 Republican convention. See Malcolm C. Moos, *The Republicans: A History of Their Party* (New York, 1956), pp. 468–479; William S. White, *The Taft Story* (New York, 1954), pp. 176–183; and David, Moos, and Goldman, *Presidential Nominating Politics in 1952*, pp. 69–85.

42. See Jules Witcover, *Marathon* (New York, 1977), Chapters 31–33.

43. Jack Arvey, as told to John Madigan, "The Reluctant Candidate," *The Reporter* (November 24, 1953), pp. 19–26.

44. See the articles on Symington in Eric Sevareid, ed., *Candidates, 1960* (New York, 1959); and Ralph G. Martin and Edward Plaut, *Front Runner, Dark Horse* (Garden City, N.Y., 1960). See also Nixon, *Six Crises* (New York, 1962).

45. Carl Sandburg, *Abraham Lincoln: The Prairie Years* (New York, 1926), Vol. 2, p. 330. To an Indiana leader, Lincoln wrote that Republicans should "look beyond our noses and say nothing on points where we should disagree."

46. Anthony L. Teasdale, "The Paradox of the Primaries," *Electoral Studies* 1 (1982), pp. 43–63; quotes from pp. 43–44, 49.

47. This is the number that White (*The Making of the President, 1968*, p. 259) estimates that the Democrats needed for their convention. For a more recent example, see Eric Pianin, "Democrats Pick San Francisco as Site of '84 National Convention," *Washington Post* (April 22, 1983).

48. Reeves, *Convention*, p. 32.

49. Material on the Kennedy organization in 1960 is drawn from Fred G. Burke, "Senator Kennedy's Convention Organization," in *Inside Politics: The National Conventions, 1960*, ed. Paul Tillett (Dobbs Ferry, N.Y., 1962), pp. 25–39.

50. Ibid., p. 39.

51. Recognizing the importance of communication at the Republican convention of 1860, a supporter of Abraham Lincoln carefully seated all the solid Seward states close together and as far as possible from the states whose delegates were in some doubt about whom to support (Glyndon G. Van Deusen, *Thurlow Weed: Wizard of the Lobby* [Boston, 1947], p. 253). Mayor Daley arranged for something similar at the Democratic National Convention in 1968, but the level of protest about excessive security procedures and the lack of communications facilities reached such a pitch that whatever strategic advantages Daley might have hoped for evaporated.

52. See David, Moos, and Goldman, *Presidential Nominating Politics in 1952,* Vol. 1; Robert Elson, "A Question for Democrats: If Not Truman, Who?" *Life* (March 24, 1952), pp. 118–133; Albert Votaw, "The Pros Put Adlai Over," *New Leader* (August 4, 1952), pp. 3–5; Douglass Cater, "How the Democrats Got Together," *The Reporter* (August 19, 1952), pp. 6–8; Arvey and Madigan, "The Reluctant Candidate: An Inside Story"; and Walter Johnson, *How We Drafted Adlai Stevenson* (New York, 1955).

53. F. Christopher Arterton, "Exploring the 1976 Republican Convention: Strategies and Tactics of Candidate Organizations," *Political Science Quarterly* 92 (Winter 1977–78), p. 664.

54. Democratic National Committee, *Mandate for Reform,* p. 40. The Republican party adopted language encouraging the participation of women, young people, and black people in their conventions, but it has stopped short of requiring quotas.

55. Cavala, "Changing the Rules Changes the Game," p. 37.

56. Ibid.

57. See Denis G. Sullivan, Jeffrey L. Pressman, Benjamin I. Page, and John J. Lyons, *The Politics of Representation: The Democratic Convention, 1972* (New York, 1974), pp. 41–70.

58. Jeffrey L. Pressman, "Exploring the 1976 Convention: Groups and Group Caucuses," *Political Science Quarterly* 92 (Winter 1977–78), pp. 673–682.

59. This account and the paragraphs that follow are taken from Jeane J. Kirkpatrick, "Representation in the American National Conventions: the Case of 1972," *British Journal of Political Science* 5 (1975), pp. 265–322.

60. Ibid., p. 285.

61. Commission on Presidential Nomination and Party Structure (Morley Winograd, chairman), *Openness, Participation and Party Building: Reforms for a Stronger Democratic Party* (Washington, D.C., January 25, 1978), pp. 19–20.

62. Among Republican delegates, women were only slightly favorable to ERA: 32 percent to 26 percent (Warren J. Mitofsky and Martin Plissner, "The Making of the Delegates, 1968–1980," *Public Opinion* [October/November 1980], pp. 37–43).

63. Ibid., pp. 40–42.

64. Herbert McClosky, Paul J. Hoffman, and Rosemary O'Hara, "Issue Conflict and Consensus Among Party Leaders and Followers," *American Political Science Review* 54 (June 1960), pp. 406–427.

65. Kirkpatrick, "Representation in National Political Conventions," p. 40.

66. For extensive documentation, see Everett Carll Ladd, Jr. (with Charles D. Hadley), *Transformation of the Party System: Political Coalitions from the New Deal to the 1970's* (New York, 1975). See also their "Political Parties and Political Issues: Patterns in Differentiation since the New Deal," a Sage Professional Paper, *American Politics Series* (Beverly Hills, Calif., 1973), pp. 4–11.

67. William R. Shafer, Romano E. Weber, and Robert S. Montjoy, "Mass and Political Elite Beliefs about the Policies of the Regime" (paper delivered at the annual meeting of the American Political Science Association, 1973).

68. Thomas Roback, "Political Attitudes among Republican Leaders: The Case of Delegates to the 1972 National Convention" (paper delivered at the annual meeting of the American Political Science Association, 1974). See also Roback, "Amateurs and Professionals: Delegates to the 1972 Republican National Convention," *Journal of Politics* 37 (May 1975), p. 462.

69. Ranney, *Curing the Mischiefs of Faction: Party Reform in America* (Berkeley, 1975), p. 153. The italics are Ranney's.

70. See Ostrogorski, *Democracy and the Party System in the United States,* pp. 145–60, for excellent descriptions of convention confusion. Tillett, ed., *Inside Politics,* contains more up-to-date material in the same vein. Theodore H. White, *Making of the President, 1964* (New York, 1965), in contrast, describes the order and efficiency of conventions, like those in 1964, when there was no real contest for the nomination; see especially pp. 201–202. See also Ralph G. Martin, *Ballots and Bandwagons* (Chicago, 1964).

71. See Roy V. Peel and Thomas C. Donnelly, *The 1932 Campaign: An Analysis* (New York, 1935), pp. 92–93. Arthur Schlesinger, Jr., writes that strategist James Farley opposed the attempt to attack the two-thirds rule, "knowing well that not all delegates who were for Roosevelt were against the rule, and fearing that a defeat on this issue might set back the whole Roosevelt drive." Roosevelt backed down just in time (*The Crisis of the Old Order, 1919–1933* [Boston, 1957], pp. 299–300). See also Robert Morss Lovett, "Big Wind at Chicago," *The New Republic* (July 13, 1932), p. 228.

72. Wesley Bagby, "The 'Smoke-Filled Room' and the Nomination of Warren G. Harding," *Mississippi Valley Historical Review* 41 (March 1955), pp. 657–674.

73. Caroline T. Harnsberger, *A Man of Courage—Robert A. Taft* (Chicago, 1952), p. 146. See also Joseph Martin's memoirs, *My First 50 Years in Politics,* as told to Robert J. Donovan (New York, 1960).

74. Peel and Donnelly, *The 1932 Campaign: An Analysis,* pp. 95–96.

75. For instance, on the Roosevelt election of 1932: "Farley had held a few votes in reserve for the second ballot, knowing the importance of showing an increase each time round." Schlesinger, *The Crisis of the Old Order, 1919–1933,* p. 306.

76. Eugene B. McGregor, Jr., "Rationality and Uncertainty at National Nominating Conventions," *The Journal of Politics* 35 (1973), pp. 472–477.

77. Harry Daugherty, *The Inside Story of the Harding Tragedy* (New York, 1932), pp. 36, 46; and Mark Sullivan, *Our Times* (New York, 1926–1935), Vol. 2, p. 54. See also Bagby, "The 'Smoke-Filled Room' and the Nomination of Warren G. Harding," pp. 657–674.

78. Arthur Vandenberg, Jr., ed., *The Private Papers of Senator Vandenberg* (Boston, 1952), p. 6.

79. Frank R. Kent, *The Democratic Party* (New York, 1928), p. 493.

80. See Jules Abels, *Out of the Jaws of Victory* (New York, 1959), pp. 65–68.

81. See Aaron Wildavsky, "What Can I Do? Ohio Delegates View the Democratic Convention," in Tillett, ed., *Inside Politics,* pp. 112–130.

82. See Edward Stanwood, *A History of the Presidency from 1788 to 1897* (Boston, 1898), pp. 206–225.

83. Mark Sullivan, *Our Times,* Vol. 6, pp. 35–67. See also Daugherty, *The Inside Story of the Harding Tragedy,* pp. 41–55.

84. See Kent, *The Democratic Party,* pp. 483–505.

85. Ferdinand Lundberg, *Imperial Hearst* (New York, 1936), pp. 273–275, and Schlesinger, *The Crisis of the Old Order, 1919–1933,* pp. 304–308.

86. See Irving G. Williams, *The American Vice-Presidency: New Look* (New York, 1954); and Joel K. Goldstein, *The Modern American Vice Presidency* (Princeton, 1982).

87. The best accounts of the selection of Spiro Agnew are in White, *Making of the President, 1968,* pp. 244–253, and Witcover, *The Resurrection of Richard Nixon,* pp. 349–55. See also Richard Cohen and Jules Witcover, *A Heartbeat Away* (New York, 1974).

88. Most of the 130-odd Goldwater delegates we interviewed at the 1964 Republican convention were prepared to sacrifice victory if victory meant becoming a "me-too" party or "going against principles" by adopting what they termed the "devious and corrupt" balanced tickets of the past.

89. Quoted in Ross K. Baker, "Outlook for the Reagan Administration," in Marlene Michels Pomper, ed., *The Election of 1980* (Chatham, New Jersey, 1981), p. 167.

90. This was noticeable even before the reforms of the 1968–1972 period. See William Carleton, "The Revolution in the Presidential Nominating Convention," *Political Science Quarterly* 72 (June 1957), pp. 224–240.

91. Loch K. Johnson and Harlan Hahn, "Delegate Turnover at National Party Conventions, 1944–68," in Donald R. Matthews, ed., *Perspectives on Presidential Selection* (Washington, D.C., 1973), p. 148.

92. Obviously this entails risks as well as opportunities. George Romney was the first serious Republican candidate in the field in 1968, and the early exposure before he could put together a fully coherent position on the Vietnam issue almost certainly caused his downfall. See White, *Making of the President, 1968*, pp. 54–61, and Witcover, *The Resurrection of Richard Nixon*, pp. 171–191.

☆ Chapter 4: The Campaign

1. See Seymour M. Lipset, Paul F. Lazarsfeld, Allen H. Barton, and Juan Linz, "The Psychology of Voting: An Analysis of Political Behavior," in Gardner Lindzey, ed., *Handbook of Social Psychology* (Cambridge, Mass., 1954), pp. 1124–1175; Lazarsfeld, Pennard Berelson, and Hazel Gaudet, *The People's Choice* (New York, 1944), pp. 87–93; Berelson, Lazarsfeld, and William N. McPhee, *Voting* (Chicago, 1954), pp. 16–17; and Richard A. Brody, "Change and Stability in Partisan Identification: A Note of Caution" (paper delivered at the 1974 annual meeting of the American Political Science Association).

2. See Angus Campbell, Philip E. Converse, Warren E. Miller, and Donald E. Stokes, *The American Voter* (New York, 1960), pp. 124, 532–53. On p. 124, Table 6–1, they summarize the highly consistent results of seven separate national sample surveys taken by the Center for Political Studies Survey Research Center from October 1952 to October 1958. Below are C.P.S./S.R.C. figures for October 1958, November 1968, November 1974, November 1976, November 1978, November 1980, and November 1982, taken from unpublished C.P.S./S.R.C. tables.

3. There is another possibility: that voters who turn out only by being dinned at by the media are likely to be less stable in their political orientations and will therefore vote less for the party and more for the candidate whose name or personality seems more familiar to them. This, in a year when an Eisenhower is on the ticket, might well mean Republican votes. The most thoroughly documented research on the question suggests that increasing turnout by relaxing registration rules would have little or no effect on the partisan distribution of the vote. See Steven J. Rosenstone and Raymond E. Wolfinger, "The Effect of Registration Laws on Voter Turnout," *American Political Science Review* 72 (March 1978), pp. 22–48.

4. See Philip E. Converse, Angus Campbell, Warren E. Miller, and Donald E. Stokes, "Stability and Change in 1960: A Reinstating Election," *American Political Science Review* 55 (June 1961), pp. 269–80, especially p. 274.

Table 4.5
Party Affiliations Are Stable

	Oct. 1958	Nov. 1968	Nov. 1974	Nov. 1976	Nov. 1978	Nov. 1980	Nov. 1982
	(percent)	(percent)	(percent)	(percent)	(percent)	(percent)	(percent)
Strong Rep.	13	10	8	9	8	10	10
Weak Rep.	16	14	14	14	13	14	14
Independent Rep.	4	9	9	10	9	12	8
Independents	8	11	15	14	10	12	11
Independent Dem.	7	10	13	12	14	11	11
Weak Dem.	24	25	21	25	24	23	24
Strong Dem.	23	20	17	15	15	16	20
Apolitical, don't know	5	1	3	2	6	2	2

5. Wolfinger and his associates analyzed the voting behavior of independents and found some surprising results. Breaking all independents into three categories, independent Democrats, independent Republicans and true independents (leaning toward neither party), they found that the partisan independents generally vote like normal Democrats or Republicans. True independents, however, act as swing voters, generally always voting for the winner. True independents have not increased in importance despite their growth in numbers, because that growth has been offset by a decline in their turnout rate. The turnout rate for true independents averaged nearly 10 percentage points lower than that for either partisan independents or true partisans over the period from 1952 to 1974, and in the election years of 1972 and 1974 the difference was 20 percentage points. See Bruce E. Keith et al., "The Myth of the Independent Voter" (paper delivered at the 1977 Annual Meeting of the American Political Science Association).

6. See Campbell et al., *The American Voter,* pp. 537–538; and Herbert H. Hyman and Paul B. Sheatsley, "The Political Appeal of President Eisenhower," *Public Opinion Quarterly* 19 (Winter 1955–56), pp. 26–39.

7. For indications that this strategy is feasible despite the existence of the general stereotypes, see Campbell et al., *The American Voter,* pp. 44–59, 179–187. See also American Institute of Public Opinion News Releases (Princeton, N.J.), February 6, 1963; October 9, 1964; and October 25, 1964.

8. For a striking demonstration of this, see Ithiel de Sola Pool, Robert P. Abelson, and Samuel Popkin, *Candidates, Issues and Strategies* (Cambridge, Mass., 1964), pp. 117–118.

9. Recall Senator Dirksen's famous castigation of Thomas E. Dewey at the Republican convention of 1952: "We followed you before, and you took us down the path to defeat." Richard Nixon in 1968 did pursue a modified "me-too" strategy. The main thrust of his campaign, however, was more like the first strategy we discussed: emphasizing dissatisfaction with the incumbent party's handling of a new issue, "law and order." Furthermore, there is some reason to suppose that rather than scoring a clear win what Nixon really did was sneak through to victory because the Democrats tore themselves apart. In 1972, running as an incumbent against the very controversial choice of only a minority of Democrats, Nixon's strategy strongly deemphasized party. "Reelect the President" was his slogan, thus ignoring not only the Republican party but even Mr. Nixon's own name.

10. For indications that this is so, see in particular Herbert McClosky, Paul J. Hoffman, and Rosemary O'Hara, "Issue Conflict and Consensus among Party Leaders and Followers," *American Political Science Review* 54 (June 1960), pp. 406–427.

11. Good accounts of debates over strategy among Republicans can be found in such sources as Charles O. Jones, *The Republican Party in American Politics* (New York, 1965); Robert Donovan, *The Future of the Republican Party* (New York, 1964); Malcolm C. Moos, *The Republicans: A History of Their Party* (New York, 1956); Robert D. Novak, *The Agony of the G.O.P. 1964* (New York, 1965); and Conrad Joyner, *The Republican Dilemma* (Tucson, 1964).

12. The *Congressional Quarterly* (November 20, 1964), p. 2709, estimated that Republicans lost more than 500 seats in state legislatures in the 1964 election. Republicans gained one governor (for a total of 17), lost two United States senators (reducing their senatorial representation to 32), and sustained a net loss in the House of Representatives of 38 seats, reducing their strength to 140 members, the lowest since the Roosevelt landslide of 1936.

13. See, for example, Jones, *The Republican Party in American Politics,* pp. 66–71. The Michigan Survey Research Center estimates that an overwhelming 96 to 98 percent of such Republicans typically vote (Philip E. Converse, Aage R. Clausen, and Warren E. Miller, "Electoral Myth and Reality: The 1964 Election," *American Political Science Review* 59 [June 1965], pp. 322–323).

14. The research of Keith et al. in "The Myth of the Independent Voter" underscores the need for distinguishing between true independents and partisan independents. The latter groups behave more or less as normal partisans in their degree of political participation, civic interest, and partisan loyalty. For earlier descriptions of independent voters, see Berelson, Lazarsfeld, and McPhee, *Voting,* pp. 333–347, e.g., propositions 39, 50, 51, 66, 68, 70, 71, 78, 79; and Campbell, et al., *The American Voter,* pp. 142–145.

15. The study of right-wing ideologues and their supporters is more speculative than empirical. Nevertheless, there are a few straws in the wind, and all blow in the same direction. In 1962, Raymond E. Wolfinger and his associates administered a questionnaire to 308 "students" at an anticommunism school conducted by Dr. Fred Schwarz's Christian Anti-Communism Crusade in Oakland, California. Among the findings of this study were that 278 of the 302 persons in this sample who voted in 1960 (or 92 percent of those who voted) had voted for Nixon, and that 58 percent of those who answered the question chose Goldwater over Nixon for 1964. At about the same time, a nationwide Gallup poll showed Goldwater the choice of only 13 percent of Republicans. Raymond E. Wolfinger, Barbara Kaye Wolfinger, Kenneth Prewitt, and Sheilah Rosenhack, "America's Radical Right: Politics and Ideology," in David E. Apter, ed., *Ideology and Discontent* (New York, 1964), pp. 267–269. Analysis of various election returns and of a 1954 Gallup poll suggests that support for the late Senator Joseph McCarthy was importantly determined by party affiliation, with Republicans far exceeding Democrats or independents in the ranks of his supporters. See Nelson W. Polsby, "Towards an Explanation of McCarthyism," *Political Studies* 8 (October 1960), pp. 250–271.

16. AIPO News Releases of September 6, 1964, and October 16, 1964, suggested that Republican defections would run as high as 30 percent, but the release of December 11 indicated that a 20 percent defection figure was more accurate. This compares with defections by Republican voters of 5 percent, 4 percent, and 8 percent in the three previous elections. Democratic defections in this election were also high—13 percent of those calling themselves Democrats voted for Goldwater—but these were confined mostly to the southern states.

17. In early July, the Gallup poll (AIPO News Release, November 11, 1964) showed the following figures among Republican voters:

Preferring			
Goldwater	22 percent	Scranton	20 percent
Lodge	21 percent	Rockefeller	6 percent

Just before the Republican convention, the figures among Republicans were:

Scranton	60 percent	Undecided	6 percent
Goldwater	34 percent		

Goldwater received 23 percent of the vote in the New Hampshire primary; 18 percent in Oregon; 8 percent in Pennsylvania (fourth in a field of five write-ins); 10.5 percent in Massachusetts; 71 percent in Indiana, where Harold Stassen received the remainder; only 49 percent in Nebraska, where Goldwater's name alone was on the ballot; 51.4 percent in California; 76 percent in Texas, running in a trial heat with only Rockefeller; 31.9 percent in South Dakota; and a bit better than 60 percent in

Illinois, where he was opposed on the ballot only by Margaret Chase Smith and where there is no law requiring election officials to tabulate write-in votes.

Gallup trial heats (AIPO News Release, July 1, 1964) before the Republican convention showed Goldwater running a poorer race against President Johnson than either Scranton or Nixon:

Goldwater	18 percent	Scranton	26 percent	Nixon	27 percent
Johnson	77 percent	Johnson	69 percent	Johnson	70 percent
Undecided	5 percent	Undecided	5 percent	Undecided	3 percent

18. AIPO News Release, September 13, 1964.

19. Louis Harris Survey News Releases (New York), July 13, 1964, and September 14, 1964. Some of the Harris survey findings on foreign affairs were:

Table 4.6

Issue		Voters Describe Goldwater Position		Describe Own Position	
		July (percent)	Sept. (percent)	July (percent)	Sept. (percent)
Go to war over	For	78	71	29	29
Cuba	Against	22	29	71	71
Use atomic bombs	For	72	58	18	18
in Asia	Against	28	42	82	82
United Nations	For	42	50	82	83
	Against	58	50	18	17

20. Jules Witcover, *The Resurrection of Richard Nixon* (New York, 1970), Chapter 8.

21. Philip E. Converse, Warren E. Miller, Jerrold G. Rusk, and Arthur C. Wolfe, "Continuity and Change in American Politics: Parties and Issues in the 1968 Election," *American Political Science Review* 63 (December 1969), p. 1084.

22. See the discussion in ibid., pp. 1090–1104.

23. *Congressional Quarterly* (November 22, 1968), p. 3177.

24. This analysis of the 1980 election draws extensively on Nelson W. Polsby, "Party Realignment in the 1980 Election," *The Yale Review* 72 (Autumn 1982), pp. 43–54.

25. David S. Broder, "Is It a New Era?," *Washington Post* (November 19, 1980).

26. David S. Broder, "Election '80 Called 'Blip,' " *Washington Post* (September 5, 1981).

27. Polsby, "Party Realignment in the 1980 Election," p. 42.

28. See Table 1.8.

29. See William Schneider, "The November 4 Vote for President: What Did It Mean?," in Austin Ranney, ed., *The American Elections of 1980* (Washington, D.C., 1981), esp. pp. 225–227.

30. See John E. Mueller, *War, Presidents, and Public Opinion* (New York, 1973).

31. Table 4.7 summarizes his Gallup popularity ratings for 1981 and 1982.

Table 4.7

Question: "Do you approve or disapprove of the way Ronald Reagan is handling his job as President?"

		Approve	Dis-approve	No opinion
1981	Jan. 30–Feb. 2	51%	13%	36%
	Feb. 13–16	55	18	27
	March 13–16	60	24	16
	April 3–6	67	18	15
	April 10–13	67	19	14
	May 8–11	68	21	11
	June 5–8	59	28	13
	June 19–22	59	29	12
	June 26–29	58	30	12
	July 17–20	60	29	11
	July 24–27	56	30	14
	July 31–Aug. 3	60	28	12
	Aug. 14–17	60	29	11
	Sept. 18–21	52	37	11
	Oct. 2–5	56	35	9
	Oct. 30–Nov. 2	53	35	12
	Nov. 13–16	49	40	11
	Nov. 20–23	54	37	9
	Dec. 11–14	49	41	10
1982	Jan. 8–11	49	40	11
	Jan. 22–25	47	42	11
	Feb. 5–8	47	43	10
	March 12–15	46	45	9

SOURCE: *Gallup Report,* No. 199 (April 1982), p. 22.

32. Broder, "Is It a New Era?"

33. Robert Axelrod, "Communication," *American Political Science Review* 72 (June 1978), p. 622.

34. See Everett Carll Ladd, "The Brittle Mandate: Electoral Dealignment and the 1980 Presidential Election," *Political Science Quarterly* 96 (Spring 1981), pp. 1–25.

35. See Robert S. Erikson and Kent L. Tedin, "The 1928–1936 Partisan Realignment—The Case for the Conversion Hypothesis," *American Political Science Review* 75 (December 1981), pp. 951–962.

36. Adam Clymer, "Displeasure With Carter Turned Many to Reagan," *New York Times* (November 9, 1980).

37. See Warren E. Miller and J. Merrill Shanks, "Policy Directions and Presidential Leadership: Alternative Interpretations of the 1980 Presidential Election," *British Journal of Political Science* 12 (July 1982), pp. 299–356.

38. See, for example, Kristi Andersen, *The Creation of a Democratic Majority, 1928–1936* (Chicago, 1979).

39. Schneider, "The November 4 Vote for President," p. 225.

40. Samuel Popkin, "The Hidden Campaign: Sea Changes in American Presidential Campaigns," *Voting and Campaigning in Presidential Elections* (typescript, June 1982), p. 4.

41. Ibid.

42. Everett Carll Ladd, "The Brittle Mandate: Electoral Dealignment and the 1980 Presidential Election"; and "The 1980 Presidential Election: In Search of Its Meaning," typescript (February 3, 1981). See also Ladd's *Where Have All the Voters Gone? The Fracturing of America's Political Parties,* 2nd. ed. (New York, 1982).

43. This would give a result similar to the "southern strategy" recommended to Richard Nixon in such publications as Kevin P. Phillips, *The Emerging Republican Majority* (New Rochelle, New York, 1969). See also Nelson W. Polsby, "An Emerging Republican Majority?," *The Public Interest* 17 (Fall 1969), pp. 119–126.

44. See Edward Tufte, *Political Control of the Economy* (Princeton, 1978) for a discussion of political effects of these sorts of activities.

45. Martin Schram, *Running for President* (New York, 1977), p. 342.

46. Ibid., pp. 352–358.

47. The report of the speech in the *New York Times,* October 6, 1956, gives no indication of how it was received. The authors heard it delivered.

48. "The records . . . revealed that the 1972 Nixon campaign effort raised a record total of $60.2 million, $8 million more than the previously acknowledged total. The committee said that $56.1 million of this amount had been spent" (*Congressional Quarterly* [October 6, 1973], p. 2659).

49. Jules Witcover, *Marathon* (New York, 1977), pp. 132–137.

50. See Table 1.8.

51. Thomas Flinn, "How Nixon Took Ohio," *Western Political Quarterly* 15 (June 1962), pp. 276–279.

52. Witcover, *The Resurrection of Richard Nixon,* pp. 237–239.

53. Schram, *Running for President,* p. 341.

54. Ibid., pp. 276–298.

55. Ibid., p. 292.

56. Ibid., pp. 337, 338–339.

57. Ibid., pp. 341–342.

58. Ibid., p. 293.

59. Ibid., p. 283.

60. See, for example, the Gallup Poll for June 25–28, 1982, in which 43 percent of a national sample said that the Democrats were the party best able to keep the country prosperous. Only 34 percent picked the Republicans. *The Gallup Report,* No. 204 (September 1982), p. 45. See Graph 4.1. See also Campbell et al., *The American Voter,* pp. 44–59.

61. See, for example, *The Joint Appearances of Senator John F. Kennedy and Vice-President Richard M. Nixon, Presidential Campaign of 1960,* Report 994, Part 3, 87th Congress, 1st Session, U.S. Senate (Washington, D.C., 1961). Especially see Mr. Nixon's opening remarks in the first joint television debate, pp. 75–78. In the 1976 debates Carter predictably accused President Ford of a lack of compassion for the unemployed, as well as guilt by association for the Depression. "I remember when Herbert Hoover was against jobs for people. . . . And we've got the highest unemployment we've had, under the Ford Administration, since the Great Depression. This affects human beings. And his insensitivity in providing those people a chance to work has made this a welfare administration, and not a work administration" (transcript of presidential debates, *New York Times* [Friday, Sept. 24, 1976]). See also Austin Ranney, ed., *The Past and Future of Presidential Debates* (Washington, D.C., 1979).

62. Transcript of Presidential Debates, *New York Times* (October 16, 1976). See also Campbell et al., *The American Voter,* pp. 44–59; and Angus Campbell, Gerald Gurin,

and Warren E. Miller, *The Voter Decides* (Evanston, Ill., 1954), pp. 44–45, especially Table 4-3, p. 45.

AIPO surveys show a more than twenty-year trend on this issue indicated in Graph 4.2. The graph is remarkably consistent in several ways. First, it testifies to the continuing perception (with many of these years under Republican presidents and many under Democrats) that the Republican party is more "the party of peace." There may have been a slight erosion of the Republican position and a gain by the Democrats over this period as a whole, although in March 1970 the Democrats were only one percentage point above where they had been twenty years earlier, while the Republicans were only four points below their 1951 reading. Second, and very revealing, is the clear periodicity of the relationship. There is a sharp peak and maximum difference between the parties as November of every presidential election year approaches, followed by a convergence over the next two years, followed by divergence toward the presidential election peak again. Just before elections we would expect voters' expressions of their accustomed stereotypes to be at their strongest because of the polarization in the attitudes of voters that normally takes place during the heat of a campaign. Senator Goldwater's extreme foreign policy positions caused the lone reversal in the positions of the two parties, but, despite the fact that both major candidates in 1968 were pledged to "end the war," and despite what was probably the more "dovish" position of Humphrey, the Republican advantage on this issue had reasserted itself within four years of the Johnson landslide.

63. The most well-publicized clashes over foreign policy occurred in the second and third television debates; see the *New York Times,* October 8, 1960, pp. 1, 12; October 9, 1960, Section 4, p. 10; and October 14, 1960, p. 22. The impression of journalists and political observers that Nixon gained in these confrontations (see, for example, the *New York Times* for October 17, 1960) was corroborated by surveys of the viewers (see the references in n. 65, following) and by Pool, Abelson, and Popkin, *Candidates, Issues and Strategies,* p. 118.

64. Converse, Miller, Rusk, and Wolfe, "Stability and Change in 1960: A Reinstating Election," pp. 269–280.

65. Elihu Katz and Jacob J. Feldman, "The Debates in the Light of Research: A Survey of Surveys," in Sidney Kraus, ed., *The Great Debates* (Bloomington, Ind., 1962), pp. 201–202. Bear in mind, however, that *issues* as such do not strongly influence voting behavior. Katz and Feldman conclude: "First of all, it seems safe to say that the debates—especially the first one—resulted primarily in a strengthening of commitment to one's own party and candidate. This was much more the case for Democrats than Republicans, but the former had much greater room for improvement" (p. 208).

66. This disability of McGovern's is vividly portrayed in the Michigan analysis: "On Vietnam, the issue most decidedly associated with him, McGovern was capable of

Graph 4.1
Which Party Best to Keep U.S. Prosperous?

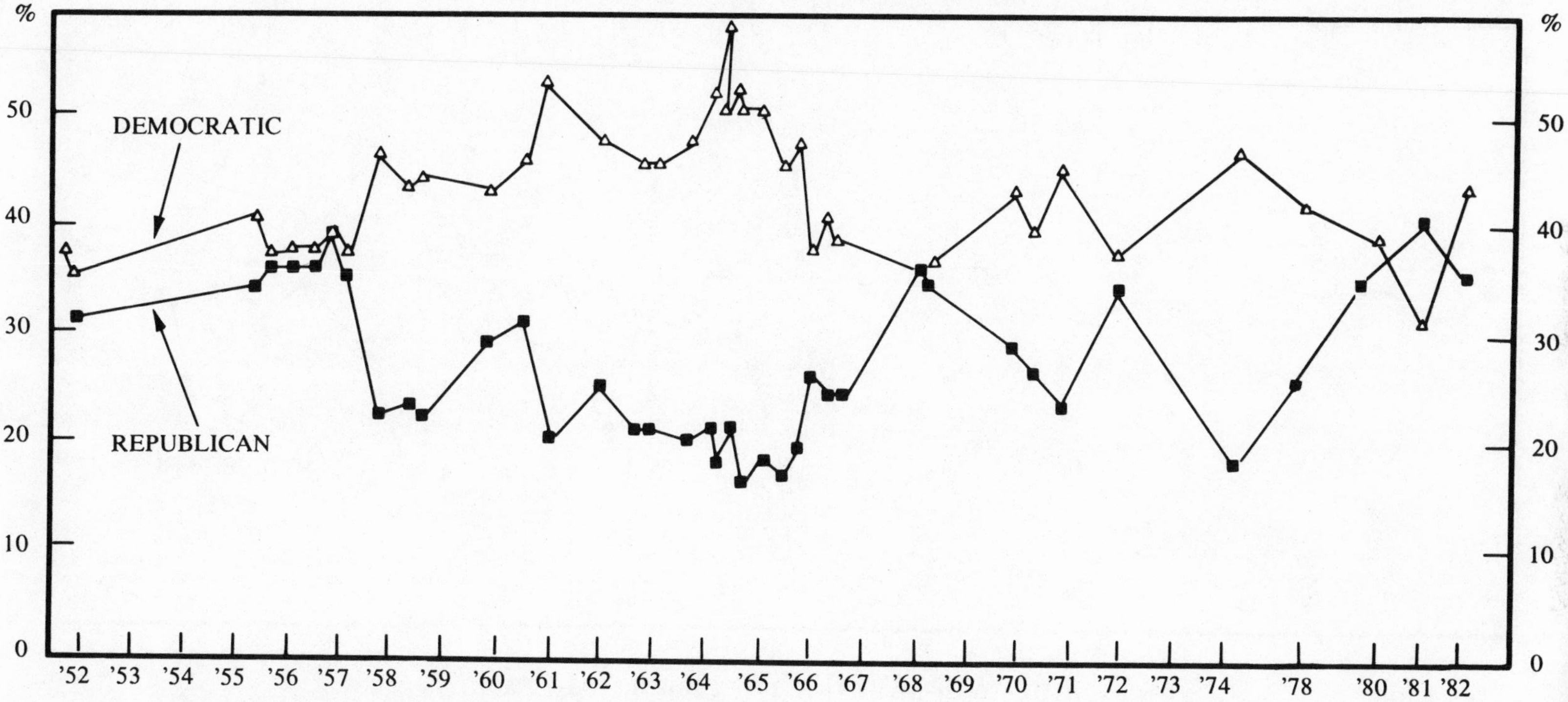

DEMOCRATIC

REPUBLICAN

SOURCE: *Gallup Opinion Index*, April 1974, November 1978, September 1982.

Graph 4.2

Which Party Best to Keep U.S. Out of World War III?

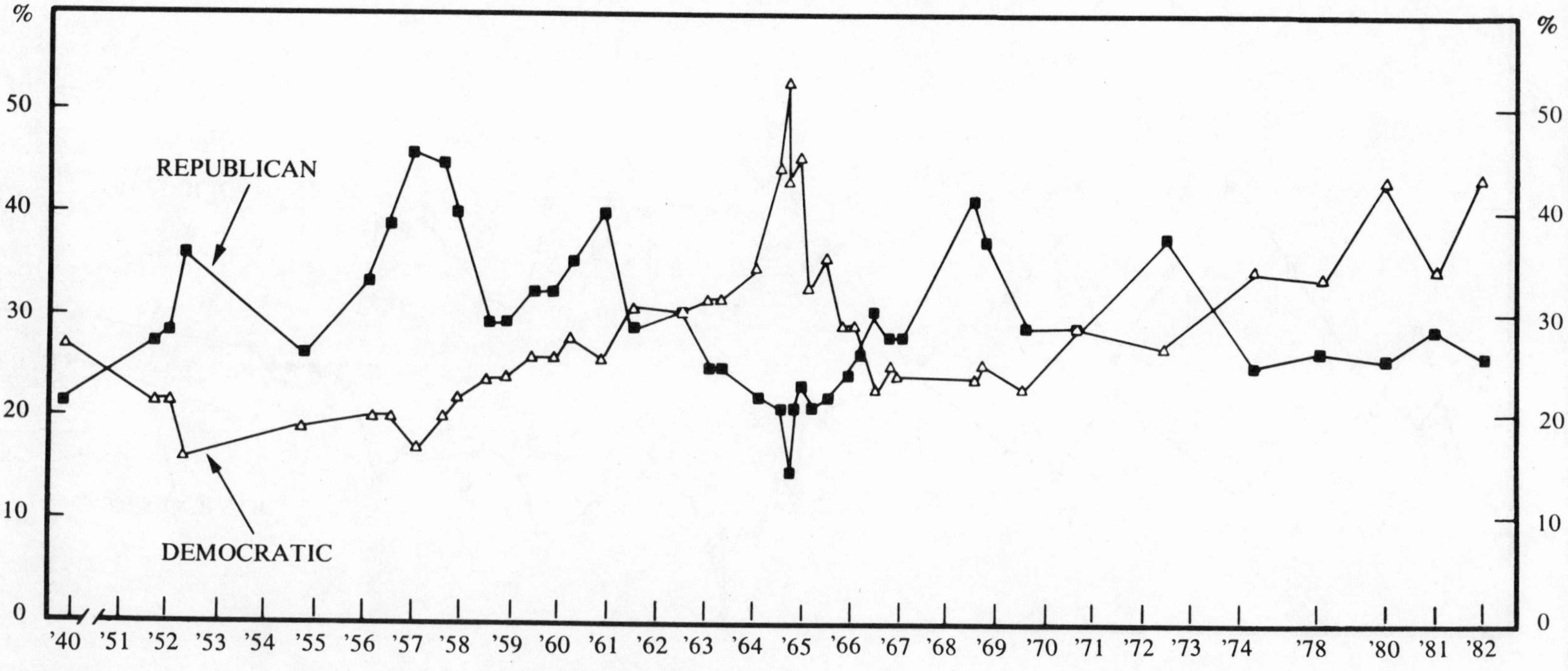

REPUBLICAN

DEMOCRATIC

%

'40 '51 '52 '53 '54 '55 '56 '57 '58 '59 '60 '61 '62 '63 '64 '65 '66 '67 '68 '69 '70 '71 '72 '73 '74 '78 '80 '81 '82

50

40

30

20

10

0

SOURCE: *Gallup Opinion Index*, April 1974, November 1978, September 1982.

securing only slightly more than his expected proportion of the two-party vote from the 29 percent of the population that most intensely favored immediate withdrawal from Vietnam. The remaining 71 percent displayed extremely high defection rates, ranging from 20 to 30 and 35 percent below the expected Democratic vote" (Arthur H. Miller, Warren E. Miller, Alden S. Raine, and Thad A. Brown, "A Majority Party in Disarray: Policy Polarization in the 1972 Election," *American Political Science Review* 70 [September 1976], pp. 19, 20).

67. Table 4.8 reports Jimmy Carter's Gallup approval ratings beginning just before the American embassy in Tehran was seized.

68. Richard Scammon and Ben Wattenberg, *The Real Majority* (New York, 1970), p. 39. See also pp. 37–43.

69. See Theodore H. White, *The Making of the President, 1960* (New York, 1961), pp. 269–275, White, *The Making of the President, 1964* (New York, 1965), passim; and Timothy Crouse, *The Boys on the Bus* (New York, 1973).

70. Department of Marketing, Miami University, Oxford Research Associates, *The Influence of Television on the Election of 1952* (Oxford, Ohio, 1954), pp. 151–160.

71. Witcover, *The Resurrection of Richard Nixon*, pp. 237–239.

72. See White, *The Making of the President, 1960*, pp. 282–283; and Herbert A. Selz and Richard D. Yoakum, "Production Diary of the Debates," in Kraus, ed., *The Great Debates*, pp. 73–126.

73. Ibid.; see also Richard M. Nixon, *Six Crises* (New York, 1962), pp. 346–386.

74. Earl Mazo, *Richard Nixon* (New York, 1959), pp. 21–22, 362–369.

75. See Katz and Feldman, "The Debates in the Light of Research: A Survey of Surveys," in Kraus, ed., *The Great Debates*, pp. 173–223.

76. See Charles Mohr, "President Tells Polish-Americans He Regrets Remark on East Europe," *New York Times* (October 9, 1976); and R. W. Apple, Jr., "Economy is Stressed by Dole and Mondale During Sharp Debate," *New York Times* (October 16, 1976).

77. See Hedrick Smith, "No Clear Winner Apparent; Scene Is Simple and Stark," *New York Times* (October 29, 1980). After the election, Terence Smith of the *Times* wrote:

> The continual emphasis on Mr. Reagan's image as a hair-trigger proponent of American military intervention—the "war and peace issue" as it came to be called—may have been overdone, in the opinion of some Carter aides.
> In June, Mr. Powell was telling reporters that Mr. Reagan was "too be-

Table 4.8
Carter Approval Trend

	Approve	Dis- approve	No opinion
1979 Oct. 12–15	31%	55%	14%
Nov. 2–5	32	55	13
American Embassy in Tehran Seized			
Nov. 16–19	38	49	13
Nov. 30–Dec. 3	51	37	23
Dec. 5–6	61	30	9
Dec. 7–10	54	35	11
1980 Jan. 4–7	56	33	11
Jan. 18–21	58	32	10
Feb. 1–4	55	36	9
Mar. 7–10	43	45	12
Mar. 28–31	39	51	10
Apr. 11–14	39	50	11
Hostage Rescue Attempt Fails			
May 2–5	43	47	10
May 16–19	38	51	11
May 30–June 2	38	52	10
June 13–16	32	56	12
June 27–30	31	58	11
July 11–14	33	55	12
July 14–25	21	63	16

SOURCE: *The Gallup Poll—Public Opinion 1980* (Wilmington, Del., 1981), p. 159.

nign" a figure to be painted as a warmonger, à la Barry Goldwater in 1964. "It wouldn't be believable," he said then.

But beginning with his Middle Western swing the day after Labor Day, Mr. Carter stressed this point above all others, warning that the election was a choice between "war and peace." He did so because of private polls taken by Mr. Caddell that showed this to be the public's greatest hidden fear about the Republican candidate. The President was hoist by his own hyperbole, in the view of some Carter aides, who feel the President grossly overstated Mr.

Reagan's record and aroused the public's skepticism about his argument. In the end, they feel, Mr. Reagan's cool, collected, nonthreatening performance in the debate defused the issue.

"Carter Post-Mortem: Debate Hurt But Wasn't Only Cause for Defeat," *New York Times* (November 9, 1980).

78. See Ranney, *The Past and Future of Presidential Debates.*

79. See Nixon, *Six Crises,* and especially White, *The Making of the President, 1960,* for a discussion of two candidates' contrasting attitudes toward their "camp" of reporters. For the 1964 election, see White, *The Making of the President, 1964.* For 1968, see Theodore H. White, *The Making of the President, 1968* (New York, 1969), pp. 327ff. For 1972, see Crouse, *The Boys on the Bus.* For 1976, see Jules Witcover, *Marathon* (New York, 1977). For 1980, see Jack W. Germond and Jules Witcover, *Blue Smoke and Mirrors* (New York, 1981), pp. 213–215, 260–264.

80. Schram, *Running for President,* passim.

81. See Stephen Hess, *The Washington Reporters* (Washington, D.C., 1981); and S. Robert Lichter and Stanley Rothman, "Media and Business Elites," *Public Opinion* (October/November 1981), pp. 42–46, 59–60.

82. "In elections at home, which Muskie contests vigorously and wins by handsome margins despite the state's strong Republican orientation, he rarely mentions his opponent's name, let alone attack him. He dwells instead on his own positive (and pragmatic) approach to problems. . . . Throughout the campaign he waits hopefully for his opponent to strike, in desperation, some more or less low blow in response to which Muskie can become magnificently outraged. Then, voice trembling with indignation but still without mentioning his opponent's name, he chastises the opposition for stooping to such levels, and thus manages to introduce a little color into the campaign. Usually the opposition obliges him: 'I can always count on the Republicans doing something stupid,' he once said with satisfaction" (David Nevin, *Muskie of Maine* [New York, 1972], p. 27).

83. Robert E. Sherwood, *Roosevelt and Hopkins* (New York, 1948), p. 821.

84. The effectiveness of underhanded tactics remains unknown. Dan Nimmo (*The Political Persuaders* [Englewood Cliffs, N.J., 1970], p. 50), argues that deviating from a vague sense of "fairness" that exists in the electorate may backfire. There is plenty of evidence on the other side as well. For a treasure trove of such material, see Stanley Kelley, *Professional Public Relations and Political Power* (Baltimore, 1956).

85. Schram, *Running for President,* p. 369.

86. Ibid., pp. 362–363.

87. See Carl Bernstein and Bob Woodward, *All The President's Men* (New York, 1974), pp. 112–162, 197, 199, 251–253, 273–274, 285–286, 328; and Senate Select Committee on Presidential Campaign Activities, *The Senate Watergate Report* (Washington, D.C., 1974).

88. For further examples see Hugh A. Bone, *American Politics and the Party System* (New York, 1955), pp. 457–69. Readers may not be aware that Al Smith had thought of moving the Vatican to Washington or that Herbert Hoover had a black concubine, yet these ridiculous allegations were made (p. 458).

Perhaps it is a sign of the times that in 1976 the following doggerel was sung to Carter by members of the campaign press corps, and a good time appears to have been had by all:

> Lust in my heart, how I love adultery
> Lust in my heart, it's my theology
> When I was young, at the Plains First Baptist Church
> I would preach and sermonize
> But oh how I would fantasize
>
> Oh, Lust in my heart, who cares if it's a sin . . .
>   (it has never been)
> Leching's a noble art
> It's OK if you shack up
> 'Cause I won't get my back up
> I've got mine
> I've got lust in my heart

Carter and his wife smiled as the reporters launched into the second chorus:

> Lust in my heart, oh it's bad politic'ly
> Lust in my heart, but it brings publicity.

Schram, *Running for President,* p. 345.

89. It seems likely, for example, that Jimmy Carter's disastrous "crisis of confidence" episode in the summer of 1979 was set off by a public opinion analysis by his poll taker, Pat Caddell. Later on, Caddell's analysis would seem to equally well qualified observers to have been alarmist. See Nelson W. Polsby, *Consequences of Party Reform* (New York, 1983), pp. 115–128, and note 91.

90. See Flinn, "How Nixon Took Ohio."

91. "One-Man Truck Tour to Poll Farmers," *New York Times* (August 1, 1948), p. 49.

92. See Abels, *Out of the Jaws of Victory.*

93. Robert Alford, "The Role of Social Class in American Voting Behavior," *Western Political Quarterly* 16 (March 1963), pp. 180–194; and Campbell et al., *The American Voter,* Chapter 13.

94. White, *The Making of the President, 1960,* pp. 203–204.

95. Ibid., p. 315.

96. White, *The Making of the President, 1968,* p. 331.

97. See Nixon, *Six Crises,* pp. 315–461.

98. Everett Carll Ladd, "The 1980 Presidential Election: In Search of its Meaning," typescript (February 3, 1981); see also "Face Off: A Conversation with the Presidents' Pollster Patrick Caddell and Richard Wirthlin," *Public Opinion* 3 (December/January 1981), p. 5.

99. See, for example, Samuel Lubell, *The Future of American Politics* (New York, 1951); his "Personalities and Issues," in Kraus, ed., *The Great Debates,* pp. 151–162; and Joseph Alsop, "The Negro Vote and New York," *New York Herald-Tribune* (and elsewhere) August 8, 1960. Reporting of this sort has become a feature of the election year coverage of the *Washington Post.* See, for example, Rowland Evans and Robert Novak, "Stronghold Lost," *Washington Post* (August 4, 1980).

100. Louis H. Bean, *Ballot Behavior* (Washington, D.C., 1940).

101. IBM published a pamphlet, *The Fastest Reported Election,* in 1961 describing their operations.

102. These suggestions are drawn in part from a reading of the Report of a Committee of the Social Science Research Council, Frederick Mosteller et al., *The Pre-Election Polls of 1948,* Social Science Research Council Bulletin 60 (New York, 1949). The misfortunes of the British polls in the 1970 general election underscores the usefulness of these suggestions.

103. Joseph Alsop, "The Wayward Press: Dissection of a Poll," *The New Yorker* (September 24, 1960), pp. 170–184.

104. There are several sources about the technology and tactics of polling. George Gallup has published *A Guide to Public Opinion Polls* (Princeton, 1948). More recently, see *Opinion Polls, Interviews by Donald McDonald with Elmo Roper and George Gallup* (Santa Barbara, 1962); and Charles W. Roll, Jr., and Albert H. Cantril, *Polls* (New York, 1972). In 1972, Representative Lucien Nedzi held congressional hearings on the possible effects of information about polls on subsequent voting. See *Public Opinion Polls,* Hearings before the Subcommittee on Library and Memorials, Committee on House Administration, House of Representatives, 93rd Congress on

H.R. 5503 (September 19, 20, 21, October 5, 1972). A further flap occurred in 1980, as the result of Jimmy Carter's concession of defeat and the television network predictions of a Reagan victory before voting was completed on the west coast. See Raymond Wolfinger and Peter Linquiti, "Tuning In and Turning Out," *Public Opinion* (February/March 1981), pp. 56–60; John E. Jackson, "Election Night Reporting and Voter Turnout," *American Journal of Political Science* 27 (November 1983); *Election Day Practices and Election Projections,* Hearings before the Task Force on Elections of the Committee on House Administration and the Subcommittee on Telecommunications, Consumer Protection, and Finance of the Committee on Energy and Commerce, U.S. House of Representatives, 97th Congress, December 15, 1981 and September 21, 1982 (Washington, D.C., 1982); and Percy H. Tannenbaum and Leslie J. Kostrich, *Turned-On TV/Turned-Off Voters* (Beverly Hills, 1983).

105. Sherwood, *Roosevelt and Hopkins,* p. 86. See also Archibald M. Crossley, "Straw Polls in 1936," *Public Opinion Quarterly* 1 (January 1937), pp. 24–36; and a survey of the literature existing at that time, Hadley Cantril, "Technical Research," *Public Opinion Quarterly* 1 (January 1937), pp. 97–110.

106. Maurice C. Bryson, "The Literary Digest Poll: Making of a Statistical Myth," *The American Statistician* 30 (November, 1976), pp. 184–185. As a matter of fact, this method produced a correct prediction in 1932, when the *Literary Digest* said that Roosevelt would win. Sampling error is tricky; an atypical sample may still give the correct prediction—by luck; but sooner or later, the law of averages is bound to catch up with it.

107. Mosteller et al., *The Pre-Election Polls of 1948.*

108. Election day exit polls often come close to offering answers to the "why" questions. For an analysis of four different 1980 exit polls, see Mark R. Levy, "The Methodology and Performance of Election Day Polls," *Public Opinion Quarterly* 47 (Spring 1983), pp. 54–67.

109. See Paul F. Lazarsfeld, "The Use of Panels in Social Research," *Proceedings of the American Philosophical Society* 92 (November 1948), pp. 405–410.

☆ Chapter 5: Reform

1.   There are many examples of the party reform school of thought. See, for example, Woodrow Wilson, *Congressional Government* (Boston, 1889); Henry Jones Ford, *The Rise and Growth of American Politics* (New York, 1898); A. Lawrence Lowell, *Public Opinion and Popular Government* (New York, 1913); William MacDonald, *A New Constitution for a New America* (New York, 1921); William Y. Elliott, *The Need for Constitutional Reform* (New York, 1935); E. E. Schattschneider, *Party Government*

(New York, 1940); Henry Hazlitt, *A New Constitution Now* (New York, 1942); Thomas K. Finletter, *Can Representative Government Do the Job?* (New York, 1945); James M. Burns, *Congress on Trial* (New York, 1949); Committee on Political Parties, American Political Science Association, *Toward a More Responsible Two-Party System* (New York, 1950); Stephen K. Bailey, *The Condition of Our National Political Parties* (New York, 1959); James M. Burns, *The Deadlock of Democracy* (Englewood Cliffs, N.J., 1963); Lloyd N. Cutler and C. Douglas Dillon, "Can We Improve on Our Constitutional System?," *Wall Street Journal* (February 15, 1983); and Cutler, "To Form a Government," *Foreign Affairs* 59 (Fall 1980), pp. 126–143. The work of the Committee on Political Parties, representing the collective judgment of a panel of distinguished political scientists in 1950, is the statement we shall refer to most often. In 1971 a member of the committee published a thoughtful reconsideration of its main ideas. See Evron M. Kirkpatrick, "Toward a More Responsible Two-Party System: Political Science, Policy Science, or Pseudo Science?" *American Political Science Review* 65 (December 1971), pp. 965–990.

2. Committee on Political Parties, *Toward a More Responsible Two-Party System*, p. 1.

3. Ibid., p. 66.

4. Ibid., p. 15.

5. A sample of this literature might include E. Pendleton Herring, *The Politics of Democracy* (New York, 1940); Herbert Agar, *The Price of Union* (Boston, 1950); Malcolm C. Moos, *Politics, Presidents and Coattails* (Baltimore, 1952); Austin Ranney and Willmoore Kendall, *Democracy and the American Party System* (New York, 1956); David B. Truman, *The Governmental Process* (New York, 1953); John Fischer, "Unwritten Rules of American Politics," *Harper's* (November 1948), pp. 27–36; Peter Drucker, "A Key to American Politics: Calhoun's Pluralism," *Review of Politics* 10 (October 1948), pp. 412–426; Ernest F. Griffith, *Congress: Its Contemporary Role* (New York, 1951); Murray Stedman and Herbert Sonthoff, "Party Responsibility: A Critical Inquiry," *Western Political Quarterly* 4 (September 1951), pp. 454–486; Julius Turner, "Responsible Parties: A Dissent from the Floor," *American Political Science Review* 45 (March 1951), pp. 143–152; William Goodman, "How Much Political Party Centralization Do We Want?" *The Journal of Politics* 13 (November 1961), pp. 536–561; and Austin Ranney, *The Doctrine of Responsible Party Government* (Urbana, Il., 1954).

6. Herring, *The Politics of Democracy*, p. 327.

7. Ibid., p. 420.

8. Committee on Political Parties, *Toward a More Responsible Two-Party System*, p. 19.

9. Bailey, *The Condition of Our National Political Parties,* p. 20.

10. This situation is deplored in Cutler and Dillon, "Can We Improve on Our Constitutional System?" One remedy, changing the term of office of congressmen and senators to coincide exactly with presidential elections, is analyzed in Nelson W. Polsby, "A Note on the President's Modest Proposal," in Polsby, *Political Promises* (New York, 1974), pp. 101–107.

11. This is not at all uncommon. See, for instance, examples in Raymond A. Bauer, Ithiel de Sola Pool, and Lewis Anthony Dexter, *American Business and Public Policy* (New York, 1963), Chapters 16, 18, and 19; and Richard F. Fenno, *Home Style* (Boston, 1978).

12. A careful history of this process is Byron E. Shafer, *Quiet Revolution: Reform Politics in the Democratic Party, 1968–1972* (New York, forthcoming). For an analysis of consequences, see Nelson W. Polsby, *Consequences of Party Reform* (New York, 1983).

13. For strong evidence on this point, see Samuel Stouffer, *Communism, Conformity and Civil Liberties* (Garden City, N.Y., 1955), passim; and Julian L. Woodward and Elmo Roper, "Political Activity of American Citizens," *American Political Science Review* 44 (December 1950), pp. 872–875. Two recent studies have examined the voters' desire not to be interfered with by the government as well as the importance of their private lives to them as compared with national issues. See Paul M. Sniderman and Richard A. Brody, "Coping: The Ethic of Self-reliance," *American Journal of Political Science* 21 (August 1977), pp. 501–521; and Richard A. Brody and Paul M. Sniderman, "From Life Space to Polling Place: The Relevance of Personal Concerns for Voting Behavior," *British Journal of Political Science* 7 (July 1977), pp. 337–360.

14. See, for example, Jack Citrin, Herbert McClosky, J. Merrill Shanks and Paul M. Sniderman, "Personal and Political Sources of Alienation," *British Journal of Political Science* 5 (January 1975), pp. 1–31; and Arthur H. Miller, "Political Issues and Trust in Government: 1964–70," along with the "Comment" by Jack Citrin, both in *American Political Science Review* 68 (September 1974), pp. 951–1001.

15. An earlier statement of main themes in this section is Aaron B. Wildavsky, "On the Superiority of National Conventions," *Review of Politics* 24 (July 1962), pp. 307–319.

16. See V. O. Key, Jr., *American State Politics* (New York, 1956), Chapter 6.

17. V. O. Key, Jr., *Southern Politics* (New York, 1950), e.g., Chapter 3 (Alabama) and Chapter 9 (Arkansas).

18. Key, *American State Politics,* p. 216.

19. See Austin Ranney, *The Federalization of Presidential Primaries* (Washington, D.C., 1978), pp. 5–7; see also Commission on Presidential Nomination and Party Structure (Morley Winograd, Chairman), *Openness, Participation and Party Building: Reforms for a Stronger Democratic Party* (Washington, D.C., 1979), pp. 32–37.

20. Quoted in Joel Fleishman, ed., *The Future of American Political Parties: The Challenge of Governance* (Englewood Cliffs, N.J., 1982), p. 163.

21. Quoted in ibid., p. 164.

22. Ibid., p. 162.

23. Quoted in Everett Carll Ladd, "A Better Way to Pick Our Presidents," *Fortune* (May 8, 1980), pp. 132–136.

24. See Edward Stanwood, *A History of the Presidency from 1788 to 1897* (Boston, 1898), pp. 125–141.

25. A classic statement is Moisei Ostrogorski, *Democracy and the Party System in the United States* (New York, 1910), pp. 158–160. See also Elmo Roper, "What Price Conventions?" *Saturday Review* (September 3, 1960), p. 26.

26. The most famous account is still Ostrogorski, *Democracy and the Party System in the United States,* pp. 141–142.

27. At least one representative of the media apparently feels as we do about this problem. Walter Cronkite argues that "it is not necessary that we be admitted to the actual floor of the convention. There is a better way (such as the use of immediate off-floor interview booths) to cover the non-podium action in order to permit a more orderly convention procedure" (*The Challenges of Change* [Washington, D.C., 1971], p. 75).

28. See Herbert McClosky, Paul J. Hoffman, and Rosemary O'Hara, "Issue Conflict and Consensus among Party Leaders and Followers," *American Political Science Review* 54 (June 1960), pp. 406–427; and Jeane Kirkpatrick, *The New Presidential Elite: Men and Women in National Politics* (New York, 1976).

29. Other rules changes among the Democrats include moving up the filing deadline in any given state to thirty to ninety days before the primary. The number of delegates allotted to each state was increased by 10 percent to allow for state party and elected officials. Cross-over primaries have been banned, restricting the primary process to registered Democrats. Single-member districts have been ruled out for delegate selection, thereby eliminating the last form of winner-take-all primary. In addition, Democrats have devised a formula for proportional allocation of the delegates from each of a state's districts using a threshold percentage of the vote, which varies up or down with the number of delegates per district up to a maximum of 25 percent. Finally, demographic quotas have been instituted; the Democrats have decreed that every

state delegation must be evenly divided between men and women. *Congressional Quarterly Weekly Report,* June 17, 1978, p. 1571, and December 16, 1978, p. 3433. See also the Report of the Commission on Presidential Nomination and Party Structure, *Openness, Participation and Party Building,* pp. 42–57; Democratic National Committee, *Delegate Selection Rules for the 1980 Democratic National Convention* (Washington, D.C., June 9, 1978); and the Report of the Commission on Presidential Nomination (Governor James B. Hunt, Jr., chairman) (Washington, D.C., March 26, 1982).

30. John Morris, "Negro Delegates Drop Plans to Walk Out as a Demonstration Against Goldwater," *New York Times* (July 16, 1964), p. 1.

31. Gerald M. Pomper, *Elections in America: Control and Influence in Democratic Politics,* revised ed. (New York, 1980).

32. Alan D. Monroe, "American Party Platforms and Public Opinion," *The American Journal of Political Science* 27 (February 1983), p. 38.

33. Ibid., pp. 27–42.

34. Stanley Kelley, Jr., Richard E. Ayres, and William G. Bowen, "Registration and Voting: Putting First Things First," *American Political Science Review* 61 (June 1967), p. 362. A more recent and equally comprehensive study of this subject leading to similar results is found in Raymond E. Wolfinger and Steven J. Rosenstone, "The Effect of Registration Laws on Voter Turnout," *American Political Science Review* 72 (March 1978), pp. 22–48.

35. The general outline of this argument has been known in this country for at least fifty years. For example, in 1924, Harold G. Gosnell wrote, "In the European countries studied, a citizen who is entitled to vote does not, as a rule, have to make any effort to see that his name is on the list of eligible voters. The inconvenience of registering for voting in this country has caused many citizens to become non-voters." *Why Europe Votes* (Chicago, 1930), p. 185. See also Raymond E. Wolfinger and Steven J. Rosenstone, *Who Votes?* (New Haven, 1980).

36. In Richard E. Ayres, *Registration 1960: Key to Democratic Victory?* (unpublished senior thesis, Princeton University, 1964), cited in Kelley, Ayres, and Bowen, "Registration and Voting: Putting First Things First," p. 375, the author cites the correlation between convenience of registration and percent of the vote for the Democratic party as proof of the Daley machine's awareness of this phenomenon. By making registration extremely convenient, the State of Utah has succeeded in getting nearly total registration. See "Registration Procedures in the State of Utah," *Election Laws of the Fifty States and the District of Columbia* (Washington, D.C., June, 1968), pp. 247–248. Similarly, Edmond Costantini and Willis Hawley estimate that turnout in California could be raised by more than 5 percent simply by keeping registration open

until the last week before the election ("Increasing Participation in California Elections: The Need for Electoral Reform," *Public Affairs Report* 10, Bulletin of the Institute of Governmental Studies [June 1969]). A 1968 registration figure of 97.8 percent was attained by holding registrations open until the Wednesday before the election (when political interest, which would stimulate the voter to register and the party activists to get him registered, is highest) and by having publicized locations in every district.

37. Kelley, Ayres, and Bowen, "Registration and Voting: Putting First Things First," p. 373.

38. Some suggestions for a comprehensive program along these lines came from the Freedom to Vote Task Force of the Democratic National Committee, *That All May Vote* (Washington, D.C., 1969) and were embodied in House and Senate bills: The Universal Voter Enrollment Act of 1970 (House Resolution 19010 and Senate 4238). See the statement by Representative Morris Udall in the *Congressional Record* (August 13, 1970), pp. H8319–32.

39. Kelley, Ayres, and Bowen, "Registration and Voting: Putting First Things First," pp. 374–375.

40. Ibid., p. 363.

41. Recent evidence shows, for example, that white youths who have not attended college are much more conservative on stylistic questions than are their peers with higher education. See the issue of *Esquire* (January 1970) devoted to this question. In general, young people divide more or less as their elders do, except more of them are neutral or undecided. See Jerald G. Bachman and Elizabeth Van Duinen, *Youth Looks at National Problems* (Ann Arbor, 1971), especially Table 3-2, p. 33, which shows the results from three surveys of teenagers conducted in 1970.

Table 5.6

Michigan Survey 19-Year-Old Males		Purdue Study High-School Seniors		Harris Survey 15–21-Year-Old Youths	
	(percent)		(percent)		(percent)
Republican	21	Republican	14	Republican	18
Democratic	32	Democratic	26	Democratic	35
Haven't Thought About It	20	Wallace A.I.P.	7	Wallace	4
		No Difference	18	Other or Not Sure	40
Neutral	14	Undecided	30	Will Refuse to Vote	3
Other	6	Missing Data	5		
Missing Data	7				

42. "Poll Finds Residency Rules Cut Vote of Young and Democrats," *New York Times* (December 6, 1969). Most universal automatic voter enrollment programs include a provision whereby the enrollee can at least vote for president even if he has moved within the week before election. For example, see Freedom to Vote Task Force, *That All May Vote.*

43. Rosenstone and Wolfinger, "The Effects of Registration Laws on Voter Turnout," p. 41; see also their response to a challenge to their conclusions in "Comment," *American Political Science Review* 72 (December 1978), pp. 1361–1362.

44. *U.S.* v. *Arizona,* 91 S. Ct. 260 (1970).

45. William G. Andrews, "American Voting Participation," *Western Political Quarterly* 19 (1966), p. 643.

46. *The California Poll* (San Francisco), Release #1201, February 1, 1983.

47. Although we know of no effort to review the situation, there seems no compelling reason why felons—"ex-" or otherwise—should be denied the ballot. Voting may be a small way of maintaining their connection with society. Their ability to vote should make politicians more interested in their welfare, including the structure and management of penal institutions. The view that loss of the right to vote penalizes would-be felons and is, therefore, a deterrent to crime is hardly worth considering. If their having a vote constitutes a danger to society even after they are released from prison, then what is the rationale for letting them wander about at large where the rest of their behavior can also menace honest folk?

48. There were, of course, many other plans for "reform," involving almost all possible combinations of these three alternatives. For example, President Nixon at one point recommended that the 40 percent plurality plank which usually goes with the direct election proposal be applied instead to the present Electoral College setup (David S. Broder, "Mitchell Recommends Electoral Compromise," *Washington Post* [March 14, 1969], p. A2). A second example is the "federal system plan" of Senators Dole and Eagleton, which states:

1. A president would be elected if he (a) won a plurality of the national vote and (b) won *either* pluralities in more than 50 percent of the states and D.C., *or* pluralities in states with 50 percent of the voters in the election.

2. If no candidate qualified, the election would go to an Electoral College where the states would be represented as they are today, and each candidate would automatically receive the electoral votes of the states he won.

3. In the unlikely event that no candidate received a majority of the electoral votes, the electoral votes of states that went for third-party candidates would be divided between the two leading national candidates in proportion to their share of the popular votes in those states (*Congressional Record,* March 5, 1970, p. S3026).

These plans have the following characteristics: (a) They are too complicated to solve any problems of public confusion or public perception that they are not "democratic." (b) They have no significant body of congressional support.

49. *Baker* v. *Carr,* 369 U.S. 186 (1962); *Wesberry* v. *Sanders,* 376 U.S. 1 (1964); and *Reynolds* v. *Sims,* 377 U.S. 533 (1964).

50. For example, Ed Gossett, original cosponsor of the district plan, asked, "Is it fair, is it honest, is it democratic, is it to the best interests of anyone in fact to place such a premium on a few thousand labor votes or Italian votes or Irish votes or Negro votes or Jewish votes or Polish votes, or Communist votes or big city machine votes, simply because they happen to be located in two or three industrial pivotal states? Can anything but evil come from placing such temptation and power in the hands of political parties and political bosses? Both said groups and said politicians are corrupted as a nation suffers." Cited in David Brook, "Proposed Electoral College Reforms and Urban Minorities" (paper delivered at the Annual Meeting of the American Political Science Association, 1969), p. 6.

51. In "The South Will Not Rise Again Through Direct Election of the President, Polsby and Wildavsky Notwithstanding," *Journal of Politics* 31 (August 1969), pp. 808–811, Professor Harvey Zeidenstein shows that the winner's margin of victory in eight large northern urban states—taken together—was greater than in the eleven states of the old Confederacy—taken together—in four of the six presidential elections between 1948 and 1968. From this he concludes that the influence of northern urban states, where the votes are, is likely to be very great under a system of direct elections. We agree, but we argue in the text that direct elections do improve the strategic position of one-party states (including some southern states), as compared with the Electoral College winner-take-all system. On this issue Zeidenstein is silent.

52. On September 18, 1969, by a vote of 339 to 70, a direct-election plan with a 40 percent plurality runoff provision was passed by the U.S. House of Representatives. See *Congressional Record* (September 18, 1969), pp. H8142–8143; for the content of the bill, see *Congressional Record* (September 10, 1969), pp. H7745–7746. For a more recent discussion of proposed reforms, see "Hearings on the Electoral College and Direct Election," Committee on the Judiciary, U.S. Senate, 95th Congress (Washington, D.C., 1977).

53. The Michigan Survey Research Center finds that only 1.5 percent of the voters in 1968 had felt that Senator Eugene McCarthy was the best man for president in the spring and still felt that way after the election. If all participants in the system had known that he was not going to be defeated and disappear but would be a serious candidate at least through the first election, it is at least possible to conjecture that he could have picked up an additional 4 percent or 5 percent (Philip E. Converse, Warren E. Miller, Jerrold G. Rusk, and Arthur C. Wolfe, "Continuity and Change

in American Politics: Parties and Issues in the 1968 Election," *American Political Science Review* 63 [December 1969] p. 1092). Cf. Richard N. Goodwin, "Reflections: Sources of the Public Unhappiness," *The New Yorker* (January 4, 1969), pp. 38–58.

54. The article that deals most clearly with the Electoral College in terms of its virtues of conciliation and broad coalition building is John Wildenthal, "Consensus after L.B.J.," *Southwest Review* 53 (Spring 1968), pp. 113–130. Wildenthal argues in part, "Rather than complain about being deprived of a choice when both parties wage 'me too' campaigns, the American people should be thankful that the interests of a wide variety of Americans can be reconciled by both parties with similar programs."

55. One summary of this position is given by Representative Thomas Kleppe of North Dakota in the *Congressional Record* (February 3, 1969), p. H648. An interesting sidelight, and a tribute to the change of perspective a change of office can bring, is his citation of Senator John F. Kennedy, who said, "After all, the states came into the Union as units. Electoral votes are not given out on the basis of voting numbers, but on the basis of population. The electoral votes belong to each state. The way the system works now is that we carry on a campaign in fifty states, and the electoral votes of that state belong to that party which carries each state. If we are going to change that system, it seems to me it would strike a blow at states rights in major proportions. It would probably end states rights and make this country one great unit."

56. Roscoe Drummond, "Perils of the Electoral System," *Washington Post* (November 14, 1960). An argument in some ways parallel to our own is contained in Anthony Lewis, "The Case Against Electoral Reform," *The Reporter* (December 8, 1960), pp. 31–33. See also Allan P. Sindler, "Presidential Election Methods and Urban-Ethnic Interests," *Law and Contemporary Problems* (Spring 1962), pp. 213–233.

57. See Estes Kefauver, "The Electoral College: Old Reforms Take A New Look," *Law and Contemporary Problems* (Spring 1962), p. 197.

58. Despite popular misconceptions, even the 1964 Republican platform, written by supporters of Barry Goldwater, contained explicit promises to preserve these programs.

59. See Kirk H. Porter and Donald Bruce Johnson, *National Party Platforms, 1840–1956* (Urbana, Ill., 1956). There are immense differences between party platforms of both 1932 and 1952. Note, for example, the subheadings under domestic policy in the 1952 platforms dealing with a range of topics entirely missing in 1932. The Democratic 1952 platform includes subheadings on full employment, price supports, farm credit, crop insurance, rural electrification, the physically handicapped, migratory workers, river basin development, arid areas, wildlife, recreation, Social Security, unemployment insurance, public assistance, needs of our aging citizens, health, medical education, hospitals and health centers, costs of medical care, public housing, slum clearance, urban redevelopment, aid to education, school lunches, day-care facilities,

specific steps under civil rights, and many other subjects completely absent in 1932. Most of these worthy causes were also supported in the 1952 Republican platform and were missing from the 1932 Republican platform. Nevertheless, there are differences *between* the parties in 1952 in regard to use of the public lands, public housing, labor legislation, farm legislation, public power, aid to education, and much more. In regard to education, for example, the 1952 Republican platform reads: "The tradition of popular education, tax-supported and free to all, is strong with our people. The responsibility for sustaining this system of popular education has always rested upon the local communities and the states. We subscribe fully to this principle." The corresponding Democratic plank reads in part: "Local, State, and Federal governments have shared responsibility to contribute appropriately to the pressing needs of our education system. . . . We pledge immediate consideration for those school systems which need further legislation to provide Federal aid for a new school construction, teachers' salaries and school maintenance and repair" (pp. 485, 504). See also Gerald M. Pomper, *Elections in America* (New York, 1968), pp. 149–178.

60. This is one of the main conclusions of Arnold Rogow, *The Labour Government and British Industry* (Oxford, 1955). See also Geoffrey Smith and Nelson W. Polsby, *British Government and its Discontents* (New York, 1981).

61. See Julius Turner, *Party and Constituency: Pressures on Congress* (Baltimore, 1951); and David B. Truman, *The Congressional Party* (New York, 1959).

62. For a general discussion of presidential control of foreign policy, see Aaron Wildavsky, "The Two Presidencies," *Transaction* 4 (December 1966), pp. 7–14.

63. See Bauer, Pool, and Dexter, *American Business and Public Policy*, pp. 9–79.

☆ Chapter 6: American Parties and Democracy

1. This parallels in many respects an argument to be found in Robert A. Dahl, *A Preface to Democratic Theory* (Chicago, 1956).

2. Angus Campbell, Philip E. Converse, Warren E. Miller, and Donald E. Stokes, *The American Voter* (New York, 1960), pp. 525–527.

3. Richard A. Brody and Benjamin I. Page, "Policy Voting and the Electoral Process: The Vietnam War Issue," *American Political Science Review* 66 (September 1972), p. 979. For the 1980 election, the evidence is clear that no special benefit with voters was conferred on Ronald Reagan by virtue of his conservatism. See William Schneider, "The November 4 Vote for President: What Did It Mean?," in Austin Ranney, ed., *The American Elections of 1980* (Washington, D.C., 1981), pp. 212–262; and Nelson W. Polsby, "Party Realignment in the 1980 Election," *The Yale Review* 72 (Autumn 1982), pp. 43–54.

4. See Dahl, *A Preface to Democratic Theory,* pp. 124–31.

5. See Nelson W. Polsby, *Consequences of Party Reform* (New York, 1983).

6. See Jack Dennis, "Trends in Public Support for the American Political Party System," *British Journal of Political Science* 5 (April. 1975), pp. 187–230.

Index

Abels, Jules, 317
Abelson, Robert P., 319
Abortion, 31, 44, 45, 128, 160, 180
Abramson, Paul, 285, 288, 293
Absentee ballots, 245
Access
    campaign contributions and, 68
    defined, 36, 295
Accountability, of political parties, 36–37
Activists
    control of candidates by, 38
    at convention, 120, 121
    in Democratic party, 35, 44
    party platform and, 237
    polarization of, 278
    policy impact of, 15
    policy preferences of, 43–44
    in primaries, 109–10
    public interest, 32, 34–35
    in Republican party, 44
    shifting role of, 3–4, 274–75
    specialized interests of, 6
    See also Purists

Adams, John, 87
Adrian, Charles R., 306
Advertising, campaign, 58, 73, 81
Advocacy, 274–81
Affirmative action, 160
AFL-CIO. *See* American Federation of Labor–Congress of Industrial Organizations
Agar, Herbert, 335
Age
    vote by (1952–1980), 10–12, 289
    and voter turnout, 26–29
Agger, Robert, 287
Agnew, Spiro, 88, 138, 317
Alabama, 248
Alaska, 51
Aldrich, John H., 293
Alexander, Herbert, xi, 65, 299, 300, 301, 302, 303
Alford, Robert R., 296–97, 333
Alienation, from political system, 220
Aliens, 245
Alioto, Joseph, 304
Alsop, Joseph, 199, 333

American Federation of Labor–Congress of Industrial Organizations (AFL–CIO), Committee on Political Education (COPE) of, 33
American Institute of Public Opinion, 244
American Voter, The (Campbell), 19, 30, 285, 286, 290, 291, 293, 294, 307, 318, 319, 343
Andersen, Kristi, 284, 287, 324
Anderson, John, in 1980 election, 12, 64, 80, 99, 163, 186
Andrews, William, 245
Apathy, political, 219–20
Apple, R. W., 82
Apter, David E., 284, 321
Arieff, Irwin B., 303
Aristotle, 220
Arterton, F. Christopher, 120, 315
Arvey, Jack, 112
Athens, political participation in, 220–21
Axelrod, Robert, 24, 158, 288, 294, 324
Ayres, Richard E., 338, 339

Bachman, Jerald G., 339
Bagby, Wesley, 316
Bailey, John, 302
Bain, Richard C., 283, 309
Baker, Howard, 96
Baker, James, 101
Baker, Ross K., 317
Baker v. Carr, 247, 341
Balanced ticket, 90, 227
Baldwin, Stanley, 263
Balloting, convention, 131–37
Bancroft, George, 136
Bandwagon behavior, 131–32, 160
Bargaining process, 116, 135–36, 144, 145
Bartels, Larry, 108, 312
Barton, Allen H., 293, 318
Bauer, Raymond A., 293, 336
Bayh, Birch, 60, 79, 101, 157
Bayley, Edwin, 305
Bean, Louis, 333
  forecast method of, 200–1
Belknap, George, 287
Benton, William, 302
Bentsen, Lloyd, 110
Berelson, Bernard, 285, 287, 288, 318
Berry, Jeffrey, M., 293

Bibby, John F., 295, 296
Biffle, Les, 193
Blacks
  candidacy of, 166–67
  delegate attitude towards, 128
  as delegates, 123, 124
  party identification of, 8–9, 24–25, 30, 166, 167, 289
  voter turnout for, 25, 26–29
Blackwood, George, 300
Bloom, Howard S., 308
Blumberg, Nathan B., 304
Boll weevils, 39
Bone, Hugh A., 309, 332
Bowen, William G., 338, 339
Brady, Henry, xi
Brams, Steven J., 298
Bricker, John, 130
Brock, William, 40
Brodbeck, Arthur J., 285
Broder, David, 154–55, 157, 322, 324, 340
Brody, Richard A., xi, 108, 286, 292, 318, 336, 343
Broh, C. Anthony, 80, 307
Brown, Jerry, 60, 98–99, 115, 186
Brown, Thad A., 291, 329
Bryan, William Jennings, 139, 173
Bryce, James, 210
Bryson, Maurice C., 334
Buckley v. Valeo, 33
Budde, Bernadette A., 62
Burdick, Eugene, 285
Burke, Fred G., 314
Burns, James M., 231, 335
Burns v. Forston, 244
Burr, Aaron, 89
Bush, George, 88, 90, 100–1, 138
Business, regulation of, 39
Busing issue, 128

Caddell, Pat, 45, 197, 332
Calhoun, John C., 89, 136
California, 51, 98, 106, 107, 120–22, 129, 158, 172, 245, 248, 279
California Committee on Party Renewal, ix
Cambodia, invasion of, 83
Campaigns, 147–98
  advertising in, 58, 73, 81
  blunders in, 174–75, 194

candidate organizations in, 110–11, 169–71, 191
celebrity role in, 55
contributions
  benefits of, 68–69
  fund raising for, 70–71
  limitations on, 32, 33–34, 61, 67–68
  monied interests and, 55–56
  by political action committees (PACs), 32–35, 61–62
  reporting requirements for, 65, 66–67
costs of, 54
Democratic strategy in, 148
domestic issues in, 175–77
feedback from, 191–98
foreign policy issues in, 176, 177–80
incumbent *vs.* challenger in, 168–69
media coverage of, 50, 58, 71–72, 79–82, 96
  candidate-media relations and, 186–88
mud-slinging and heckling in, 188–91, 259, 332
party identification during, 148–49
party role in, 4, 197–98
preconvention strategies in, 111–14
in preprimary period, 95–96
professionalization of, 63
public funding of, 54–55, 64–67, 71
Republican strategies in, 149–52
in 1964–1980, 152–61
selection of states for, 171–72
self presentation in, 181–83
social issues in, 180–81
spending on, 55, 59
  electoral outcomes and, 56–61
  limits on, 67
television debates in, 58, 178–79, 183–86
theory and action in, 167–68
whistle-stop methods in, 172–73
See also Primaries
Campbell, Angus, 285, 286, 287, 290, 291, 293, 294, 307, 318, 319, 343
Candidates
  black, 166–67
  campaigns of, See Campaigns
  in Congressional elections, 265
  dark horse, 113–14

early announcement by, 95, 97–98, 142, 144
ethical standards for, 188–89
insurgent, 85
and party organization, 36–37
personal organizations of, 110–11, 116–20, 142–43, 169–71, 191
policy preferences of, 17, 45, 68
political parties and, 50
press relations with, 186–88
public image of, 181–83
selection of. See Nomination process
speeches by, 174–75, 182–83
See also specific names
Cantor, Joseph E., 294
Cantril, Hadley, 290
Carter, Jimmy, 83–84, 85
  campaign spending of, 59
  deflationary policy of, 180
  in 1976 election, 60, 72, 96, 142, 332
    campaign, 51, 55, 113, 172, 174–75, 190
    media impact on, 144, 187
    nomination of, 119, 144
    policy committments of, 44–45
    primaries, 95, 107, 108, 110
    at state conventions, 108
    vice presidential choice of, 138
    vote received by, 12, 79, 241
  in 1980 election, 14, 111, 146, 164
    campaign strategy of, 197
    Iranian hostage crisis and, 15, 58, 83, 179, 186, 330
    nomination of, 129–30
    in primaries, 98
    television debates of, 185–86
    vote received by, 12, 241
  public image of, 181, 183
Cass, Lewis, 136
Catholic vote, 8, 25, 289
  1952–1980, 10–12
Caucus, party, 230–31, 280
Cavala, William, xii, 120, 121, 310
Ceaser, James, 296
Celebrities, donated services of, 55
Center for Political Studies, 148
Center party, formation of, 233
Chairman, convention, 130
Chamberlain, Neville, 263
Chicago (Il.), 115–16

Chief executives
  political powers of, 36, 37
  See also Presidency; specific names
Church, Frank, 157
Citrin, Jack, 293, 336
Civil rights, 128, 134, 164, 194, 221
Civil War, 8, 140
Clague, Christopher, 306
Clausen, Aage, R., 320
Cleveland, Grover, 190
Clymer, Adam, 294, 324
Coattail, presidential, 41
Cohen, Bernard C., 78, 305
Colatoni, Claude S., 299
Columbia Bureau of Applied Social Re-
  search, 285
Committee on Political Education
  (COPE), 33
Committees, Congressional, chairmen of,
  215
Committee to Reelect the President
  (CREEP), 57, 69, 171
Common Cause, 34, 62
Communism issue, 270–71
Computer, election forecast by, 201–2
Congress
  apportionment in, 246–47, 265
  campaign finance legislation in, 32,
    33–34
  and electoral college reform, 250–51
  political action committees and, 62
  party cohesion in, 260–61
  and party reform, 213–15
  proposal for presidential nomination
    by, 232
Congressional elections, 20, 78, 145
  of 1964, 46
  of 1968, 153
  of 1970, 153, 158
  of 1972, 153
  of 1974, 153, 158
  of 1978, 95
  of 1980, 153–54, 157–61
  of 1982, 84
  political action committees and,
    32–33
  quality of candidates in, 265
Connally, John, 59
Connecticut, 157
Connelly, Gordon M., 285

Consensus government, vs. policy government, 211–12
Conservative party (British), 259–60
Conservative vote, mobilization of,
  151–52
Conventions
  chairman of, 130
  mid term, 240–41
  policy formation at. See Party plat-
    form
  public funding of, 64, 65, 66, 115
  site selection for, 66, 114–16, 131
  time of, 116
  See also Nomination process
Converse, Philip E., 284, 285, 290, 291,
  292, 307, 318, 320, 322, 326, 343
Cook, Rhodes, 309–10
Cooper, Homer C., 288
Cornwell, Elmer E., 290
Corporations, political action committees
  of, 32–33
Cotter, Cornelius P., 296
Cox, Archibald, 89
Cranston, Alan, 158, 310
CREEP. See Committee to Reelect the
  President
Crime issue, 128, 161, 180
Cronkite, Walter, 337
Crossley, Archibald M., 334
Crossley poll, 205
Crotty, William J., 293, 302
Crouse, Timothy, 306, 329
Cuba, 178, 261
Cummings, Milton C., Jr., 291
Cutler, Lloyd N., 335

Dahl, Robert A., 284, 290, 343, 344
Daley, Richard, 314
Dark horse candidates, 113–14, 238
Daugherty, Harry, 133, 136, 317
David, Paul T., 283, 309
Davis, Morton D., 297
Dawes, Charles, 89
Debates, televised, 58, 178–79, 183–86
Defense spending, 39, 264
Delegates
  to Democratic National Convention,
    120–24, 125, 144, 145, 312–13,
    337–38
  elected officials as, 47, 49, 144, 145

in multiballot conventions, 128–31
party controls and, 46–47
policy preferences of, 49, 125–27, 128, 146
to Republican National Convention, 123, 124–27
rewards for support of, 135
seating of, 129–30
selection of, 94, 97, 111, 238–39, 312–13. *See also* Primaries
turnover of, 141–42
Democracy
deliberative, 276–77
election and policy mandates in, 268–74
participatory, 217–22
plebiscitary, 279
Democratic Commission on Party Structure and Delegate Selection, 120
Democratic National Committee, 39–40
Democratic party
activists in, 35, 44
campaign spending by, 55, 56, 57
campaign strategy in, 148, 243
in Congress, 153–54
Committee chairmen and, 215
Republican landslide of 1980 and, 157–61
domestic policy and, 175–76
fund raising by, 70–71
identification with, 91
mean vote of (1952–1980), 286
media coverage of, 58, 72
membership characteristics of, 7
midterm conference of, 241
New Deal coalition in, 158, 163
platform of, 240, 259
political resources of, 90–91
in presidential elections (1952–1980), 10–12
primaries of, 94–95, 104–8, 231
See also Primaries
reform in, 215, 216–17, 337–38
in nomination process, 49, 145, 208, 209, 233, 238
voting blocs in, 24–25, 30
voting strength of, 8–9
See also specific candidates
Demonstrations, convention, 131, 234
Dennis, Jack, 344

Dewey, Thomas E., 150, 320
in 1940 election, 134
in 1948 election, 135, 173, 194, 205–6, 305
Dexter, Lewis Anthony, 293, 336
Dillon, C. Douglas, 335
Direct-election plan, 248–51, 254
Dirksen, Everett, 320
District conventions, 108–11
Dixiecrats, 39, 250
Dole, Robert, 170, 177, 185, 340
Domestic policy
as election issue, 16, 17, 175–77
policy government and, 263–64
Donnelly, Thomas C., 316
Donovan, Robert, 320
Downs, Anthony, 292, 295
Drew, Elizabeth, 294, 300
Drucker, Peter, 335
Drummond, Roscoe, 342
Dunn v. Blumstein, 244
Durbin, Thomas M., 313

Eagleton, Thomas, 139, 196, 277, 340
Eastern states, vote in (1952–1980), 10–12
Ecological interest groups, 24, 180
Economic issues, 14
Education
of delegates, 123, 124
vote by, 10–12, 289, 339
and voter turnout, 26–29
Eisenhower, Dwight, 58, 88
in 1952 election, 10, 59, 226, 311
in 1956 election, 10, 17, 77
personal appeal of, 9, 56, 150
Eisenhower Doctrine, 261
Eizenstat, Stuart, 174
Elderly voter, 165
Elections
forecasts. *See* Forecasts, election
and public policy, 268–74
See also Congressional elections; Gubernatorial elections; Presidential elections
Electoral College, 50–51, 91
abuses of, 255
checks and balances in, 255–56
reform of, 246–56, 340–41
direct-election plan and, 248–51, 254

Electoral College *(Cont.)*
    district plan in, 253–54, 341
    electoral outcomes under, 254–
      55
    proportional plan in, 251–52, 254
    unit rule in, 51, 150, 247–48, 298
Electoral vote, 51
    actual *vs.* proportional, 252
    vs. popular vote (1976), 249
Electorate, exclusion from, 245, 340
Elites, rule by, 278–79
Elliott, William Y., 334
Energy prices, 179
Environmental issues, 24, 161
Epstein, Edwin M., 294, 300, 302
Equal Rights Amendment, 31, 39, 124,
      161, 315
Ericson, Robert S., 78, 287, 307, 324
Ernst, Harry W., 301, 302, 310
Erskine, Hazel Gaudet, 288, 290
Ethnic groups
    and balanced ticket, 227
    party identifcation of, 9, 166
European Common Market, 262

Farley, James A., 110, 313
Federal Communications Commission,
      72
Federal Elections Campaign Act
      (FECA), 32, 34, 61, 64–67
Federal Elections Commission, 66
Feldman, Jacob J., 326
Felons, 245, 340
Field, Harry M., 285
Finifter, Ada W., 288
Finletter, Thomas K., 335
Fiorina, Morris, 19, 292
First-ballot nominations, 142
Flanigan, William H., 287
Fleishman, Joel, 231, 337
Floor demonstrations, 131, 234
Florida, 95, 144
Ford, Gerald
    as campaigner, 81–82
    in 1976 election, 72, 82, 84, 138
    campaign of, 51, 168–69, 190
      mistakes in, 174
    nomination of, 119
    public image of, 174, 175, 181,
      187

    television debate of, 185
    vote received by, 12, 241
    and Nixon pardon, 190
Ford, Henry Jones, 334
Forecasts, election
    Bean method of, 200–1
    by electronic computers, 201–2
    from historical statistics, 201
    interview technique of, 199–200
Foreign policy, 16, 176, 177–80, 326
    and party reform, 216
    and policy government, 261–63
Frankovic, Kathleen, 294
Frick, Henry C., 69
Front porch campaign, 173
Front runners
    in convention, 133, 134
    in early primaries, 97–98

Gallup, George, 333
Gallup poll, 152, 203, 205, 306, 325
Game analogy, in primary campaigns,
      103
Garner, John Nance, 87, 136
Gender gap, 3
German-Americans, 9, 166
Gibson, James L., 296
Gilbert, Charles E., 306
Gill, Joe, 112
Glenn, John, 310
Goldberg, Arthur S., 287
Goldman, Ralph M., 283, 309
Goldstein, Joel K., 317
Goldwater, Barry, 157
    in 1964 election, 46, 55, 142, 177, 265,
      317
    campaign strategy of, 150–51
    foreign policy issues and, 322
    nomination of, 47, 49, 240
    in primaries, 98
    state conventions and, 108
    vice presidential choice of, 140
    vote received by, 11, 321–22
    organization of, 110
    supporters of, 127
Goodman, William, 309
Goodwin, Richard N., 342
Gorman, John W., 290
Gorman, Joseph, xi
Gormond, Jack W., 311

Gosnell, Harold G., 309, 338
Gossett, Ed, 341
Government spending, 24
    cuts in, 15
    public opinion on, 161
Governors
    in nomination process, 47, 49
    and party organization, 37, 47
Great Britain, 189, 242, 259–60, 263
Great Depression of 1929, 8, 176
Greek-Americans, 138
Greenstein, Fred I., 288, 306
Griffith, Ernest F., 335
Gubernatorial elections, 78, 145
    in presidential election years, 47, 48
Gulf of Tonkin incident, 308
Gulf of Tonkin Resolution, 261
Gun control, 31, 160, 180
Gurin, Gerald, 325–26

Hadley, Charles D., 296
Haggerty, Brian, 65, 302
Hahn, Harlan, 318
Halleck, Charles, 135
Handgun registration, 160
Harding, Warren G., 133, 136, 173
Harnsberger, Caroline T., 316
Harris poll, 152, 160, 203, 322
Harrison, William Henry, 190–91
Hart, Gary, 310
Harvard Law School Forum, 140
Hatch Act, 86
Hawley, Willis, 338
Haynes, Paul R., 285
Hazlitt, Henry, 335
Heard, Alexander, 55, 299, 300, 303
Hebert, Edward, 215
Heckling, in campaigns, 188–91
Helms, E.A., 309
Helms, Jesse, 63
Herring, E. Pendleton, 295, 309, 335
Hess, Stephen, 331
Hidden vote theory, 151–52, 219, 278
Hispanic voters, 167
Hoffman, Paul J., 295, 315, 320, 337
Hoover, Herbert, 83, 154
House of Representatives. See Congress
Houston (Texas), 131
Hucker, Charles W., 300
Huckshorn, Robert J., 296

Humphrey, Hubert, 89
    campaign organization of, 110
    in 1960 election, 138, 298
        campaign spending by, 60
    in 1968 election, 85, 86, 99, 128, 138,
        185, 189
        campaign contributions to, 56–57,
            70, 301–2, 303
        campaign feedback and, 193
        issue forces and, 16–17
        vote received by, 11
    in 1972 election, 105, 106
    public image of, 181–82
Hunt Commission (1980–1982), 49, 145,
    209, 238
Huntington, Samuel P., 308
Huthmacher, J. Joseph, 290
Hyman, Herbert H., 290
Hyman, Sidney, 302

Idaho, 158, 242
Illinois, 99, 144, 157
Illiterates, 245
Incumbency
    as liability, 86–90, 169
    as resource, 82–86, 168–69
Independents, 99
    issue oriented, 13
    mobilization of, 151
    partisan and pure, 18–19, 149, 320
    voting record of (1952–1980), 10–12,
        319
Inflation, 14, 83–84, 128, 176
Insurgent candidates, 85
Interest groups, 4, 22–35
    campaign contributions by, 32–35
    characteristics of, 22
    defined, 22
    function of, 31–32
    influence of, 22–23
    and political parties, 44
    press of, 187
    public interest, 32, 34–35
    single-issue, 33
    and voting blocs, 23–31
Inter-University Consortium for Political
    and Social Research, 50
Iowa, 82, 95, 101, 108
Iranian hostage crisis, 15, 58, 83, 179,
    186, 330

Irish-Americans, 8, 9, 166
Issues
  electoral outcomes and, 16–17
  gender related, 31, 165
  interest groups and, 24, 33
  national scope of, 213, 214
  and party preference, 45–46
  party realignment and, 160–61
  in voting decision, 9, 13–17, 269–73
  See also Policy government; Public
    policy; *specific issues*
Italian-Americans, 166
ITT Corporation, 66

Jackson, Andrew, 139, 190
Jackson, Henry, 59, 60, 101
Jackson, John E., 334
Jacobson, Gary C., 78, 293, 300, 302, 307
Jefferson, Thomas, 190, 298
Jewish vote, 8, 289
Johnson, Andrew, 137
Johnson, Donald Bruce, 342
Johnson, Loch K., 318
Johnson, Lyndon B., 60, 88, 174
  fund raising by, 70
  in 1960 election, 90, 134, 137
  in 1964 election, 55, 185, 272
    vice-presidential choice of, 137–38
    vote received by, 11, 152
  in 1968 election, 79, 85, 86
    primaries, 100
Johnston, Richard, 287
Jones, Charles O., 311
Jordan, Hamilton, 98, 172, 175

Kalmbach, Herbert, 171
Katz, Elihu, 306
Kefauver, Estes, 59, 112, 139, 225
Keith, Bruce E., 287, 319
Keller, Bill, 303
Kelley, Stanley, Jr., 242, 307, 338, 339
Kendall, Willmoore, 309, 335
Kennedy, Edward M., 241
  in 1972 election, 95
  in 1980 election, 58, 61, 83, 85, 98, 99,
    129–30, 196
Kennedy, John F., 139
  in 1960 election, 55, 142, 272
    campaign of, 173
    foreign policy in, 178

media and, 75, 77
  money available to, 60, 70
  nomination of, 134
  organization of, 117–19, 170
  in primaries, 60, 100
  public image of, 181, 184
  religious issue and, 98
  television debates of, 178–79,
    183–86
  vice-presidential choice of, 135, 137,
    138
  vote received by, 10
Kennedy, Robert F.
  and 1960 election, 118
  in 1968 election, 17
  primaries of, 99, 224
Kent, Frank R., 317
Kentucky, 8
Key, V.O., 15, 284, 285, 287, 288, 290,
  291–92, 295, 296, 297, 336
Keynes, John Maynard, 168
Kiewiet, Roderick, 292
Kinder, Donald, 19, 292, 293
King, Anthony, 286
King, Martin Luther, 194
Kirkpatrick, Evron M., 335
Kirkpatrick, Jeane, 124, 126, 291, 297,
  315
Kleppe, Thomas, 342
Korea, 270–71
Koster, Richard M., 295
Kostrich, Leslie J., 334

Labor unions
  delegates from, 124
  political action committees of, 32, 33
  voting record of (1952–1980), 10–12,
    25
Labour party (British), 259–60, 280
Ladd, Everett, 161, 197, 231, 296, 297,
  316, 324, 333, 337
La Follette, Robert, 99
Lake, Celinda, 31, 294
Landslide victories. *See* Eisenhower,
  Dwight D., in 1956 election;
  Johnson, Lyndon B., in 1964
  election; Nixon, Richard M., in
  1972 election; Roosevelt, Frank-
  lin D., in 1936 election
Lane, Robert E., 286, 288

Lawson, Kay, 302
Lazarsfeld, Paul F., 285, 287, 306, 318, 334
Lengle, James, 97, 106, 310
Levesque, Terrence J., 299
Levin, Murray, 300
Levy, Mark R., 334
Lichter, Robert, 305, 331
Liebling, A.J., 304
Life-style issues, 160, 161, 164, 180
Lincoln, Abraham, 137, 190, 314
    dark-horse strategy of, 113
Lindblom, Louise, xi
Lindsay, John, 144
Linz, Juan, 293, 318
Lipset, Seymour M., 293, 318
Literary Digest, 204–5, 334
Livingston, William S., 296
Lobbies. See Interest groups
Lockard, Duane, 290
Lodge, Henry Cabot, 99, 130, 137
Lodge-Gossett Resolution, 251–52
Long, Russell, 157
Longley, Lawrence D., 299
Los Angeles (Cal.), 115
Lowden, Frank, 133
Lowell, A. Lawrence, 334
Lubell, Samuel, 199, 290, 333
Lucy, William H., 102, 311
Lundberg, Ferdinand, 317
Lyons, John J., 315

McCarthy, Eugene, 85, 216
    in 1968 election, 17, 79, 341
        primaries of, 99, 100, 110, 224
    in 1972 election, 144
    in 1976 election, 12
McCarthy, Joseph, 321
McClosky, Herbert, 38, 125, 293, 295, 297, 315, 320, 336, 337
McCorkle, Pope, 231
MacDonald, William, 334
McGovern, George, 85, 120
    in 1972 election, 59, 108, 142
        issues and, 14, 17, 275–76, 326, 329
        foreign policy, 179
    nomination of, 121–22, 124, 125, 126, 127, 128, 129, 216
    organization of, 119, 170–71
    primaries of, 95–96, 100, 105–6, 107, 110, 144–45
    vice-presidential choice of, 139, 196, 277
    vote received by, 11, 241
McGovern-Fraser Commission (1969–1972), 209, 312–13
McGregor, Eugene B., Jr., 133, 317
McKean, D.D., 309
McPhee, William N., 285, 287, 288, 318
McWilliams, Wilson Carey, 230–31
Magleby, David B., 287
Mail solicitation, 71, 276
Maine, 201
Malbin, Michael, 63, 294, 302, 303
Manatt, Charles, 115, 241
Manhattan Project, 87
Mann, Thomas, 231
Marcus, George E., 284
Markus, Gregory B., 285
Marshall, Thomas Riley, 87
Marshall Plan, 261
Marston v. Lewis, 244
Martin, Joseph, 130, 305
Martin, Ralph G., 314
Massachusetts, 248
Matsu-Quemoy issue (1960), 84, 178, 196
Mazo, Earl, 329
Media
    campaign coverage of, 50, 58, 71–72, 81–82, 144, 174–75
        candidate-media relations and, 186–88
    in preprimary period, 96
    in primaries, 99, 100, 101, 102–3
    convention coverage of, 235–36
    political impact of, 307
    See also Newspapers; Radio; Television
Meehl, Paul E., 293
Merriam, C.E., 309
Me-too strategy, 150, 152, 243, 320
Miami Beach (Fla.), as convention site, 115, 116
Michigan Center for Political Studies, 17, 24, 148, 162, 285, 291, 341
Michigan Survey Research Center. See Michigan Center for Political Studies
Middle Atlantic states, 8

Midwest, 8, 9, 289
  voting record of (1952–1980), 10–12
Mikulski Commission (1972–1973), 209
Miller, Arthur H., 291, 329
Miller, Warren E., 285, 291, 296, 307,
  318, 320, 324, 326, 329, 341, 343
Miller, William, 140
Minor parties, public funding of, 64, 67
Missile gap issue (1960), 84
Mitchell, Robert Cameron, 35, 295
Mitofsky, Warren J., 315
Mohr, Charles, 329
Mondale, Walter
  in 1976 election, 138, 185, 225–26
  in 1980 election, 90
  in 1984 election, 38–39, 96, 310
  as vice president, 88
Monroe, Alan D., 338
Montjoy, Robert S., 316
Moos, Malcolm C., 309, 314, 335
Morehouse, Sarah McCally, 295
Morison, Elting E., 311
Morris, John, 338
Mosteller, Frederick, 333, 334
Mott, Stewart, 303
Mud-slinging, in campaigns, 188–91, 259
Mueller, John E., 323
Muskie, Edmund, 138, 331
  in 1972 election, 95, 96, 106, 128, 144,
    188
  in 1976 election, 113

Nadel, Mark V., 303
Nader's Raiders, 34
Natchez, Peter B., 285
National Citizen's Action Committee,
  33
National Congressional Club, 63
National convention. *See* Conventions;
  Delegates; Nomination process
National direct primary, 223–25, 226–27,
  228–29
National Education Association (NEA),
  124–25
National Independent Conservative Polit-
  ical Action Committee (NIC-
  PAC), 62
National Opinion Research Center, 161
National Security Council, 88
Nebraska, 99, 311

Nedzi, Lucien, 333
Nelson, Candice F., 287
Nevada, 158
New Deal, 8, 9, 45–46, 154, 259
  coalition, 158, 163
New England, 9
Newfield, Jack, 311
New Hampshire, 79, 82, 95, 97–98, 99,
  100, 101, 157–58, 224
Newspapers, 58
  convention coverage by, 235–36
  favorable coverage from, 186–87
  as feedback source, 192
  of interest groups, 187
  manipulation of, 74
  partisan, 72–75, 78
  political impact of, 75–78, 307
  political news in, 73
News services, 74
New York, 51, 172
New York City, 115
New York Daily News, 76
New York Times, 77
Nie, Norman H., 284, 286, 291
Nimmo, Dan, 331
Nixon, Richard M., 150
  and media, 75, 83, 183
  in 1960 election, 56, 137, 152, 163, 183
    campaign strategy of, 194–96
    foreign policy in, 178–79
    public image of, 181, 184
    television debates of, 178–79, 183–
      86, 326
    vice-presidency as liability to, 86, 89
    vote received by, 10, 30
  and 1964 election, 99, 113
  in 1968 election, 84, 99, 113, 142
    campaign strategy of, 152, 173–74,
      183, 320
      Southern, 195
    issue forces and, 16–17
    media and, 75
    in primaries, 98
    vice-presidential choice of, 138
    vote received by, 11, 152–53, 158
  in 1972 election, 185
    campaign contributions to, 57, 69,
      171
    mud-slinging tactics of, 190
    vote received by, 11, 17, 158

organization of, 190
pardon of, 190
Nomination process, 2, 42, 93–146
at convention, 116–41
balloting in, 131–37
1928–1980, 143
bargaining in, 116, 135–36
candidate organization and, 116–20
delegates and caucuses in, 120–27
floor demonstrations in, 131, 234
multiballot, 128–31
future of, 141–46
governors in, 47, 49
political parties and, 109, 144, 145, 230–31, 239, 274–75
preconvention period and, 93–108, 142–43, 230
at state and district conventions, 108–11
before primaries, 93–96
candidate strategies and, 111–14
presidential powers over, 85–86
reform of, 94, 114, 208, 209, 216
candidate selection in, 237–38
Congressional nomination in, 232–33
delegate selection in, 238–39
media role and, 235–36
mixed system in, 239
party leaders and, 225–26, 227–28
separation of business and ceremonial functions in, 234–35
standards for, 223–25
See also Primaries, reform of
television impact on, 79–81
for vice-president, 111–12, 133, 137–41
See also Conventions
Nonvoters, 26–29, 162, 272
North Carolina, 8
North Dakota, 99, 158
Novak, Robert D., 311
Nuclear freeze campaign, 15

Occupation, voting record by, 10–12
Odegard, Peter H., 309
O'Hara, Rosemary, 295, 315, 320, 337
Ohio, 173

Opinion polls, 23, 82, 152
by commercial organizations, 203
election forecasts by, 202–7
sampling error in, 204–6
voting behavior and, 334
in 1980 election, 156
on party affiliation, 160–61
on policy preferences, 273
and primary elections, 101–2
private, 147, 203
reliability of, 192
techniques of, 206–7, 333
Ordeshook, Peter D., 299
Oregon, 99
Orr, Elizabeth, 287
Ostrogorski, Moisei, 309, 316, 337

PACs. See Political action committees
Page, Benjamin I., 292, 315, 343
Panama Canal Treaty, 261
Panel survey, 206
Participatory democracy, 217–22
Party identification, 42–43
basis for, 7–8
benefits of, 18, 228
during campaigns, 148–49
candidate appeal and, 9
changes in, 19, 91, 100. See also Political parties, realignment of
decline in, 18–19, 20, 148–49
voter turnout and, 21
demographic characteristics in, 10–12, 166
of ethnic groups, 9, 166
historical roots of, 8–9
vs. issue voting, 13–17
media impact on, 76
by partisan independents, 18
and voting behavior, 7–8, 20
by voting blocs, 24–25, 30–31
Party platform
accomodation process in, 236–37
cyclical changes in, 258–59, 342–43
delegate support for, 146
enforcement of, 239–40
public opinion and, 240
reform in, 237
policy government and, 212–13
Patman, Wright, 215
Patronage, 37, 41, 135

Patterson, Thomas, 103
Pauley, Edwin, 69
Peel, Roy V., 316
Penniman, H.R., 309
Pennsylvania, 105, 157
Petrocik, John R., 284, 285, 291
Philadelphia (Pa.), as convention site, 115
Phillips, Charles, 290
Phillips, Kevin P., 324
Pianin, Eric, 314
Pierce, John L., 285
Pierson, James E., 214
Pillow, Gideon, 136
Plaut, Edward, 314
Playboy magazine, Carter interview in, 174
Plissner, Martin, 315
Policy. *See* Public policy
Policy government
  domestic policy impact of, 263–64
  elite rule and, 278–79
  false premises of, 277–78
  foreign policy and, 261–63
  needs for consensus and, 276
  participatory democracy and, 217–18
  parties as agents of, 274–75
  political theory of, 210–15
Polish-Americans, 8, 138
Political action committees (PACs), 55
  campaign contributions by 32–35, 61–62
  political parties and, 63
  rise of, 33
Political participation
  decline in, 220–22
  time and energy costs of, 6, 220–21
  See also Activists
Political parties, 2, 3–4, 36–50
  accountability of, 36–37
  of advocacy *vs.* intermediation, 274–81
  affiliation with. *See* Party identification
  and campaign strategy, 197–98
  centralized structure of, 40–41
  Congressional, 39, 260–61
  decline of, 50
  democracy and, 267–81
  differences between, 256–60
  fund raising by, 69–71
  goals of, 36
  and interest groups, 44
  membership characteristics of, 6–7
  in nomination process, 109, 230–31, 239, 274–75
  policy preferences of, 13, 38–39, 43–47. *See also* Party platform
  political action committees and, 63
  primaries and, 114
  realignment of, 154
    center party and, 233
    Congressional election of 1980 and, 153–54, 157–60
    policy issues in, 160–61
    Presidential election of 1980 and, 155–56
    theory of, 161–63
  reform of. *See* Reform, party
  relations of elected officials with, 37–38
  resources of. *See* Resources, political
  state organizations of, 37, 40, 41–42, 46–47, 109
  See also Democratic party; Republican party; *specific names*
Political strategies
  defined, 1
  in presidential elections, 1–2, 3
  See also Campaigns
Polk, James, 136
Polls. *See* Opinion polls
Polsby, Nelson W., 292, 297, 307, 308, 309, 313, 343, 344
Pomper, Gerald, 107, 283, 295, 312, 338
Poor people, voting record of, 24
Popkin, Samuel, 164, 165, 290, 318, 324
Popular vote, *vs.* electoral vote, 249
Porter, Kirk H., 342
Powell, Jody, 44
Power, political parties and, 36–37
Preconvention period, 59, 93–108
Predictions. *See* Forecasts, election
Prendergast, William, 296
Presidency
  incumbency as political resource in, 82–86
  power over nomination process, 85–86
  two-term limit and, 86
Presidential Election Campaign Fund, 64

Presidential elections
    direct election plan for, 248–51, 254
    and policy mandate, 269–74
    political strategies in, 1–2, 3
    vote by group in (1952–1980), 10–12
    See also Campaigns; Nomination pro-
        cess; Reform, party; *specific
        names and subjects*
President's Club, 70
Press. *See* Newspapers
Pressman, Jeffrey L., 122, 315
Prewitt, Kenneth, 321
Price, H. Douglas, 308
Primaries, 97–108
    campaign strategy in, 112–13
    Democratic, 94, 95, 104–8
    early participation in, 97–98
    increased number of, 97, 103–4
    media coverage of, 100, 101
        television, 102–3, 142
    opinion poll impact on, 101–2
    political parties and, 114
    public funding of, 55, 64
    reform of, 223–30
        national direct primary in, 223–25,
            226–27, 228–29
        regional direct primaries and, 229
        state primaries and, 226, 227, 229
        time limitations in, 230, 231–32
    television coverage of, 79, 80–81
    vote counting rules for, 105–7
    voter turnout in, 104–5, 108
    write-in strategy for, 99–100
Prohibition, 133
Proposition 13
Protestant vote, 8, 30, 166, 289
    1952–1980, 10–12
Public interest
    consensus *vs.* policy government on,
        211–12
    groups, 32, 34–35
Public opinion
    and party platform, 240
    in policy decisions, 218
    polling of. *See* Opinion polls
Public policy
    activist role in, 15
    elections and, 268–74
    party differences and, 13, 46
    referenda on, 279

Public spending. *See* Government
    spending
Purists
    changes favoring, 274–75
    defined, 36
    in nomination process, 132, 238, 239,
        280
    policy committment of, 38
Putnam, Robert D., 288

Race, vote by, 10–12
    See also Blacks
Radio, 72, 78, 176, 183, 236, 307
Raine, Alden S., 291, 329
Ranney, Austin, 104–5, 127, 231, 335, 337
Reagan, Ronald, 38, 181, 182, 222
    and Bush, George, 88
    economic policy of, 46
    and foreign trade, 179–80
    gender gap of, 31
    in 1976 election, 61, 82, 85
        nomination of, 120
        vice-presidential choice of, 112, 138,
            140
    in 1980 election, 59, 84, 142, 150
        campaign strategy of, 196–97
        media coverage of, 75
        opinion polls on, 156
        party realignment and, 155–57, 162
        primaries, 100, 101
        television debate of, 186
        vote received by, 12, 30, 155–56,
            162, 241
            motivation for, 164
            from women, 165
    policy issues and, 15, 177
    popularity of, 156, 323
    public image of, 329–30
    and responsible government model,
        265–66
Reconstruction period, 8
Reeves, Richard, 312, 314
Referenda, 279
Reform, 3, 208–66
    in campaign finance, 54–55, 61
    of Electoral College, 246–56, 340–41
    of nomination process. *See* Nomina-
        tion process, reform of
    participatory democracy and, 217–22
    party differences and, 256–60

Reform *(Cont.)*
  policy government theory of, 210–15
  and policy preference, 215–17
  post-Watergate, 54, 188
  relevancy of, 260–66
  universal automatic voter enrollment
    and, 241–46, 340
  in voter registration, 241–46
Regional primaries, 229
Regional vote (1952–1980), 10–12
  See also specific regions
Religion, vote by (1952–1980), 10–12
Remmers, H.H., 288
Repass, David, 285
Republican National Committee, 39–40
Republican party
  activists in, 44
  campaign spending by, 55, 56, 57
  campaign strategies of, 149–52, 243
    from 1964–1980, 152–61
  in Congress, 154–55
    party realignment and, 157–61
  domestic policy and, 176–77
  foreign policy and, 177–78
  fund raising by, 70
  in gubernatorial elections, 47, 48
  identification with, 148, 149
  media coverage of, 58, 72
  membership characteristics of, 7
  minority groups and, 167
  platform of, 240, 259
  political resources of, 91–92
  in presidential elections (1952–1980),
    10–12
  voting blocs in, 30–31
  voting strength of, 8, 9
  See also specific candidates
Resources, political
  benefits from, 218–19
  convertability of, 90–92
  distribution of, 53–92
  incumbency as, 82–86
  information control as, 71–79
  money, 54–71
  television, 79–82
Reston, James, 310
Reuss, Henry, 215
Reynolds v. Sims, 247, 341
Ribicoff, Abraham, 302
Richards, Richard, 63

Richardson, Elliot, 89
Right-to-life movement, 180
Rivers, William L., 305
Roback, Thomas, 316
Roberts, Steven V., 155
Robinson, Michael J., 74, 305, 307
Rockefeller, Nelson, 59, 60, 61, 88, 138
Rogow, Arnold, 343
Roll, Charles W., Jr., 333
Romney, George, 75, 318
Roosevelt, Franklin D., 189
  in 1932 election, 110, 136
  nomination of, 129
  in 1936 election, 204–5
  in 1940 election, 139
  press attacks on, 76
  Truman and, 87, 138
Roosevelt, Theodore, 69, 99
Roper, Elmo, 284, 306, 336
Roper poll, 205
Rosenhack, Sheilah, 321
Rosenstone, Steven J., 285, 318
Rossi, Peter H., 285
Rothenberg, Larry, 108, 312
Rothman, Stanley, 305, 331
Rovere, Richard, 305
Rubin, Richard, 102–3, 307, 312
Ruml, Beardsley, 69
Running mate. *See* Vice-president
Rusk, Jerrold G., 341

Sabato, Larry J., 307
Sandburg, Carl, 314
San Diego (Cal.), 66
San Francisco (Cal.), 115
Saturday Night Massacre, 89
Scammon, Richard, 180, 298, 311, 329
Schattschneider, E.E., 309, 334–35
Schram, Martin, 297, 301, 324
Schweiker, Richard, 112, 140
Scranton, William, 240
Seitzinger, Michael V., 313
Senate. *See* Congress
Sex
  vote by (1952–1980), 10–12, 294
  and voter turnout, 26–29
  See also Women
Shafer, Byron, xi–xii, 97, 106, 309, 310,
  336
Shafer, William R., 316

Shanks, J. Merrill, 293, 324, 336
Shannon, Jasper B., 303
Sheatsley, Paul B., 290
Sheehan, Margaret H., 307
Sheraton Corporation, 66
Sherwood, Robert E., 331, 334
Sindler, Allan P., 314
Smith, Al, 131, 135
Smith, Eric R.A.N., 284–85
Smith, Hedrick, 329
Smith, Jeffrey, 290
Smoke-filled room, 136, 232–33
Smoot, Reed, 130
Sniderman, Paul M., 293, 336
Social issues, 180–81
Social Security, ix, 176
Sola Pool, Ithiel de, 293, 318, 319, 336
Sonthoff, Herbert, 335
Sorauf, Frank J., 295
South and southern vote
    campaign strategy and, 194, 195
    civil rights issues and, 194
    under direct-election plan, 250
    1952–1980, 10–12
    party identification in, 8, 25
    primaries in, 227
    turnout of, 26–29
South Dakota, 158
Speeches, 174–75, 182–83, 192
Stagflation, 84
Stans, Maurice, 171
Stanwood, Edward, 317, 337
State conventions, 108–11
State party organization, 37, 40, 41–42,
    46–47
Stedman, Murray, 335
Stevenson, Adlai, 134
    in 1952 election, 59, 86, 112
    campaign contributions of, 69
    media impact on, 78
    nomination of, 119
    vote received by, 10
    in 1956 election, 10, 139, 170
    party leaders and, 225
    speeches of, 182–83
Stokes, Donald E., 285, 307, 318, 343
Stouffer, Samuel, 284, 336
Strunk, Mildred, 290
Sullivan, Denis G., 315
Sullivan, John L., 284

Sullivan, Mark, 317
Supply-side economics, 46
Supreme Court, 244, 245
    See also specific decisions
Symington, Stuart, 60, 113, 314

Taft, Robert A., 59, 61, 226
Tannenbaum, Percy H., 334
Tariffs, 179–80, 262
Tate, James, 115
Taxation, cuts in, 15, 46
Teasdale, Anthony, 114, 314
Tedin, Kent L., 287, 324
Television, 15, 77, 176
    campaign advertising on, 81
    candidate debates on, 58, 178–79,
        183–86
    favorable coverage on, 187–88
    in nomination process, 79–81, 146,
        235, 236, 304
    political impact of, 78–79, 307
    primary coverage of, 102–3, 142
    self-presentation on, 182–83
    third-party candidates on, 80
Tennessee, 8
Texas, 110, 137
Third-party candidates, 254–55
    under direct-election plan, 250–51
    television coverage of, 80
    See also Wallace, George
Ticket balancing, 90, 138–39, 140–41
Truman, David B., 295, 335
Truman, Harry S., 58, 134, 138, 308
    in 1948 election, 77, 82, 173, 193, 255
    and 1952 election, 86
    as Vice-president, 87–88
Tufte, Edward, 324
Turner, Julius, 335, 343

Udall, Morris, 59, 60, 82, 101, 236, 310,
    313
Uncertainty, indicators of, in nomination
    process, 133
Undecided vote, in election forecasts, 203,
    204
Underdog strategies, 149–52
Underwood, Oscar, 135
Unemployed, voter turnout of, 26–29
Unemployment, 14, 24, 84
Ungovernability, crisis of, 86

Unit rule, 51, 150, 247–48, 298
Universal automatic voter enrollment, 241–46, 340
Unruh, Jesse, xi
Urban issues, 16
Utah, 158, 338

Van Buren, Martin, 131, 136, 139, 191
Vance, Cyrus, 89
Vandenberg, Arthur, 134, 317
Van Deusen, Glyndon G., 314
Van Duinen, Elizabeth, 339
Verba, Sidney, 284, 285, 286, 291
Vice-president
    constitutional functions of, 87
    election to presidency of, 137
    incumbency as liability to, 86–87, 89–90
    independence of, 89
    nomination of, 133, 137–41
        balanced ticket in, 90, 138–39, 140–41
        early disclosure in, 111–12
    updating role of, 87–88
    See also specific names
Vietnam War, 16–17, 57, 70, 83, 89, 92, 128, 177, 179, 216, 221, 261, 308
Virginia, 8
Voter registration, 20, 220
    residence requirements in, 244–45
    turnout and, 242, 338, 340
    universal automatic, 241, 242–44
Voters and voting, 5–21
    elderly, 165
    first-time, 30, 162–63
    party preferences of (1952–1980), 2, 9–12
    political commitment of, 5–6
    requirements for, 244–46, 338
        See also Voter registration
    with special interests, 6
    timing of decisions by, 216
    women, 164–65
    youth, 165–66
    See also Nonvoters
Voter turnout
    decline in, 20–21, 241
    differential, 204
    by first-time voters, 30

1968–1980, 21, 156
    by population characteristics, 21, 26–29
    party affiliation and, 7
    in primaries, 104–5, 108
    registration rule impact on, 242–43, 245, 338, 340
Voting age, 25, 245
Voting behavior,
    group membership and, 10–12
    ideology in, 162, 270
    of independents, 319
    issues in, 9, 13–17, 269–73
    media impact on, 76–77, 78–79
    opinion poll impact on, 334
    and party identification, 7–8
    and political interest, 6–7
    by voting blocs, 23–31
    See also Political parties, re-alignment of
Voting studies, 23

Wallace, George, 255
    in 1968 election, 17, 25, 153, 189, 195
        campaign contributions to, 70
        vote received by, 11
    in 1972 election, 106, 128, 144
Wallace, Henry, 139, 140
Watergate, 57, 66, 115, 171, 188, 221
Wattenberg, Ben, 180, 311, 329
Wattenberg, Martin, 50, 293, 298
Wayne, Stephen J., xi, 310, 311
Weber, Romano E., 316
Weisberg, Herbert F., 293
Welfare issue, 24, 128, 161, 221–22, 264
Wertheimer, Fred, 62
Wesberry v. Sanders, 247, 341
Westlye, Mark, 287
West Virginia, 8, 98
Western states, vote in (1952–1980), 10–12
Whispering campaigns, 136
Whistle-stop methods, 172–73
White, Theodore, 195, 301, 302, 306, 311, 314, 329, 333
Wildavsky, Aaron B., 309, 317, 336, 341, 343
Wildenthal, John, 342
Wilkie, Wendell, 130, 131, 150

Williams, Irving, 317
Wilson, James Q., 290
Wilson, Woodrow, 87, 210, 334
Window plan, 230
Winner-Take-All rule, 105, 106, 143–44
Winograd Commission (1975–1980), 209
Wirthlin, Richard, 155, 196–97
Wisconsin, 99, 100, 231
Witcover, Jules, 75, 308, 311, 314, 322, 329
Wolfe, Arthur C., 341
Wolfinger, Barbara Kaye, 321
Wolfinger, Raymond E., 285, 287, 306, 318, 319, 321
Women
    as delegates, 121, 123, 124
    group interests of, 31, 165
    party identification of, 30–31, 164–65, 289

voter turnout of, 26–29
voting record of (1952–1980), 10–12
Women's movement, 164
Wood, Leonard, 133
Woodward, Julian L., 284, 336
Write-in strategy, 99–100

Youth
    age requirements for, 245
    as delegates, 123, 124
    party identification of, 25, 30, 165–66, 339
    voter turnout of, 26–29
Yunker, John A., 299

Zeidenstein, Harvey, 341
Zingale, Nancy H., 287